BOXING

HEROES & CHAMPIONS

BOXING

HEROES & CHAMPIONS

BOB MEE

CHARTWELL
BOOKS, INC.

A QUINTET BOOK

Published by Chartwell Books, Inc.
A Division of Book Sales, Inc.
114 Northfield Avenue
Edison, New Jersey 08837

This edition produced for sale in the U.S.A., its
territories and dependencies only.

ISBN 0-7858-0778-0

This book was designed and produced by
Quintet Publishing Limited
6 Blundell Street
London N7 9BH

Creative Director: Richard Dewing
Art Director: Silke Braun
Designer: Steve West
Senior Editor: Anna Briffa
Editor: Sean Connolly

Typeset in Great Britain by
Central Southern Typesetters, Eastbourne
Manufactured in Singapore by Eray Scan Pte Ltd
Printed in China by Leefung-Asco Printers Ltd

CONTENTS

FOREWORD

In April 1997, George Foreman, age 48, defeated a previously undefeated heavyweight named Lou Savarese, testing the floor boards by bouncing in the 12th round as his 31-year-old opponent was bicycling backward and huffing and puffing in anticipation of the final bell. A few days before, a 63-year-old woman had given birth. I still haven't decided which event was more amazing.

We're fascinated by prize fighters. That hasn't changed in 100 years, and it won't change over the next 100. We make sure to watch them win and lose, and rise and fall, and if you've ever been in a boxing gym or a dressing room, you know we also make sure to watch them do nothing at all. Ever wonder why? The answer is simple. Who else so readily risks their dignity and welfare every time they punch the clock? Who else competes with such passion? Who else sweats and bleeds whether the reward is $100 or $1-million? We watch because we are compelled to watch.

From John L. Sullivan and Jack Johnson to Evander Holyfield and Prince Naseem Hamed, the greatest of the great fighters intrigue us, entertain us, infuriate us, and inspire us, but never, ever bore us. Rough, hard men who find themselves hopelessly exposed by the nature of their trade, they're both vulnerable and impervious. Most of all, they're honest in their work.

The greatest of the great fighters become symbols of their time. Jack Dempsey in the Roaring Twenties, Joe Louis in the uncertain 1930s and early-1940s, Muhammad Ali in the turbulent 1960s, Sugar Ray Leonard in the greed-infested 1980s, Oscar De La Hoya and his personalized internet web site in the 1990s—could any of these champions have thrived in a different era? Perhaps, perhaps not. But on the rare occasions when time and fighter merge, the result is pure magic.

Bob Mee, who has written several features for *KO Magazine* (*The Ring*'s sister publication), is among the most experienced and respected boxing scribes on either side of the pond. Who better, then, to chronicle the greatest fighters of the modern era? In truth, there aren't as many great fighters as there used to be. Mee is doing his part to make sure the same isn't said of writers.

April 29, 1997
Steve Farhood, Editor-in-Chief, *The Ring*

INTRODUCTION

THE IMAGE OF BOXING

Someone once analyzed sport as a reflection of the struggle between life and death. The winner lives, the loser dies. As civilization supposedly progresses, the need to identify life with victory is diluted or submerged, and so the definition of sport widens to allow the introduction of activities which carry lower risk.

Or so runs the theory.

Boxing, one of the oldest sports of all, dilutes little. Its heroes bleed, risk their health, indeed their lives, in the pursuit of wealth, fame, recognition, and, weird as it seems, fun. Boxers are the most ordinary and most extraordinary of men, who understand the cost of their sport perhaps better than most. They understand it, not in any pretentious, academic way, but by instinct.

Boxers have received an unfair press over the years. Sometimes they are not as articulate as some from other worlds, but talk to them long enough and each one of them knows what a special world it is they inhabit.

Glenn McCrory, who won the IBF world cruiserweight title in 1989 and is now a highly respected television analyst, came perhaps the nearest to explaining it in a published conversation with Robert Phillip of the London *Daily Telegraph*, shortly after the death of Scottish boxer James Murray following a fight in October 1995. At the time, still only 31 but with so much already achieved, he was contemplating a comeback.

"Will I fight again? God, I don't know. Part of the problem is I've never had boxing beaten out of me. It's still my first love... I know I could die. I know I could end up on a life-support machine. I know I could end up shuffling around like Ali. Of course I know the risks...

"Why do I love boxing so much, even at dreadful times like this? Because it's the story of life. The pain, the honour, the nastiness, the nobility. Life's every ingredient. What other sport could have given the world Ali? I'm proud, really proud, to be a fighting man."

For years, boxers have suffered from the image of men with bent noses, cauliflower ears, and busted hands, men who fought because there was nothing else for them. Nothing could be further from the truth, although many do seek it out initially as a way out of the poverty trap, and many, like the late Johnny Owen, who was painfully shy and rarely spoke in company, find a way of expression in a boxing ring that they simply cannot command outside it.

Tony Sibson, one of the most exciting British boxers of the late 1970s and 1980s, thrived in a boxing ring. Yet even now, as a successful businessman approaching 40 years of age who is sometimes invited to functions as a "Guest of Honor," he finds it extremely difficult to stand in a room full of boxing people and answer questions from the floor. This is not out of any difficulty with the English language, but simply a tendency to shrink back in company. In December 1996 in his home city of Leicester, England, where he has a place of honor at the Grand Hotel Sporting Club and is among his own people, he said to me with a rueful grin after taking the microphone two or three times in a question-and-answer session: "That was far tougher than going into a ring... was it all right?" Yet one-to-one, Sibson has an almost poetic vision.

At the end of his career, we wrote a book together that for one reason and another was never published. When we first sat down, he said: "Maybe this will be a book, whether it does any good or not, I don't know. But I don't want this to be just about Tony Sibson. It might be a speech for a lot of fighters. We're not daft. We know what's going on. We know we're cogs for the machinery. Whatever happens, the machine must go on. We're just bits that wear out. But the people who run it, the people who make the real money, can't ever have what I really am. It's like if you're a rock singer. They can pay you what they like, but they can never have the one thing you'll have—that moment on stage."

Perhaps the wrong-headed, stereotyped assessment of boxers was summed up best by the British and Commonwealth welterweight champion Sylvester Mittee with his oft-celebrated remark: "There is a popularly held misconception that fighters are monosyllabic buffoons. And that myth is perpetuated when fighters are thrown in front of a microphone and they freeze."

Boxers are exceptional people. What follows here is a tribute to all of them—including those who did not make it into the honored list of 250 fighters. With a handful of exceptions, these things are to some extent arbitrary. What makes one man better than another, or his achievements worth more? There will be arguments over the boxers we have chosen to represent the sport in this unofficial "Hall of Fame," yet were the time and space available for a succession of volumes, there would be 250 boxers from each decade who had a story worth the telling. The luxury is not available, of course, and we hope that the selection is of a more general interest than some of the narrower interpretations of the phrase "Hall of Fame." We have not succumbed to the myth that such an honor belongs only to the dead or those who have not boxed for 30 years.

BOXING HISTORY

Boxing's story begins way back in the fog of time, in the civilizations of Ancient Greece and then Rome. A description of a fight scene in the *Iliad* is the first known record, but as nobody is quite sure when Homer was writing it's difficult to put any kind of date on it. Nevertheless, anyone who thinks Muhammad Ali was an innovator in the art of psyching out opponents should read what Homer's character Epeius had to say about his forthcoming fight.

"The mule is mine," he said, referring to the prize at stake. "I'm going to tear the fellow's flesh to ribbons and smash his bones. I recommend him to have all his mourners standing by to take him off when I've done with him!"

Bare-knuckle boxing certainly existed in Britain in the seventeenth century, and the first commercially acknowledged champion was James Figg of Thame, who set up his own academy at the Adam And Eve tavern near the corner of what is now Tottenham Court Road and Oxford

Street in London around 1719. Four years later King George I ordered a permanent ring be erected, surrounded by railings, in Hyde Park for the use of any members of the public who wished to box. It was torn down by religious zealots in the 1820s. The first rules were drawn up in the name of John Broughton, the most successful of those who followed Figg, and followed the first major ring fatality in 1741 when Broughton injured George Stephenson of Hull so severely that he died of his injuries.

In the middle years of the century a series of scandals seriously damaged the sport, but it revived in the 1780s and was at its peak for the next 40 years, rivaled in popularity only by the great horse races of the day. Champions like Jem Belcher, Daniel Mendoza, Tom Cribb, and Henry Pearce were national heroes. An obituary of one J. J. Braysfield, a wealthy eccentric from Camberwell, in the *Sporting Magazine* in 1820, illustrates how much a part of daily life pugilism had become:

"Almost from his infancy, he was an attendant upon all the fairs, boxing matches, races and diversions of every kind round London, from the ring made by the first class amateurs, of the Fancy, down to the weekly badger baiting in Black Boy Alley. He was no less a constant attendant upon the execution of criminals..."

And in his essay "The English Admirals" in 1881, Robert Louis Stevenson said boxing was still central to the ordinary working man's sporting interests at that time.

"Almost everybody in our land, except humanitarians and a few persons whose youth has been depressed by exceptionally aesthetic surroundings, can understand and sympathize with an Admiral or a prize-fighter. I do not wish to bracket Benbow or Tom Cribb; but, depend upon it, they are practically bracketed for admiration in the minds of many frequented alehouses. If you told them about Germanicus and the eagles, or Regulus going back to Carthage, they would very likely fall asleep; but tell them about Harry Pearce and Jem Belcher, or about Nelson and the Nile, and they put down their pipes to listen."

As social reformers had their way and old country sports like badger-baiting and cock-fighting were outlawed, prize-fighting drew increasing attention from abolitionists. In 1845, *The Illustrated London News* called it "a practice revolting to mankind." It almost died out as fights became increasingly long-winded and dull, decided increasingly often by foul blows. With the exception of the astonishing fight between Tom Sayers and John Camel Heenan in 1860, when Parliament was virtually emptied of members wanting to see the event, boxing declined slowly, until the acceptance of the Marquess of Queensberry Rules allowed it to survive and prosper as a sport with gloves. Before this, rules were basic and sometimes loosely applied. Broughton was no doubt keen to avoid another tragedy, but his rules were probably to some degree a result of social pressure. He and his friends knew what a lucrative business they had, the wealthy patrons enjoyed it as a spectacle and a gambling diversion, and took measures enough to protect it. Broughton's Rules, published in August 1743, outlawed the more grotesque fouls like gouging at the eyes, "purring" or raking a man with spiked boots, and landing blows when the opponent was on the floor.

These rules did well for almost a century, until the "London Prize Ring Rules" were introduced in 1838, following the death of a boxer known as "Brighton" Bill Phelps. They were more specific than Broughton's efforts, but stuck to his guidelines. They were updated in 1853 and 1866, but the following year the Marquess of Queensberry changed boxing forever by putting his name to a set of rules drawn up by John Graham Douglas. These were intended for amateurs, but suited the professional sport admirably, and for the first time imposed a duration on individual rounds, and a "ten" count.

Boxing, both amateur and professional, increased in popularity rapidly as the century drew to a close, and with the founding of the National Sporting Club in Covent Garden in 1891, it found a powerful home that could fight its corner as and when required.

It was required often: deaths from boxing at the NSC were appallingly frequent. Walter Croot in 1897, Tom Turner in 1898, Mike Riley in 1899 and Billy Smith, alias Murray Livingstone, in 1901. After the last fatality eight people involved, including the club officers, the seconds of the boxers, the referee, and the winning boxer, Jack Roberts, were accused of "feloniously killing and slaying Murray Livingstone." After a full hearing at the Old Bailey, the jury took two minutes to find each defendant not guilty, ruling that Livingstone's death was an accident as a result of a boxing contest.

Boxing in Britain was not legalized by that landmark judgment, but the precedent was established. Its position strengthened, it developed rapidly.

In the United States, bare-knuckle fighting had developed throughout the century, in spite of the opposition of would-be abolitionists, anxious that their new country grew along supposedly civilized lines. British boxers plied their trade in America from the 1830s and the last of the acknowledged London Prize Ring Rules champions was American-born, the great John L. Sullivan, a gregarious, larger-than-life character who was adored by his fans and despised by the "right-thinking, moral majority." He reigned from 1882 to 1892, and was involved in the last bare-knuckle champion-ship fight, when he defeated Jake Kilrain in the 75th round in Richburg, Mississippi, in July 1889.

When he lost the title in New Orleans in September 1892, it was in a gloved bout. James J. Corbett, a young, scientific boxer from San Francisco, knocked him out in the 21st round.

Way back in the early nineteenth century, the lightweight class was generally acknowledged as a sensible alternative for those too small to box the giants of the day, but weight divisions developed only gradually as the century wore on. By 1900, there were men claiming to be champions of the world at heavyweight, middleweight, welterweight, light-weight, featherweight, and bantamweight. Actual weight limits for these categories settled down with time, but at first were by no means rigidly defined.

In the first years of the century gloved boxing spread from Britain to Europe, and was established in France largely on the reputation of the glamorous Georges Carpentier, who fought from 1908 until 1926. In the years immediately preceding World War I, European champions began to appear. By 1920, the structure of boxing was recognizable. In South Africa and Australia, it had been popular since bare-knuckle times.

THE SURVIVAL OF THE SPORT

Any sport can exist because of its competitors, but it thrives and matures only by the extent of its popular support. Because of the intensity of the opposition boxing has attracted, its success has depended more than most on how well it draws. Fortunately, this has never been a prolonged problem. From bare-knuckle days, when "The Fancy" would travel hundreds of miles and tramp across inhospitable terrain to witness a big fight, knowing all the while that magisterial intervention could force everyone to rush into the next county, or even cancel it completely, people have felt compelled to watch boxing in huge numbers.

The first great promoter to tap into these resources in the gloved era was George "Tex" Rickard, a legendary Texan who in his time raised cattle, mined gold, ran a gambling hall, blew one fortune at poker and in unsuccessful digs, and then made another promoting fights. He made $30,000 on a lightweight championship fight in 1906 between Battling Nelson and Joe Gans in the boomtown of Goldfield, Nevada, and even more when he shelled out $101,000 in cash to clinch the heavyweight championship fight in Reno, Nevada, in 1910 between Jack Johnson and James J. Jeffries.

Rickard promoted Jack Dempsey in the Manassa Mauler's great years, beginning with his three-round win over Jess Willard for the heavyweight championship near Toledo, Ohio, in July 1919. Dempsey's defense against Carpentier in 1921 brought boxing its first million-dollar gate when 80,183 paid to watch the fight in a stadium Rickard had built specially at Boyle's Acres, Jersey City. The total receipts were an astonishing $1,789,238.

Dempsey and Luis Firpo drew 82,000 to the Polo Grounds in New York in 1923, but Rickard's biggest draw in terms of sheer volume of people was on a rainy night in Philadelphia in September 1926 when 120,757 paid to watch Dempsey lose his title to Gene Tunney. The rematch 12 months later at Soldier Field, Chicago, attracted 104,953 and gross receipts of an incredible $2,658,660. This was the famous "Battle of the Long Count," in which Tunney was knocked down for a controversial count of nine in the seventh round, but then got up to drop Dempsey and win the decision. Afterward Tunney's share came to just short of $1 million, and he paid Rickard the difference so that he could enjoy the kick of receiving a million-dollar check. "He was the great man of my life," said Dempsey, referring to Rickard in his autobiography *Massacre In The Sun.*

Rickard's death in 1929, the Wall Street crash, and the retirement of Dempsey and Tunney left a huge gap, which was not properly filled until the arrival of Joe Louis, who attracted three million-dollar live gates—for his non-title fight against Max Baer in 1935, and for his world title defenses against Max Schmeling in 1938 and then Billy Conn in 1946.

It was a quarter of a century before it happened again, this time for an indoor fight—the classic first meeting between Joe Frazier and Muhammad Ali at Madison Square Garden, New York, in 1971 when a capacity crowd of 20,455 paid

$1,352,951, with ringside seats selling for an unprecedented $150. Frank Sinatra took photographs from a press pitch beneath the ropes!

Television took boxing into a new era and projected Ali as a worldwide star. The Ali–Ken Norton fight in 1976 at Yankee Stadium produced the first $2 million gate since the Tunney–Dempsey rematch, and the rematch between Ali and Leon Spinks in the New Orleans Superdome drew a huge indoor crowd of 63,350 as well as a gross of $4.8 million. Ali's final world title fight against Larry Holmes broke the $5 million barrier, even though the Caesars Palace arena in Las Vegas had a capacity of less than 25,000.

For as long as it does business like this, boxing would seem to have too much financial clout for the abolitionists to make much impact. In 1993 in the Aztec Stadium, Mexico City, national hero Julio Cesar Chavez drew an astonishing live crowd which was estimated as high as 136,000 for a defense against Greg Haugen of the United States which brought him his 84th consecutive win.

In Britain, television viewing figures for 1995 reflected boxing's popularity, as it filled three of the top five places in the listings for sporting events. The ill-fated fight between Nigel Benn and Gerald McClellan topped the list with 13 million viewers, more than a million ahead of The Grand National horse race, a cherished favorite. A Frank Bruno fight came third, with Naseem Hamed fifth.

REGULATION

Boxing led a maverick existence, run by individual promoters, then promotional groups, US state commissions, and national governing bodies, and surviving persistent Mob interference from the 1920s until the early 1960s. There were several attempts to bring it into some kind of logical order, but nothing was totally effective.

British boxing has been regulated better than most, although never drawing government backing or legal standing. The National Sporting Club considered itself the natural guardian of the sport and arrogantly refused to recognize contests held elsewhere as having British championship status. While this was unjustified, the social strength of the NSC gave it a powerful voice. In 1909 it fixed weight divisions that would provide the base for championship boxing from then on. The categories were, as follows:

Heavyweight—any weight
Light-heavyweight—up to 175 lb.
Middleweight—160 lb.
Welterweight—147 lb.
Lightweight—135 lb.
Featherweight—126 lb.
Bantamweight—118 lb.
Flyweight —112 lb.

The NSC also provided belts, sponsored by their president, Lord Lonsdale, for British champions. When the British Boxing Board of Control was first formed in 1918 it was no more than a puppet of the NSC, but as the club declined, so the Board increased in strength and in 1929 it was reconstituted, taking full control of the sport. The Board continued the tradition of awarding Lonsdale Belts to British champions.

In Paris in 1920, the first attempt to found a worldwide governing body was made with the establishment of the International Boxing Union. France, Denmark, Holland, Italy, Switzerland, Sweden, Norway, Brazil, Argentina, Canada, Australia, Britain, and the United States all put their names to the founding of the new body, but the US commitment was no more than token, and in 1922 Britain withdrew support.

In the United States, the National Boxing Association was formed in 1921 to take power away from the New York State Athletic Commission, which had assumed responsibility for the sport. By 1927, the NBA was declaring its own world champions... and the divisive nature of the sport at the top level was set on course, with separate factions within the United States itself, as well as alternative ideas coming from Britain and the countries represented by the International Boxing Union.

Boxing is a notoriously difficult sport to regulate and historians still argue over the claims and counterclaims of men purporting to be world champions in the days before any governing bodies existed at all. Boxing is about boxers, however, and they have always risen above the petty arguments of those whose no doubt well-meaning attempts to regulate the sport become bogged down in red tape.

Gradually, more weight categories were added to the eight originals until by the late 1980s there were 17, from strawweight or mini-flyweight (105 lb.) upward. The strawweight divison was introduced in 1987, light-flyweight (108 lb.) in 1975, super-flyweight (115 lb.) in 1980, super-bantamweight (122 lb.) in 1976, super-featherweight in 1921 when it was called junior-lightweight, light-welterweight in 1922, light-middleweight in 1962, super-middleweight in 1984, and cruiserweight in 1979.

After Rickard the next major promoter was Mike Jacobs, a former ticket agent, who made his fortune with Joe Louis. He died of a heart attack in 1952, and was succeeded by Jim Norris, a millionaire whose International Boxing Club ran the sport... with help from Underworld figures like the notorious Frankie Carbo, Blinky Palermo, Truman Gibson, and others. Mob involvement was high in the 1920s when stories of fixed fights abounded, and again after the War when they seemed to have an unusual amount of pull in the lightweight, welterweight, and middleweight divisions. The IBC failed to persuade the fiercely independent Cus D'Amato, manager of heavyweight champion Floyd Patterson, to play their way.

BOXING WORLDWIDE

In 1957 the IBC was brought down by US Senator Estes Kefauver for the offense of running an illegal monopoly. It was disbanded the following year after an investigation and prosecution from the US Department of Justice and the FBI. The Kefauver Committee also investigated mob involvement in boxing and former world middleweight champion Jake La Motta testified that he had thrown a fight in the 1940s in return for a shot at the title, which he then won against Marcel Cerdan of France. In December 1961, five of the leading mobsters, including Carbo and Palermo, were jailed.

Carbo received the heaviest punishment—25 years and a $10,000 fine. Palermo was jailed for 15 years, with another $10,000 fine. Norris died shortly afterward, a broken man.

As a result of this scandal, boxing attempted to put its house in order. The ineffective National Boxing Association was replaced by the World Boxing Association, founded in Tacoma, Washington, in August 1962. The WBA had widespread support in the United States, with the exception of New York, which had always run in opposition to the old NBA anyway, and also drew good support from Latin America.

As a result of that move, the rest of the major forces in the boxing world formed the World Boxing Council, based in Mexico City, in February 1963. Leading members were the British Board of Control, the European Boxing Union, the British Commonwealth, and it also enjoyed a working agreement with the New York Commission.

Designed to save boxing, the fact that these two organizations rarely agreed on anything eventually led to the ludicrous situation in the 1990s where four or five boxers call themselves "world champion" at the same weight at any time. The opportunity to provide boxing with an all-embracing body like, say FIFA in soccer, was lost 30 years before.

A split in the WBA led to disgruntled members, led by Bobby Lee of New Jersey, forming the International Boxing Federation, and their operations began in 1984. They survived because of their American platform. They claimed the WBA was biased toward South and Central American nations, at the expense of the interests of the United States, which promoted most championship fights. The IBF also survived because it attracted the patronage of Larry Holmes, who was acknowledged at the time as the best heavyweight in the world, but who had fallen out with the WBC over his decision to give a title shot to Joe Frazier's young son, Marvis. The WBC refused to sanction the fight, which ended inside a round, and although that had a non-title status, when Holmes returned it was as IBF champion.

Another breakaway group walked out of the 1988 WBA Convention and formed the WBO, run by Pepe Cordero, who had once been denounced by promoter Bob Arum as the "bagman" for the WBA. That is, if any promoter wanted anything done in the WBA Cordero, who had no official position, had to be paid. Even so, the WBO flourished from its Puerto Rican base and on Cordero's death the business passed on to his son. Among their early champions was the great but declining Thomas Hearns. By the early 1990s they were well established.

Other organizations followed—including the IBC, IBO, WBF, and, in January 1995, the British-based World Boxing Union. The proliferation of sanctioning bodies, known collectively as "The Alphabet Boys," heaped scorn on the administrative side of a sport which seemed absolutely chaotic. One sensible, overdue move came in the mid-1990s when the American Boxing Commissions formed an association, which promoted a unity that had previously been lacking in the United States. From that point, any fight which took place in a commission-less state was regarded as a non-sanctioned, in other words, unlicensed fight. Suspensions were respected by all members, and a level of communication was reached which had never been achieved before. Results from all commissions were submitted by the New Jersey-based organization Fight Fax, which ensured the records of all American licensed boxers were kept up to date.

The major international promoters of recent times have been Don King, Bob Arum, the Main Events team headed by the late Dan Duva and Cedric Kushner, all of whom have benefited enormously from the proliferation of governing bodies. Television companies can sell world championship fights to audiences more easily than meaningful non-title fights as the latter demand of the viewer some knowledge of boxing's pecking order, whereas the former can be marketed on the falsehood that the two fighters in the ring are the best two at their weight in the world. While the discerning viewer may notice the difference in initials of the sanctioning bodies, most will not. In 1995, for another project, I calculated the increase in number of world championships contested (at ten-year intervals) during the century. The figures are revealing:

1904	—	8
1914	—	11
1924	—	11
1934	—	21
1944	—	10
1954	—	13
1964	—	19
1974	—	40
1984	—	89
1994	—	177

In 1993, writing for the trade paper *Boxing News*, I discovered that statistics bore out the notion that particular governing bodies favored or worked closely with certain promoters. At the time the IBF was dominated by Cedric Kushner, the WBC by Don King, the WBA worked mostly with Dan Duva, and the WBO with Britain's Barry Hearn.

Boxing is now a far more complex business than it was at the beginning of the gloved era when men grew slowly accustomed to three-minute rounds, but still fought long, grueling fights. In 1891, James J. Corbett and Peter Jackson boxed themselves to a standstill after 61 rounds, with no winner, and 15 years later Joe Gans and Battling Nelson slogged out a 42-round epic for the lightweight championship before Gans won on a foul. The 1915 heavyweight championship bout between Jack Johnson and Jess Willard was scheduled for 45 rounds—Willard won in the 26th. In 1914, former champion Bob Fitzsimmons wrote to boxing journalist Nat Fleischer, who would later found *Ring* magazine in New York. Fitzsimmons said:

"The cavemen of the ring are extinct. Champions such as we had in my prime are gone, never again to return. The champions of the future will be as children compared to the rough and ready battlers of 20 or more years ago. Fighting, like all other sports, is reaching out along lines of improvement. The men of today realize than boxing is more important than slugging. They are beginning to see the advantages of knowing how to block and feint and those who still can retain their punch are the ones who will reach the top. You'll find as the years pass that fighting will become more and more scientific and championships will change hands on points and not on knockouts."

(Fleischer, 50 Years At Ringside, 1958).

Fitzsimmons was right. After 10 rounds, he and his contemporaries might have considered a fight was just beginning to develop, yet both of the heavyweight championship bouts between Gene Tunney and Jack Dempsey in 1926 and 1927 produced points wins for Tunney over the 10-round course. The last world title fight to last more than 15 rounds was in 1923 when Mike McTigue outpointed Battling Siki in Dublin for the light-heavyweight belt, and the last world title fight to be scheduled for 20 rounds was between Joe Louis and Abe Simon in Detroit in 1941. Louis won in the 13th. After that, the world championship distance settled down to 15 rounds, which was accepted as a fair test until the 1980s when, officially on the grounds of medical safety, the distance was shortened by the WBC to 12 rounds. Coincidentally, a 12-round fight fits in to a one-hour TV slot, whereas a 15 rounder does not.

The more senior world sanctioning authorities, in particular the WBC, have made considerable improvements in the sport, especially in medical areas. They also from time to time fund medical needs of their former champions—for example, Thai flyweight Sot Chitalada had a bill for eye surgery paid by the authority recently—and they also showed their interest in boxing history by backing a more eccentric campaign to return the body of Battling Siki from its New York burial ground to his native Senegal. Their political bias has been questioned from time to time, but few would suggest that president Jose Sulaiman and his team do not love the sport.

But when all the external issues are summed up, they seem no more than peripheral, unnecessarily complex diversions. Boxing's lure is in its boxers and in the fights for which they are remembered. I hope this book will serve as a tribute, not just to the 250 highlighted here, but to all of them, from the best to the worst, to the most successful champions to the rawest novices. For boxers are a special breed, and it's been my privilege to work among them for almost 20 years. Thank you, one and all.

MUHAMMAD ALI

FACT FILE

1942 Born Cassius Marcellus Clay, Jr., Louisville, Kentucky

1960 Won Olympic light-heavyweight gold medal

1964 Beat Sonny Liston to win world heavyweight title

1967 Exiled from boxing for refusing to be drafted into US Army

1971 Lost to Joe Frazier in world title comeback

1974 Regained championship by knocking out George Foreman

1978 Lost to novice Leon Spinks

1978 Champion for a third time by outpointing Spinks

Career record: Fights 61, Won 56, Lost 5

For two controversial decades Muhammad Ali made the world sit up and pay attention to his extrovert, wonderful genius.

"I shocked the world!" he yelled on the night in 1964 when supposedly invincible heavyweight champion Sonny Liston retired at the end of the sixth round in Miami. And Ali, who changed his name from Cassius Clay the day after that epic triumph, went on shocking and delighting, astonishing and occasionally irritating his public for another generation and more.

In a sense he was two fighters. Before 1967 he was built for speed and youthful exuberance. When he returned from his three-year exile, which had been forced on him by his refusal to be drafted into service in the Vietnam War, he was slower than before but more cunning. He took more punches, too many in the end, but he proved that as well as his incredible talent he had a huge heart and solid jaw. He lost to a peak Joe Frazier in a 15-round classic in Madison Square Garden, but regained the title by knocking out George Foreman in the "Rumble in the Jungle" in Zaire in 1974.

His 14-round triumph over Frazier in "The Thrilla in Manila" in 1975 was his last great performance. He should have retired then, but fought on too long, losing and regaining the title against near-novice Leon Spinks, and losing a sad, one-sided fight with Larry Holmes in 1980. His last fight was a points defeat to Trevor Berbick in the Bahamas in December 1981, by which time he was chronically sick. Parkinson's Syndrome was pronounced soon afterward.

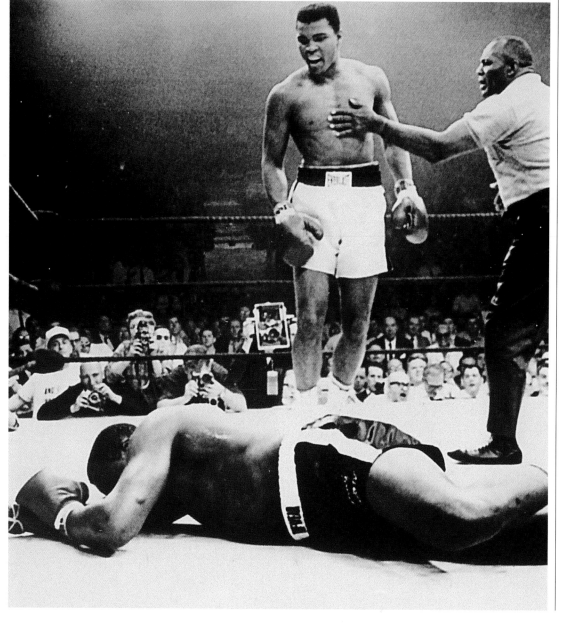

SNEERING ALI TAUNTS THE FALLEN SONNY LISTON IN THEIR 1965 REMATCH. JERSEY JOE WALCOTT IS THE REFEREE

SEE ALSO ◆ GEORGE FOREMAN 118 ◆ JOE FRAZIER 122 ◆ SONNY LISTON 196

TERRY ALLEN

Terry Allen from Islington in north London, England could have spent most of his life in prison, yet had the character and determination to find a different path—one that took him straight to the flyweight championship of the world.

Allen's real name was Edward Govier, but he changed it when he was on the run from the Navy during World War II. He deserted after six weeks, swapped ID cards with an acquaintance—and "Terry Allen" was born.

After he had won 16 pro fights, he was arrested and sent to serve his country in Egypt, but by the end of 1945 he was home, and combined his boxing career with a day job as a barrow boy selling fruit and vegetables.

There were setbacks along the way, including a 15-round draw with world flyweight champion Rinty Monaghan in Belfast's intimidating King's Hall, but after the Irishman retired, Allen was matched for the vacant title with Honore Pratesi of France. And on April 25, 1950, 24-year-old Allen outpointed Pratesi at Harringay Arena in north London. A pre-fight underdog, Allen outwitted the Frenchman to win a 15-round decision—and the next morning was back at work on his barrow!

He was champion for only 98 days, losing the title on points to 34-year-old Dado Marino before a 10,000 crowd in Honolulu. In a rematch in November 1952, Allen lost again.

He never regained the form that had taken him to the title, but he was given one last crack in Tokyo against Marino's successor, Yoshio Shirai, in 1953. He lost—and retired the following year.

FACT FILE

1925 Born Edward Albert Govier, Islington, London

1949 Drew with Rinty Monaghan in first world title attempt

1950 Won world flyweight title by outpointing Honore Pratesi

1950 Lost world title to Dado Marino in Honolulu

1954 Retired after European title defeat in Milan

Died: London, age 61, April 8, 1987

Career record: Fights 77, Won 62, Lost 14, Drawn 1

ALLEN (RIGHT) ATTACKS HONORE PRATESI IN THEIR FLYWEIGHT TITLE FIGHT AT HARRINGAY, LONDON, IN APRIL 1950

SEE ALSO ◆ DADO MARINO 212 ◆ RINTY MONAGHAN 220

THE GREAT FIGHTS

SONNY LISTON
V.
CASSIUS CLAY

MIAMI BEACH CONVENTION HALL.
FEBRUARY 25, 1964.

Boxing was getting a terrible press. People questioned its validity following the high-profile deaths of Benny Paret and Davey Moore, and pointed out that its heavyweight champ, Sonny Liston, was an unsmiling ex-con with rumored underworld connections. Now came Cassius Clay, a boy, a brash, bewitching, funny, annoying 22-year-old to make the whole thing seemed more like a circus than ever.

At the weigh-in Clay raved so wildly a doctor pronounced him "living in mortal fear."

Some said Liston was frightened of what he perceived as a crazy man, others said he bet his entire $720,000 purse on Clay, or that he was told to throw the fight by the mob, but the truth is probably mundane. Eddie Machen, who took Liston 12 rounds in 1960, said when you called Liston names in the ring, when you did things he didn't expect, when you displayed that you were not intimidated, he lost his concentration and his temper.

Clay made it plain he was not afraid, drilling home jabs and fast hooks to win round one. Liston took the second, but in round three was cut beneath the left eye. He landed heavily again in the fourth, and at the bell Clay told trainer Angelo Dundee: "Cut the gloves off!" He had something in his eyes and couldn't see—but was shoved out for the fifth and told to run.

He backed off, taking body blows, doing nothing. He seemed ready to fall. By round six he could see again, and dazzlingly outboxed Liston, who suddenly looked slow, old, and uninterested. The official cards were split three ways: the fight was level.

And then it was over. Clay leaped to his feet, shouting uncontrollably: "I shocked the world!"

Liston sat placidly on his stool, claiming a damaged left shoulder. This was a pathetic surrender from a misunderstood man.

The next day Clay announced he was Muhammad Ali, a Black Muslim. And 15 months later he knocked out Liston in the first round of another strange, confusing fight. By then, hesitantly, boxing was recovering.

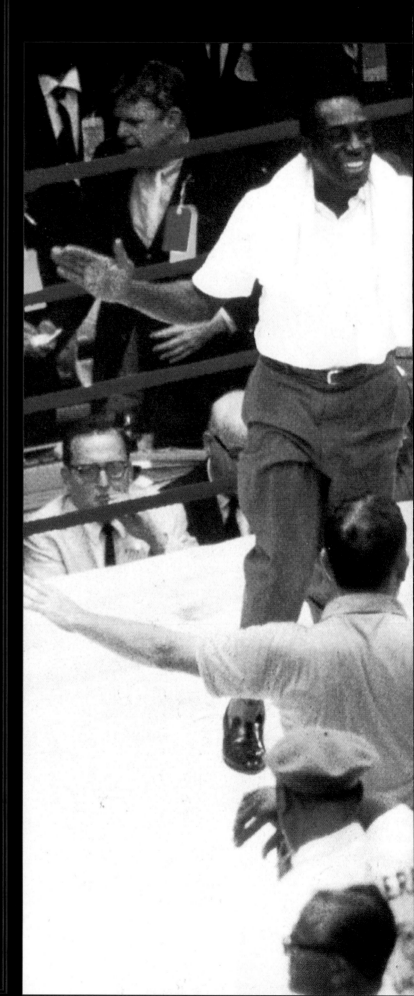

LOU AMBERS

Known as "The Herkimer Hurricane," Lou Ambers was the son of a saloon keeper who lost everything in the Wall Street Crash in 1929. The same year Lou began boxing in bootleg shows for $5 a time to help out with the family finances.

Lou, whose real name was Luigi Giuseppe D'Ambrosio, slogged his way to a world lightweight title fight by 1935, after losing only one decision in his first 46 fights. On this occasion Champion Tony Canzoneri outpointed him. In his next fight he beat future welterweight champion Fritzie Zivic in spite of a broken jaw that was wired up for six weeks afterwards.

He was deeply affected by the death of an opponent in 1936 but six months later beat Canzoneri for the championship in front of a crowd of 18,026 at Madison Square Garden. It was a unanimous decision. Surprisingly, he won only five of nine non-title fights but when the championship was on the line, he managed to regain his form and outpointed Canzoneri again.

Henry Armstrong beat Ambers on a split decision to take away his title in July 1938, but Ambers won the rematch in Yankee Stadium, a unanimous decision that rankled with Armstrong for years afterward. He lost the title to Lew Jenkins in three rounds—his first stoppage defeat—in May 1940. When Jenkins stopped him again in February 1941, he retired. Although his official record showed 100 fights, Ambers said including the bootleg bouts it was really 238, of which he lost only eight in total.

"I loved to fight," he said. He moved to Phoenix, Arizona, with his wife and family, and worked for a metal company, ran a restaurant and did some public relations until he retired.

A VETERAN AMBERS (RIGHT) FACES LEW JENKINS IN 1940

SEE ALSO ◆ **HENRY ARMSTRONG 21** ◆ **TONY CANZONERI 54**

DENNIS ANDRIES

DENNIS ANDRIES could be ungainly and clumsy, but more than made up for his lack of natural talent with his fanatical dedication and ruthless self-belief. He could look the crudest, most disorganized of fighters, and yet kept learning, kept working, kept believing until he won the World Boxing Council light-heavyweight title not once, but three times.

Born in Guyana, his actual age was often a matter of conjecture, but officially he was 24 when he began his professional career. And he was still licensed at the age of 43! His first two British title bids ended in disappointment: Bunny Johnson and Tom Collins both outpointed him. But he plodded on and in April 1986 in Edmonton, north London, he slugged out a split decision win over former US Marine J. B. Williamson to become WBC

champion. The next morning this down-to-earth man traveled to his first press conference as world champion on the underground, his belt laid across his lap in a shopping bag.

After he lost the title to Thomas Hearns in 10 rounds in Detroit in 1987, Andries moved to the Kronk Gym to work alongside his conqueror. Trainer Emanuel Steward guided him to two more WBC title reigns. He overpowered Tony Willis in Tucson in February 1989, then lost on a last-round stoppage to Australian substitute Jeff Harding. He traveled to Melbourne and stunned the boxing world by knocking out Harding in a return, but their third fight in London went to the Australian on a majority decision. Five years later, Andries was still fighting, and had won and lost the British cruiserweight championship.

FACT FILE

1953 Born Buxton, Guyana
1986 Beat J. B. Williamson to become WBC champion
1987 Lost title to Thomas Hearns, moved from London to Detroit
1989 Regained WBC title by beating Tony Willis
1989 Lost title on last round stoppage to Jeff Harding
1990 Won WBC title a third time by knocking out Harding
1991 Lost "decider" with Harding on majority decision
Career record: Fights 65, Won 49, Lost 13, Drawn 3

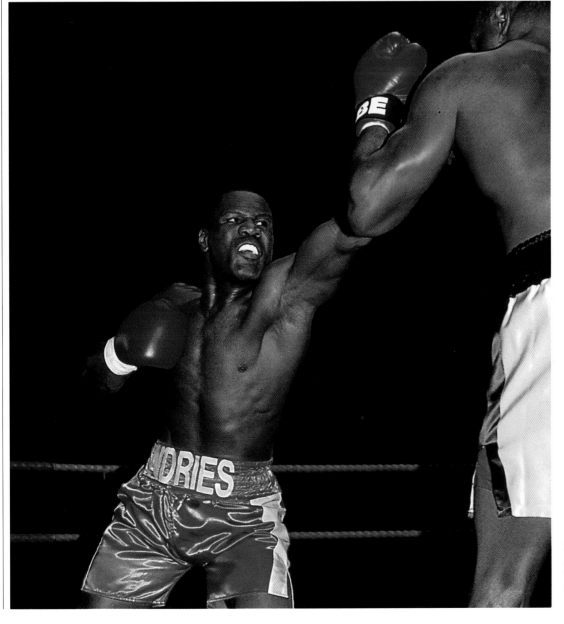

THE HACKNEY ROCK: ANDRIES FOUGHT PROFESSIONALLY FOR ALMOST 20 YEARS, AND HAD THREE SPELLS AS WORLD LIGHT-HEAVYWEIGHT CHAMPION

SEE ALSO ◆ THOMAS HEARNS 153

YURI ARBACHAKOV

Mechanical, almost programmed, as one might expect of the old Soviet Union amateur coaching system, Yuri Arbachakov is nevertheless a hugely successful fighting machine who has adapted magnificently to the demands of the professional boxing ring.

Arbachakov is a solid puncher, who thumps home a hard jab to set up his attacks, and although he has tended to take more punches as he has grown older, his chin has not yet let him down.

He sprang to prominence in 1989 when after winning the Soviet flyweight championship, he won gold medals at both the European and World Championships. Mikhail Gorbachov's "Glasnost" policy opened up the country to capitalist influences, but professional boxing was initially a haphazard, disorganized sport. Arbachakov, along with several of his contempories, accepted offers to move base to Japan, where he made his debut in February 1990. Most of the others returned home, but Arbachakov stuck it out, enduring bouts of homesickness and in June 1992 winning the WBC flyweight title, the first of the old Soviet boxers to claim a professional world championship. His eighth round knockout of Thailand's Muangchai Kittikasem was ruthlessly effective, and provided a perfect platform upon which he built his reputation as the best flyweight of his time. Arbachakov complained from time to time of his life in Tokyo, once having to play host to a stream of journalists who, following his criticism that it was too cramped, were invited to inspect the home provided by his promoter. In the ring, however, he was flawless. He had a tight squeeze against Mexican counterpuncher Ysaias Zamudio, but dealt with all-comers whenever required, earning star status in his adopted country.

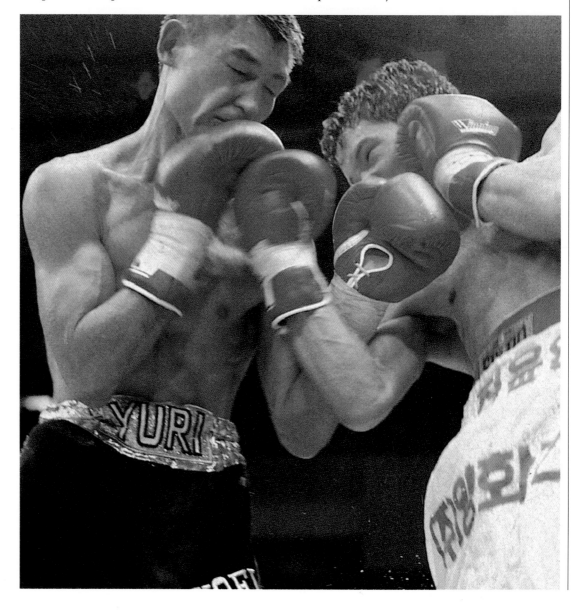

ARBACHAKOV—A TRUE FIGHTING MACHINE WHO WAS DECEPTIVELY CLEVER AND A HURTFUL PUNCHER

BRUNO ARCARI

Bruno Arcari was a tough, organized southpaw from Latina, south of Rome. He made an inauspicious start, losing his debut on a cut eye in December 1964. Although he won his next 11, including a decision over the veteran former world lightweight champion Joe "Old Bones" Brown, he was stopped again on cuts when he challenged Massimo Consolati for the Italian light-welterweight title in August 1966.

However, from this time until his retirement 12 years later, Arcari remained unbeaten in a run of 61 fights. He beat Consolati on a disqualification to become Italian champion, and won the European title in 1968 by stopping Johann Orsolics of Austria in Vienna.

Arcari, stocky and clever but rarely spectacular, built up a sizable following at home and when he challenged Pedro Adigue of the Philippines for the WBC title in Rome in January 1970, a crowd of 17,000 turned out. Arcari won a hard fight on points, and went on to turn back all-comers for the next four years. Rene Roque of France, the Brazilian Joao Henrique, and Enrique Jana, Domingo Barrera, and Everaldo Costa Acevedo all failed to dethrone him.

On a rare foray outside his home country, Arcari retained his title by knocking out hard-hitting but erratic Jorgen Hansen in five rounds in Copenhagen. Six months after defending for the eighth time, against Tony Ortiz of Spain in February 1974, he gave up the title because he could no longer make light-welterweight, but in spite of some promising results, his plans to fight for the welterweight championship never fully materialized and in 1978 he retired.

FACT FILE

1942 Born Latina, Italy

1964 Made professional debut

1968 Won European light-welterweight title

1970 Won WBC title by outpointing Pedro Adigue in Rome

1974 Relinquished WBC title after eight successful defenses

1978 Announced retirement, age 36

Career record: Fights 73, Won 70, Lost 2, Drawn 1

BRUNO ARCARI LIFTED BY FANS AFTER HIS TRIUMPH AGAINST PEDRO ADIGUE IN 1970

SEE ALSO ◆ JOE BROWN 43

ALEXIS ARGUELLO

FACT FILE

1952 Born Managua, Nicaragua

1974 Won WBA featherweight title

1978 Won WBC super-featherweight belt

1981 Won WBC lightweight title

1982 Failed against Aaron Pryor in bid for fourth world championship

Career record: Fights 88, Won 80, Lost 8

Outside the ring, Alexis Arguello had more than his share of hardship. Inside it, he was a master. A dignified, poised man, he clawed his way up from poverty in Managua. He was working on a dairy farm at 14, and by 16 was a boxer.

His first world title bid in 1974 ended in a narrow points defeat by the Panamanian, Ernesto Marcel, but Marcel was so chastened by the experience he retired almost immediately. Arguello challenged Marcel's successor, the great Mexican Ruben Olivares, in Los Angeles in 1974, and won a dramatic fight in 13 rounds to become WBA featherweight champion at the age of 22.

He was tall and upright, and not over-hard to hit, yet panther-like in his approach and with the rare ability to take a man out with one shot. He was featherweight champion for three years, then moved up to super-featherweight and beat the long-established WBC champion Alfredo Escalera of Puerto Rico on a 13th-round stoppage.

This time there were eight defenses in two years before he relinquished again to move up to lightweight. His points victory over Scotland's Jim Watt at Wembley in June 1981 was a masterclass. His ambition to win a fourth title was foiled when he lost twice to Aaron Pryor, after which he retired.

When the Sandinistas confiscated his lands in Nicaragua, Arguello returned to boxing. After two wins a heart condition was diagnosed and he gave up. He was based in Florida, but struggled to stay afloat financially and in 1994 was back again when past his 40th birthday. After losing his second comeback fight in 1995, he retired for good.

ARGUELLO RAISES THE NICARAGUAN FLAG AFTER A WORLD TITLE TRIUMPH. POLITICAL EVENTS IN HIS HOMELAND EVENTUALLY FORCED HIM TO EMIGRATE

SEE ALSO ◆ RUBEN OLIVARES 257 ◆ AARON PRYOR 273

HENRY ARMSTRONG

Henry Armstrong, otherwise known as Homicide Hank, was the nearest thing to perpetual motion ever seen in a boxing ring. Neither wild nor clumsy, he steamed forward throwing a succession of educated and accurate punches that were not particularly heavy in themselves, but had a cumulative effect. Many good, skillful fighters were worn out by Armstrong simply because they couldn't keep him off.

Some say his extraordinary stamina was a result of a freakishly low heartrate, but for whatever reason, Armstrong achieved the incredible feat of holding three world titles at the same time.

First, he flattened Petey Sarron in six rounds in New York in October 1937—he only man to do that in 143 fights. That gave him the featherweight title. Then he took the welterweight title from Barney Ross at Long Island Bowl on a 15-round decision in May 1938.

Perhaps the most remarkable of all was his split decision over Lou Ambers for the lightweight crown three months after he had beaten Ross. Ambers gashed Armstrong's mouth so badly that blood gushed on to the canvas from the third round on. By the 12th referee Arthur Donovan wanted to stop the fight because "the ring's full of blood—your blood." Armstrong promised "I won't bleed no more," and carried on without his mouthpiece, swallowing his blood as he fought.

Armstrong relinquished his featherweight title and Ambers regained the lightweight belt the following year, but Henry continued to defend the welterweight championship until he lost to Fritzie Zivic in October 1940. Before that he had been foiled by a controversial draw verdict when he tried to win a version of the middleweight title from Ceferino Garcia in Los Angeles. From 1951 he spent his life as a Baptist minister, but died in poverty.

FACT FILE

1912 Born Henry Jackson, Columbus, Mississippi

1937 Knocked out Petey Sarron to win world featherweight title

1938 Beat Barney Ross for the welterweight title

1938 Completed the set by dethroning lightweight champion Lou Ambers

Died: Los Angeles, age 75, October 24, 1988

Career record: Fights 181, Won 152, Lost 21, Drawn 8

ARMSTRONG DUCKS A RIGHT HAND FROM ERNIE RODERICK IN THEIR FIGHT FOR THE WELTERWEIGHT CHAMPIONSHIP AT HARRINGAY, 1939

SEE ALSO ◆ LOU AMBERS 16 ◆ BARNEY ROSS 287 ◆ FRITZIE ZIVIC 351

THE GREAT FIGHTS

RUBEN OLIVARES
V.
ALEXIS ARGUELLO

INGLEWOOD FORUM,
LOS ANGELES.
NOVEMBER 23, 1974.

Ruben Olivares fought with his soul. Win or lose, he offered a piece of himself to everyone who paid to see him.

Arguello possessed an altogether more composed spirit, a more careful, patient personality. He thought about his business, about his strategy, and about when to box and when to fight. In the end a far more complete fighter than Olivares, he was admired, and popular in his native Nicaragua, but neverthelesss did not touch the heart.

Together, before Olivares's faithful followers at the Inglewood Forum, Los Angeles, in November 1974 their styles intertwined to provide a marvelous fight, drawing gate receipts of $186,400.

Although only 27, Olivares had been fighting for 10 years, and had slugged his way out of Mexico to become one of the all-time Forum favorites—this was his 16th appearance at the arena since 1968. The Forum fans were his people.

He had moved out of the bantamweight division after two spells as world champion, and had been WBA featherweight champ for only four months when he met Arguello, a 22-year-old from Managua whose precocious talents had brought him 39 wins in 42 fights.

Arguello, in his first appearance in the United States, began as a big underdog, but grew up as the fight developed. He refused to be intimidated by the partisan atmosphere, boxed capably behind his jab and took whatever Olivares dished out.

By the 13th the old champion had become ragged and tired. Trailing on points, he still fired his punches, but without zip, without venom—and Arguello stepped in, outpunched him and floored him twice, the second time for the count with a clean left hook 80 seconds into the round.

Arguello would go on to win three world titles at separate weights over the next seven years and become a revered ring artist. But Olivares, for all his flaws and reckless ways, would always be loved.

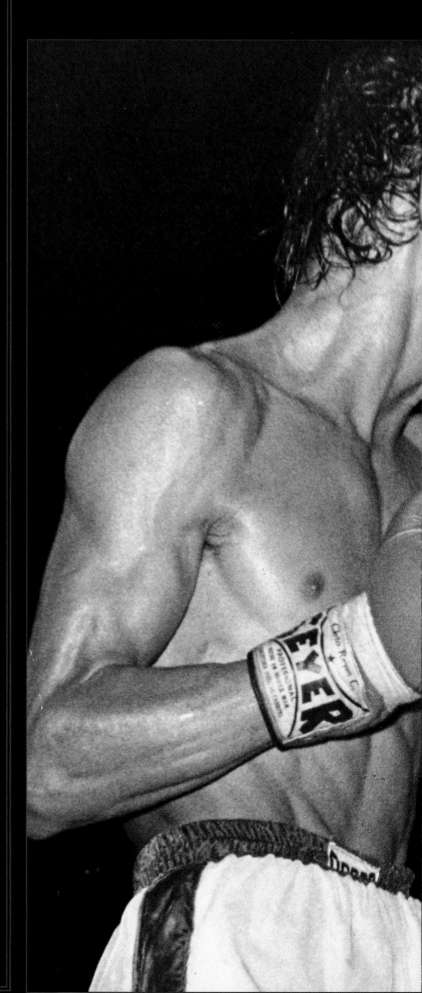

RICARDO ARRENDONDO

FACT FILE

1949 Born Apatzingan, Mexico

1966 Made professional debut

1971 Won WBC super-featherweight title in Japan

1974 Lost WBC title in 6th defense in Japan

Died: Morelia, Mexico, age 42, September 29, 1991

Career record: Fights 99, Won 76, Lost 22, Drawn 1

Ricardo Arrendondo was a speedy, exciting Mexican who at his best was a tough, uncompromising fighter with a big punch. Born in Apatzingan, west of Mexico City, he made his debut in the capital as a 17-year-old and quickly developed a reputation as one of the most impressive young talents in the country.

His first title attempt brought disappointment—he took a good champion, Hiroshi Kobayashi, 15 rounds for the WBA super-featherweight title in Tokyo, but lost the decision. He put that one down to inexperience, rattled off half a dozen knockout wins in a three-month spell, and then returned to Japan to defeat the WBC champion, Yoshiaki Numata, in 10 rounds.

Arredondo didn't mind where he fought. His first defense was in Costa Rica—a decision over Jose Isaac Marin—and although he did return to Mexico City to knock out William Martinez, he enjoyed fighting in Japan. He was well paid to defend there three times, but the fourth trip proved one too many: he was outpointed by Kuniaki Shibata. By then he had lost his edge, and at only 24 years of age had in effect burned himself out.

He continued to box on at lightweight and light-welterweight and always competed well, but slid rapidly from the top. He won only three of his last 12 fights and retired after a 10th-round knockout in Seoul by the Korean Sang-hyun Kim in March 1978. His younger brother Rene Arrendondo later held the WBC light-welterweight title.

Ricardo was killed when he drove his car into a concrete bridge over Rio Chiquito outside his hometown of Morelia. He was 42.

ARREDONDO ... THREE YEARS AS CHAMP, BUT BURNED OUT TOO SOON

SEE ALSO ♦ HIROSHI KOBAYASHI 179

ABE ATTELL

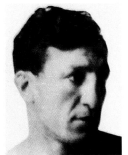

Abe Attell was a gambling man and a great raconteur, who was blessed with enough business sense as well as boxing ability to keep a grip on the world featherweight title for a total of nine years.

From the famous fighting area known as "South of the Slot"—the Powell Street cable car line in San Francisco—Attell would happily win amateur medals that could be traded in for $15. He tired of that, and by 16 was fighting professionally. Only 5 ft. 4 in., he was a tough, clever fighter with a sharp punch. When he was 17 he outpointed former champion George Dixon, but his title claims were not taken seriously until 1903, when he outpointed Johnny Reagan in a 15-rounder in St. Louis. He worked conveniently behind the No Decision law when the need arose, as when he was outboxed in every round by the brilliant Welshman Jim Driscoll, and was also lucky to get a draw in two fights with Owen Moran of Birmingham.

Nevertheless, he knew what he was doing, and was never afraid to risk his money. He gambled his entire $5,000 purse in a 1904 fight with Harry Forbes on a win inside five rounds. He just managed it. Beginning with a rogue named "Bad Jack" McKenna, he went through a string of managers, and learned every trick a fighter needed to know—including how to flatten a referee in a clinch! Eventually, he lost the title on points to Johnny Kilbane over 20 rounds at Vernon, California, in February 1912. His last fight was in 1917. He ran bars in New York and was named in the notorious World Series baseball fix of 1919 (the "Black Sox" scandal), but was never charged. He died in a nursing home in the Catskill Mountains in 1970.

FACT FILE

1884 Born San Francisco, California

1901 First claimed world featherweight title, age 17

1903 Widely acknowledged as champion after beating Johnny Reagan

1912 Lost title to Johnny Kilbane in Vernon, California

Died: New Paltz, New York, age 85, February 7, 1970

Career record: Fights 171, Won 124, Lost 19, Drawn 24, No Decision 2, No Contests 2

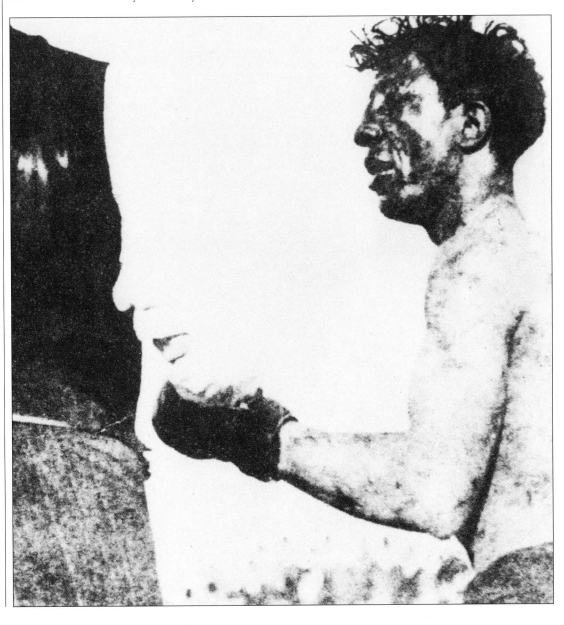

THE BLOODIEST OF BRAWLS: ATTELL IN A GORY 20-ROUNDER WITH "HARLEM" TOMMY MURPHY IN 1912

SEE ALSO ◆ JIM DRISCOLL 95 ◆ JOHNNY KILBANE 177 ◆ OWEN MORAN 231

MAX BAER

Max Baer wasn't the greatest heavyweight who ever lived, but he was probably one of the happiest. "I'm a ham at heart," he said once. "Life's serious, so why not lighten it up a little?"

When he humiliated the giant Primo Carnera in the Madison Square Garden Bowl at Long Island, New York, in 1934, his fame escalated. He was called "The Playboy of the Ring" or "Madcap Maxie," and he did his best to live up to expectations. In his championship winning fight, he dropped poor Carnera repeatedly, once tripping over him and yelling out: "Last one up's a cissy!" Carnera was eventually rescued in round 11.

Baer confined himself to exhibitions for the next 12 months, then failed to take his first challenger, the then modestly talented but hungrily ambitious James J. Braddock, at all seriously. Baer cracked jokes as Braddock piled up points, and found out much too late that he couldn't knock him out with his trademark overhand right. The heavyweight title changed hands.

In his next fight he was knocked out in four rounds by Joe Louis. He could have got up, but said later: "If people want to see the execution of Max Baer, it will cost more than $50 a seat."

He tried to revive his career with an incredible 24-fight, three-month tour in 1936, but lost to Tommy Farr in London in April 1937 and never came close to another title shot. He retired in 1941 after losing to Lou Nova, but stayed a celebrity, earning cash by refereeing wrestling bouts, and lived comfortably with his wife and three children until his sudden death from a heart attack in a Hollywood hotel.

BAER (RIGHT) IN SPARRING BEFORE DEFENDING AGAINST JAMES J. BRADDOCK

SEE ALSO ◆ JAMES J. BRADDOCK 37 ◆ PRIMO CARNERA 59 ◆ JOE LOUIS 204

IRAN BARKLEY

Iran Barkley, who made his name with a remarkable third round win over Thomas Hearns in Las Vegas in 1988, once said: "What separates me from others fighters is true madness."

Before he fought Hearns, the champion's trainer Emanuel Steward knew Barkley had the attitude to be dangerous. "He's not that skillful, but he just don't give a damn." Sure enough, battered and on the brink of defeat, Barkley found the right hand of a lifetime to drop Hearns on to his back. Seconds after regaining his feet, Hearns was rescued by the referee.

Four years later Barkley became the only man to beat Hearns twice, when he outpointed him over 12 rounds to win the WBA light-heavyweight title. This victory also made Barkley the unlikeliest member of the elite band who have won world titles at three separate weights.

Nicknamed "The Blade," he was taught to box in the Bronx by his sister Yvonee. Later he overcame a detached retina in his left eye, and gave up driving after twice surviving frightening car crashes.

He was erratic—Nigel Benn walked through him in a round, and James Toney stopped him in nine when he was weight-drained—but on his night, as he showed against Hearns, he was one to avoid. He was supposedly finished when he whacked out Darrin Van Horn in two rounds to win the IBF 168 lb. belt, and he followed that by beating Hearns a second time.

But after Toney trounced him in his last fight as a super-middle, his weight ballooned. By 1996, he was reduced to earning small money in club fights.

FACT FILE

1960 South Bronx, New York

1988 Stopped Thomas Hearns to win WBC middleweight title

1989 Lost title to Roberto Duran

1992 Won IBF super-middleweight title against Darrin Van Horn

1992 Beat Hearns again, this time for WBA light-heavyweight belt

Career record: Fights 48, Won 36, Lost 12

BARKLEY BLASTS OUT THOMAS HEARNS IN THEIR AMAZING FIRST FIGHT

SEE ALSO ◆ ROBERTO DURAN 99 ◆ THOMAS HEARNS 153 ◆ JAMES TONEY 310

MARCO ANTONIO BARRERA

FACT FILE

1974 Mexico City
1989 Made professional debut at 15
1992 Won Mexican super-flyweight title at 18
1995 Became WBO super-bantamweight champion by outpointing Daniel Jimenez
1996 Lost WBO title to Junior Jones
Career record: Fights 44, Won 43, Lost 1

Known as "The Baby-Faced Assassin," Marco Antonio Barrera was an intelligent, ruthlessly efficient fighter from Mexico City who seemed sure to become one of the greatest ring technicians of the modern era.

A former law student who put his education to one side as he pursues fame and considerable fortune as a boxer, Barrera was a serious, organized man. He won five national junior titles in a 60-bout amateur career, but at 15 he turned professional under top manager Ricardo Maldonado.

By the time Marco Antonio Barrera was 18 he was Mexican super-flyweight champion and he added the North American Boxing Federation belt in 1993. Gradually, he moved up the weight divisions and in March 1995 won the WBO super-bantamweight championship by outpointing the tough Puerto Rican Daniel Jimenez.

Barrera looked capable of reigning for as long as he can make the weight. He was a busy champion, crushing ordinary challengers like Frankie Toledo and Maui Diaz, outpointing the resilient Agapito Sanchez and then putting on a punch-perfect display to stop the capable Eddie Croft in seven rounds at Caesars Palace, Las Vegas, in November 1995.

He survived a torrid battle with former IBF champion Kennedy McKinney, and went on to turn back other one-time world titleholders Jesse Benavides and Orlando Fernandez, before taking 10 rounds to wear down No.1 contender Jesse Magana. But his reign came to an end in November 1996, when former WBA bantamweight champion Junior Jones beat him in five rounds in Tampa, Florida.

BARRERA WAS AN EXCEPTIONAL CHAMPION WHO WON 43 CONSECUTIVE FIGHTS

CARMEN BASILIO

Carmen Basilio loved a fight. Not an exhibition of fancy-dan skills—a no-frills, barnstorming, tear-up was his specialty. Basilio was cunning and crafty, and prepared to fight all night, beyond normal levels of pain and endurance. That's why the 5 ft. 6½ in. son of a New York State onion farmer not only won the world welterweight title, but outpunched the legendary Sugar Ray Robinson for the middleweight crown in spite of weighing less than 154 lb.

Basilio began as a 21-year-old lightweight after a spell in the US Marines. In 1953 he floored world welterweight champion Kid Gavilan but lost a close decision, and had to wait until June 1955 for another chance. This time he stopped Tony DeMarco in 12 rounds in Syracuse. Return clauses were formalities in world title contracts then, and Basilio had to stop DeMarco again before he lost to Johnny Saxton in Chicago in May 1956. Six months later he stopped Saxton in nine rounds to become champion for a second time. Inevitably, Saxton was given another shot, but Basilio's superiority was established. Carmen won in two rounds.

In September 1957 he stepped up to middleweight to win one of the greatest fights of all time when he dethroned Ray Robinson via a split decision in front of a 38,000 crowd at Yankee Stadium, New York. The return in Chicago six months later went the other way, Basilio fighting one-eyed for the last nine rounds, yet losing by a 2-1 split. He was past 30 years old by then, and Gene Fullmer stopped him twice and Paul Pender outpointed him before he retired in 1961. He went on to be a college physical education instructor in Syracuse, a sales rep, and managed one or two local fighters, his place in boxing history is safe.

FACT FILE

1927	Born Canastota, New York
1955	Won world welterweight title at second attempt
1956	Lost and regained title against Johnny Saxton
1957	Beat Ray Robinson to win world middleweight title
1958	Lost rematch with Robinson
1961	Retired after last world title defeat by Paul Pender

Career record: Fights 79, Won 56, Lost 16, Drawn 7

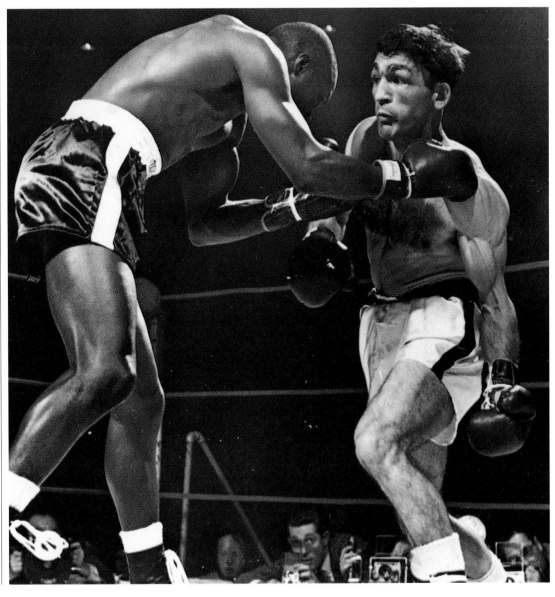

BASILIO SWARMS ALL OVER A DISORGANIZED JOHNNY SAXTON. HE WON TITLES AT WELTERWEIGHT AND MIDDLEWEIGHT

SEE ALSO ◆ GENE FULLMER 123 ◆ PAUL PENDER 268 ◆ RAY ROBINSON 278

HOGAN BASSEY

Hogan Bassey was a short, stocky battler who traded on pressure, durability and strength. He knew the art of working the body, of controlling the pace of a fight and wearing a man down. His greatest hour was in Paris on June 24, 1958 when he climbed up from an early knock-down to stop the stylish Algerian Cherif Hamia in 10 rounds for the vacant world featherweight title.

Bassey's first known fight was in 1949, but his early record is obscure. He won Nigerian titles at flyweight and bantamweight before sailing for Liverpool early in 1952. He found work immediately and had 19 fights in his first year in England.

In 1955 he won the British Empire 9 stone (126 lb.) title by knocking out Billy "Spider" Kelly in eight rounds in Belfast, and when Saddler retired in 1956, he showed he could box as well as fight, setting up his world title chance by outpointing Percy Lewis and Miguel Berrios.

He made one successful defense, destroying the undefeated Mexican sensation Ricardo "Pajarito" Moreno in three rounds before 20,034 fans in Wrigley Field. Bassey grossed $70,000.

Bassey earned well in four non-title fights, including a ninth-round stoppage of the veteran former champ Willie Pep, but then lost his title when he retired after 13 rounds against Davey Moore at the Olympic Auditorium, Los Angeles, in March 1959. Five months later Moore beat him again, and Bassey's career was over at the age of 27.

He returned to Nigeria, and in 1963 this polite, intelligent but firm man was appointed a director of physical education by the government. He was also involved in the coaching of the national amateur team.

HIS LAST WORLD TITLE FIGHT: BASSEY (LEFT) FAILS TO REGAIN THE CHAMPIONSHIP AGAINST DAVEY MOORE IN 1959

SEE ALSO ◆ DAVEY MOORE 227

JOE BECERRA

Joe Becerra paved the way for generations of great Mexican bantamweights when he knocked out Alphonse Halimi of France in eight rounds in Los Angeles in July 1959.

The victory, in the newly built $6.5 million Memorial Sports Arena, was the first world title success by a Mexican-born bantamweight, and set off jubilant celebrations, especially in Becerra's home city of Guadalajara, where thousands had heard the radio broadcast of the fight in bars and restaurants. Becerra's parents, who lived in a house their son had bought for them, promised to walk a round trip of 160 miles to a shrine to offer thanks to God.

Becerra was contracted to give Halimi a rematch, and this time took out the Algerian with a clean left hook in round nine in the Los Angeles Coliseum in February 1960. The fight drew a huge crowd of 31,830, which paid a Californian gate record of $383,060. Yet for all his huge popularity, Becerra was paid only $30,000 plus expenses—the same fee as Halimi.

Three months later Becerra retained the title on a split decision in Tokyo against Kenji Yonekura, a slick, defensive counterpuncher who cut Joe's eye during their tough contest and left him with a heavy nose bleed.

In Juarez in August 1960 he was floored three times and stopped in the eighth round of a non-title fight with Eloy Sanchez and announced his retirement. He came back briefly, but in reality his career was over at the age of 24. A loner who would sit for hours in contemplation, some say he never got over the death of Walter Ingram, whom he stopped in what should have been a routine celebration appearance in Guadalajara after dethroning Alphonse Halimi.

FACT FILE

1936 Born Jose Becerra, Guadalajara, Mexico

1953 Professional debut in Guadalajara

1959 Won world bantamweight title by knocking out Alphonse Halimi

1960 Retired as undefeated champion

Career record: Fights 79, Won 72, Lost 5, Drawn 2

BECERRA: MEXICAN HERO WHOSE CAREER ENDED SUDDENLY

WILFRED BENITEZ

FACT FILE

1958	Born Bronx, New York
1973	Professional debut at 15 in Puerto Rico
1976	Won WBA light-welterweight title at 17
1979	Won and lost WBC welterweight title
1981	Won his third world title—at light-middleweight
1990	Lost last fight in Canada

Career record: Fights 62, Won 53, Lost 8, Drawn 1

Wilfred Benitez became the youngest-ever world champion in the Hiram Bithorn Stadium in San Juan in 1976 when, age 17 years and six months, he outpointed Antonio Cervantes for the WBA light-welterweight title.

Benitez, who was coached by his ruthless father Gregorio, had wonderful boxing skills—and his natural talent was enough to take him to world titles in three weight divisions. Sadly, he was unable to match his intelligence inside the ring with wisdom out of it. His ring earnings were squandered and by the 1990s he was living in Puerto Rico on state support, officially recognized as having suffered seriously debilitating brain damage.

Yet he was a supreme talent. After beating Cervantes, he made three successful WBA title defenses, outgrew the division and took the WBC welterweight belt from quality fighter Carlos Palomino, in San Juan in January 1979.

It took the genius of Ray Leonard to snap his unbeaten run in his 40th fight. Leonard stopped him with only six seconds to spare in the 15th round at Caesars Palace, Las Vegas, in November 1979.

Benitez kept on filling out and in May 1991 he returned to Las Vegas to knock out Britain's WBC light-middleweight champion Maurice Hope in the 12th round. He had enough left to outbox Roberto Duran in January 1982, but Thomas Hearns took away his title with a points decision the following December.

Benitez fought on for another eight years, and paid the price for it, even though he was only 32 when he retired.

BENITEZ CELEBRATES VICTORY OVER ROBERTO DURAN IN LAS VEGAS

SEE ALSO ◆ ANTONIO CERVANTES 62 ◆ ROBERTO DURAN 99 ◆ RAY LEONARD 187 ◆ CARLOS PALOMINO 262

NIGEL BENN

One of the hardest-hitting of all British middle-weights, Nigel Benn also turned out to be a lasting world champion who fought in the very highest class for six years.

With Benn, action was always guaranteed. He did his job in the simplest possible way, looking for openings for big punches and letting fly as soon as he found the range. As his career developed, so too did his defensive abilities, but his relish for a head-to-head, all-or-nothing confrontation remained un-dimmed. Part of his attraction was his occasional vulnerability—Michael Watson and Chris Eubank both counterpunched him to defeat. He climbed off the floor to stop normally durable Doug De Witt in eight rounds in Atlantic City for the WBO middleweight title in April 1990. He dropped Iran Barkley three times to score a stoppage win inside a round in Las Vegas, but lost the title to Eubank in a marvelous battle in Birmingham in November 1990. He then moved up to super-middleweight, looking for a rematch with Chris Eubank, but had to make do with the WBC championship, which he convincingly ripped from the Italian Mauro Galvano in three rounds in October 1992.

The return with Eubank drew a crowd of 42,000 at Old Trafford soccer stadium, Manchester, in October 1993—and Benn left the ring angrily after the fight was scored a draw. He won a tumultuous struggle with Gerald McClellan at the London Arena in February 1995, a magnificent fight soured by a terrible ending. McClellan suffered acute brain damage. Benn's championship reign ended with a surprise points defeat by South African Sugarboy Malinga in March 1996, and he was then stopped twice in WBO title bids by Steve Collins.

FACT FILE

1964	Born London
1988	Won Commonwealth middleweight title with 17th consecutive knockout
1990	Became WBO champion in Atlantic City
1990	Lost WBO title in classic with Chris Eubank
1992	Won WBC super-middleweight title in Italy
1996	Lost WBC title to Sugarboy Malinga of South Africa

Career record: Fights 48, Won 42, Lost 5, Drawn 1

BENN BLASTS OUT LOU GENT IN LONDON IN 1993

SEE ALSO ◆ IRAN BARKLEY 27 ◆ STEVE COLLINS 74 ◆ CHRIS EUBANK 106

NINO BENVENUTI

FACT FILE

1938 Born Giovanni Benvenuti, Isole d'Istria, Trieste, Italy

1960 Olympic welterweight gold medal

1965 Won world light-middleweight title

1967 Won and lost world middleweight title fights with Emile Griffith

1970 Second reign ended by Carlos Monzon

Career record: Fights 90, Won 82, Lost 7, Drawn 1

A stylish, smooth boxer with a steely determination and, in his peak years, a stout chin, Benvenuti overshadowed even the 18-year-old Cassius Clay at the Rome Olympics in 1960 when he won the Best Boxer Trophy.

After winning the welterweight gold medal—his 120th consecutive amateur victory—Benvenuti turned professional in his home town of Trieste, where his father was a fisherman.

By 1965 he had beaten compatriot Sandro Mazzinghi for the world light-middleweight title, but it was for his three-fight series with Emile Griffith for the middleweight championship that he is mostly remembered, especially in the United States. Benvenuti, who had lost the light-middleweight title to Ki-soo Kim in South Korea for a $35,000 payday, won the first fight with Griffith in Madison Square Garden in April 1967 on a unanimous decision, despite being floored in round four.

The rematch, in New York's Shea Stadium in September 1967, saw Griffith regain the belt on a majority verdict in front of 20,000 fans. The third bout marked the opening of the present Madison Square Garden in March 1968—and again after 15 marvelous rounds it was a majority decision—this time to Benvenuti, who had the edge after dropping Griffith in round nine.

He was popular in Italy, but grew more erratic as the decade wore to a close, even if he did usually put it all together for defenses. Finally, he took one too many and was knocked out in 12 rounds by Carlos Monzon in November 1970. When Monzon demolished him in the return inside three rounds, Benvenuti knew it was time to go. In retirement he went into politics and in 1995 was reported to have gone to work as a helper in Mother Theresa's hospital in Calcutta.

BENVENUTI ON THE WAY TO A KNOCKOUT WIN OVER LUIS RODRIGUEZ IN ROME IN 1969

SEE ALSO ◆ EMILE GRIFFITH 144 ◆ CARLOS MONZON 222

JACK "KID" BERG

Boxing was a simple art to Jack "Kid" Berg. It required immense stamina, speed, a bottomless pit for a heart, and the ability to toss punches relentlessly from whatever angle presented itself. Berg could jab and follow up with a textbook right cross, but preferred if such niceties were not required.

Berg, born in London's East End Jewish quarter, was still short of his 15th birthday when he made his professional debut at the Premierland Arena. Within months he was fighting 15-rounders.

By the time he was 18, he had crossed the Atlantic to make his name, doing his best to live up to his tag of the "Whitechapel Whirlwind." American fans loved him because he was nothing like the traditional British technician. His trainer, the legendary Ray Arcel, said years later: "He had the face of an angel and the heart of a devil!"

Ironically, it was back in London at the Royal Albert Hall in February 1930 that Berg won the world junior-welterweight title, as it was called then, by stopping Mushy Callahan of New York in 10 rounds.

Berg twice beat the great Cuban, Kid Chocolate, but was knocked out in three rounds by Tony Canzoneri in a lightweight title bid, which some said cost him his 140 lb. belt. He argued that it hadn't, but lost a return at 135 lb. with Canzoneri and was then outpointed by Sammy Fuller in New York in May 1932. He returned home and won the British lightweight title against Harry Mizler, and finally retired in 1945, when he was 36.

FACT FILE

1909	Born Judah Bergman, London, England
1924	Began professional career, age 14
1930	Won world junior-welterweight title against Mushy Callahan
1931	Twice lost to Tony Canzoneri
1932	Relinquished all title claims after defeat by Sammy Fuller
1945	Last professional fight, in Coventry
Died:	London, age 81, April 22, 1991

Career record: Fights 192, Won 157, Lost 26, Drawn 9

ALWAYS A POPULAR FIGHTER, BERG DREW FANS TO HIS WORKOUTS WHEN HE RETURNED TO ENGLAND TO FIGHT MUSHY CALLAHAN IN 1930

SEE ALSO ◆ TONY CANZONERI 54 ◆ KID CHOCOLATE 72

RIDDICK BOWE

Riddick Bowe overcame proverty, tragedy and heartbreak to win the undisputed heavyweight championship of the world.

He was brought up in the same Bedford-Stuyvesant ghetto of New York that spawned Mike Tyson. Rock Newman, who managed him throughout his professional career, said that as soon as he saw where Bowe was raised—"it was basically a crack supermarket" —he knew the man had character.

Bowe was slaughtered by American critics when he lost to Lennox Lewis in the 1988 Olympic final, but had previously been a world junior champion and medalist in both the Pan-American Games and World Cup. His Olympic effort was marred by a nagging injury and by emotional turmoil: a brother was dying of cancer. His sister was also murdered when she

tried to stop a crack addict stealing her welfare check.

Out of all of this chaos came a good, positive man. Boxing cynics predicted that he would "unravel like a piece of twine" when the game got rough, but he showed his character in winning a marvelous 12-rounder with Evander Holyfield when he became undisputed champion in 1992.

Sadly, he found it hard to sustain the dedication that had taken him to the top, and lost the title back to Holyfield in his third defense. By the time he stopped Holyfield in another tremendous fight in November 1995, the glory days seemed behind them both. Holyfield had lost the title to Michael Moorer and Bowe had beaten Herbie Hide to win the lightly regarded WBO title, though he later gave that up.

BOWE KEEPS EVANDER HOLYFIELD AT BAY WITH HIS LEFT JAB. THEY HAD THREE GREAT FIGHTS

SEE ALSO ◆ EVANDER HOLYFIELD 159 ◆ LENNOX LEWIS 194 ◆ MICHAEL MOORER 230 ◆ MIKE TYSON 319

JAMES J. BRADDOCK

James J. Braddock, a well-schooled, determined, and disciplined family man, had one chance to change his life. And he grabbed it, overturning odds of 10-1 to dethrone the then current world heavyweight champion Max Baer at the Long Island Bowl, New York, on June 13, 1935.

Braddock was born in the chaotic Hell's Kitchen area of west New York, and was then raised across the Hudson River in New Jersey, during which time he had more than 100 amateur contests.

He was a professional at 19, but after a challenge for the world light-heavyweight title failed against Tommy Loughran in 1929, his career drifted. He lost as many as he won, and retired to work on the waterfront at Hoboken, New Jersey. When there was no work, he claimed $17 a week relief.

In 1934, he was persuaded to take a payday against prospect Corn Griffin and scored a stunning upset in three rounds. Twelve months later he beat Baer, piling up points as the champion posed and clowned. Writer Damon Runyon called him "The Cinderella Man" and it stuck.

Braddock was sensible enough to know he would probably lose to Joe Louis, but finally clinched a deal that gave him 10 percent of the profits of Mike Jacobs' promotions of Louis's heavyweight title fights for the next 10 years. Braddock estimated it earned him an extra $150,000. Louis did beat him in eight rounds, but not before Braddock had knocked him down.

Braddock and his wife lived the rest of their lives in the home they bought in North Bergen, New Jersey, when he was champion.

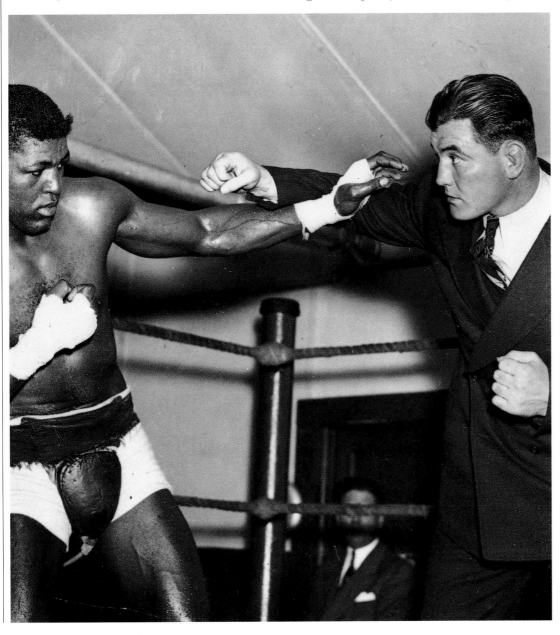

WHILE STILL CHAMPION, BRADDOCK FINDS TIME TO TEACH A YOUNG HOPEFUL A TRICK OR TWO

SEE ALSO ◆ MAX BAER 26 ◆ TOMMY LOUGHRAN 203 ◆ JOE LOUIS 204

THE GREAT FIGHTS

EVANDER HOLYFIELD
V.
RIDDICK BOWE

THOMAS & MACK CENTER, LAS VEGAS.
NOVEMBER 13, 1992.

Heroism in defeat is not an attribute that would attract many fighters, but after a lifetime of victories Evander Holyfield found his career enriched from the moment he lost to Riddick Bowe in one of the greatest fights in heavyweight championship history.

Holyfield was perceived before this fight as a good, rather colorless champion. After a one-punch knockout of a barely interested Buster Douglas in October 1990, Holyfield outboxed slow, old George Foreman, survived a scare to stop late sub Smokin' Bert Cooper, and then outpointed ancient Larry Holmes.

He stood accused of being dull, a blown-up cruiserweight, too much nice-guy, a man who took no risks.

And then came the Bowe fight.

One writer memorably predicted that when the going got rough Bowe would "unravel like a piece of twine," an unforgiving, unfair reference to his silver medal-winning performance in the 1988 Olympic Games when, distracted by injury and personal problems, he lost in the final to Lennox Lewis.

Together these two doubted men proved themselves warriors of the highest order. Bowe reached a peak he was never to match again, showing technical skills few believed he possessed, and eventually overpowering a champion who showed a cold, intelligent courage in refusing to quit. No, Holyfield did more than that. He constantly sought out a way to win, even when there was none. He took a terrible pasting in the 10th round, yet finished it on top with Bowe sucking in huge gulps of air. Bowe rallied to drop Holyfield with a left hook in the 11th and went on to clinch a unanimous points win, but had been pressed to his limit the whole way.

"I kept saying 'Lay down, lay down' but he wouldn't," said the new champion. And Holyfield, sadly and with typical dignity, announced a retirement that didn't last. Twelve months later he pulled off a surprise win over Bowe in a return and in November 1995, Bowe won a third meeting, climbing off the floor to stop Holyfield in eight breathtaking rounds.

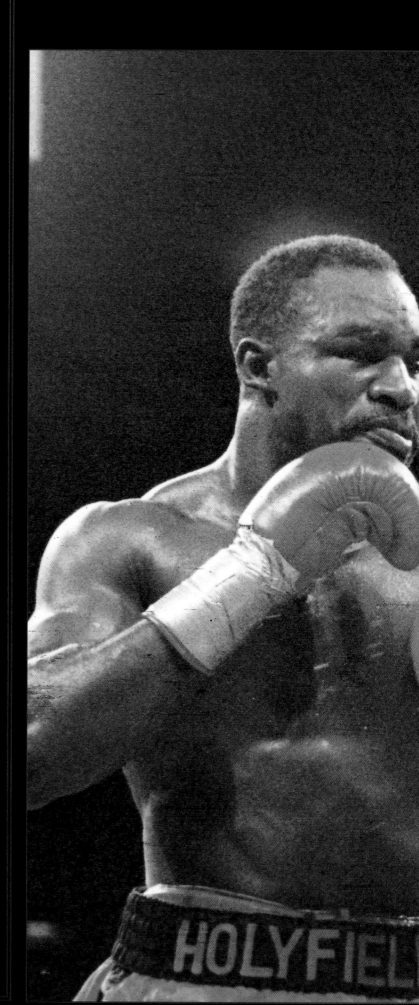

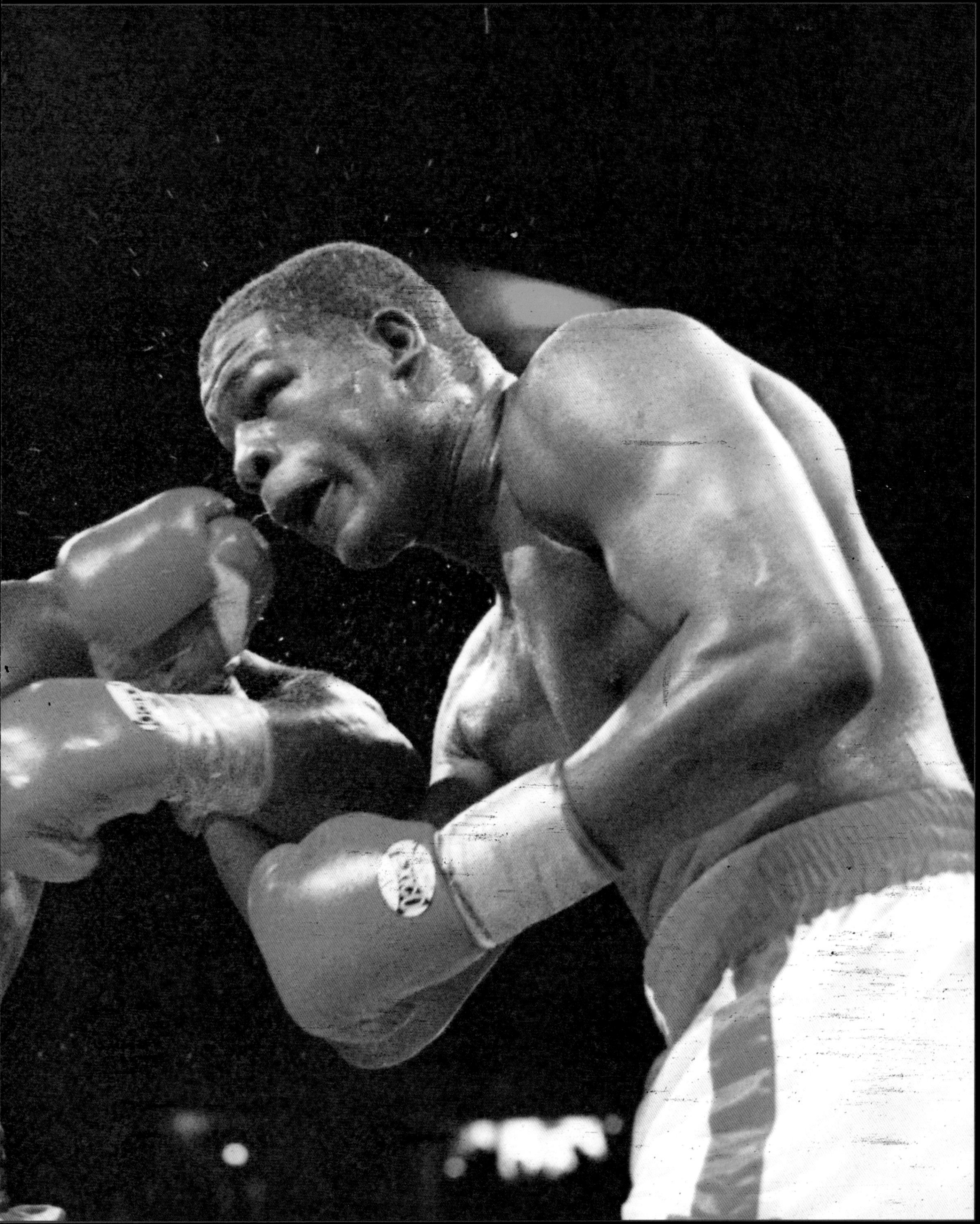

BENNIE BRISCOE

FACT FILE

1943 Born Augusta, Georgia

1962 Professional debut in Philadelphia

1967 Held Carlos Monzon to a draw in Buenos Aires

1971 Lost 15-round decision to Monzon in title fight

1977 Beaten for vacant title by Rodrigo Valdez

1983 Announced retirement

Career record: Fights 96, Won 66, Lost 24, Drawn 5

For two decades, Bennie Briscoe plied his trade as one of the most fearsome middleweights of his time, a prowling, bald-headed menace with a wrecking ball of a left hook.

"Bad" Bennie wasn't the fastest middleweight the world ever saw, but he knew how to wear a man down, how to chew him up and spit out the bits, better than anybody else in his day.

He failed to win a world title because he had the misfortune to peak at the same time as the great Carlos Monzon. And when they fought for the middleweight championship in 1972 in front of a packed house at Luna Park in Buenos Aires, Monzon won clearly on points.

Five years earlier, before Monzon was champion, Briscoe was widely thought to have beaten the Argentine, but was given a 10-round draw.

Briscoe fought them all, champions and rising stars alike. Some, like Marvin Hagler and Emile Griffith, managed to box well enough to outpoint him, but he ruined the aspirations of many others along the way, men whose names have come to mean little to history but whose reputations were growing rapidly... until they bumped into "Bad Bennie."

He was knocked out only once, by the Colombian Rodrigo Valdez in Monte Carlo in 1974 when the WBC stripped Monzon. In a rematch after Monzon had retired, Briscoe took Valdez the full 15 rounds. He finally retired when just short of his 40th birthday.

BRISCOE, IN A TYPICAL CROUCH, HUNTS DOWN "IRISH" TED MANN ON THE WAY TO A POINTS WIN

SEE ALSO ◆ EMILE GRIFFITH 144 ◆ MARVIN HAGLER 147 ◆ CARLOS MONZON 222 ◆ RODRIGO VALDEZ 322

JACK BRITTON

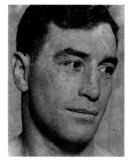

If you are looing for a glimpse of how tough old-time fighters were, look no further than Jack Britton. An accomplished, stylish boxer who made up for his lack of a big punch with his ability to out-think almost anyone he met, Britton fought professionally for more than a quarter of a century, from the smoky clubs of Milwaukee and Chicago to the grandest venue of his time, Madison Square Garden. In the 1920s, the New York State Athletic Commission raised its age limit for boxers from 38 to 45 to accommodate him.

Britton was acknowledged as a master of his trade long before he became a world champion. Old record books are still being revised as researchers work on archive material, but a February 1916 points win over Ted Kid Lewis led to Britton's being recognized as welter-weight champion. By a conservative estimate, it was Jack's 163rd professional fight! He and Lewis fought 20 times in a rivalry that stretched from 1915 to 1921, with the championship being swapped between them until Britton established his superiority with a ninth-round knockout in Canton, Ohio, in March 1919.

Britton was lucky to retain his title in June 1922 when the great lightweight Benny Leonard was disqualified for hitting him after knocking him down, but in his next defense 37-year-old Britton was floored three times and outpointed over 15 rounds by Mickey Walker in November 1922. Sadly, his investments flopped and he was forced to go on boxing for another eight years, eventually moving on to life as a trainer in New York City and then running a drugstore in Miami with his wife.

FACT FILE

1885 Born William J. Breslin Clinton, New York

1916 Won world welterweight title against arch-rival Ted Kid Lewis

1917 Lost title back to Lewis

1919 Beat Lewis to become champion for third time

1922 Finally dethroned by Mickey Walker

1930 Retired, age 44

Died: Miami, Florida, age 76, March 27, 1962

Career record: Fights 343, Won 220, Lost 55, Drawn 50, No Decisions 16

A CRAFTY, EDUCATED BOXER, BRITTON WAS ONE OF THE MOST RESPECTED TEACHERS OF HIS DAY AS WELL AS A FINE CHAMPION

SEE ALSO ♦ BENNY LEONARD 186 ♦ TED KID LEWIS 195 ♦ MICKEY WALKER 330

PANAMA AL BROWN

Al Brown was a spidery, almost impossibly thin man who somehow crammed a 5 ft. 11 in. frame into a bantamweight's body. He made the 118-lb. limit in order to prolong his control of the division for a remarkable six years, from 1929 to 1935.

"Panama Al" learned to box in Panama, where he worked as a shipping clerk on the canal-front. He learned quickly, and by 1923 was living in New York, where he developed into a world-class boxer, a cunning technician who knew how to use his height and reach, as well as a sharp hitter with exquisite timing.

In the mid-1920s he visited Paris, and after he won the world bantamweight title by giving a sound boxing lesson to Gregorio Vidal in Long Island, New York, on June 18, 1929, he moved his permanent base to France.

From the days when as a boy he used to box before US sailors, he was a natural entertainer. His flashy, extrovert style served him well in Paris, where he switched comfortably between nightclub and ring as the moment required. He also took his bantamweight crown on the road, defending in New York, Paris, Montreal, Marseille, Milan, London, and Tunis, before a 23-year-old Spaniard, Baltazar Sangchilli, out-slugged him in Valencia on June 1, 1935. His skills faded slowly, and he still had enough to beat Sangchilli in a rematch three years later, but by then the Spaniard was no longer champion. By 1939, Brown was back in New York, and he ended his career in Panama in 1942. The fortune he earned in the ring long spent, he died of tuberculosis in New York on April 11, 1951. He was only 48.

PANAMA AL STAVES OFF BALTAZAR SANGCHILLI IN VALENCIA IN 1935 ON THE NIGHT HIS LONG REIGN CAME TO AN END

JOE BROWN

Known affectionately as "Old Bones," Joe Brown was a 30-year-old father of three sons by the time he won the world lightweight title... and yet managed to hold on to it until he was almost 36.

Brown was one of a multitude of quality black professionals in the late 1940s and early 1950s who had skill but no political connections and who therefore languished in the boxing shadows. Unlike most of them, Brown emerged to outpoint a reigning champion, Wallace "Bud" Smith, in a non-title fight in Houston, Texas, in May 1956.

In a rematch for the championship the following August, this carpenter's son from Baton Rouge, Louisiana, delighted a packed house in New Orleans by outpointing Smith again, in spite of breaking his right hand in round two. Smith chased him hard all night, but Brown was much too quick and too clever,

and dropped him twice in round 14 to seal a split decision.

In February 1957 he stopped Smith in 11 rounds, and then turned back a further 10 challenges, including two from the best British lightweight of the era, Dave Charnley. "Old Bones" beat the London southpaw on a cut eye in five rounds in Houston in 1959, and then beat him on a close decision in London in April 1961. He also survived a torrid struggle with Michigan southpaw Kenny Lane in 1958.

The years caught up with him in April 1962, when he lost the title to the classy Puerto Rican, Carlos Ortiz, in Las Vegas. Brown was a boxer by trade, however, and continued earning, from Manchester to Monterrey, from Rio to Johannesburg, for the next eight years. He was 44 years old when he had his last fight, a 10-round decision over Ramon Flores in Tucson, Arizona.

FACT FILE

1926 Born New Orleans, Louisiana

1943 Professional debut

1956 Won world lightweight title at the age of 30

1962 Lost world title to Carlos Ortiz in Las Vegas

1970 Retired after winning a 10-round fight in Tucson, Arizona

Career record: Fights 161, Won 104, Lost 42, Drawn 13, No Contests 2

OLD BONES: BROWN WAS LIGHTWEIGHT CHAMPION FOR SIX YEARS

SEE ALSO ◆ DAVE CHARNLEY 66

FRANK BRUNO

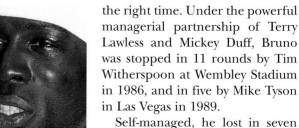

I f ever a man made the best of his talents, it was Frank Bruno. After losing three world heavyweight title attempts, the 6 ft. 3 in. Londoner might easily have been content to have played out the role of Britain's favorite sporting son for the rest of his days.

But Bruno wanted more than to be remembered affectionately as the greatest of his country's embarrassingly long list of heroic losers. He had set his heart on becoming world champion—and on an emotionally charged night at Wembley Stadium in September 1995, Bruno's dream came true: he outboxed and outworked the defending WBC titleholder, Oliver McCall, to win a unanimous decision.

Bruno achieved his ambition because of his unflagging dedication to the job, and eventually because he had the right connections at the right time. Under the powerful managerial partnership of Terry Lawless and Mickey Duff, Bruno was stopped in 11 rounds by Tim Witherspoon at Wembley Stadium in 1986, and in five by Mike Tyson in Las Vegas in 1989.

Self-managed, he lost in seven rounds to Lennox Lewis in Cardiff in 1993, and the distressing manner of his defeat—propped on the ropes taking full-blooded blows to the head—led to calls for his retirement. But Bruno wanted to go on, switched to be promoted by Frank Warren, whose American associate Don King controlled the new WBC champion, McCall. And finally, at the age of 33, Bruno won the title. His reign didn't last. In his first defense he was bludgeoned to one-sided defeat by Mike Tyson and retired because of an eye condition six months later.

NOT CONTENT WITH HIS ROLE AS BRITAIN'S FAVORITE SPORTING SON, BRUNO DEFIED HIS CRITICS BY WINNING A WORLD TITLE AT THE FOURTH ATTEMPT

SEE ALSO ◆ LENNOX LEWIS 194 ◆ MIKE TYSON 319

KEN BUCHANAN

A dazzling boxer with a beautiful left hand, Ken Buchanan became the first Briton to win a world title abroad since the legendary Ted Kid Lewis more than 50 years earlier.

Buchanan traveled to San Juan, Puerto Rico, to outpoint Ismael Laguna of Puerto Rico for the WBA lightweight championship, overcoming searing heat and a quality fighter to earn a split decision on September 26, 1970.

In spite of a petition from boxing fans and representations from his management team, the British Board of Control refused to recognize him because they were not affiliated to the WBA.

He was a huge hit in New York, however, when he beat the Canadian Donato Paduano in a non-title fight in Madison Square Garden. In Los Angeles, he beat late substitute Ruben Navarro in his first world title defense, which was also recognized by the WBC—and therefore Britain.

The WBC stripped him for giving Laguna a return, which he won on points, but his WBA reign ended against 21-year-old Roberto Duran in June 1972. The marauding Duran hit him anywhere and at the end of 13 brutal rounds, after shipping one final low punch, the Scot was ruled unable to continue.

A 1975 WBC title attempt against Ishimatsu Suzuki in Japan failed. After being thumbed in the eye by a Japanese sparring partner, Buchanan lost a 15-round decision.

He gave up completely for almost four years, but a divorce followed by a failing hotel business forced him to return. He was 36 when he finally retired in 1982, but in order to clear his debts took two more unlicensed fights. He ran a pub, and later returned to his old trade as a carpenter.

FACT FILE

1945 Born Edinburgh, Scotland

1965 Won ABA featherweight title

1970 Beat Ismael Laguna for the WBA lightweight title in Puerto Rico

1972 Lost championship in third defense to Roberto Duran

1975 Lost world title bid against WBC champion Ishimatsu Suzuki

Career record: Fights 69, Won 61, Lost 8

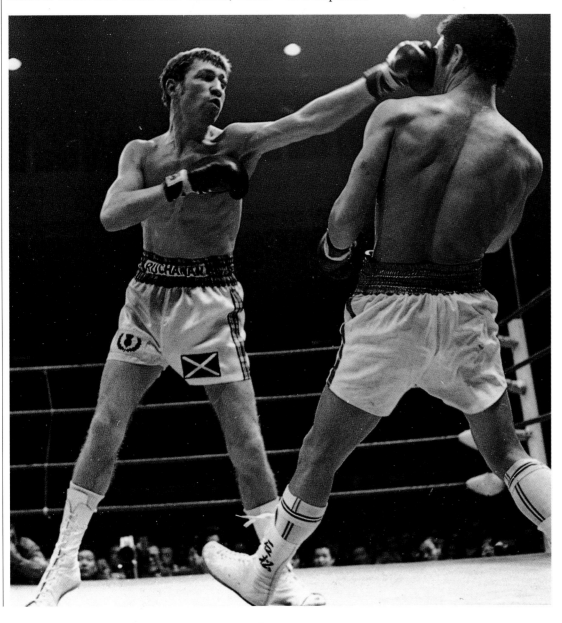

CLASSIC STYLIST: BUT BUCHANAN HAD STEEL IN HIS BELLY WHEN IT MATTERED

SEE ALSO ◆ ROBERTO DURAN 99 ◆ ISMAEL LAGUNA 183

THE GREAT FIGHTS

KEN BUCHANAN V. ROBERTO DURAN

MADISON SQUARE GARDEN. JUNE 26, 1972.

Roberto Duran's swarming, brawling, brutally ruthless victory over Scotland's Ken Buchanan made him a world champion at the age of 21 and signaled the arrival of one of the greatest fighters ever.

It was boxing in the raw, a display of naked violence that rendered Buchanan's smooth skills impotent in the 13 rounds the fight lasted in Madison Square Garden. The fight drew $570,000—record receipts at the time for a lightweight fight.

In the end Duran was lucky not to be disqualified as referee Johnny LoBianco seemed oblivious to a horribly low final punch on the bell to end the round. LoBianco ruled Buchanan unable to continue before the start of the 14th—a verdict that still rankles with the Scot, who had showed his quality in three wonderful championship wins against Ismael Laguna (twice) and Ruben Navarro.

Buchanan was on the floor from a right hand in the opening round, but got up to give Duran a sustained argument. The marauding, merciless young Panamanian crowded persistently, but had his gumshield knocked flying out of the ring in the fifth, and was caught frequently by immaculate left hooks.

People forget how fast Duran was as a lightweight, but his rushes took away the effectiveness of Buchanan's best weapon, his left jab, and gradually even this ferociously competitive champion was worn down. He was cut over the left eye in round seventh, and hurt two or three times in the 12th.

Duran had the better of the 13th, then drove a right hand into Buchanan's groin after the bell. The Scot dropped in agony, got up and walked to his corner as his father Tom and trainer Gil Clancy raced in and argued frantically with LoBianco.

"I'm not a dirty fighter," said Duran through an interpreter.

Two contracts were signed for return fights, which never materialized. Duran continued to rule the division for the rest of the decade.

CHARLEY BURLEY

FACT FILE

1917 Born Charles Duane Burley, Bessemer, Pennsylvania

1939 Beat Fritzie Zivic, ranked in world top 5 by Ring magazine

1942 Twice lost to Ezzard Charles, in world middleweight top 3

1944 Beat Archie Moore

1950 Retired after victory in Lima, Peru, age 32

Died: October 16, 1992, age 75

Career record: Fights 98, Won 84, Lost 11, Drawn 2, No Contest 1

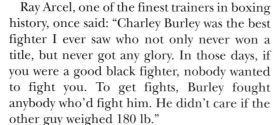

Sometimes fate, but more often boxing politics, conspire to prevent the best fighter of a generation from becoming a world champion. It happened to lightweight Packey McFarland early in the century, and in the 1940s it happened to middleweight Charley Burley.

Ray Arcel, one of the finest trainers in boxing history, once said: "Charley Burley was the best fighter I ever saw who not only never won a title, but never got any glory. In those days, if you were a good black fighter, nobody wanted to fight you. To get fights, Burley fought anybody who'd fight you. He didn't care if the other guy weighed 180 lb."

Arcel said even Sugar Ray Robinson avoided Burley. Eddie Futch, who came to prominence later than Arcel, remembered Burley alongside another brilliant black middleweight, Holman Williams, as the best of his generation. "Burley was really something to see," said Futch. "He was a true master at slipping punches, counterpunching."

Archie Moore, the long-time light-heavyweight champion who had more than 200 fights and boxed Rocky Marciano and Floyd Patterson for the heavyweight title, said Burley was the best man he met. Never knocked out or stopped in 98 fights spread across 14 years, Charley began fighting in Pittsburgh as a teenager. He lost to Fritzie Zivic in 1938, but twice beat him in rematches. World-class heavyweight Jimmy Bivins couldn't stop him, and Ezzard Charles, who went on to become heavyweight champion, outpointed him twice. Nevertheless, whatever he did, Burley could never get a title fight. Even when he retired, just short of his 33rd birthday, he was on a seven-fight winning run and had lost only one of his last 19.

A BOXING MASTER, BUT BURLEY WAS AVOIDED BY EVERY MIDDLEWEIGHT CHAMPION OF HIS TIME

SEE ALSO ◆ EZZARD CHARLES 65 ◆ ARCHIE MOORE 226 ◆ FRITZIE ZIVIC 349

Tommy Burns

Tommy Burns was a smart, if somewhat maverick businessman as well as a tough, uncompromising fighter who held the world heavyweight title from 1906 to 1908. Out of necessity— because he couldn't command huge single purses and so had to accumulate his wealth—he was a busy champion. He was also the first man to take the championship on the road, defending it in Los Angeles, London, Dublin, Paris, Melbourne, and Sydney.

Burns dabbled with ice hockey and lacrosse before taking up boxing at the turn of the century. Only 5 ft. 7 in. tall (the shortest heavyweight champion) he matured from a teenaged lightweight until by 1906, when he beat Marvin Hart over 20 rounds to become heavyweight champion, he scaled 180 lb.

He stopped Fireman Jim Flynn, twice beat the clever light-heavyweight Philadelphia Jack O'Brien, and knocked out unbeaten Australian champion Bill Squires in 129 seconds. "I got a bloody good lickin' and I'm goin' 'ome," said a disconsolate Squires.

Burns outclassed British hopes Gunner Moir and Jack Palmer, flattened portly Irishman Jem Roche in Dublin, and beat the South African, Jewey Smith, in Paris. In Australia, Burns beat Squires twice more, and Bill Lang, but then accepted $30,000 from promoter Hugh D. McIntosh to defend in Rushcutter's Bay, near Sydney, against Jack Johnson. Burns was trounced in 14 one-sided rounds, and some said he gambled away most of his fortune before leaving Australia.

He boxed only occasionally after that, the last time in 1920 when he was knocked out by British champion Joe Beckett. In retirement he bought pubs in Britain and a speakeasy in New York, then in 1948 turned to evangelism. He was on a religious visit to Vancouver when he died of a heart attack.

Fact File

1881 Born Noah Brusso, Chesley, Ontario, Canada

1906 Beat Marvin Hart to becomoe world heavyweight champion

1908 Lost championship to Jack Johnson in Australia

1920 Last fight in London, age 39

Died: Vancouver, British Columbia, Canada, age 73, May 10, 1955

Career record: Fights 60, Won 46, Lost 5, Drawn 9

Burns (right) walks out to defend his world heavyweight crown against Jem Roche in Dublin

JOHN CALDWELL

FACT FILE

1938	Born Belfast, Northern Ireland
1956	Olympic flyweight bronze medal, age 18
1960	Won British flyweight title
1961	Won European recognition as world bantamweight champion
1962	Beaten in unification bout by Brazilian Eder Jofre
1964	Won British and Empire bantamweight titles
1965	Announced retirement

Career record: Fights 35, Won 29, Lost 5, Drawn 1

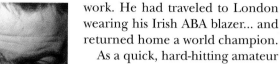

On a heady night at Wembley in May 1961, John Caldwell outboxed and outpunched Algerian Alphonse Halimi for 15 rounds to win European recognition as bantamweight champion of the world.

For Caldwell, a Belfast plumber who called himself "The Cold-Eyed Killer" inside the ring, it was a huge gamble that paid off handsomely. He was the British flyweight champion, and had never previously weighed more than 115 lb., but promoter Jack Solomons offered him the fight against a man who had previously edged out his compatriot and former amateur international teammate Freddie Gilroy on a close decision.

Caldwell snapped up the opportunity, beefed himself up to a little less than 116½ lb., still well inside the bantamweight limit, and went to work. He had traveled to London wearing his Irish ABA blazer... and returned home a world champion.

As a quick, hard-hitting amateur Caldwell won 243 of 250 bouts, including a bronze medal in the 1956 Olympics in Melbourne. He had gone on to win the British flyweight title in 1960. But as a bantamweight, although his success was greatest, it did not endure. He beat Halimi in a rematch in October 1961, but outside Europe, the tough, hard-hitting Brazilian, Eder Jofre, was acknowledged as champion. They fought for the undisputed title in Sao Paulo in January 1962, and Caldwell was stopped in ten rounds. The Irishman was never the same again, and although he won and lost the British and Empire bantamweight titles, he retired in 1965 when still only 27.

CLASSICIAL LEFT LEAD: JOHNNY CALDWELL OUTBOXES ALPHONSE HALIMI, 1961

SEE ALSO ◆ EDER JOFRE 169

HECTOR CAMACHO

One of the most outrageous extroverts ever to hold a world championship, Puerto Rican southpaw Hector Camacho could also box beautifully and fight like an alley cat. If he grew more cautious and negative as the years went by, then he matured outside the ring too—and by 1996 was speaking fondly of the joys of family life and fatherhood.

Camacho, who reveled in his tag of "Macho Man," could be insensitive, but when in the right mood, and especially in his youth, was a supremely skilled boxer. He won the WBC super-featherweight title by knocking out Rafael "Bazooka" Limon in five rounds in 1983, and two years later stepped up to lightweight and dethroned another Mexican Jose Luis Ramirez, winning a 12-round decision.

But he was lucky to scrape home on points over fellow Puerto Rican Edwin Rosario in a fight some said totally changed his approach. Suddenly, he became more of a runner, less carefree and more cunning. By 1989 he was the WBO light-welterweight champ after a win over Ray Mancini, but he lost his title and his unbeaten record in his 40th fight when a point deducted for refusing to obey the referee's instructions at the start of the last round cost him the verdict against Greg Haugen.

Haugen failed a post-fight dope test, and Camacho beat him in the rematch for the vacant title. But a one-sided drubbing from Julio Cesar Chavez in 1992 persuaded him to move up. In 1996 he was still fighting, mostly as a light-middleweight.

FACT FILE

1962 Born Bayamon, Puerto Rico
1980 Professional debut in New York City
1983 Won WBC super-featherweight title
1985 Won WBC lightweight title
1989 Won WBO light-welterweight title
1991 First defeat—controversially—to Greg Haugen
Career record: Fights 65, Won 61, Lost 3, Drawn 1

MACHO MAN: CAMACHO WAS OUTRAGEOUS, BUT BENEATH THE HYPE WAS AN ACCOMPLISHED BOXER WITH A CHAMPION'S HEART

SEE ALSO ◆ JULIO CESAR CHAVEZ 67 ◆ RAY MANCINI 208 ◆ EDWIN ROSARIO 283

ORLANDO CANIZALES

FACT FILE

1965	Born Laredo, Texas
1984	Professional debut
1988	Won IBF bantamweight title by stopping Kelvin Seabrooks
1994	Moved out of division after 16 championship defenses
1995	Lost WBA super-bantamweight bid against Wilfredo Vazquez

Career record: Fights 46, Won 42, Lost 3, Drawn 1

A consumate professional from the border town of Laredo, Texas, on the banks of the Rio Grande, Orlando Canizales was the best bantamweight in the world in the late 1980s and early 1990s.

He came from a solid, respectable background—his father Robert traveled to San Antonio every day to work in hotels, while his brother Gaby, who also twice held versions of the bantamweight championship, had a day job as a Laredo sheriff. Orlando once said he had never had a street fight in his life.

He was 18 when he turned professional, and after winning North American and United States titles at flyweight and super-flyweight, he became IBF world bantamweight champion with a 15th-round stoppage of Kelvin Seabrooks in Atlantic City in July 1988.

Canizales built his reputation steadily.

Sometimes he was explosive, sometimes no better than workmanlike, but he did what was required. His closest call was when he brought his title to freezing Sunderland in Britain's Northeast and turned back local hero Billy Hardy on a split decision that had the home fans chanting "Fix, Fix."

Hardy was given a rematch on a hot afternoon in Laredo in May 1991, and was knocked out in eight rounds. Canizales went on defending until he beat the record of consecutive defenses set by Manuel Ortiz in the 1940s, but as soon as he moved up to super-bantamweight at the start of 1995, he was beaten on a close verdict by WBA champion Wilfredo Vazquez of Puerto Rico.

He suddenly looked all of his 30 years, and in 1996 also lost to former WBA champion Junior Jones of New York in a fight that would have been a classic two years earlier.

CANIZALES DEFENDED THE
IBF BANTAMWEIGHT TITLE 16
TIMES IN SIX YEARS

SEE ALSO ◆ WILFREDO VAZQUEZ 323

MIGUEL CANTO

In the mid-1970s, respected British referee Harry Gibbs called Miguel Canto the best defensive counterpuncher, pound-for-pound, in boxing.

The little ring general from the sprawling industrial suburbs of Merida, the capital of Yucutan State in southeast Mexico, held the WBC flyweight title for four years and made a record 14 successful defenses.

Miguel Canto was a masterly boxer with quick hands and feet, an educated jab, and fast combination punches, Canto stood only 5 ft. 1 in., but had an unusually long reach, which he used effectively. Although he was stopped in two of his first three fights, he went on to become Mexican flyweight champion in January 1972, but lost his first world title attempt in 1974 when he was outpointed by Betulio Gonzalez of Venezuela.

In January 1975, he outboxed Japanese southpaw Shoji Oguma, who had succeeded Gonzalez, for a majority decision win in Sendai. By then he owned a restaurant named "Los Venados"—literally, The Deers—and was building a hotel in the fashionable resort of Cancun. But his promise to be out of boxing within two years came to nothing, as he piled up defenses and pay-days which averaged around $80,000 a time.

Canto, the first man from Yucutan to win a world title, twice beat old rivals Gonzalez and Oguma as well as two from the Chilean Martin Vargas. By 1979, however, he was slow and looked old. He lost the title in a poor display in South Korea against Chan-hee Park, and although he drilled himself into shape one last time the rematch ended in a draw. Canto was finished, but boxed on until 1982 when he retired, aged 34, after a stoppage defeat by Rodolfo Ortega in Merida.

FACT FILE

1948 Born Miguel Angel Canto Solis, Merida, Mexico

1972 Won Mexican flyweight title

1975 Won WBC flyweight title against Shoji Oguma in Japan

1979 Lost championship in 15th defense to Chan-hee Park in South Korea

1982 Announced retirement, age 34

Career record: Fights 74, Won 61, Lost 9, Drawn 4

CANTO'S CHAMPIONSHIP TROPHY IS ALMOST AS BIG AS HE IS!

SEE ALSO ♦ BETULIO GONZALEZ 137

TONY CANZONERI

FACT FILE

1908 Born Slidell, Louisiana

1927 Won world featherweight title by outpointing Johnny Dundee

1930 Knocked ou Al Singer in 66 seconds for world lightweight title

1931 Also recognized as world light-welterweight champion

1935 Won lightweight championship for second time from Lou Ambers

Died: New York City, December 9, 1959, age 51

Career record: Fights 175, Won 141, Lost 24, Drawn 10

Tony Canzoneri could box with the best, but loved nothing better than a toe-to-toe tear-up. The ready-smiling former shoeshine boy from Slidell, Louisiana, was also widely regarded as one of the straightest men in what in the 1930s was often a dirty business, and won world titles at three separate weights.

An Italian-American from a large family, Canzoneri was taught to box in New Orleans by world bantamweight champion Pete Herman. At 16 he faked his age to turn professional, at 18 he twice fought unsuccessfully for the NBA bantamweight title against Bud Taylor, and at 19 won the world featherweight championship against Johnny Dundee. After losing the belt in his second defense—when still only 19—he moved up to lightweight. In 1930 he lost a split decision to world champ Sammy Mandell and was outpointed in a classic with Britain's Jack "Kid" Berg. Finally, he won the world lightweight title with a sensational 66-second knockout of Al Singer in Madison Square Garden, New York.

Canzoneri twice beat Berg in 1931 and twice held the world junior-welterweight title, but lost both crowns to Barney Ross in Chicago in June 1933. Canzoneri outpointed Lou Ambers to regain the lightweight title in May 1935. Ambers beat him twice in rematches, but old-timers also talked for years of his 10-round wars with the welterweight champion Jimmy McLarnin in 1936. Canzoneri won the first, McLarnin the second. He retired in November 1939, worked as an actor in vaudeville, then ran a summer theater on Long Island, New York. Eventually he opened a sportsmen's bar on Broadway, but died from a heart attack in a New York hotel room in 1959.

CANZONERI, ONE OF THE GREAT RING TECHNICIANS OF ALL TIME, SLAMS A RIGHT TO THE BODY OF EDDIE ZIVIC

SEE ALSO ◆ LOU AMBERS 16 ◆ JACK "KID" BERG 35 ◆ JOHNNY DUNDEE 98 ◆ JIMMY MCLARNIN 246

Michael Carbajal

A brilliant amateur, Michael Carbajal proved he had the immense courage of a great professional champion when he climbed off the canvas twice to knock out Mexican hero Humberto Gonzalez in the seventh round of a classic battle in 1993.

Until that night, Carbajal was considered by many to be a product of a well-oiled publicity machine run by promoter Bob Arum. But Carbajal showed a 7,000 crowd at the Las Vegas Hilton as well as millions of TV viewers that he was for real. Arum billed it "La Explosion"—and for once the hype was matched by the product. Carbajal was floored in rounds two and five, but urged on by trainer-brother Danny, pressed on to an inspired triumph. "God couldn't have given me a better brother," said Michael.

Carbajal was born in a house filled with brothers, sisters, cousins, nephews, and nieces in a rundown quarter of Phoenix, and learned his boxing from his father Manuel. While working as a truck driver, he became an amateur star, his career culminating in a silver medal at the 1988 Olympics. He stopped Thailand's Muangchai Kittikasem in seven rounds to win the IBF light-flyweight belt in Phoenix on July 29, 1990. He turned back six challenges before his epic win over Gonzalez, and then made two more defenses before he was outsmarted in the rematch with the Mexican in February 1994. Carbajal was in the boxing wilderness until March 1996 when he regained the IBF belt by outpointing Mexican Melchor Cob Castro. He lost it in 1997 to Mauricio Pastrana.

CARBAJAL HELD TWO VERSIONS OF THE LIGHT-FLYWEIGHT TITLE AND PUT ON A THREE-FIGHT SERIES WITH HUMBERTO GONZALEZ

FACT FILE

1967	Born Phoenix, Arizona
1988	Light-flyweight silver medalist in Seoul Olympics
1990	Won IBF light-flyweight title
1993	Beat WBC champ Humberto Gonzalez in classic confrontation
1994	Lost rematch with Gonzalex
1996	Regained IBF title

Career record: Fights 43, Won 41, Lost 2

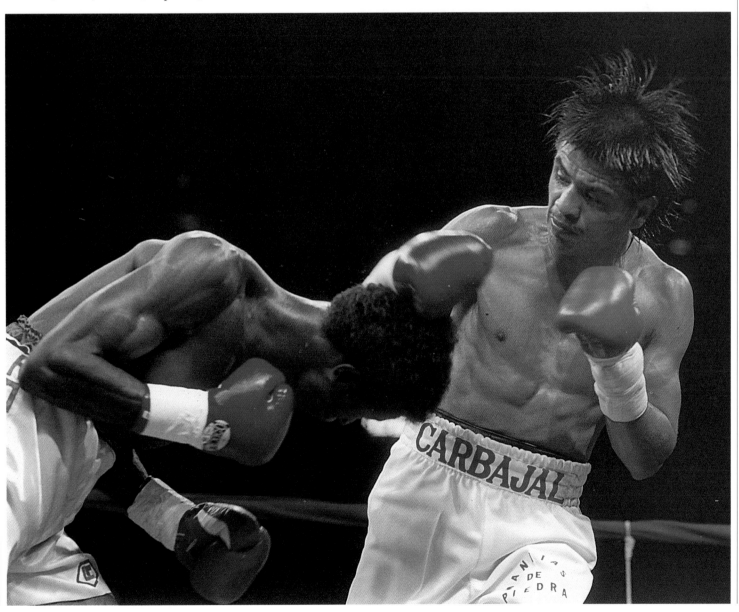

SEE ALSO ◆ **HUMBERTO GONZALEZ 138**

THE
GREAT
FIGHTS

HUMBERTO GONZALEZ
V.
MICHAEL CARBAJAL

HILTON HOTEL, LAS VEGAS.
MARCH 13, 1993.

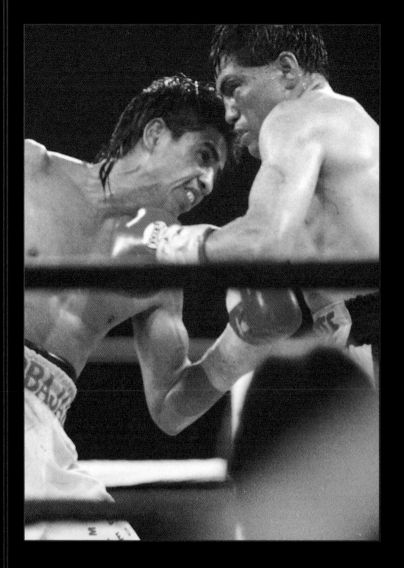

Michael Carbajal fought his way from the back-streets of Phoenix, Arizona, to earn a dream $1 million payday against Mexican favorite Humberto "Chiquita" Gonzalez.

And Carbajal, who was labeled "Little Hands of Stone," shrugged off his doubters by clawing his way back from the brink to knock out Gonzalez in seven rounds before 7,000 fans at the Las Vegas Hilton.

Promoter Bob Arum said Carbajal would become the first little man to earn $1 million for a single fight—and Michael achieved it here as he added Gonzalez's WBC light-flyweight belt to the IBF version he already owned in a showdown Arum billed as "La Explosion."

There were those who said the light-flyweight silver medalist at the 1988 Olympics was a manufactured product of the Top Rank hype machine, who won his IBF belt against an undermotivated champion, Muangchai Kittikasem of Thailand, and then built his reputation on hand-picked challengers. Here, he laid down the truth once and for all.

Gonzalez, second in popularity in Mexico only to Julio Cesar Chavez, put Carbajal under pressure from the start, ripping into him and making light of a four-inch height gap. In the second round, Carbajal was put down by a left to the chin, nodded calmly to his inspirational trainer-brother Danny, and hauled himself up.

In round five, he slumped down, seriously hurt this time and Gonzalez appeared on the verge of a great win. But from somewhere Carbajal found the nerve and desire to lash back. Gonzalez tried to knock him out, failed, and bled from an inch-long cut on his left eyelid.

In round seven Carbajal landed a fight-winning left hook. "Chiquita" kept himself up somehow, but had nothing left and after a barrage of punches, one final left hook sent him crashing to the canvas to be counted out.

Gonzalez would prove his own greatness by twice beating Carbajal on points in rematches which, while admirable and intriguing, never reached the heights of this magnificently raw, head-to-head struggle.

PRIMO CARNERA

Primo Carnera was the most manipulated and exploited of all world heavyweight champions and became the barely disguised role model for the popular novel and film "The Harder They Fall".

A simple, gigantic Italian, who stood 6 ft., 5¾ in. and scaled more than 250 lb., he was ridiculed for his ponderous style.

First spotted as a circus strongman with a working name of Juan the Unconquerable Spaniard, he became a boxing freakshow, bowling over opponents who had been paid in advance to lose.

Carnera had some ability, however, and did beat some top-class men fairly. Jack Sharkey, whom he knocked out in six rounds to win the world heavyweight title in Madison Square Garden Bowl, New York, in June 1933, was adamant that he was underrated. Nevertheless, however much Sharkey protested, he was still widely accused of taking a dive.

Carnera defended his title with points wins over Paolino Uzcudun of Spain, and former light-heavyweight champ Tommy Loughran, but was then humiliated by Max Baer, being floored repeatedly before the fight, in New York in June 1934, was stopped in the 11th. And in 1935 he was butchered in six rounds by Joe Louis.

Carnera was tossed on to the scrapheap with only a fraction of the fortune his managers claimed he had earned. When he returned to Italy in 1936, he was sick and disillusioned, yet through all his problems retained his dignity and sense of honor. After the war, he made a short-lived comeback, then turned to wrestling and settled with his family in California. In 1967 he returned to his home village to die, age 60, of liver disease.

CARNERA, AN HONEST MAN WHO RETAINED HIS DIGNITY IN THE FACE OF TERRIBLE EXPLOITATION

SEE ALSO ◆ MAX BAER 26 ◆ JOE LOUIS 204 ◆ JACK SHARKEY 298

Georges Carpentier

Georges Carpentier was the most glamorous athlete of his generation, a French war hero who called himself "The Orchid Man." His popularity was immense, and he drew as much attention from social critics as he did from boxing scribes.

Society writer Beverley Nichols described Carpentier as "extraordinarily amusing" and revealed that whenever the Frenchman was in London he was so popular that he became the recipient of sackfuls of mail from women "who had fallen in love with him."

A miner's son, Carpentier was a brilliant boxer who learned from childhood in northern France. He fought for money from the age of 14, and within five years had held European titles at four weights, from welterweight to heavyweight.

He won the world light-heavyweight title in October 1920 by knocking out Battling Levinsky in four rounds, but was way out of his depth when thrown to world heavyweight champion Jack Dempsey in the first of promoter Tex Rickard's "Million Dollar Gate" epics near Jersey City in July 1921. A crowd of 80,183 paid a total of $1,789,238 to see Dempsey knock out the Frenchman in four rounds.

Carpentier returned to Europe, knocked out Ted Kid Lewis in one round, then lost his world light-heavyweight title to Battling Siki in Paris in a "fix that went wrong" in September 1922. Siki was supposed to lose spectacularly— on the grounds that the film would do enormous business. But Carpentier hurt Siki by mistake, and Siki forgot the script and knocked out the ill-conditioned champion in the sixth round.

Carpentier faded from the world scene after he lost to Gene Tunney in New York in 1924, and had his last fight in 1926.

FACT FILE

1894	Born Lens, France
1920	Won world light-heavyweight title against Battling Levinsky
1921	Knocked out by world heavyweight champion Jack Dempsey
1922	Lost world light-heavyweight title
Died:	Paris, France, October 28, 1975, age 81

Career record: Fights 109, Won 88, Lost 14, Drawn 6, No Decision 1

THE ORCHID MAN'S FLOWER IS FADING. HE PREPARES TO LEAVE THE RING AFTER HIS 1924 FIGHT WITH TOMMY GIBBONS IN MICHIGAN CITY

SEE ALSO ◆ JACK DEMPSEY 88 ◆ TED KID LEWIS 195 ◆ BATTLING SIKI 300 ◆ GENE TUNNEY 313

JIMMY CARRUTHERS

Jimmy Carruthers was a masterful southpaw known as "Shoulders" because of his awkward style. He was unlucky not to win a medal in the 1948 Olympics, when he withdrew because of a cut in sparring, but made up for it later in the professional ranks.

On November 15, 1952 he challenged world bantamweight champion Vic Toweel of South Africa in front of a 30,000 crowd at the Rand Stadium in Johannesburg. Carruthers was given little chance, but he stunned Toweel with a perfect left hand in the opening seconds, and in two minutes, 19 seconds it was all over. Carruthers was world champion at the age of 23.

In a rematch four months later, also in Johannesburg, Carruthers won in ten rounds, and then took the title home. In spite of suffering from a tapeworm and fighting with a severely cut eye, he outpointed American challenger Henry "Pappy" Gault in front of a 32,500 crowd at the Sydney Sports Ground. His last fight as champion was in a rainstorm in Bangkok in May 1954, when he beat local slugger Chamrern Songkitrat in a fight restricted to 12 rounds. It drew a crowd of more than 50,000, but the ferocity of the rain meant both men boxed barefoot. Carruthers had also been sick with a stomach upset for three days. Twice light bulbs above the ring shattered on to the canvas, and at one point Carruthers hopped around trying to remove broken glass from his foot. He won clearly and afterwards shocked and stunned the boxing world by announcing his retirement.

A comeback in 1961 failed, and he settled down to run a health drink business in Sydney. He died of lung cancer in 1990.

CARRUTHERS SUFFERED A BADLY CUT EYE IN HIS FIGHT AGAINST ALDO PRAVISANI IN SYDNEY 1961

MARCEL CERDAN

A rugged, persistent, and cunning fighter, Marcel Cerdan stands alongside Georges Carpentier as the most enduring of French boxing heroes.

Cerdan was born in Sidi-bel-Abbes, headquarters of the French Foreign Legion in Algeria, and turned professional in Casablanca with the man who had taught him to box, family friend Lucien Roupp. Marcel was established as a world class welterweight before the War interrupted his career. He served with the French Navy until the nation fell, and in 1942 was ordered to defend his European title for the entertainment of Nazi troops in Paris, but short-changed them by disposing of Jose Ferrer inside a round, leaving Paris without permission on false papers. After that he fought in the Free French Navy.

After the War, he picked up the pieces of his career, won both French and European middleweight titles, and in Jersey City, New Jersey, on September 21, 1948, he battered defending world champion Tony Zale to defeat after 11 one-sided rounds.

By now Cerdan, married with children, was heavily involved in a love affair with French singer Edith Piaf, a scandal that seemed, like Piaf's songs, to touch the soul of the French people. He was forgiven for it. Cerdan lost the world title when he damaged a shoulder and fought Jake La Motta one-armed until his corner pulled him out at the end of the ninth round in Detroit in June 1949. A rematch was arranged and as Cerdan left Paris he told reporters: "I will win, or I will die." A dreadful prophecy. The plane crashed into a mountain on the island of Sao Miguel in the Azores. All 48 on board were killed.

FACT FILE

1916 Born Sidi-bel-Abbes, Algeria

1939 Won European welterweight title

1947 Won European middleweight title

1948 Won world middleweight title against Tony Zale

1949 Lost world title to Jake La Motta

Died: The Azores, October 27, 1949, age 33

Career record: Fights 109, Won 105, Lost 4

ALWAYS THE EXTROVERT ... MARCEL CERDAN ENJOYS A BREAK WITH THE BOYS OF THE CATHOLIC YOUTH ORGANIZATION IN NEW YORK BEFORE HIS FIGHT WITH GEORGE ABRAMS IN 1946

SEE ALSO ◆ JAKE LA MOTTA 182 ◆ TONY ZALE 342

ANTONIO CERVANTES

FACT FILE

1945	Born San Basilio de Palenque, Bolivar, Colombia
1964	Professional debut
1978	Won WBA light-welterweight title against Alfonso Frazer
1976	Lost title to Wilfred Benitez
1977	Regaiined WBA title against Carlos Giminez
1980	Lost title in 21st world title fight against Aaron Pryor
1983	Retired, age 37

Career record: Fights 79, Won 66, Lost 12, Drawn 1

Antonio Cervantes once claimed to astonished boxing writers that he was a descendant of Miguel Cervantes, the seventeenth-century Spanish novelist who wrote *Don Quixote* but was almost certainly joking!

A Colombian who moved his base to Venezuela in the late 1960s, he was 26 when he won the WBA light-welterweight title by stopping defending champion Alfonso Frazer in Panama in October 1972. For the next eight years, he was acknowledged as the best light-welterweight in the world, his reign interrupted only briefly by the 17-year-old genius from Puerto Rico, Wilfred Benitez. Cervantes consolidated his position in 1973 with five defenses, one against the former champion Nicolino Loche, who had turned back Antonio's first title bid by outpointing him in Buenos Aires in 1971.

One of his finest victories was a points win over Esteban De Jesus in May 1975. A classy stand-up boxer, Cervantes could also punch. When he won the title, Frazer was reportedly out cold for two minutes. He also stopped tough, ambitious men like the Australian Hector Thompson, and defended his title in Puerto Rico, Venezuela, Panama, and Japan.

He lost the WBA title on a split 15-round decision to Benitez in San Juan in March 1976, but when Benitez moved up to welterweight, Cervantes was paired with old rival Carlos Giminez of Argentina, and became champion again with a sixth-round stoppage. This time he kept it until, at the age of 34 and in his 21st world title fight, he was knocked out in four rounds by Aaron Pryor in Cincinnati. He retired in 1973.

CERVANTES FLATTENS SHINCHI KADOTA IN TOKYO IN 1974

SEE ALSO ◆ **WILFRED BENITEZ 32** ◆ **ESTEBAN DE JESUS 84** ◆ **NICOLINO LOCHE 197** ◆ **AARON PRYOR 273**

JEFF CHANDLER

oltin' Jeff Chandler was a carpenter's laborer from the mean streets of south Philadelphia who took up boxing when he wandered into the city's Juniper Gym at the advanced age of 19 years.

After only two amateur bouts, a win and a split decision defeat to the experienced Johnny Carter, he turned professional in February 1976. After drawing his debut, he settled down to learn the business the hard way, on the tough, preliminary circuit around Philadelphia and Atlantic City.

After nine fights he signed for a 4 ft., 8 in. former vaudeville performer and national jitterbug champion, "KO" Becky O'Neill, and with the help of Philadelphia promoter Russell Peltz, she guided Chandler to the USBA and NABF titles.

Finally, in November 1980, he won the WBA bantamweight title by stopping Julian Solis of Panama in the 14th round in Miami. Even then, he kept boxing in perspective —he worked eight hours a day for a Philadelphia construction firm.

In his first defense he outpointed former WBC champ Jorge Lujan, then was held to a draw in Tokyo by Eijiro Murata. He knocked out Solis again, and then brought Murata to Atlantic City and stopped him in the 13th round.

Stylish and hard-hitting, in March 1982 he stopped old amateur rival and fellow Philadelphian, Johnny Carter, in six, and continued to dominate the division through a total of nine defenses until April 1984, when he lost in the 15th round to Californian Richard Sandoval in Atlantic City. Chandler, a family man, took a beating and retired.

FACT FILE

1956 Born Philadelphia
1976 Professional debut
1980 Won WBA bantamweight title against Julian Solis
1984 Lost WBA title in 10th defense and retired, aged 27
Career record: Fights 37, Won 33, Lost 2, Drawn 2

JOLTIN' JEFF CELEBRATES A 1983 WIN OVER ELIJIRO MURATA

JUNG-KOO CHANG

FACT FILE

1963 Born Pusan, South Korea

1983 Won WBC light-flyweight title against Hilario Zapata

1988 Relinquished WBC title

1991 Retired after failing to regain title for third time

Career record: Fights 42, Won 38, Lost 4

Known as the Korean Hawk, Jung-koo Chang was a ruthlessly efficient fighting machine who made 15 successful defenses of the World Boxing Council light-flyweight title in the mid-1980s.

Fast and tricky, Chang wore down opponents with prolonged, furious attacks. He fought his way up from the four-round novice class, making such rapid progress that in September 1982, when still only 19, he lost a split decision to reigning WBC light-flyweight champion Hilario Zapata in Chonju.

His backers tempted Zapata back to South Korea and in March 1983, a month past his 20th birthday, he avenged his first professional defeat by stopping the talented Panamanian in the third round in Daejon.

That was the launchpad for a sensational career that made him one of the most popular Korean sportsmen in history. He beat the Mexican, German Torres, over 15 rounds and when the WBC cut the championship distance to 12 rounds, he also outpointed the rising Thai star Sot Chitalada in spite of a badly cut eye in Pusan in March 1984.

He went on to defeat Torres twice more, and beat other world title claimants in Japan's Hideyuki Ohashi (twice) and the Mexican Isidro Perez, before out of the ring worries forced him to relinquish the title in 1988. His wife invested a large sum of their money in a restaurant business, which then collapsed, and the ensuing family strife left Chang unable to concentrate on boxing. When he returned in 1989, the fire had left him.

He lost on points to new champion Humberto Gonzalez of Mexico, and subsequent attempts at flyweight against Sot Chitalada and Muangchai Kittikasem brought further disappointment. He retired after Kittikasem stopped him in the 12th round in May 1991.

JUNG-KOO CHANG SHOUTS FOR JOY AFTER DEFEATING JAPANESE CHALLENGER HIDEYUKI OHASHI

SEE ALSO ◆ SOT CHITALADA 71 ◆ HUMBERTO GONZALEZ 138 ◆ HILARO ZAPATA 346

EZZARD CHARLES

ome say Ezzard Charles was the best light-heavyweight in history, who was never given the chance to prove it in a world title fight.

When his opportunity did arise, it was as a heavyweight in the wake of the retirement of Joe Louis. Although he scaled less than 180 lb., Charles was paired with Jersey Joe Walcott for the vacant NBA title in Chicago's Comiskey Park in June 1949 and won a unanimous 15-round decision.

When Louis was forced back into the ring by his financial difficulties, a bout with Charles was inevitable. And on September 27, 1950, Charles outclassed the faded old champ to earn universal recognition, handing him a 15-round drubbing that he admitted later gave him no pleasure at all. Louis had been his long-time hero.

Charles, who was known as the Cincinnati Cobra, was an underrated champion. He made eight defenses of the heavyweight championship, before a supposedly routine affair against 37-year-old Walcott in Pittsburgh in July 1951 went horribly wrong. He was knocked out in the seventh round.

That took something out of him. Walcott beat him again, and although he gave Rocky Marciano a grueling 15-rounder in June 1954, he was knocked out in eight rounds in the return only three months later. Charles faded rapidly after that and announced his retirement in 1956, tried a comeback and quit for good in 1959, by which time he was losing on club shows in places like Boise, Idaho, and Oklahoma City. In his 40s he developed multiple sclerosis and spent his last years in a wheelchair. He died in Chicago when only 53.

FACT FILE

1921	Born Lawrenceville, Georgia
1939	National AAU and National Golden Gloves middleweight champion
1949	Beat Jersey Joe Walcott for vacan NBA world heavyweight title
1950	Defeated Joe Louis on Points
1951	Lost title to Walcott
1954	Twice lost challenges to Rocky Marciano

Died: Chicago, Illinois, May 27, 1975, age 53
Career record: Fights 122, Won 96, Lost 25, Drawn 1

CHARLES (RIGHT) A VASTLY UNDER-VALUED CHAMPION FIGHTS JERSEY JOE WALCOTT

SEE ALSO ◆ JOE LOUIS 204 ◆ ROCKY MARCIANO 209 ◆ JERSEY JOE WALCOTT 328

DAVE CHARNLEY

FACT FILE

1935	Born Dartford, Kent, England
1957	Won British lightweight title
1959	Won Empire lightweight title
1959	Lost first world title bid on cut to Joe Brown
1960	Won European lightweight title
1961	Lost highly controversial decision in rematch with Brown

Career record: Fights 61, Won 48, Lost 12, Drawn 1

Henry Cooper called Dave Charnley the greatest of Britain's postwar fighters. The tough Dartford southpaw was desperately unlucky in his two attempts at the world lightweight title, both against Joe "Old Bones" Brown, in 1959 and 1961.

In the first he lost on a cut eye in five rounds in Houston, Texas, but in the second at Earls Court in London on April 18, 1961, Charnley outfought the veteran craftsman from Louisiana. Referee Tommy Little thought otherwise and raised Brown's hand, sparking an angry demonstration of boos, jeers and foot stamping from the 18,000 crowd. The protests did not subside even when the next contest was announced and Little needed a police escort from ringside. The normally strait-laced trade paper *Boxing News* reported: "We felt like leaving the Press seats and joining in the demonstration!"

Charnley did beat Brown in their third fight, but by then the American had lost his world title. Charnley, a neat, clean-cut married man, made a habit of fighting the best in the world. He won the British lightweight title by out-pointing Joe Lucy in 1957, added the Commonwealth championship by knocking out Willie Toweel of South Africa in 1959, and became European champion with a ten-rounds win over Mario Vecchiatto in 1960. He also beat future world welterweight champions Don Jordan and Kenny Lane, another perennial lightweight contender.

He retired in 1964 after the only stoppage defeat of his life, against reigning world welterweight champion Emile Griffith in a non-title fight at Wembley. In retirement, he became a successful property developer, building on the sum he made in the ring.

CHARNLEY PILES ON THE PRESSURE AGAINST JOE BROWN IN 1961

SEE ALSO ◆ JOE BROWN 43 ◆ EMILE GRIFFITH 144

Julio Cesar Chavez, perhaps the greatest of all Mexican fighters, once said: "I started fighting before I was one minute old!" He went on to compete in more world title fights than anyone in history. By the end of 1996, with his career almost done, the tally had reached 34.

He knocked out compatriot Mario Martinez in eight rounds to become the WBC super-featherweight champion in September 1984, and in November 1987 he moved up to lightweight and took the WBA title from Puerto Rican Edwin Rosario with a brilliant, probably peak performance. The fight was stopped in round 11. A relentless, prowling aggressor with an especially destructive left hook, Chavez became a three-weight world champion in 1989 when he stopped Roger Mayweather in 10 rounds for the WBC light-welterweight crown.

He showed a champion's heart and composure to floor and stop IBF champion Meldrick Taylor with two seconds left in the 12th round in Las Vegas in March 1990. If Taylor had survived, Chavez would have lost on points. As he went into the 1990s, Chavez gradually slowed. He was lucky to draw with WBC welterweight champion Pernell Whitaker and finally lost his unbeaten record—and his WBC title—to Frankie Randall in January 1994. A disputed technical decision gave him the championship back, but he was eventually cut to fourth-round defeat by Oscar De La Hoya in the summer of 1996. For all he had earned, Chavez was beset by financial and personal problems. His wife divorced him, and in October 1996 he handed over his entire $1 million purse for a win over Joey Gamache to the tax officials. "Why has this happened? Because I'm a boxer, not an accountant," he said.

FACT FILE

1962	Corn Ciudad Obregon, Mexico
1984	Won WBC super-featherweight title against Mario Martinez
1987	Won WBA lightweight title by stopping Edwin Rosario
1989	Won WBC light-welterweight title against Roger Mayweather
1990	Won a classic with Meldrick Taylor with two seconds to spare
1994	Lost & regained title against Frankie Randall
1996	Beaten by Oscar De La Hoya

Career record: Fights 100, Won 97, Lost 2, Drawn 1

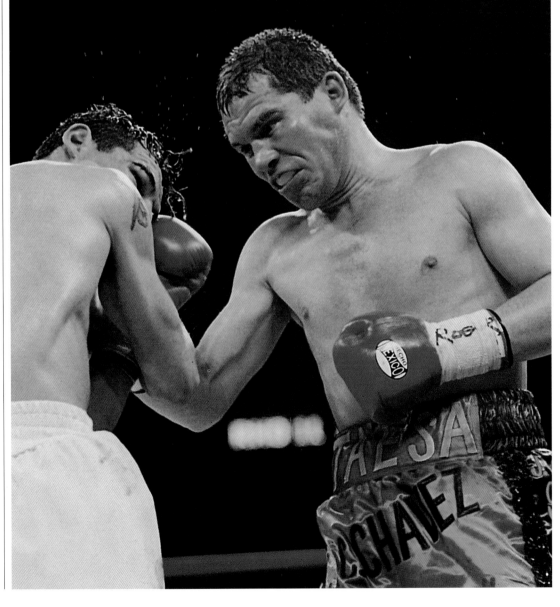

CHAVEZ, ONE OF THE GREAT PRESSURE FIGHTERS OF ALL TIME, HAD MORE WORLD TITLE FIGHTS THAN ANYBODY

SEE ALSO ◆ OSCAR DE LA HOYA 85 ◆ EDWIN ROSARIO 283

THE GREAT FIGHTS

JULIO CESAR CHAVEZ V. MELDRICK TAYLOR

HILTON CENTER, LAS VEGAS. MARCH 17, 1990.

The standard for dramatic finishes was set by Julio Cesar Chavez and Meldrick Taylor in their light-welterweight title showdown in Las Vegas in March 1990.

Going into the 12th and final round Taylor, who held the International Boxing Federation version of the championship, looked set for victory.

Chavez, the Mexican idol who was the World Boxing Council champion with 68 consecutive victories behind him, had looked extraordinarily slow in the first half of the fight as Taylor had sped into a big lead, and the Mexican's second half trawling back had not been effective enough for two of the three judges. While Chuck Giampa did have Chavez in front by a strangely generous scoreline of 105-104 after the 11th, Jerry Roth and Dave Moretti had Taylor in surprisingly big leads, respectively, at 108-101 and 107-102. The truth seemed somewhere in between.

Taylor was fading, but only needed to get through the final round and the decision was his. Pressing relentlessly, and knowing he was behind, Chavez took everything out of Taylor with an amazing last round surge. Taylor slipped over in mid-round, then in the last 20 seconds was badly shaken by a right hand. Chavez piled in, smashing home another right to put the American down. Taylor got up at five, his eye closing, his mouth bleeding, and referee Richard Steele asked him: "Are you all right?" He answered the question, himself: "You're not all right," and crossed his arms. There were two seconds left on the clock.

Steele's decision outraged Taylor's team and manager Lou Duva had to be restrained as he ducked into the ring to remonstrate with the official. At the post-fight press conference, he received more criticism, but said the following day: "When a guy doesn't respond, what are you going to do? I asked him twice. It's a shame."

The fracture to the orbital bone of his eye mended, but Taylor never got over the psychological hurt of defeat when just two seconds from victory. When they fought again in 1994, Taylor was stopped in eight rounds.

CHARTCHAI CHIONOI

FACT FILE

1942 Born Bangkok,
Thailand

1966 Won world flyweight
title against Walter
McGowan

1969 Lost world flyweight
title to Efren Torres

1970 Regained it, lost it
again

1973 Won WBA flyweight
title against Fritz
Chervet

1974 Lost championship
for third time to
Susumu Hanagata

Career record: Fights 85,
Won 63, Lost 19, Drawn 3

Thai flyweight Chartchai Chionoi was one of the most enduring of world champions ever, who held the 112 lb. title three times between 1966 and 1974.

The son of a policeman, Chionoi was inspired to box as an 11-year-old by the world-class exploits of compatriot Chamrern Songkitrat. He turned professional at 15, but came of age when he challenged Scotland's Walter McGowan for the world championship before an ecstatic 16,000 crowd in Bangkok on December 30, 1966. McGowan was stopped because of a horribly cut nose in the ninth round, and the fight was watched by the King of Thailand from a throne that had been erected specially for the occasion.

Chionoi beat McGowan on cuts again in a rematch in seven rounds at Wembley in September 1967. He didn't mind boxing abroad—in January 1968 he beat Efren "Alacran" Torres in 13 bloody rounds in Mexico City. He was well beaten in eight rounds by Torres in a return in February 1969, toyed with the idea of retirement but instead opted for a decider with the tough little Mexican in Bangkok in March 1970. This time 25,000 fans —again, including the King—turned out to see Chionoi collect a deserved unanimous decision.

Surprisingly, he lost the title to Erbito Salavarria in two rounds in December 1970. The talented Japanese fighter Masao Ohba stopped him in 12 rounds in a WBA fight in January 1973, but when Ohba was killed in a car crash, Chionoi beat Fritz Chervet of Switzerland for the vacant title. Susumu Hanagata of Japan deprived him of the belt with a sixth-round win in Tokyo in October 1974, by which time Chartchai was 32 years old. He retired the following year after a defeat in Panama.

CHIONOI (RIGHT) IN ACTION AGAINST MEXICO'S EFREN TORRES, WON THE FLYWEIGHT TITLE THREE TIMES

SEE ALSO ◆ WALTER MCGOWAN 241

SOT CHITALADA

Technically accomplished, with a flashing left hand, a sharp straight right and an iron chin, Sot Chitalada was one of the best of modern flyweight champions, although he fought a constant battle against the scales.

Chitalada regularly took off a sixth of his body weight to make the 112 lb. championship limit, and under such circumstances it's astonishing that he boxed at the top for seven years, competing in 16 world title fights.

Trained by Englishman Charles Atkinson, Chitalada soon displayed his talents. The Thais were so confident of his ability that they put him in a WBC light-flyweight contest against the great Korean Hawk, Jung-koo Chang, in only his fifth professional fight. He gave Chang all the trouble he needed before losing the match on points.

Chitalada won the WBC flyweight title by outboxing Mexican Gabriel Bernal in Bangkok in October 1984. He traveled to London in February 1985 and stopped former champ Charlie Magri on cuts in four rounds, and then set about establishing his reputation. Surprisingly, his rematch with Bernal was a draw, but then proved his superiority over the Mexican in a third fight in December 1986. He found weight-making increasingly tough, and when he lost the title to Yong-kang Kim in South Korea in 1988, Atkinson wanted him to move up to bantamweight. However, he stayed at 112 lb., outboxed Kim in a return in Thailand, and went on to make four more defenses. Long estranged from Atkinson, he was eventually stopped in six rounds by fellow Thai Muangchai Kittikasem in February 1991. In a rematch Kittikasem beat him in the ninth, and Sot retired. In retirement his eyesight began to fail and in the mid-1990s the WBC paid for corrective surgery.

FACT FILE

1962	Born Bangkok, Thailand
1984	Won WBC flyweight title against Gabriel Bernal
1988	Lost title on points to Yong-kang Kim in Korea
1989	Regained title by beating Kim in Bangkok
1991	Lost to compatriot Muangchai Kittikasem

Career record: Fights 31, Won 26, Lost 4, Drawn 1

CHITALADA (RIGHT) ON HIS WAY TO A FOUR-ROUND WIN OVER BRITAIN'S CHARLIE MAGRI

KID CHOCOLATE

FACT FILE

1910 Born Eligio Sardinias Montalbo in Cerro, Cuba

1931 Won world junior-fliyweight title by beating Benny Bass

1932 Beat Lew Feldman for New York recognition as fetherweight champ

1933 Lost junior-lightweight title to Frankie Klick

1938 Last fight in Havana

Died: Cuba, August 8, 1988, age 78

Career record: Fights 148, Won 132, Lost 10, Drawn 6

Kid Chocolate was an immaculate boxer who could punch his weight, a student of the techniques of boxing who fought exuberantly, as if he never wanted to stop living; and, for the depressingly short span of his youth, he was one of the greatest fighters of his time.

Chocolate began boxing at the age of ten. By 18 he was a professional in Havana and within six months was plying his flamboyant talent in New York. He beat Fidel La Barba, Al Singer, and Bushy Graham.

His first defeat, after 52 victories, was when Jack Berg made the most of an 11 lb. pull in weight to win a close decision in a classic struggle in August 1930.

After failing to dethrone featherweight champ Battling Battalino, he won the world junior-lightweight title with a seventh-round stoppage of Benny Bass in Philadelphia in July 1931. He lost to Tony Canzoneri for the lightweight championship, but in 1932 only Berg beat him in 20 fights, and he stopped Lew Feldman in 12 rounds to become the New York-recognized world featherweight champ. But his lifestyle was catching up with him, and at the end of 1933 he suffered a bad defeat against Tony Canzoneri and then lost his junior-lightweight title on a seventh round stoppage to Frankie Klick. In February 1934 he gave up the featherweight title, no longer able to make the weight. Nobody gave him another title chance, even though from 1934 to his retirement in Cuba in 1938, he lost only two decisions in 48 fights. He ran a gym for a time, and lived with his memories in a rambling house until his death in 1988.

CUBAN GENIUS KID CHOCOLATE LIVED LIFE TO THE FULL

SEE ALSO ◆ JACK BERG 35 ◆ TONY CANZONERI 54 ◆ FIDEL LA BARBA 181

CURTIS COKES

A clever, crafty ring general, Curtis Cokes was an underrated world welterweight champion who went on to become a highly respected coach.

Cokes was born in Dallas, began fighting as a 20-year-old lightweight, and learned the business in the tough rings of Texas in the late 1950s and early 1960s. He fought world-class men such as Luis Rodriguez, Kenny Lane, and his greatest early rival Manuel Gonzalez, whom he met five times.

His chance came when the WBA decided on an elimination tournament after Emile Griffith had moved up to middleweight and vacated the 147 lb. title.

Cokes stopped Luis Rodriguez in the 15th round in New Orleans in July 1966, and then won the vacant WBA title by outpointing Gonzalez a month later. He rounded off a watershed year by clearly outboxing aggressive Frenchman Jean Josselin in Dallas in November 1966 to win deserved universal recognition.

He could be erratic—in 1967 he drew and lost in non-title fights against François Pavilla and Gypsy Joe Harris respectively—but when the title was on the line, he proved himself the best welterweight of his time. Pavilla was stopped in a return for the title and he turned back challenges from Californian champ Charlie Shipes, Willie Ludick of South Africa, and Ramon LaCruz before in April 1969, he lost in 13 rounds to the great Cuban, Jose Napoles.

Cokes lost a return with Napoles, but boxed until 1972, when he finally accepted that at 35 another chance would not come his way. In retirement he trained fighters, co-wrote an instructional book, and in 1995 took Dallas-born Quincy Taylor to the WBC middleweight championship.

FACT FILE

1937	Born Dallas, Texas
1958	Professional debut, age 20
1966	Won world welterweight title
1969	Lost title to Jose Napoles
1972	Announced retirement

Career record: Fights 80, Won 62, Lost 14, Drawn 4

COKES CELEBRATES AFTER HIS DEFEAT OF FRANCOIS PAVILLA SUCCESSFULLY DEFENDING HIS WORLD WELTERWEIGHT TITLE

SEE ALSO ◆ EMILE GRIFFITH 144 ◆ JOSE NAPOLES 250 ◆ LUIS RODRIGUEZ 279

STEVE COLLINS

Two magnificently planned victories over Chris Eubank brought the career of "Celtic Warrior" Steve Collins to a late but extremely lucrative peak.

Collins was separated from the pack of talented contenders by an intense hunger and, when it mattered most, the ability to hold his nerve and adapt his style to a subtly changing situation. Collins always was his own man. A good, but not great amateur, he went to Massachusetts to learn alongside the best in the business, Marvin Hagler.

The red-headed Dubliner stayed for four years and won both the Irish and USBA middleweight titles, but his first three attempts to win major championships ended in disappointment. WBA champion Mike McCallum outboxed him in 1990. Reggie Johnson beat him on a majority decision after McCallum had vacated the title, and Sumbu Kalambay also beat him on a majority in a European title.

After linking up with British promoter Barry Hearn in 1993, he won the WBO middleweight title by stopping Chris Pyatt in five rounds in May 1994, but his career came alive through his two wins over Eubank in 1995.

Collins outpsyched Eubank in their first meeting in County Cork by claiming he had been hypnotized, and then mixed smart counterpunching with controlled aggression to win a points verdict in a fight where both men were floored.

In the rematch Collins bullied Eubank out of the fight in a display of furious, sometimes reckless aggression in Cork City. After victories over Cornelius Carr and Neville Brown, Collins stopped Nigel Benn in four rounds in Manchester in July 1996 and beat him again in a sixth-round retirement four months later.

THE CELTIC WARRIOR PINS CHRIS EUBANK ON THE END OF HIS JAB IN THEIR SECOND FIGHT ON A RAINY NIGHT IN CORK CITY

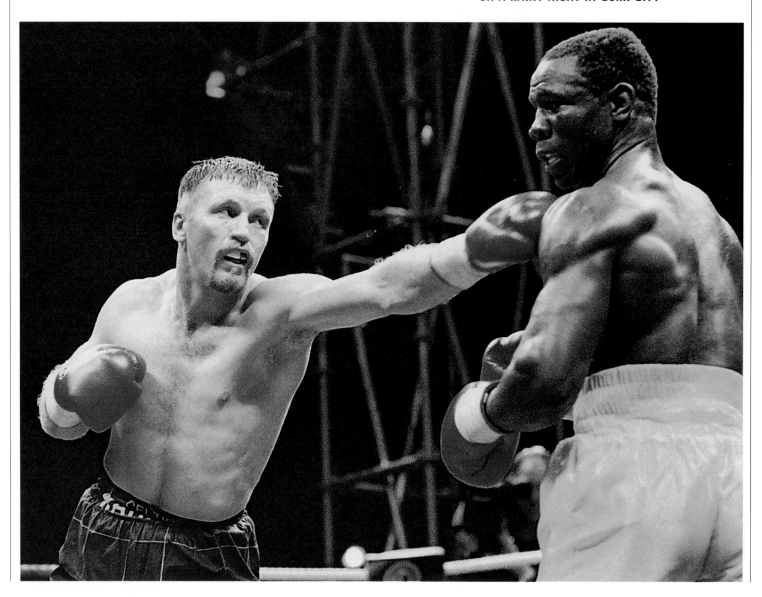

SEE ALSO ◆ NIGEL BENN 33 ◆ CHRIS EUBANK 106 ◆ MIKE McCALLUM 238

BILLY CONN

Billy Conn will always be remembered as the man who came closest to beating the prime Joe Louis. He was ahead on points after 12 rounds against Louis in front of a crowd of 54,486 at the New York Polo Grounds on June 18, 1941, collecting points with a sensational display of counterpunching.

But in the 13th he became overconfident and, in spite of being a light puncher even among light-heavyweights and 25 lb. lighter than Louis, went for the knockout. That was exactly the kind of gift Louis needed, and the fabled Brown Bomber put Conn down for the count just before the end of the round. "What's the point in being Irish if you can't be thick," was Conn's rueful post-fight attempt at self-mockery. He had blown the chance of a lifetime.

The War prevented their boxing again until 1946, by which time both were well past their best. Conn had deteriorated further and was easily knocked out in round eight. Conn was of Irish stock and born in Pittsburgh. A professional fighter at 16, he won the world light-heavyweight title by outpointing Melio Bettina from Connecticut in July 1939, and defended it three times, against Bettina and Gus Lesnevich twice. He relinquished it to take the fight with Louis.

He also beat world-class heavyweights such as Lee Savold, Bob Pastor, and Al McCoy, as well as top middleweights Fred Apostoli, Solly Krieger, and Teddy Yarosz.

BEFORE HIS SECOND FIGHT WITH JOE LOUIS, CONN IS VISITED BY FREDDIE MILLS IN HIS TRAINING CAMP IN NEW JERSEY

FACT FILE

1917 Born William David Conn, Jr., in Pittsburgh, Pennsylvania

1939 Beat Melio Bettina to become world light-heavyweight champ

1941 Relinquished light-heavyweight title, lost to Joe Louis

1946 Lost long-awaited rematch with Louis

Died: May 29, 1993 age 75

Career record: Fights 76, Won 63, Lost 12, Drawn 1

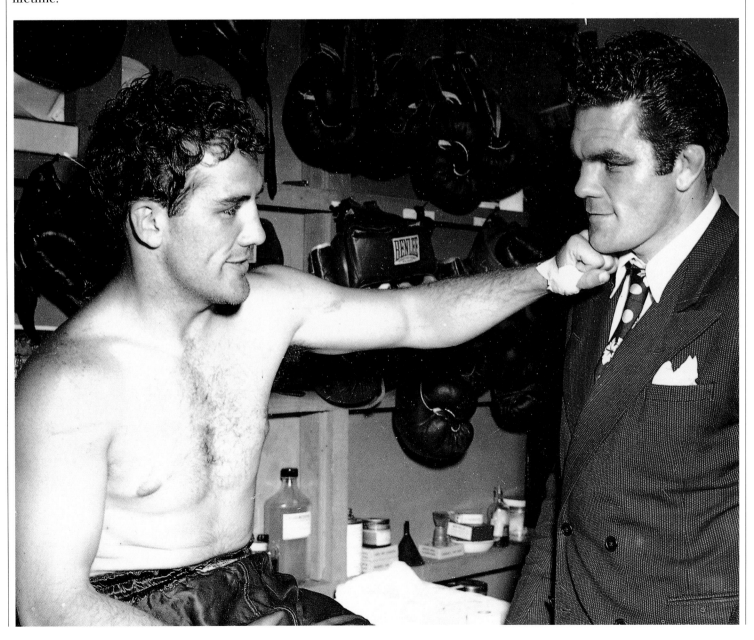

THE GREAT FIGHTS

JOE LOUIS

V.

BILLY CONN

POLO GROUNDS, NEW YORK CITY. JUNE 18, 1941.

By 1941 Joe Louis was ruthlessly destroying all-comers, who were cruelly condemned by writers as the "Bum of the Month" club.

Since June 1937, when he had dethroned James J. Braddock, Louis had made an incredible 17 world title defenses, including the celebrated first round thrashing of Germany's Max Schmeling.

Nevertheless, one man was convinced he could beat Louis—Billy Conn of Pittsburgh, and 54,487 paid to see him try at the Polo Grounds in the summer of 1941.

For the first two rounds, the champion pressed forward steadily, landing solidly, but from round three Conn, who had given up his light-heavyweight title to concentrate on this fight, began to drill home his left hand. A sharp right buckled Louis' knees in round four, but the champion responded in the fifth, staggering Conn with a left hook and leaving him so confused that he went to the wrong corner at the bell. They revived him with smelling salts.

Conn was hurt again in the sixth, and cut over the right eye, but regained control in round seven. Louis looked bewildered as Conn darted in and out, as the champ said later "stinging like a mosquito," and by the ninth Conn was chatting contentedly in the clinches. In the 12th Louis wobbled again and at the bell it was his turn to be given smelling salts. Two officials had Conn ahead 7-4-1 in rounds and 7-5, while the third saw it even at 6-6. Louis needed the last three rounds to salvage a majority decision, while one more for Conn would seal his victory.

But instead of continuing to box sensibly, Conn went for a knockout in round 13. Suddenly Louis had a standing target, opened up venomously and Conn was badly battered before a right hand put him down on his face. He was counted out two seconds before the bell. "If he'd stayed cool, he might have become champion," said Louis.

Five years later they fought again, but a washed-up Conn was knocked out in eight rounds.

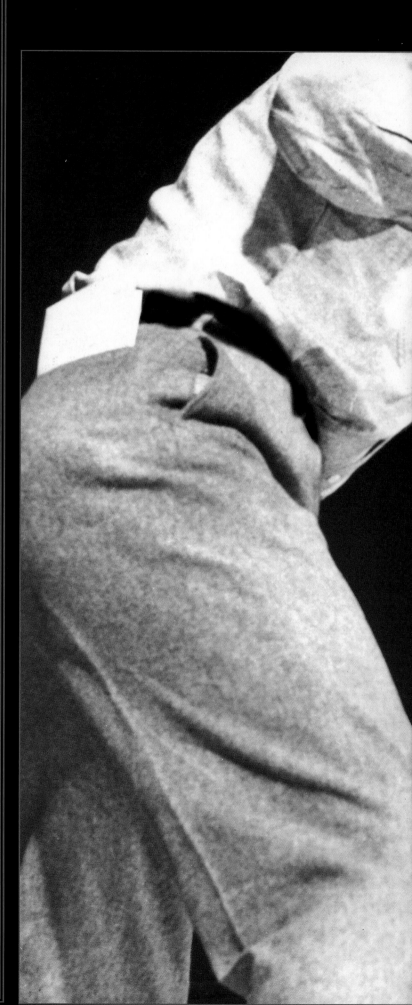

JOHN CONTEH

FACT FILE

1951 Born Liverpool, England

1973 Won British, Commonwealth and European light-heavyweight titles

1974 Outpointed Jorge Ahumada to win WBC title

1977 Stripped of world title by WBC

Career record: Fights 39, Won 34, Lost 4, Drawn 1

John Conteh was arguably the most talented British boxer of modern times, whose two-and-a-half year reign as WBC light-heavyweight champion was marred by bad luck, bad living, and bad advice.

Conteh had everything before him when he outpointed a rugged Argentine named Jorge Ahumada to win the WBC light-heavyweight title at Wembley's old Empire Pool in October 1974.

But after one defense against American Lonnie Bennett, he fell out with the formidable empire fronted by promoter Harry Levene. In those days, Levene enjoyed almost complete control of the major promotions in London. Conteh's resistance was revolutionary.

He twice broke his right hand, which sidelined him for 14 months, then his business-manager brother Tony negotiated a deal that resulted in Conteh being paid £2,000 (about

$3,000) for a 15-round points win in defense of his title against a tough Californian-Mexican named Yaqui Lopez.

On an emotional night in Liverpool, he defended his title with a third-round stoppage of Len Hutchins in March 1977, but was stripped for refusing to honor a contract to defend against an unknown Argentine, Miguel Cuello, in Monte Carlo two months later.

He failed narrowly in title fights against Mate Parlov and Matthew Saad Muhammad, but Saad stopped him quickly in a return. Conteh retired after a final night before a sellout crowd in Liverpool in May 1980, when he easily stopped American import James Dixon.

In his retirement, he overcame his self-destructive out of the ring habits, eventually found a meaning in religion and went on to earn a living as an after-dinner speaker.

CONTEH, A STYLISH, CONTROLLED BOXER WHO WAS WBC LIGHT-HEAVYWEIGHT CHAMP FOR THREE YEARS

SEE ALSO ◆ MATTHEW SAAD MUHAMMAD 234

HENRY COOPER

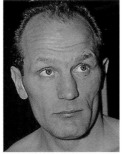

enry Cooper is one of the great folk heroes of British boxing.

Although he was the dominant European heavyweight of the 1960s, British sports fans celebrate one moment above all others—that tiny fragment of time in which his left hook floored a brash 21-year-old named Cassius Clay at Wembley Stadium in 1963.

Clay went down heavily, was saved by the bell and then given extra recovery time by a stroke of opportunism from trainer Angelo Dundee, who admitted years later he had aggravated a tear in Clay's glove.

When they came out for the next round, the fifth, Clay had recovered and stopped Cooper because of a horrible cut over his eye.

Clay, who became Muhammad Ali a year later, promised him a rematch for the world title—and in 1966 at Arsenal soccer stadium in London, a dreadful gash above Cooper's left eye cut short his challenge in round six.

Cooper was denied a second world title fight against WBA champion Jimmy Ellis, during Ali's three-year ring exile, because the British Board of Control did not recognize the organization. Cooper gave back the British title he had held for 10 years in protest, then regained it from Jack Bodell in 1970.

As an amateur he won two ABA titles and boxed in the 1952 Olympics, and as a professional he was European champion three times between 1964 and 1971, as well as British and Empire champion from 1959. He lost all three belts on a bitterly disputed decision to Joe Bugner in March 1971 and retired.

He continued to enjoy enormous popularity, working as a fight anaylist for the BBC, and in advertisements and personal appearances.

FACT FILE

1934	Born London
1952	Boxed in Helsinki Olympics
1959	Began 10-year reign as British heavyweight champion
1963	Floored Cassius Clay at Wembley
1966	Lost rematch for world title
1971	Retired after bitter defeat by Joe Bugner

Career record: Fights 55, Won 40, Lost 14, Drawn 1

COOPER SMASHES A GLASSY-EYED CASSIUS CLAY TO THE CANVAS IN 1963. CLAY WON IN THE NEXT ROUND

SEE ALSO ◆ MUHAMMAD ALI 12

JAMES J. CORBETT

FACT FILE

1866 Born San Francisco, California

1892 Knocked out John L. Sullivan to win world heavyweight title

1897 Lost the title to Bob Fitzsimmons

1903 Lost last fight to James J. Jeffries in world title challenge

Died: Bayside, New York, February 18, 1933, age 66

Career record: Fights 20, Won 11, Lost 4, Drawn 3, No Contests 2

An innovative boxer who brought scientific technique to a peak, "Gentleman" Jim Corbett was a strangely remote man.

He ended the bare-knuckle era once and for all by finishing the marauding reign of the belligerent, often boorish but essentially big-hearted John L. Sullivan. In New Orleans in September 1892, Corbett knocked out Sullivan in 21 rounds. Stylish and upright, Corbett held the title for five years, apart from a brief interlude when he retired and then changed his mind.

Always patient and calculating, Corbett had drawn a 61-round epic with the greatest black heavyweight of the day, Peter Jackson, before beating Sullivan. As champion he made money on the stage, outclassed British challenger Charley Mitchell in 1894, and then lost the title to Bob Fitzsimmons in Carson City, Nevada, in March 1897. Corbett floored and outboxed Fitzsimmons in the early rounds, but was knocked out in the 14th round by a short left to the pit of the belly, an area labeled by a medic and celebrated ever after as "the solar plexus."

Corbett described the effect in *The Roar of the Crowd*, his autobiography. "I was conscious of everything... the silence of the crowd, the agony on the faces of my seconds, the waiting Fitzsimmons, but my body was like that of a man stricken with paralysis."

He twice failed to regain the title from Fitzsimmons' successor James J. Jeffries and in retirement appeared on the stage, wrote articles on big fights for newspapers, and stayed on the fringes of the sport.

CORBETT (LEFT) DEMONSTRATES HIS SKILLS FOR THE CAMERA

SEE ALSO ◆ BOB FITZSIMMONS 114 ◆ JAMES J. JEFFRIES 168

PIPINO CUEVAS

Pipino Cuevas, a thunderous puncher from Mexico City who took the welterweight division by storm in the late 1970s, enjoyed enormous popularity in his own country.

Like so many who rise to stardom young, however, he did not endure. A burn-out was hardly surprising—he was fighting professionally just a few days after his 14th birthday; by 17 he was the Mexican welterweight champion and he won the WBA welterweight title by trouncing Angel Espada of Puerto Rico in two rounds, when still only 18, in July 1976.

A boy with a chilling temperament, he was slightly upright in style, but had natural punching power in either hand. When he connected cleanly, he usually finished the fight.

However, he was not at his best against cunning, slippery technicians, and, as a result, he lost several early decisions, but in 11 successful title defenses spread over four years, only one man took him the distance: American Randy Shields, who was a clever, knowledgable boxer who defended stoutly for the full 15.

But good fighters like the Canadian Clyde Gray, Americans Harold Grey and Pete Ranzany, and former champions Billy Backus and, in two rematches, Espada, were all overpowered. Cuevas's time at the top came to a shocking end in August 1980 in Detroit when he was chopped down in two rounds by Thomas Hearns. He faded slowly, grasping at the past and trying to relive it, but Hearns had destroyed his self-belief. He lost in four rounds to Roberto Duran in 1983, but struggled on until 1989 when he finally accepted the inevitable and retired. He was 31, and his great days were already a decade behind him.

FACT FILE

1957 Born Mexico City
1972 Professional debut, age 14
1975 Won Mexican welterweight title at 17
1976 Stopped Angel Espada of Puerto Rico to win WBA title
1980 Lost title to Thomas Hearns in 12th defense
Career record: Fights 50, Won 35, Lost 15

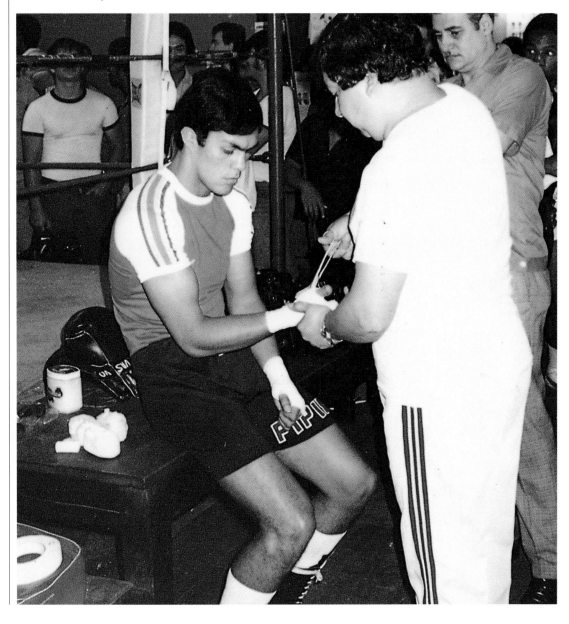

A VERY YOUNG CUEVAS PREPARES FOR A SPARRING SESSION AT THE GYM

SEE ALSO ♦ ROBERTO DURAN 99 ♦ THOMAS HEARNS 153

DONALD CURRY

When Donald Curry trained in Britain for a fight with Colin Jones in 1985, hardened pros stopped to watch in amazement.

Curry, a gentle, softly spoken Texan whose lithe skills and venomous punch were aptly described by his "Cobra" nickname, was the best welterweight in the world from 1983 until 1986, when the combination of weight-making and a marauding Englishman named Lloyd Honeyghan effectively ruined him.

Curry, whose elder brother Bruce was WBC light-welterweight champion, was trained out of Fort Worth, Texas, by local manager Dave Gorman. Donald won a National AAU title at 17, turned pro at 19, and was World Boxing Association champion at 21.

He won the title by outpunching and outboxing a tough Korean named Jun-sok Hwang in Fort Worth in February 1983. He quickly set about establishing a dominance of the division, stopping Roger Stafford in one round and outpointing Marlon Starling, who was also one of the best 147-lb. boxers of the generation. He stopped in turn Elio Diaz, Nino LaRocca, and Colin Jones, and then unified the division in December 1985 with a sensational knockout of the current WBC champ Milton McCrory in two rounds in Las Vegas.

Curry was considered a genuine threat to middleweight champion Marvin Hagler, but stayed at welterweight for one fight too long—he took a hammering from Honeyghan in Atlantic City in September 1986 and was never as good again. He was knocked out by WBA light-middleweight champ Mike McCallum, and although he stopped Italy's Gianfranco Rosi for the WBC version, he lost it quickly to Rene Jacquot of France, a man with whom he would have toyed in his prime. He retired after losing to Terry Norris in 1991, but returned to the ring in early 1997.

A POLITE, SOFTLY SPOKEN MAN, CURRY WAS TRANSFORMED INTO A DICTATORIAL RING GENERAL ONCE THE BELL RANG

SEE ALSO ◆ LLOYD HONEYGHAN 162 ◆ MIKE MCCALLUM 238 ◆ GIANFRANCO ROSI 286

LES DARCY

Old-timers will tell you Les Darcy died of a broken heart. In fact the terrible streptococcus virus killed the legendary Australian middleweight at the age of 21, but technicalities like that don't matter to the multitudes who still place the farmer's son from New South Wales among the elite of Australian sporting heroes.

At 15, this quiet, smiling, slow-thinking youth was earning spare cash in the ring, where he quickly developed a reputation as one of the toughest men who laced on gloves. Apparently impervious to pain, he was stocky, long-armed, and a ferocious in-fighter.

He won recognition in his homeland as world champion when he beat American Jeff Smith on a foul in May 1915, and went on to beat the top men of his day, George Chip, Eddie McGoorty, and Jimmy Clabby. Most of his earnings were plowed back into the family farm.

Darcy's mother twice refused him permission to fight in the World War and at the end of 1916 he stowed away to America, in spite of the government restrictions on men over the age of 17 leaving the country.

He was pilloried by newspaper writers at home and the United States, and the promoters who had promised fights turned their backs on him. Even his exhibitions brought jeers and taunts of cowardice. Misunderstood and rejected, he sank into depression. He was in Memphis, planning to become an American citizen and join the US Signal Corps, and at last training for a fight, when he fell ill. Within a month he was dead. His embalmed body was returned to Australia where an estimated half a million people paid their respects.

FACT FILE

1895	Born Stradbroke, New South Wales, Australia
1915	Won Australian recognition as world middleweight champion
1916	Last fight, successful eighth defense against George Chip
Died:	Memphis, Tennessee, May 24, 1917, age 21

Career record: Fights 49, Won 45, Lost 4

DARCY: NAIVE, MISUNDERSTOOD, AND DIED TOO YOUNG

ESTEBAN DE JESUS

FACT FILE

1951 Born Carolina, Puerto Rico

1972 Beat Roberto Duran in 10-rounder in New York

1974 Lost to Duran in world title fight

1976 Won WBC lightweight title against Ishimatsu Suzuki

1978 Lost undisputed title fight to Duran

Died: San Juan, Puerto Rico, May 11, 1989, age 37

Career record: Fights 62, Won 57, Lost 5

A skillful boxer with a sharp fast array of punches, Esteban De Jesus was the first man to beat the great Roberto Duran, but whose ability could not save him from a tragic end.

He was a fresh-faced 21-year-old when he outpointed the Panamanian "Hands of Stone" in a 10-round non-title fight in New York in November 1972, when Duran held the world lightweight championship.

In a rematch for the title in Panama City in 1974, De Jesus dropped Duran in the first round, but was knocked out in the 11th of a classic battle that is still rerun on TV "Great Fights" shows.

After also missing out in a WBA light-welterweight challenge against Antonio Cervantes, De Jesus dropped back to 135lb. and won the WBC lightweight title by outpointing Japan's defending champion Ishimatsu Suzuki in Bayamon. For a while he was celebrated, retaining his title through three defenses and then earning $150,000 for a unification fight with Duran, who was the WBA champion. Duran knocked him out in the 12th round in Las Vegas in January 1978.

He won six more fights, but was stopped in 13 rounds by WBC light-welterweight champion Saoul Mamby in July 1980. It was to be his last fight. Already a cocaine and heroin addict, he shot dead a teenager in a petty traffic dispute and was jailed for life. While in prison, he contracted the HIV virus from sharing needles with fellow prisoners and died of AIDS. As he lay dying, his old adversary Duran visited him and kissed him farewell.

DE JESUS WAS THE FIRST MAN TO BEAT ROBERTO DURAN, BUT HIS DRUG HABIT LED TO HIS DEATH

SEE ALSO ◆ ROBERTO DURAN 99

OSCAR DE LA HOYA

O scar De La Hoya is a national treasure, a bright-eyed, intelligent boxer with the style and looks to become the next fighting superstar.

Born in Los Angeles of Mexican stock, he was the only American boxing gold medalist in the Barcelona Olympics. He signed a $500,000 deal to turn professional, with a car and van, and half the down payment on a house thrown in!

As a schoolboy he used to mail his homework back from wherever he was on international duty, and intended to become an architect if boxing didn't work out.

It did. When a lanky super-featherweight he looked a little vulnerable, but as he filled out into a light and then light-welter, looked less so. And his skills ripened until he was more or less flawless. He beat Jimmi Bredahl of Denmark to win the WBO super-featherweight title in his 12th professional fight in March 1994, and four months later moved up to take the WBO lightweight title, flattening the normally durable Mexican veteran Jorge Paez in two.

He had to go the full 12 rounds for the first time when he outpointed Puerto Rican Juan Molina, then trounced IBF champ Rafael Ruelas in two rounds. He rounded off 1995 by headlining at the reopening of Madison Square Garden, trouncing former WBC 130-lb. champ James Leija in two. De La Hoya came of age when he defeated WBC light-welter champion Julio Cesar Chavez in four one-sided rounds in Las Vegas in June 1996, in effect taking boxing into its next generation, and began 1997 by outpointing previously unbeaten Miguel Angel Gonzalez.

FACT FILE

1973 Born Los Angeles, California
1992 Olympic lightweight gold medal
1994 Won WBO super-featherweight and lightweight titles
1996 Dethroned WBC light-welterweight champ Julio Cesar Chavez
Career record: Fights 23, Won 23

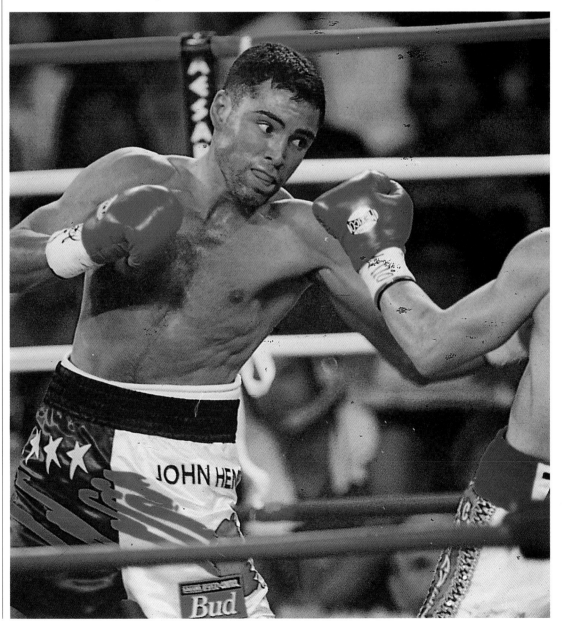

AMERICA'S GOLDEN BOY OF THE 1992 OLYMPICS, DE LA HOYA WENT ON TO FULFIL HIS TALENTS AS A MULTI-WORLD TITLEHOLDER AS A PROFESSIONAL

SEE ALSO ♦ JULIO CESAR CHAVEZ 67 ♦ JUAN MOLINA 219 ♦ JORGE PAEZ 260

CARLOS DE LEON

Carlos De Leon came from the Puerto Rican town of Rio Piedras to become a four-time world champion and the most persistent cruiserweight of the 1980s.

A soldier's son and the oldest of ten children, he began boxing at ten, after watching his local hero, bantamweight Francisco Villegas, in the gym. He turned professional as a 15-year-old lightweight and moved gradually through the weight divisions.

The cruiserweight category was introduced for those too big to be light-heavyweights but not strong enough to handle the increasingly muscular and bulky heavyweights. While never fashionable, its acceptance was largely because of De Leon, who was a constant face on the scene for an entire decade and fought in 16 world championship bouts.

He first won the WBC title by outpointing tough Flathead Native American Marvin Camel on a majority decision over 15 rounds in the vast New Orleans Superdome on November 25, 1980, alongside the Ray Leonard–Roberto Duran rematch.

A surprise defeat against S. T. Gordon cost him the title in June 1982, but 13 months later he outboxed the American in the Dunes Hotel in Las Vegas. His second reign went on to 1985, when he lost on points to Alfonso Ratliff, but within nine months he was back on top following a points win over Ratliff's successor, Bernard Benton.

He lost a unification fight with Evander Holyfield on cuts, but when Holyfield moved up to heavyweight, he regained the WBC belt by stopping Sammy Reeson in London. He lost it for the last time to Italy's Massimiliano Duran in July 1990. Five years on, he was still trading on his reputation, earning small purses as a journeyman heavyweight.

DE LEON: A RECORD 16 WORLD CHAMPIONSHIP FIGHTS AT CRUISERWEIGHT

Jack Delaney

A smooth, slick boxer, Jack Delaney was one of the most colorful and knowledgable ring technicians of the 1920s who should have been light-heavyweight champion long before he was, in 1926.

Delaney was a French-Canadian whose real name was Ovila Chapdelaine. Born in Quebec, he moved to Connecticut with his family when a boy, and began boxing in Bridgeport as a teenager.

He quickly developed a reputation as one of the most naturally skilled boxers on the scene, and a 1924 win over Tommy Loughran in Boston established him as a world-class operator, even though he rarely weighed even 170 lb.

In an all-action fight with the brawling Paul Berlanbach, Delaney climbed off the canvas to win on a fourth-round knockout, but the following year it was Berlanbach, known as the Astoria Assassin, who was given the title shot against Mike McTigue. He won on points.

Delaney twice knocked out the marvelous middleweight Tiger Flowers, but when he challenged Berlanbach for the title in December 1925 in New York, he conceded 7½ lb. and lost a majority decision.

He won 11 fights in the next six months, then at last beat Berlanbach for the title in front of a crowd of 41,000 in Ebbets Field, Brooklyn, on July 16, 1926.

After three more fights, he gave up the world championship to try his luck where the money was—in the heavyweight division. But although he was tall enough at 5 ft. 11½ in., he was too light. He beat some good men, but defeats by Tom Heeney and Jack Sharkey consigned him to the scrapheap. He retired in 1932, ran a New York bar and had various business interests, but died of cancer when only 48.

FACT FILE

1900 Born Ovila Chapdelaine, in St. Francis du Lac, Quebec

1926 Won world light-heavyweight title against Paul Berlanbach

1927 Gave up title to chase heavyweight championship

1932 Announced retirement

Died: Katonah, New York, November 27, 1948, age 48

Career record: Fights 93, Won 79, Lost 11, Drawn 1, No Contents 2

REMARKABLY POPULAR, DELANEY DREW 41,000 FANS WHEN HE WON THE WORLD LIGHT-HEAVYWEIGHT TITLE IN BROOKLYN

SEE ALSO ◆ TIGER FLOWERS 115 ◆ TOMMY LOUGHRAN 203 ◆ MIKE MCTIGUE 247 ◆ JACK SHARKEY 296

JACK DEMPSEY

FACT FILE

1895 Born William Harrison Dempsey, Manassa, Colorado

1919 Battered Jess Willard in 3 rounds for world heavyweight title

1921 First million-dollar gate against Georges Carpentier

1926 Lost title to Gene Tunney in Philadelphia

1927 Lost "Battle of Long Count" to Tunney in Chicago

Died: New York City, May 21, 1983, age 87

Career record: Fights 81, Won 66, Lost 6, Drawn 9

There will never be another heavyweight like the fabled Manassa Mauler.

Jack Dempsey was the greatest boxing hero of the Jazz Age, the tumultuous Twenties when ordinary men really did dream they could be anything they wanted .

Dempsey was their role model, the proof that dreams came true, a man who rode the rails and lived in the hobo jungles, who fought for his supper in small-town saloons, and went on to win the heavyweight championship of the world.

On a scorching summer day near Toledo, Ohio, on July 4, 1919, Dempsey battered the giant Jess Willard to the canvas seven times in a terrible first round. Willard eventually retired, blood pouring from his face and mouth, with a broken cheekbone, after the third.

Dempsey beat a dying friend Billy Miske to give him a payday, struggled to overcome Bill Brennan, another boxer who died young, and then at Boyle's Acres, Jersey City, in 1921 knocked out the glamorous French war hero Georges Carpentier in just four rounds.

He and manager Jack Kearns broke the banks in the little town of Shelby, Montana, when they insisted on a $100,000 guarantee to fight Tommy Gibbons, and went on from there to win the wildest of all championship fights in two rounds against Luis Firpo.

To Kearns's annoyance, Dempsey married film star Estelle Taylor, concentrated on making movies, and when he next fought, in 1926 against Gene Tunney, his spark had gone. He lost on points.

In the rematch he put Tunney down for the infamous Long Count, but lost again and retired. After the war, he ran his restaurant in New York for many years.

DEMPSEY FOUGHT HIS WAY UP FROM THE HOBO JUNGLES TO THE WORLD TITLE

SEE ALSO ◆ GEORGES CARPENTIER 59 ◆ GENE TUNNEY 315

Jack Dempsey "The Nonpareil"

Known as "The Nonpareil," Jack Dempsey was one of the pioneer fighters who didn't mind too much whether he boxed with or without gloves, and wasn't above a spot of wrestling when the opportunity, or payday, arose. Weight disparities didn't bother him either, and although he rarely scaled more than 147 lb. he is usually regarded as the first of the world middleweight champions.

Dempsey was born plain John Kelly in County Kildare, but his parents took the boat to New York when he was a boy and settled in Brooklyn. He took the name Dempsey because they disapproved of boxing, won his first bout in the 21st round in 1883, and a year later claimed the middleweight title after defeating George Fulljames of Canada. Later historians tend to pour scorn on this bout, but after he defeated Jack Fogarty in 27 rounds in New York in 1886, he earned $1,500 and the championship belt.

Apart from when he was knocked out by an elbow punch from George LaBlanche in 1889—the punch was outlawed immediately afterward—he beat all-comers for the rest of the decade.

In 1890 he stopped English-born Australian Billy McCarthy in 28 rounds in San Francisco, but then his health began to fail. He lost the title for a $12,000 purse against Bob Fitzsimmons in New Orleans in January 1891, taking a terrible beating in a one-sided fight. In his dressing room he wept uncontrollably. He retired after losing to welterweight champion Tommy Ryan in January 1895, and died of tuberculosis.

FACT FILE

1862 Born John Kelly, near Clane, County Kildare, Ireland

1884 Claimed world middleweight title by defeating George Fulljames

1886 Presented with world title belt after defeating Jack Fogarty

1890 Defeated Australian Billy McCarthy in San Francisco

1891 Lost middleweight title to Bob Fitzsimmons in New Orleans

1895 Last fight against welterweight champion Tommy Ryan

died: Portland, Oregon, November 2, 1895, age 32

Career record: Fights 64, Won 50, Lost 3, Drawn 8, No Contests 3

THE FIRST JACK DEMPSEY: THE NONPAREIL, BORN IN COUNTY KILDARE AND WORLD MIDDLEWEIGHT CHAMP IN THE 1880S

SEE ALSO ◆ BOB FITZSIMMONS 114

THE GREAT FIGHTS

JESS WILLARD
V.
JACK DEMPSEY

TOLEDO, OHIO.
JULY 4, 1919.

Jess Willard, the giant cowboy who had beaten the hated Jack Johnson in 1915, had not boxed for 40 months when he walked into the Bay View Park arena on the shores of Maumee Bay to box Jack Dempsey for a massive $100,000 payday.

Willard was a 37-year-old family man, and out of shape at 245 lb., but Dempsey was considered too small, even though he was sharp and had trained for months. Public perception was that Dempsey's blows would bounce off the giant and he would gradually be worn down.

They did not. He was not. Dempsey tore into the champion from the first bell and hurled heavy blows at his head. Willard, undertrained as he was, could not absorb them and was down in a matter of seconds.

He was floored seven times in an astonishing first round, which ended with Dempsey believing he had won the title. In the din, he and manager Jack "Doc" Kearns believed referee Ollie Pecord had completed the count as Willard sat on the floor in a corner, his mouth open, blood streaming from his nose, and his cheekbone shattered in seven places. But the bell had interrupted his count. The fight was not over. Kearns had to call Dempsey back into the ring—he was already being ushered away by a group of celebrating friends—to avoid a disqualification.

Dempsey's rush of adrenalin faded but his attacks were systematic instead of frenzied in rounds two and three. Willard tried to throw punches, but the right side of his head was horribly swollen, and at the end of the third, both of his eyes were shut. Two of his teeth lay on the canvas.

His corner retired him as he repeated, almost in shock, over and over like a mantra: "I have a farm in Kansas and one hundred thousand dollars... I have a farm in Kansas and one hundred thousand dollars..."

Dempsey reigned for the next seven years.

JACK DILLON

FACT FILE

1891 Born Ernest Cutler Price, Frankfurt, Indiana

1908 Professional debut, age 17

1914 Claimed world light-heavyweight title

1916 Lost title back to Battling Levinsky

1923 Last fight, age 32

Died: Chattahoochee, Florida, August 7, 1942, age 51

Career record: Fights 245, Won 162, Lost 24, Drawn 36, No Decisions 2, No Contest 1

Known as the Hoosier Bearcat or Jack The Giant Killer, Jack Dillon was a smart fighter who had the technical ability, durability and sheer strength required to cope with the toughest men of his time, whatever they weighed.

Dillon, who was born plain Ernest Price in Indiana, was only 5 ft. 7½ in. tall, and was never more than a light-heavyweight. He fought for his living for 15 years, traveling wherever fights took him, and boxing as often as possible. In 1911 alone, there were 27 fights, and in 1912 there were 29, mostly in world class against the likes of Frank Klaus, George Chip, Jack "Twin" Sullivan, Battling Levinsky, and Eddie McGoorty.

By 1914 he was recognized as the world light-heavyweight champion after a 12-round points win over Levinsky in Butte, Montana. His new status didn't affect his habits at all. He moved around, fighting as often as possible, averaging a bout every ten days, usually over ten rounds, sometimes longer. The same year he began to take on heavyweights, and beat top men like Fireman Jim Flynn, Gunboat Ed Smith, and Billy Miske.

In 1916 he fought Levinsky for the ninth time, and lost the light-heavyweight title on a 15-round decision in Boston. His slide was gradual, and understandable. A new generation was taking over, and Dillon's long career was slowing him. Nevertheless, he kept trundling away, never changing his aggressive style, until 1921 when he drifted out of the sport. He made one comeback fight in 1923 in a no-decision bout in Indiana, and then retired for good, age 32. He ran a small restaurant in Florida until he died.

JACK THE GIANT KILLER: DILLON DIDN'T CARE WHO HE FOUGHT, OR HOW BIG THEY WERE

GEORGE DIXON

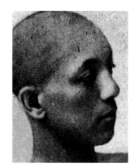

A fast, stylish boxing master, George Dixon was a photographer's apprentice who drifted into the sport because his employer had regular contracts with local fighters.

He saw boxing as an art, and it gave him his living for all of his adult life. Even when there was no official competition to be had, he boxed exhibitions in dance halls and theaters, and his manager Tom O'Rourke estimated that his ring appearances totaled around 800. In his prime he was virtually flawless.

Born in Halifax, Nova Scotia, he was boxing at 16, and moved south to Boston a year later. In February 1890, he drew a 70-round epic with Cal McCarthy and then traveled to England for the first time to defeat Nunc Wallace in 18 rounds to claim the world featherweight title.

In September 1892, Dixon featured in the three-day festival of boxing in New Orleans headlined by James J. Corbett's win over John L. Sullivan. George knocked out Jack Skelly in eight rounds the day before.

He fought the greatest men of his day—the wayward Australian genius Young Griffo, England's Billy Plimmer and Pedlar Palmer, included—and dominated the division for the rest of the decade. There were times when others claimed the championship, as when he lost to both Frank Erne and Solly Smith, but he remained at the top until Terry McGovern beat him in eight rounds in January 1900.

He somehow squandered the money he earned—an estimated $250,000—boxed in Britain for two years, and retired after losing a 15-round decision to Monk The Newsboy in Providence in December 1906. He was more or less penniless when he dropped dead just over two years later.

FACT FILE

1870	Born Halifax, Nova Scotia, Canada
1890	Won world featherweight title against Nunc Wallace
1896	Lost title to Frank Erne
1897	Regained and lost title, but continued to press claims
1900	Lost title to "Terrible" Terry McGovern
1906	Last fight, age 36
Died:	New York City, January 6, 1909, age 38

Career record: Fights 146, Won 78, Lost 25, Drawn 37, No Decisions 3, No Contests 3

DIXON (LEFT) IN A BARE-KNUCKLE POSE. IN HIS PRIME HE WAS FLAWLESS

SEE ALSO ◆ YOUNG GRIFFO 145 ◆ TERRY McGOVERN 240

JAMES DOUGLAS

FACT FILE

1960	Born Columbus, Ohio
1981	Professional debut
1987	Lost first world title attempt against Tony Tucker
1990	Upset Mike Tyson, lost to Evander Holyfield
1996	Returned to ring, age 36

Career record: Fights 37, Won 31, Lost 5, Drawn 1

BUSTER DOUGLAS: THE MAN WHO TAMED MIKE TYSON

Buster Douglas will be remembered as the man who showed the world Mike Tyson was human.

A 40-1 outsider when he traveled to Tokyo in February 1990, Douglas staged an inspired performance to climb off the canvas to knock out Tyson in the 10th round.

Scandalous attempts to dethrone him on the grounds that he had been given a long count when he was put down in the 8th were howled down, and he kept the title.

He was paid a gross $24 million to defend against Evander Holyfield in October 1990, but fought a court battle to free himself from the demands of promoter Don King, which cost him dearly. Other commitments cut into the gross, but he still picked up a payday estimated at around $10 million.

But disillusioned by his experiences of the past eight months, Buster failed to prepare adequately and was knocked out in the third round by Holyfield. Both the referee and even his own father intimated that he could have got up.

In retirement, his weight ballooned to the point where he eventually collapsed in a diabetic coma. The shock forced him back into training, and he returned to the ring in 1996. How serious the intent remained to be seen.

Buster was the son of 1960s middleweight Bill Douglas. A genuine heavyweight at 6 ft. 4 in. and, in shape, 230 lb., he lost his first world title attempt when Tony Tucker stopped him in 10 rounds for the vacant IBF belt in May 1987. But he fought his way back and peaked on that amazing day in Tokyo when he left the self-appointed "baddest man on the planet" scrambling around madly for his gumshield on the canvas.

SEE ALSO ◆ **EVANDER HOLYFIELD 159** ◆ **MIKE TYSON 319**

JIM DRISCOLL

"Peerless" Jim Driscoll was a classical boxer with a wonderful left hand and a near-perfect defense.

He outboxed reigning world featherweight champion Abe Attell so comprehensively in New York in 1909 that some observers said the American didn't win a round. Unfortunately for the Welshman, the ridiculous no-decision rule applied in New York State at the time, which meant that unless a knockout occurred, a fight was technically an exhibition with no result given.

Driscoll was born and raised in Cardiff, and in his teens would work a boxing booth, challenging anyone to hit him on the nose while he stood on a handkerchief with his hands tied behind his back!

In 1907 he won the British featherweight title by knocking out Joe Bowker of Salford in the 17th round. The following year he beat Charlie Griffin of New Zealand on a foul to win the Empire title. Driscoll moved to New York, was a sensation and hailed, after his "win" over Attell, as the real world champion. He returned home instead of staying for a rematch because he had given his word that he would attend a charity event.

In 1912 he easily defeated Frenchman Jean Poesy in 12 rounds to win the European title and restate his claim to the world crown. Early in 1913 he drew with Owen Moran of Birmingham over 20 rounds, and retired, but after World War I he made a brief comeback, quitting for good after Frenchman Charles Ledoux stopped him in 17 rounds at the National Sporting Club. He was only 44 when he died of tuberculosis, following pleurisy and pneumonia, and more than 100,000 lined the streets of Cardiff as his funeral procession passed through.

FACT FILE

1880	Born Cardiff, Wales
1907	Beat Joe Bowker for British featherweight title
1908	Won Empire title against Charlie Griffin
1909	Outclassed world champion Abe Attell in no-decision bout
1912	Won European title against Jean Poesy
1919	Last fight against Charles Ledoux
Died:	Cardiff, Wales, January 31, 1925, aged 44

Career record: Fights 69, Won 59, Lost 3, Drawn 7

ONE OF THE GREATEST RING ARTISTS OF ALL TIME: DRISCOLL WEARS HIS PRECIOUS LONSDALE BELT IN 1910

SEE ALSO ◆ ABE ATTELL 25

THE
GREAT
FIGHTS

MIKE TYSON
V.
JAMES "BUSTER"
DOUGLAS

TOKYO DOME, JAPAN.
FEBRUARY 10, 1990.

"I ron" Mike Tyson, the fearsome, sneering, self-styled "Baddest Man on the Planet," came apart in the bizarre, Sunday afternoon setting of the Tokyo Dome, in a fight timed to fit HBO's American scheduling. If there was a sense of unreality about the housing of a world heavyweight championship at this time of day, it was nothing compared to the result. James "Buster" Douglas, a 40-1 no-hoper, wrecked Tyson's planned multimillion dollar showdown with Evander Holyfield on June 18 by knocking the champion out in the 10th round.

The sight of Tyson scrambling around on the canvas, trying to cram his gumshield back into his mouth, was hauntingly pathetic... but matched only by the post-fight antics of promoter Don King, Tyson, and the heads of the WBC and WBA, who were Jose Sulaiman and Gilberto Mendoza, respectively.

King, who also promoted Douglas and who therefore should have been happy, called the result a "tragedy" and argued that Mexican referee Octavio Meyran had given Douglas a long count when he had been floored by a perfect uppercut at the end of round eight. Meyran was wheeled out to meet the press and offer his humble apologies for a human error. Tyson joined in, claiming: "I am still the legitimate champion... You guys know me. You know I walk like I talk. I've never cried or bitched about anything. I knocked Buster out fair and square."

Howls of public protest followed as soon as the news began to filter through. Douglas was furious, both with King and the governing bodies. "What more can I do than knock him out?" he said. His manager John Johnson called the attempted manipulation of the situation "sickening." "Buster kicked his ass, it's as simple as that," he said. "These guys can go to hell." Eventually public pressure enabled Douglas to keep the heavyweight championship and he agreed to defend against Holyfield, leaving Tyson... and King... out in the cold.

JOHNNY DUNDEE

One of the ring's most slippery, unorthodox of tricksters, Johnny Dundee was a flashy, extrovert character who was typical of the hard-boiled professionals of his day.

He boxed for his living, and therefore as often as possible —for example, 47 times in 1911! He didn't punch too hard, partly because he didn't see the point in risking damage when there may be another engagement only a few days ahead, but he had a great chin. In his 337 registered bouts over 22 years, he was knocked out only twice.

Dundee was born in Sicily and raised in the infamous "Hell's Kitchen" ghetto in New York. He lost his professional debut against a youth known only as Skinny Bob in New York in August 1910. A week later he beat Bob in a return and set about his ferocious schedule.

He drew with Johnny Kilbane in a world featherweight title fight in 1913, put the disappointment behind him and slogged away again, mixing with champions like the great Benny Leonard, Willie Ritchie, Matt Wells, Lew Tendler, and Rocky Kansas.

In 1921 he beat George "KO" Chaney on a fifth-round foul to win the world junior-lightweight title, and lost and regained it against Jack Bernstein in 1923. That year also saw him stage a dazzling display before a 40,000 crowd at New York Polo Grounds to win the undisputed featherweight crown by outpointing Eugene Criqui of France.

Kid Sullivan took away his junior-lightweight crown in 1924, and he outgrew the featherweight division. Tony Canzoneri outscored him in one last title bid at junior-lightweight in 1927, but by then he was declining. He retired at the end of 1932.

EUGENE CRIQUE LOST HIS TITLE TO JOHNNY DUNDEE JUST FOUR WEEKS AFTER CLAIMING IT FROM JOHNNY KILBANE

SEE ALSO ◆ TONY CANZONERI 54 ◆ JOHNNY KILBANE 177

ROBERTO DURAN

oberto Duran's black eyes lit up when he had a man hurt. This cunning, dynamic Panamanian known as "Hands Of Stone" loved nothing more than the scent of a man about to crack.

Duran learned to fight on the waterfront as a boy, by 15 he was a professional fighter, and at 21 he stopped Ken Buchanan with a brutal, rough-house onslaught to win the world lightweight title.

He held it for the next seven years against all-comers. For most of that span the WBC failed to recognize him, but that was their loss. Everybody knew Duran was the best lightweight for many generations.

Eventually he outgrew the division, and in June 1980 in Montreal he won the WBC welterweight crown by inflicting the first defeat on Ray Leonard, although his weird "No Mas" walkout in the rematch five months later was one of the most puzzling episodes in ring history. Duran just stopped fighting and turned away from Ray Leonard in the eighth round.

In disgrace in Panama, he was not forgiven until 1983 when he bludgeoned loose the WBA light-middleweight title from Davey Moore. Marvin Hagler outpointed him for the middleweight crown, and he retired after Thomas Hearns put him out, face first, in two rounds in Las Vegas in June 1984.

He couldn't keep away, however. In February 1989, he outpointed defending WBC middleweight champ Iran Barkley to become a four-weight world champ at the age of 37. Slowly he drifted into middle age, losing sometimes to those who were too quick on their feet, but mostly winning. And as he moved toward the 30th anniversary of his professional debut, he steadfastly ignored the gradual dying of the flame in his belly and the graying of his hair. Even at 45 he fought on with conviction.

FACT FILE

1951	Born Guarare, Panama
1972	Beat Ken Buchanan to win world lightweight title
1979	Gave up lightweight title after 12 defenses
1980	Beat Ray Leonard for welterweight title, lost rematch
1983	Stopped Davey Moore to win WBA light-middleweight belt
1989	Beat Iran Barkley to become a 4-weight champ

Career record: Fights 112, Won 100, Lost 12

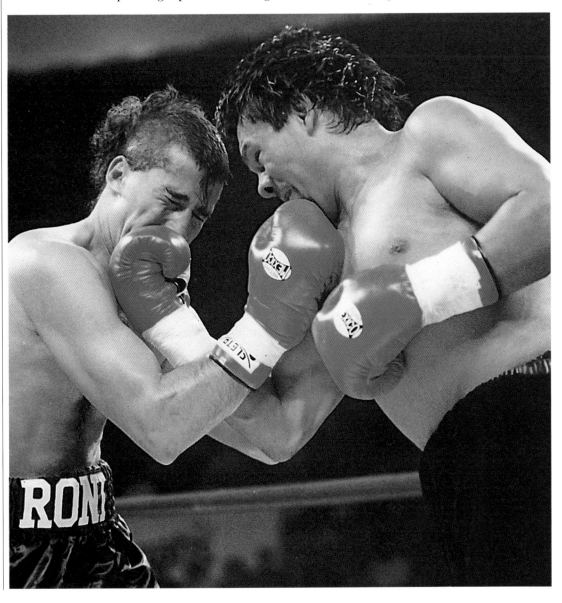

DURAN (RIGHT) WAS STILL SLOGGING AWAY IN HIS MID-40S

SEE ALSO ◆ **IRAN BARKLEY 27** ◆ **KEN BUCHANAN 45** ◆ **MARVIN HAGLER 147** ◆ **RAY LEONARD 187**

THE GREAT FIGHTS

RAY LEONARD
V.
ROBERTO DURAN

OLYMPIC STADIUM, MONTREAL, CANADA. JUNE 20, 1980.

Snarling, stomping, tormenting Roberto Duran was a man at peace. Ray Leonard, for all his skill and invention, was a man attempting to prove something to himself as well as the ever-skeptical boxing world.

Maybe that was the difference between them, which the judges identified, and so awarded "Hands of Stone" a unanimous decision after 15 wonderful, close rounds in the arena where four years earlier Leonard had won his Olympic gold medal.

It was a terribly difficult fight to score: Duran charged in, slugging, slamming, pushing, butting once or twice, and using all the ring cunning stored up from the previous decade or more, when he had been one of the greatest lightweights of all time.

Leonard landed whipping, eye-catching combinations and bounced fierce right hands off Duran's black-bearded jaw, but wanted to defend his WBC welterweight title the hard way, like a climber who deliberately chooses the most difficult face of a mountain. He so badly wanted to demonstrate his greatness; and his ego, and perhaps his very lack of certainty, drew him into Duran's territory.

The result was a magnificent encounter, which Duran won and deserved to win. At the final bell, as the 46,317 paying fans rose in a roaring salute Leonard smiled broadly and offered his glove. Duran snorted and walked past him, his passion undimmed, his enjoyment interrupted by the formality of a time limit on a fight. The judges' cards showed just how close it was: 148-147, 145-144, 146-144.

Afterwards the Panamanian camp were arrogant and jingoistic—"Duran over Leonard, Torrijos over Carter, Panama over America!"—yelled the camp interpreter. And as Leonard contemplated the reality of his first professional defeat, trainer Angelo Dundee laid the blame at his fighter's feet. "It was his plan. He had it in his head that he was stronger than Duran."

Five months later, Leonard took his revenge when Duran quit, snarling "no mas" in the eighth round.

GABRIEL ELORDE

FACT FILE

1935 Born Bogo, Cebu, Philippines

1956 Lost to Sandy Saddler for world fetherweight title

1960 Beat Harold Gomes for world junior-lightweight crown

1964 Lost world lightweight challenge to Carlos Ortiz

1966 Ortiz beat him in rematch

1967 Lost junior-lightweight title after seven years to Yoshiaki Numata

1971 Last fight, aged 36

Died: Manila, Philippines, January 2, 1985, age 49

Career record: Fights 117, Won 88, Lost 27, Drawn 2

A fast, solidly built southpaw, Gabriel "Flash" Elorde is acknowledged as the greatest sports star ever produced in the Philippines.

The youngest in a family of 15 from the island of Cebu, he earned his share for the table by shining shoes, washing dishes, selling on the street, and laboring on various construction sites.

And at 16, he began fighting for pay—a career that would last 20 years and would take him to the world junior-lightweight championship.

He found veteran featherweight champ Sandy Saddler too rough in a foul-filled encounter at the San Francisco Cow Palace in January 1956, but mixed his time between the United States, Japan, and his homeland to pick up experience and keep the money flowing in.

In 1960 he knocked out American Harold Gomes in seven rounds in Quezon City to win the junior-lightweight crown, which he proceeded to keep for the next seven years. Twice he lost lightweight challenges to Carlos Ortiz, but at 130 lb. he was unbeatable.

He made nine successful defenses over good men, including Joey Lopes, Johnny Bizzarro, and Love Allotey, and also beat the future lightweight champ Ismael Laguna in a non-title fight, before Yoshiaki Numata of Japan outpointed him to take away his championship in Tokyo in June 1967.

Elorde fought on until 1971, when he was past his 36th birthday. He used much of his ring earnings to build a church, and also opened an orphanage, a school, and a boxing gym in Manila. A chain smoker in retirement, he died of lung cancer at the age of 49.

A YOUTHFUL "FLASH" ELORDE POSES WITH SANDY SADLER BEFORE THEIR 1956 FIGHT

ANTONIO ESPARRAGOZA

A long-armed, lanky technician with a stony face, Antonio Esparragoza was a disciplined and intelligent fighter who held the World Boxing Association featherweight title for four years.

Esparragoza was a patient, organized boxer who liked to take his time before picking an opponent apart with an almost mechanical precision. Most important of all, he could punch hard and accurately.

He was from a comfortable home in Cumana and although he began to box from the age of 13, he did not have to fight his way out of poverty. He was a regular Venezuelan amateur international, peaking with a bronze medal in the 1978 World Championships in Belgrade. He also picked up silver in the King's Cup in Thailand.

Esparragoza turned professional in 1981 after winning 76 of his 93 amateur bouts, and went on to win the WBA featherweight belt with a stunning 12th-round stoppage of Steve Cruz in the Texan's home town of Fort Worth in March 1987.

With the exception of a draw against Mexican Marcos Villasana in Los Angeles in June 1988, Esparragoza was an impressive champion. He had no psychological difficulty in defending abroad and, because of economic and political problems in Venezuela, did so repeatedly. He fought Pascual Aranda in Texas, Villasana in California, Jose Marmolejo in Italy, Mitsuru Sugiya in Japan, Jean Marc Renard in Belgium, Eduardo Montoya in Mexico, and Chan-mok Park in South Korea. Finally, however, he lost on points to Yong-kyun Park in South Korea in March 1991 and acceded to his mother's long-held wish and retired.

FACT FILE

1959 Born Cumana, Venezuela

1981 Professional debut

1987 Knocked out Steve Cruz to win WBA featherweight title

1991 Lost title in eighth defense to Yong-kyun Park in South Korea

Career record: Fights 36, Won 30, Lost 2, Drawn 4

ESPARRAGOZA TAKES CARE OF BUSINESS AGAINST JAPANESE CHALLENGER MITSURU SUGIYA IN 1989

LUISITO ESPINOSA

FACT FILE

1967 Born Manila, Philippines

1984 Professional debut, age 16

1989 Knocked out Khaokor Galaxy to win WBA bantamweight title

1991 Lost bantamweight crown to Israel Contreras

1995 Won WBC featherweight title against Manuel Medina

Career record: Fights 47, Won 40, Lost 7

Boxing was an inevitable career for Luisito Espinosa: His father Dio once went the distance with the great Japanese flyweight, "Fighting" Harada, while his uncle Leo had three rather unsuccessful world title attempts in the 1950s.

One of Dio's 14 children, Luisito was sparring by the time he was seven years old and used a sackful of sand as a punchbag. However, he never bothered with an amateur career, confining himself to three bouts and then turning professional at 16. Progress was tough for the tall, lean youngster, but he fought his way up. On October 18, 1989 he was given a shot at Thailand's Khaokor Galaxy for the WBA bantamweight title. Espinosa was considered a "safe" challenger by the Thais, but knocked out Galaxy with a series of left hooks in round one.

Still only 22, he defended twice in Thailand, fulfilling the option clauses on the contract he had signed before the Galaxy fight, and disposed of American Hurley Snead and then Thanomsak Sithboabay of Thailand. He was dubbed "Golden Boy" by Filipino writers, but when he returned home to defend the title he was surprisingly knocked out in five rounds by Israel Contreras of Venezuela.

In the wilderness for a while, at least he gave his 5 ft. 8 in. frame time to fill out. In 1995 he signed with respected Japanese boxing writer and fight promoter Joe Koizumi, and then at the end of the year outpointed classy Mexican Manuel Medina to win the WBC 126 lb. featherweight belt. Three defenses followed as he established himself further in 1996, including a fourth-round knockout of former champion Alejandro Gonzalez of Mexico.

LUISITO ESPINOSA POSES FOR THE CAMERA

LUIS ESTABA

Although he won the World Boxing Council light-flyweight title in scandalous circumstances, Luis "Lumumba" Estaba went on to become a formidable champion.

The wiry, tough stylist from Venezuela was already a veteran when the WBC added an extra division with a 108-lb. weight limit in order to help those men who had plenty of ability but found themselves outweighed even in flyweight fights.

The first champion, Franco Udella of Italy, gave up the title because of illness and Estaba, by then 34, was matched with a Paraguayan named Rafael Lovera, who was the WBC's No.1 contender. Only after Estaba had battered Lovera in four one-sided rounds in Caracas in September 1975 did the WBC begin any real investigation of the credentials which Lovera's management claimed for the fighter.

The incredible truth was soon revealed. Lovera had never had a single fight.

While that made the WBC a laughing stock, Estaba set out to prove his worth. He did it in style, making 11 successful title defenses in two and a half years.

Estaba won his first defense in Okinawa, Japan, when the crowd rioted after he stopped Takenobu Shimabukuro in the 10th round. After that he defended at home, including an effortless three-round knockout of Udella in July 1976.

In October 1977 he outboxed chunky Thai southpaw Netrnoi Vorasingh over 15 rounds in Caracas, but his reign came to an end when he was knocked out in the 14th round by Mexican Freddy Castillo in February 1978. By this time Estaba was 36. Five months later, he lost in five rounds to Vorasingh, who had quickly dethroned Castillo, and retired, age 37.

FACT FILE

1941 Born Guiria, Sucre, Venezuela
1967 Professional debut
1975 Won WBC light-flyweight title, age 34
1978 Lost WBC light-flyweight title in 12th defense
Career record: Fights 52, Won 41, Lost 9, Drawn 2

ESTABA MADE 11 SUCCESSFUL DEFENCES IN SPITE OF BEING ONE OF THE OLDEST MEN TO WIN A CHAMPIONSHIP

CHRIS EUBANK

One of the most eccentric and enigmatic of champions, Chris Eubank consistently viewed boxing as a barbaric activity, yet admitted it gave him an irreplaceable buzz. He constantly counterbalanced the immense financial rewards it provided with the toll it took on his body.

Eubank could be cutting and cruel, yet was also the most sensitive of men. He genuinely attempted to use his status as a world champion to make the world a better place, whether through visits to Britain's ghettoes or by attempting to turn post-fight press conferences into sermons for world peace.

Born in London, Eubank was sent to New York to live with his father when he threatened to go off the rails. After five professional fights in Atlantic City, Eubank returned home and eventually with Barry Hearn launched one of the most successful partnerships British boxing has ever seen.

Eubank stopped Nigel Benn in nine ferocious rounds to win the WBO middleweight title in Birmingham in November 1990, and after three defenses, moved up to super-middleweight and beat Michael Watson in a tragic battle at White Hart Lane soccer stadium. Watson suffered brain damage after being stopped by Eubank in the 12th round.

Eubank made 14 successful defenses—sometimes showing what an outstanding talent he was, and at others appearing very lucky to receive the verdict—before he was dethroned by Steve Collins in County Cork in March 1995. In a rematch Eubank was again outworked by the tough, battle-hardened Irishman and then retired.

Then in October 1996, Eubank returned to the boxing world with a most bizarre enterprise, promoting himself in an easy win over a low-grade Argentine named Luis Barrera in Egypt.

MOMENT OF DESTINY: EUBANK ON HIS KNEES AFTER HIS 1990 WIN OVER NIGEL BENN

SEE ALSO ◆ **NIGEL BENN 32** ◆ **STEVE COLLINS 74**

A fast, elusive featherweight with a glorious left hand, Johnny Famechon was a master of the art of hitting without getting hit.

He was from a family of French fighters. His uncle Ray fought Willie Pep for the world title; another uncle, Emile, and his own father Andre were both world-class operators. Johnny was born Jean Pierre in Paris, and at five the family moved to Australia.

A one-time electrician's apprentice, he persuaded his father to let him box and, trained by the exceptional Ambrose Palmer, turned professional in Melbourne at 16. In the mid-1960s he won both Australian and British Empire titles, but his career took off on January 21, 1969, the night he outboxed Jose Legra at the Albert Hall, London, for the WBC featherweight championship. Legra had won 54 consecutive fights, but the Spanish-based Cuban found Famechon a shadowy target, and lost on points.

Famechon's skills were pretty to watch, but had a hard, ruthless edge to them. In Sydney in July 1969 he retained his title against Fighting Harada on a disputed decision, but in the rematch in Tokyo in January 1970 he climbed off the floor to stop Harada in the 14th round of a magnificent fight.

Famechon earned well in these defenses and in non-title fights, but was dethroned on May 9, 1970 when he lost a unanimous decision to veteran Mexican southpaw Vicente Saldivar. He retired and lived in comfortable retirement with his wife and children, staying in good enough shape to run marathons into his mid-forties.

In the 1990s Famechon suffered serious head injuries when struck by a car. His recovery has been slow but typically determined.

FACT FILE

1945	Born Jean Pierre Famechon, Paris, France
1961	Professional debut in Melbourne, age 16
1964	Won Australian featherweight title
1967	Won British Empire featherweight title
1984	Knocked out Roberto Duran in two rounds
1969	Beat Jose Legra to become WBC champion
1970	Lost championship to Vicente Saldivar

Career record: Fights 67, Won 56, Lost 5, Drawn 6

A HAPPY FAMECHON PACKS HIS BOOTS INTO HIS BAG FOR THE JOURNEY HOME TO AUSTRALIA AFTER WINNING THE WORLD TITLE AGAINST JOSE LEGRA IN LONDON

SEE ALSO ◆ FIGHTING HARADA 151 ◆ JOSE LEGRA 185 ◆ VICENTE SALDIVAR 292

THE GREAT FIGHTS

NIGEL BENN
V.
CHRIS EUBANK

NATIONAL EXHIBITION CENTRE, BIRMINGHAM.
NOVEMBER 18, 1990.

Chris Eubank and Nigel Benn bared their souls, not in pursuit of the flimsy bauble known as the World Boxing Organization middleweight title, but for something less tangible and more essential: maybe the final proof of their own fighting hearts, their strength, and their youth. Winning and losing mattered, but fighting to the bitter end, giving the last drop of themselves, mattered more.

Benn, the self-styled "Dark Destroyer," the untamed former soldier from East London and Eubank, the street-kid turned eccentric intellectual from Brighton, were somehow driven by each other's presence and on this late autumn night before 12,000 people in the NEC, reached new heights together.

Promoter Barry Hearn announced in September that Benn would be paid £1 million ($1.5 million) for the second defense of his WBO belt and Eubank, the most dramatic and enigmatic personality on the British scene, would earn a "six-figure sum."

Both were worth every penny as they fought at a fierce pace. Benn's left eye began swelling in the second, and eventually shut tight, but Nigel scored the only knockdown in the eighth when Eubank appeared to slip on water in a corner as he took a long right, and went down. He protested, but referee Richard Steele tolled out the mandatory eight.

Two judges had Benn in front going into the ninth, but then Eubank found the punches to drive him along the ropes into a corner where his defenses came apart. Referee Steele spotted the sudden slackening of his senses and jumped in to end this marvelous fight.

Eubank, his mouth bloodied, sank to his knees in delight and relief, and then, after attempting to explain the pain he had suffered from a gashed tongue, proposed to his girlfriend via the TV cameras.

Benn, who blamed the struggle of making 160 lb. for weakening him, campaigned hard for a rematch, but when it came at super-middleweight before 42,000 people in Manchester in 1993, the result was a bitterly disputed draw.

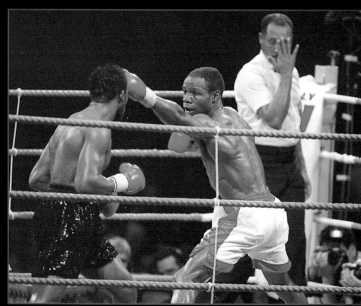

JEFF FENECH

FACT FILE

1964	Born Pyrmont, Sydney, Australia
1984	Boxed in Los Angeles Olympics
1985	Won IBF bantamweight title in seventh pro fight
1987	Won WBC super-bantamweight title
1988	Became 3-weight world champion
1991	Controversial draw with WBC super-feather champ Azumah Nelson

Career record: Fights 31, Won 27, Lost 3, Drawn 1

Jeff Fenech was a raging storm of a fighter, a pugnacious terrier who could talk as well as he fought and in the few short years of his prime grew into one of Australia's greatest sporting heroes.

The sixth child of Maltese immigrants, Fenech came out of the tough working-class backwaters of Sydney, Australia to capture the heart of a nation.

Hard work and a zest for learning were his keys to his success, as well as a trainer, Johnny Lewis, who could both channel his determination and polish his style. Robbed in the quarter-final of the 1984 Olympics, Fenech turned pro in a blaze of publicity.

In his seventh fight he battered defending IBF bantamweight champion Satoshi Shingaki of Japan for a ninth-round stoppage. For the next few years he was unstoppable. He defended the bantamweight belt three times, coming through grueling struggles against Americans Jerome Coffee and Steve McCrory, then moved up to win the WBC super-bantamweight title in 1987 with a fourth-round knockout of Thailand's Samart Payakarun.

After two more defenses, he became a three-weight champ by stopping Victor Callejas of Puerto Rico in 10 rounds for the WBC featherweight crown.

Severe hand problems hampered him greatly and after beating Marcos Villasana in April 1989 he retired, but found it impossible to stay away. Many felt he beat Azumah Nelson in a drawn WBC super-featherweight title fight in Las Vegas in 1991. He was widely expected to win the return in 1992, but Nelson broke him up in eight rounds. He retired for good after losing an IBF lightweight title fight to Philip Holiday in 1996. It was his 14th world championship bout.

FENECH ... ROSE FROM THE BACKWATERS OF SYDNEY TO BECOME AN AUSTRALIAN FOLK HERO

SEE ALSO ◆ AZUMAH NELSON 251

JACKIE FIELDS

ackie Fields was a boy of 16 when he won the Olympic featherweight gold medal at the Paris Olympics in 1924. As they played the Star Spangled Banner, he burst into floods of tears.

Five years later he won the NBA welterweight title by outpointing Young Jack Thompson as a riot raged outside the ring in Chicago Coliseum—150 people were hospitalized and one died!

Fields was born in Chicago in 1908, and the family moved to Los Angeles to open a restaurant when he was 13 because his father contracted tuberculosis. The business struggled to make money, and Jackie boxed as an amateur to earn groceries. Before he was 17, he was a professional, but almost abandoned his career when Jimmy McLarnin broke his jaw during a fight and knocked him out in two rounds. Nevertheless the purse paid off his family mortgage. He carried on.

Wins over Mushy Callahan, Vince Dundee, and Thompson brought him on, and he beat Thompson again to win NBA recognition as welterweight champion. In Detroit in July 1929 he unified the title with a second-round win over Joe Dundee, who was disqualified for a low punch after being floored twice. Fields lost the title over 15 rounds to Thompson in Detroit in May 1930, regained it by outscoring French-Canadian Lou Brouillard in Chicago in January 1932, but lost the sight in one eye in a car crash.

Not surprisingly, he lost the championship on points to crafty southpaw Young Corbett III in San Francisco in February 1933. In the dressing room afterward, Fields's manager Jack Kearns flattened the referee!

He retired after one more fight, worked in Hollywood for Twentieth Century Fox, and some years later partly owned the Tropicana Hotel in Las Vegas.

FACT FILE

1908	Born Jacob Finkelstein, Chicago
1924	Olympic featherweight gold medal
1929	Won NBA welterweight title by outpointing Young Jack Thompson, beat Joe Dundee for universal recognition
1930	Lost world title to Young Jack Thompson
1932	Regained world title against Lou Brouillard
1933	Lost title to Young Corbett III, retired age 25

Career record: Fights 87, Won 74, Lost 9, Drawn 3, No Contest 1

FIELDS WAS AN OLYMPIC GOLD MEDALIST AND TWICE WORLD WELTERWEIGHT CHAMPION

THE GREAT FIGHTS

JAMES J. CORBETT
V.
BOB FITZSIMMONS

CARSON CITY, NEVADA.
MARCH 17, 1897.

Carson City was a dangerous, edge-of-the-law mining town 7,000 feet up in the Nevada mountains, where men came to change their lives, to earn their fortunes, and to live without chains.

They were a motley, unpredictable band—and when James J. Corbett brought his heavyweight championship of the world to town to fight 34-year-old Bob Fitzsimmons in a specially constructed wooden arena, lawman Bat Masterson stood at the entrance and collected 400 guns. Wyatt Earp, six-shooters in place, sat ringside in case of any trouble.

There was none. The crowd was smaller than had been expected, but they saw a classic battle between a master boxer and a cagey, experienced man with a good ring brain and big punch.

For six rounds it was all Corbett. Fitzsimmons' lips cracked and bled, his face reddened by the sun and the champion's precise punching. In the sixth the challenger went down on one knee, blood dripping from his nose and mouth, and his wife Rose leaned through the ropes and pleaded with him to get up. Corbett laughed at her.

Fitzsimmons beat the count, survived the round, and from the seventh switched his attention from Corbett's head, which he could not hit, to the body. Gradually, the champion slowed. In the 13th round, Corbett was open enough for two of his gold teeth to be knocked out by a right hand. At the end of the round Rose Fitzsimmons yelled excited encouragement to her husband: "Hit him in the slats, Bob!"

And in the 14th he floored Corbett with a short left to the pit of the stomach. Badly winded and groaning, he crawled across the ring, reached for the ropes, missed, and fell on his face.

When he recovered Corbett demanded a rematch, telling Fitzsimmons: "You'll fight me again or I'll lick you every time we meet on the street." The new champion said: "If you ever lay a hand on me outside the ring, I'll kill you."

They never fought again.

BOB FITZSIMMONS

Bob Fitzsimmons had spindly, knock-kneed legs, a bald head rimmed by strands of red hair, and an ungainly style, yet was a formidable fighter who was the first man to win world titles at three separate weights.

His parents emigrated from Cornwall when he was nine. He did the rest of his growing up in New Zealand, and worked as a blacksmith, developing a powerful upper body, until he was spotted by bare-knuckle genius Jem Mace.

He learned in the professional rings around Sydney, but made his name in New Orleans on January 14, 1891 when he won the world middleweight title by flooring champion Jack Dempsey ("The Nonpareil") 13 times for a 13th-round knockout.

When heavyweight champ Jim Corbett retired briefly in 1896, Fitzsimmons demolished Peter Maher in one round to receive brief acknowledgment as champion. But Corbett, who disliked Ftizsimmons, quickly reclaimed the title, while the Englishman lost a chaotic fight with Tom Sharkey on a foul. When he protested, the referee—Wild West legend Wyatt Earp—pulled a gun on him!

When he knocked out Corbett with a body punch in the 14th round in Carson City, Nevada, on March 17, 1897, he was encouraged from ringside by his wife Rose. "Hit him in the slats, Bob," she yelled.

He cashed in on his title in vaudeville appearances until 1899 when he lost to the hulking "boilermaker" from Ohio, James J. Jeffries, on an 11th-round knockout. In 1903 Fitzsimmons, who rarely weighed more than 168 lb., won the light-heavyweight title by outscoring George Gardner over 20 rounds in San Francisco. He lost it to Philadelphia Jack O'Brien in 1905, boxed on for another nine years and was 54 when he died of pneumonia.

FITZSIMMONS (RIGHT) SHAKES HANDS WITH JIM JEFFRIES. THE CORNISHMAN HELD TITLES IN THREE SEPARATE WEIGHT DIVISIONS

SEE ALSO ◆ JAMES J. CORBETT 80 ◆ JAMES JEFFRIES 169 ◆ PHILADELPHIA JACK O'BRIEN 256

TIGER FLOWERS

Before every fight, the solemn-faced man known as the Georgia Deacon would recite from Psalm 144: "Blessed be the Lord my strength which teacheth my hands to war and my fingers to fight." And then Tiger Flowers would walk out to fight every opponent he came up against until he dropped.

Modest and unassuming, Flowers was a Methodist who found no conflict in boxing for his living. He fought for eight years before being allowed a title fight, beat the great Harry Greb to win the middleweight championship, but was not allowed to keep it long. He also died tragically in a New York hospital, several hours after an operation to remove scar tissue from his right eye. An anesthetic overdose was suspected, though never admitted.

Like a later hero, Marvin Hagler, Flowers found his progress was frustrated simply because he was black, a southpaw, and too good for his own good. Eventually, he lost a decision to former light-heavyweight champion Mike McTigue that provoked such a public outcry that he was given a title fight with the declining Greb two months later. The 30-year-old former shipyard worker from the Deep South outfought the champion to win a split decision.

In a rematch six months later Flowers beat Greb unanimously, but was then the victim of a dreadful verdict against former welterweight champion Mickey Walker in mob-run Chicago in December 1926. Flowers's contractual right to a rematch was also ignored.

Four days after stopping Leo Gates in his 18th fight of 1927, he died in hospital. At his funeral Gene Tunney called him an inspiration "to live cleanly, speak softly, trust in God and fight hard and fair.".

FACT FILE

1895 Born Theodore Flowers, Camille, Georgia

1918 Professional debut

1926 Beat Harry Greb for world middleweight title, lost it to Mickey Walker

Died: New York City, November 16, 1927, age 32

Career record: Fights 157, Won 116, Lost 13, Drawn 6, No Contest 1, No Decisions 21

FLOWERS, THE GEORGIA DEACON, PICTURED IN 1926, THE YEAR HE BEAT HARRY GREB FOR THE WORLD MIDDLEWEIGHT TITLE

SEE ALSO ◆ HARRY GREB 141 ◆ MIKE McTIGUE 247 ◆ MICKEY WALKER 330

The GREAT FIGHTS

GEORGE FOREMAN
V.
MUHAMMAD ALI

**TWENTIETH OF MAY STADIUM, KINSHASA, ZAIRE.
OCTOBER 30, 1974.**

Muhammad Ali made the boxing world believe in miracles again on a humid, muggy night in Zaire.

George Foreman was perceived as a monster, an unstoppable, surly brute of a human being who knocked men down until they couldn't get up any more.

His heavy, methodical swings had dropped Smokin' Joe Frazier six times in the four minutes, 35 seconds their fight had lasted in Jamaica in January 1973. After that, he had flattened Joe Roman of Puerto Rico in two minutes, and Ken Norton in five.

Now Ali and Foreman met in "The Rumble in the Jungle" in Kinshasa, with Muhammad grossing $5,450,000 and staying on the banks of the Zaire river as a guest of president Mobutu Sese Seko. As Foreman prepared sullenly, believing he would blow Ali away, the challenger played with the press, labeling George "The Mummy" and laughing at him. "George Foreman ain't nothing," he said. "He a big old bully from Texas."

Nevertheless, most critics picked Foreman to end Ali's career with a decisive knockout. The champ was a 1–3 favorite to win.

In the first round, Ali stunned 62,000 fans in the stadium and many millions on TV around the world by refusing to run, by not dancing as he said he would, and by standing in front of Foreman and beating him to the punch. In round two, he topped even that, by retreating to the ropes, cupping his gloves around his face, tucking in his elbows and letting Foreman hit him. "I felt sick when he did that," said Ali's trainer Angelo Dundee.

For round after round, he taunted and talked to Foreman, whose response was to whack away with even greater venom. And slowly, steadily, Foreman punched himself out. Ali showed what a great chin and great heart he had—and then proved his phenomenal ring brain when he judged Foreman's tiredness to perfection, and exploded off the ropes in the eighth round to knock him out, regaining the title he had first won against Sonny Liston ten long years before.

GEORGE FOREMAN

George Foreman didn't worry about subtle techniques. Once he had mastered the basics—a thudding, bone-shuddering jab, how to throw a hook, an uppercut, and a cross—he just went out and hit people. Mostly, they stayed hit.

Foreman won the 1968 Olympic heavyweight gold medal when still a novice. He spent four years learning the professional business before he won the world heavyweight title with a six-knockdown, two-round demolition of previously unbeaten Joe Frazier in Kingston, Jamaica, in January 1973.

He separated his first two challengers, Jose Roman and Ken Norton, from their senses with minimum effort. Norton, who had broken the jaw of Muhammad Ali, was knocked out in two rounds, which meant that when Foreman was matched with Ali in the "Rumble in the Jungle." Big George was a heavy favorite.

Ali's eighth-round win cast Foreman aside, and although he won five more fights to set up a rematch, those plans were destroyed by a close points defeat by Jimmy Young in 1977. Backstage, Foreman underwent a spiritual conversion and retired to a new life as a preacher.

Ten years later he began to box again, and after a long rehabilitation process in which he flattened Gerry Cooney in two rounds, he was outpointed by Evander Holyfield in 1991. He plodded along and in November 1994 pulled off the unthinkable: at the age of 45, he knocked out Michael Moorer in the 10th round in Las Vegas to regain the WBA and IBF versions of the world championship. He continued to fight and by the end of 1996 was still recognized as champion by the British-based WBU.

FOREMAN: THE PUNCHING PREACHER WHO PULLED OFF A BOXING MIRACLE

SEE ALSO ◆ MUHAMMAD ALI 12 ◆ JOE FRAZIER 122 ◆ MICHAEL MOORER 230

BOB FOSTER

A deputy sheriff from New Mexico, Bob Foster took his job so seriously that he once arrested his wife for speeding. He also tended to lack a sense of humor in his other occupation—as light-heavyweight champion of the world.

Foster had a nasty habit of flattening normally durable, until then iron-chinned fighters, usually with a lethal left hook that carried the kick of a Magnum.

Foster was a brilliant amateur while in the US Air Force, but grew disillusioned when he was asked to boil down to middleweight—he was 6 ft., 3 in. tall—because the light-heavyweight berth at the 1960 Olympics had already been given to Cassius Clay.

He turned professional in 1961, and waited seven years for a title shot. When his chance finally happened he knocked out veteran Dick Tiger in four rounds at Madison Square Garden on May 24, 1968.

For the next six years he was untouchable at 175 lb., although forays into the heavyweight division were disastrous: Joe Frazier knocked him out in two rounds in a world title fight, and Muhammad Ali beat him in eight.

It is as a light-heavyweight, arguably the finest of them all, that he will be remembered. He was stripped by the WBA for a while, but knocked out rival champion Vicente Rondon in two embarrasingly easy rounds. Britain's Chris Finnegan went down in 14, and his fourth-round blastout of Mike Quarry in 1972 was chilling in its precision.

He retired after scraping a draw with rugged Argentine Jorge Ahumada in his 14th defense in 1974.

FOSTER TRAINS IN LONDON BEFORE HIS DEFENCE AGAINST CHRIS FINNEGAN IN 1972

FACT FILE

1938	Born Albuquerque, New Mexico
1968	Knocked out Dick Tiger for world light-heavyweight title
1970	Lost heavyweight title fight with Joe Frazier
1972	Lost to Muhammad Ali, but still light-heavyweight champ
1974	Retired as undefeated champion
1978	Last fight, age 39

Career record: Fights 65, Won 56, Lost 8, Drawn 1

SEE ALSO ◆ **MUHAMMAD ALI 12** ◆ **JOE FRAZIER 122** ◆ **DICK TIGER 307**

THE GREAT FIGHTS

JOE FRAZIER
V.
MUHAMMAD ALI

MADISON SQUARE GARDEN, NEW YORK.
MARCH 8, 1971.

This was the night, above all others, that proved the greatness of Smokin' Joe Frazier.

Frazier and Muhammad Ali shared $1 million, plus ancillary rights that were said to have almost doubled that. Madison Square Garden was packed with 21,455 customers, paying $1,352,961. A ringside seat cost $150. Frank Sinatra took photographs from a pressman's pitch beneath the ropes.

As the drama unfolded, the noise of the crowd built to a shrieking crescendo. Ali won rounds with his jabs and quick flurries, but Frazier never stopped hunting him down, hooking with the left, slamming punches into his side, burying his head on Ali's chest and thumping away.

Still, Ali's jabs and right hands raised gargoyle-like lumps on Frazier's head. He kept the fight close... but then in the final round, tried a slow right hand, was beaten to it by a crunching left hook that sent him crashing on to his back, the tassels of his boots twirling.

Ali got up at four, and was like a man treading through a snowdrift until the final bell ended his torture. Referee Arthur Mercante scored 8-6-1, judge Bill Recht 11-4 and judge Artie Aldala 9-6... Smokin' Joe Frazier had proved his point.

"I did not make him crawl, I did not jibe him. He had taken enough... he tried to talk to me, but nothing came out," said Frazier.

Ali tried to put it into perspective. "You don't go mad. You don't shoot yourself. Soon this will be old news... Maybe a plane will go down... or a great man will be assassinated. That will be more important than me losing. I'm not crying."

Frazier would never be as good again. "What more can I do?" he said. "I've got to live a little. I've been working for 10 long years."

Ali would beat him twice in returns, the second time in the epic "Thrilla in Manila" in 1975.

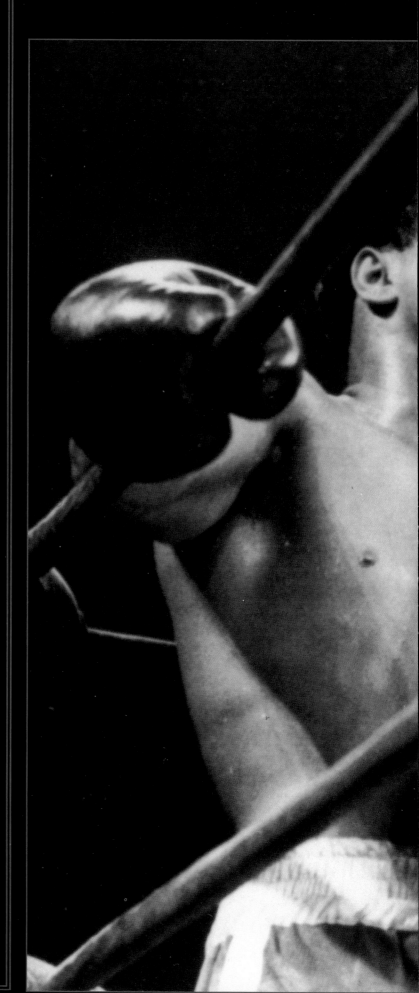

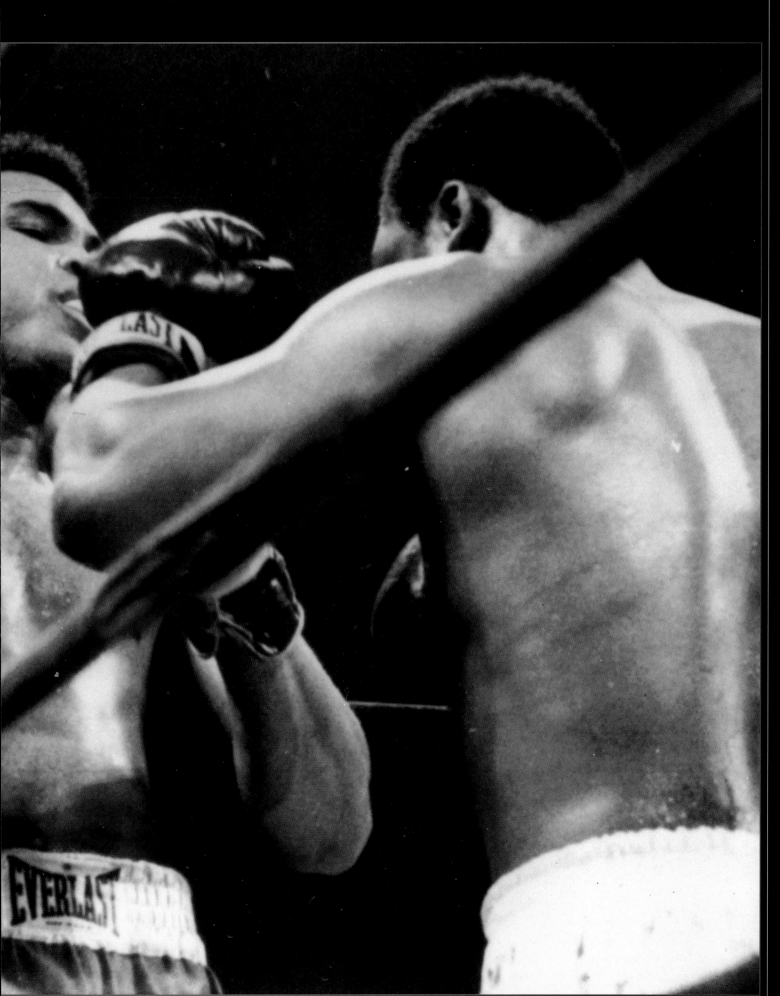

JOE FRAZIER

FACT FILE

1944 Born Beaufort, South Carolina

1964 Olympic heavyweight gold medal

1968 Won New York recognition as heavyweight champion

1970 Beat Jimmy Ellis for undisputed title

1971 Beat Muhammad Ali in "Fight of the Century"

1973 Lost title to George Foreman

1975 Lost "Thrilla in Manila" to Ali

1981 Last fight, age 37

Career record: Fights 37, Won 32, Lost 4, Drawn 1

Smokin' Joe Frazier's hour of destiny came on that magnificent night when he floored and outpointed Muhammad Ali at a packed Madison Square Garden, New York, on March 8, 1971.

It was viewed as a victory for ordinary, workaday Black America over the heart of the cultural revolution, for plain Baptist folk over the perceived Black Muslim menace. And that's something Joe Frazier has remained comfortable with in the quarter of a century that has passed since that astonishing, and very magical night.

But after the adrenalin wore off, Frazier's pain set in. He was hospitalized for several weeks in Philadelphia. When he emerged, the edge of his desire had gone, almost as if there was nothing left to prove.

Frazier was born in South Carolina, moved north to Philadelphia, where he worked as a slaughterman by day and boxed at night. He won the 1964 Olympic heavyweight gold medal in Tokyo, turned pro the following year, and won New York recognition as world champ by knocking out Buster Mathis in the 11th round in March 1968.

He beat top-quality fighters such as Oscar Bonavena and Jerry Quarry before unifying the title with a four-round win over WBA champ Jimmy Ellis in 1970. After that he knocked out light-heavy champ Bob Foster in two and beat Ali for his 27th consecutive win.

But after two more low-key defenses he was bludgeoned to defeat by George Foreman in Kingston, Jamaica, in January 1973. Ali beat him twice in returns, the second time in the marvelous "Thrilla In Manila" in 1975. After Foreman stopped him again in 1976 he retired. He came back for one fight in 1981, then stopped for good.

SMOKIN' JOE: FRAZIER IN A THOUGHTFUL MOOD

SEE ALSO ◆ MUHAMMAD ALI 12 ◆ GEORGE FOREMAN 118 ◆ BOB FOSTER 119

GENE FULLMER

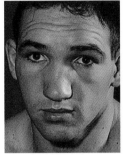

Gene Fullmer was a strict Mormon who gave his tithe—ten percent of his earnings—to the Church of Latter Day Saints. Any idea that his commitment to his faith lessened his desire to fight until he dropped was cast aside the moment anybody saw him in a ring.

Fullmer, allegedly named after former heavyweight champ Gene Tunney, was a solid brawler who hit hard and often, and who didn't worry about getting hit back.

He emerged as a world-class pro in 1955 when he fought men like Paul Pender and Gil Turner. The next year his victims included Ralph "Tiger" Jones, Rocky Castellani, and Charles Humez.

But he finally arrived on January 2, 1957, when he outpointed Sugar Ray Robinson in Madison Square Garden to win the world middleweight title.

Robinson pulled out one of the great punches in championship history, a sensational left hook, to beat him in the fifth round of the Chicago rematch four months later.

But in August 1959 Fullmer rebounded, outslugging another tough, grizzled battler, Carmen Basilio, to take the National Boxing Association title on a 14th-round stoppage in San Francisco.

He kept the NBA belt for three years, surviving draws with Joey Giardello and Robinson and beating Spider Webb, Basilio, Robinson, Florentino Fernandez, and Benny Paret, before losing what had by then become the World Boxing Association belt to Dick Tiger in October 1962.

In a return Fullmer held Tiger to a draw, but in a third match in August 1963 in Nigeria he lost in seven rounds. In retirement he made a fortune farming mink.

FACT FILE

1931	Born West Jordan, Utah
1951	Professional debut
1957	Won and lost world middleweight title against Ray Robinson
1959	Won NBA recognition as champion against Carmen Basilio
1962	Lost WBA title to Dick Tiger
1964	Announced retirement, age 33

Career record: Fights 64, Won 55, Lost 6, Drawn 3

FULLMER (RIGHT) WAS NEVER PRETTY TO WATCH, BUT FEW COULD WITHSTAND HIS RAW, AGGRESSIVE, SLUGGING STYLE

SEE ALSO ♦ CARMEN BASILIO 29 ♦ PAUL PENDER 268 ♦ RAY ROBINSON 278 ♦ DICK TIGER 307

THE GREAT FIGHTS

GENE FULLMER
V.
RAY ROBINSON

CHICAGO STADIUM.
MAY 1, 1957.

By the mid-1950s, Sugar Ray Robinson was fighting a new generation of middleweights, men who worried little about the reputation of a man who was champion a dozen years before.

Gene Fullmer, a Mormon from Utah, was one of them who knew that while Robinson would never be less than a star, his talents were fading.

Fullmer has never subscribed to the popular opinion that Robinson was the greatest fighter of all time. They fought first at Madison Square Garden on January 2, 1957 and Fullmer outworked the 35-year-old champ for a unanimous 15-round decision, cutting the ring off cleverly and applying constant pressure.

A rematch was a must—and only four months later they met again at Chicago Stadium, where Robinson had first won the middleweight title against Jake La Motta six years before that.

For four rounds, it was the same kind of fight as the first. Robinson wanted to box at long range. Fullmer pressured him and poured out punches in streams. An enthusiastic 25-year-old at the top of his game, Fullmer was winning by a single point on all three cards.

And then Robinson proved just how great he was, drawing Fullmer on to a pair of right hands to the body, and then pivoting cleanly to crash a perfect left hook to the jaw. Fullmer didn't see it and went down, knocked out. His body tried to pull itself up, but his mind was away somewhere else. He was still crouching uncomprehendingly on one knee as referee Frank Sikora spread his arms.

"Everything was going all right," said Fullmer. "And the next thing I knew I was focusing my eyes on the referee and I had been counted out."

They were to box twice more, in NBA title fights. They drew the first in Los Angeles in December 1960, and Fullmer won the second on points, in Las Vegas in March 1961, by which time Robinson was 39.

LARRY GAINS

FACT FILE

1900 Born Toronto, Canada

1925 Knocked out Max Schmeling in 2 rounds

1931 Beat Phil Scott for British Empire title

1932 Outpointed Primo Carnera in London

1934 Lost Empire title to Len Harvey

Died: Cologne, Germany, July 26, 1983, age 82

Career record: Fights 146, Won 116, Lost 23, Drawn 5, No Contests 2

For 22 years after the fall of Jack Johnson in 1915, black fighters were barred from boxing for the world heavyweight championship. Nothing was official, but this was Johnson's legacy and everyone knew it. Consequently, men like Larry Gains, Harry Wills, and George Godfrey were never given the opportunities their talents deserved.

Even when Joe Louis won the title in 1937, only one black man, the virtually blind John Henry Lewis, challenged him in the first ten years of his reign.

Gains was from Toronto, took a cattle boat to England in 1923 to seek his fortune as a fighter, and was based in Germany in 1925 when he knocked out the young Max Schmeling in two rounds.

He recrossed the Atlantic—on a luxury liner —won the Canadian heavyweight title against Soldier Jones in Toronto and sparred with Jack Dempsey, who admitted he couldn't hit him. The fast, elusive Canadian with the jolting punch returned to Europe and from 1929 until 1933 lost only once in 41 fights. Still no breaks occurred, even though he outpointed the giant Italian, Primo Carnera, in London and said: "I could have danced all night!". He drew with former light-heavyweight champion Mike McTigue, who is known to have said: "I would rather fight Jack Sharkey every week than Larry Gains once a month."

A year after Gains beat him, Carnera knocked out Sharkey to become champion. But still nothing came the way of the big Canadian and in 1934 he was conveniently removed from the picture when he lost his Empire heavyweight title on a highly controversial decision to Len Harvey. He continued to fight for another seven years before retiring at the age of 41.

GAINS, WHOSE MISFORTUNE WAS TO BE A BLACK HEAVYWEIGHT IN THE 1930S, CALLED HIS AUTOBIOGRAPHY "THE IMPOSSIBLE DREAM"

SEE ALSO ◆ PRIMO CARNERA 58 ◆ JACK DEMPSEY 88 ◆ LEN HARVEY 152 ◆ MIKE MCTIGUE 247 ◆ MAX SCHMELING 294

KHAOSAI GALAXY

A walk-in slugger, Khaosai Galaxy was almost impossible to discourage. He would march forward, throwing vicious southpaw body shots in a relentless, driving pursuit.

Sometimes he could be caught cold early on, but he was never knocked out. He went down once or twice, and had to overcome bad cuts from time to time, but at the end Galaxy would be the one standing.

His only defeat was in a Thai bantamweight title fight in his sixth paid bout when he lost on points to Sakda Saksuree. That was irrelevant by the time he won the vacant WBA super-flyweight title with a sixth-round knockout of Eusebio Espinal in November 1984.

He accumulated his reputation, steadily battering his way past everyone who was put in front of him. Mostly he fought in Bangkok, where he was a national icon, but he did venture out to Willemstad in Curaçao to knock out Israel Contreras of Venezuela in five rounds, and also turned back challenges in Korea and Japan.

In 1987 in Indonesia he knocked out local hero Ellyas Pical in 14 rounds in front of a 30,000 crowd, earning a $150,000 payday, and before his fights in Bangkok sponsors virtually lined up to drape gold around his neck.

He blew away top-class men such as Yongkang Kim of South Korea and the stylish Venezuelan, David Griman, both of whom held world titles at flyweight. In 19 defenses only compatriot Kongtoranee Payakarun, Kenji Matsumara of Japan and, in his final professional fight, Armando Castro of Mexico, lasted the distance.

Khaosai's twin brother Khaokor also held the WBA bantamweight title, making them the first twins to become world champions.

FACT FILE

1959 Born Khaosai Wangchompu, Petchaboon Province, Thailand
1980 Professional debut
1984 Won WBA super-flyweight title agaiinst Eusebio Espinal
1991 Retired undefeated champion after his 19th defense
Career record: Fights 50, Won 49, Lost 1

THE AMAZINGLY SUCCESSFUL GALAXY HELD ON TO HIS WORLD TITLE THROUGH 19 DEFENCES. HE REMAINS ONE OF THAILAND'S GREATEST EVER SPORTSMEN

VICTOR GALINDEZ

Like so many who die young, Victor Galindez lived his short, triumphant life on the edge.

As a boy he worked the fields of his uncles' farms, but by 16 he was an unlicensed professional fighter in a leopardskin robe and trunks, and at 19, hiding his past, he boxed for Argentina in the 1968 Olympics.

When his official professional career began in 1969 he learned the hard way, losing several decisions along the way, but eventually on the retirement of Bob Foster, he won the vacant WBA belt by overpowering American Len Hutchins in 12 rounds in Buenos Aires in December 1974.

Amazingly, he smashed his right knee in a car crash a month before the bout, damaged an ankle when he fell off a horse, and made himself violently sick by wolfing down a pre-fight plateful of "Frogs à la Provençal"!

He was a swashbuckling champion who reigned for almost four years, through ten successful defenses against good fighters. Among those he beat: Ahumada, Pierre Fourie twice, Richie Kates twice, Alvaro Lopez twice, and Eddie Mustafa Muhammad. He loved cars, symbols of freedom and wealth. At one point he owned 26, including five Mercedes-Benz.

Weight-making finally cost him his title against Mike Rossman in New Orleans in September 1978. He somehow beat Rossman in a rematch in spite of dislocating an elbow, but lost it again when his jaw was broken by Marvin Johnson in November 1979.

He retired after surgery for detached retinas in both eyes, and was learning to be a racing driver when he was killed in a freak accident. He was standing by his own broken-down car when another driver lost control and mowed him down.

ONE OF THE GREAT WARRIORS, GALINDEZ NEVER KNEW WHEN HE WAS BEATEN

JOE GANS

Known as The Old Master, the supremely talented Joe Gans was already a veteran of 103 fights when he won the world lightweight title with a 100-second knockout of Frank Erne in Fort Erie, Ontario, in 1902. From the next six years he dominated the division, losing only when his fatal illness—tuberculosis—weakened him seriously.

Gans had wonderful coordination and impeccable footwork, but was black... and was therefore expected to "behave himself". He came from a poor family who scraped a living selling oysters, and he did what the situation demanded in order to keep earning.

In 1900 he lost so dismally to Terry McGovern in Chicago that the city authorities banned the sport. Earlier he quit in a world lightweight title contest with Erne with a badly cut eyelid. But once he was allowed to become champion, he let his talents flow. Only heavyweight Sam Langford was able to beat him, and then on points over 15 rounds, between 1901 and 1908.

In Goldfield, Nevada, on September 3, 1906, he won an epic struggle with Battling Nelson, which ended only when the Durable Dane was disqualified for repeated low blows in the 42nd round. Gans wired home to his mother: "Your boy is bringing home the bacon with lots of gravy on it!"

By 1908 he was sick. And on July 4, at Colma, California, he was floored nine times and stopped in 17 rounds by Nelson. Two months later Nelson beat him in 21 rounds. His last fight was a 10-round newspaper decision over Englishman Jabez White, and he died the following year.

FACT FILE

1874 Born Baltimore, Maryland

1902 Won world lightweight title against Frank Erne

1904 Relinquished world title after nine defenses

1906 Regained title in 42-round epic with Battling Nelson

1908 Lost championship to Nelson in 17 rounds

Died: Baltimore, August 10, 1910, age 35

Career record: Fights 156, Won 131, Lost 9, Drawn 16

GANS, THE FINEST LIGHTWEIGHT OF HIS TIME, WHOSE LIFE WAS CUT SHORT BY TUBERCULOSIS

SEE ALSO ◆ **TERRY McGOVERN 240** ◆ **BATTLING NELSON 254**

THE GREAT FIGHTS

JOE GANS
V.
BATTLING NELSON

GOLDFIELD, NEVADA.
SEPTEMBER 3, 1906.

Goldfield, Nevada, was one of the greatest gold camps of them all. It made millionaires of ordinary man, whose only necessary attributes were the will and ability to handle a shovel and knowledge enough to recognize what they were looking for.

Drinking and gambling establishments were open around the clock, and Goldfield had a law court, a church, its own newspaper, and a school. In 1906 Tex Rickard, a high-level hustler who had already won and lost one fortune in card houses, agreed to promote a major fight to enhance its social reputation. He shelled out $33,000 to tempt Joe Gans and Battling Nelson to dispute the world lightweight championship—and advertised the fight by placing $30,000 worth of gold coins in the window of the local bank.

By fight time Goldfield was heaving with newcomers, all there to see the two greatest lightweights of the day: Gans, the consummate, stylish boxer from Baltimore; Nelson, the brawling, rock-hard "Durable Dane" whose stamina was legendary. A throng of 8,000 filed into Rickard's new arena on a baking late summer afternoon. Gans, who had received a telegram from his mother imploring him to "bring back the bacon," outsped and outboxed Nelson from the start. By round eight, Nelson spat blood, and he was floored briefly. Frustrated and impatient, he plowed on, round after round, and gradually began to rough Gans up on the inside. He outfought him, and it seemed the fight was turning his way when in round 33 Gans broke his right hand on the top of Nelson's thick skull.

Gans, however, boxed beautifully with his left and Nelson wilted slowly in the heat. By the 42nd round he was in a terrible state. Not wanting to be knocked out, he launched a furious barrage of low punches that forced referee George Siler to disqualify him.

Gans sent a message to his mother: "Mammy, your boy is bringing home the bacon with lots of gravy on it."

...test. Goldfield. Nevada. Won By Gans.

KID GAVILAN

Kid Gavilan was an exuberant ring talent. He wasn't the predatory type his ring name implied—it means Sparrowhawk in Spanish—but at his dazzling peak, there was nobody faster, more exciting or stylish. He could take a punch, too. Nobody ever knocked him out.

Gavilan was a professional in Havana at 17, but it was in New York that he settled. The city buzzed in those years immediately after the war, and Gavilan's devil-may-care, ready-smiling genius fitted the time.

Twice he outpointed reigning world light-weight champion Ike Williams. After losing his first welterweight title fight to Ray Robinson, he took over by winning the vacant championship against Johnny Bratton. He stayed champion until 1954, surviving a controversial fight with Billy Graham but also beating Bobby Dykes, Gil Turner, Graham again, Chuck Davey, Carmen Basilio, and Bratton again.

Fixed fights were rife at the time. Nobody knows exactly what happened, but Gavilan's win over Graham was considered dubious—and he certainly believed he could not beat Johnny Saxton in Philadelphia in October 1954. He was right: the unanimous decision went against him, even though ringside reporters considered he was robbed.

In his great years he would cruise Manhattan in his Cadillac, but on his retirement in 1958 and by now a Jehovah's Witness, he returned to his Cuban farm for a quieter life. After Fidel Castro's revolution, both his passport and car were confiscated and he was arrested repeatedly for preaching on the streets. In 1968 the authorities let him emigrate back to the United States, where he underwent two cataract operations but, after a brief spell working with Muhammad Ali's entourage, he suffered three strokes and in old age lived alone in a small Miami flat.

GAVILAN (RIGHT) OUTBOXES JOHNNY BRATTON FOR THE WORLD WELTERWEIGHT CROWN IN NEW YORK IN 1951

SEE ALSO ◆ CARMEN BASILIO 29 ◆ RAY ROBINSON 278

FRANKIE GENARO

A stylish, fleet-footed boxer, Frankie Genaro was the flyweight gold medalist at the 1920 Olympic Games in Antwerp, and arguably the finest professional 112 lb. fighter of the decade.

In 1922 the little man from Brooklyn moved into world class by outpointing Phil Rosenburg and Pancho Villa, and in March 1923 outboxed Villa again over 15 rounds for the American flyweight championship.

World champ Jimmy Wilde had virtually retired. When he was persuaded to take one last title defense in the United States, most expected Genaro to be his opponent. In fact, Genaro's manager asked for too much money and instead Villa battered Wilde in seven brutal rounds to take the title.

Not surprisingly, Genaro was considered the uncrowned champion until 1925 when he lost a 10-round decision in Los Angeles to Fidel La Barba. He struggled for form for a while, but came good in Toronto in February 1928 when he outboxed Frenchy Belanger over 10 rounds to earn recognition as NBA flyweight champion.

Genaro was knocked out for the first time in his life when he lost the NBA belt in 58 seconds to a Frenchman they called The Spider, Emile Pladner, in Paris in March 1929. It was a stunning upset, but Genaro regained the title from Pladner six weeks later on a fifth-round foul. This also gave him European recognition as champion.

Although he drew with his major rival, Midget Wolgast, in 1930, Genaro was generally regarded as the best flyweight in the world until Victor "Young" Perez beat him in two rounds in Paris in October 1931.

Genaro fought on until 1934, then worked at various jobs in the New York area, retaining a love of boxing, even when he retired with his wife to the upstate lakefront at Cochecton.

FACT FILE

1901 Born Frank DiGennaro, New York City, August 26, 1901

1920 Olympic Games flyweight gold medal

1923 Beat Pancho Villa for American flyweight title

1925 Lost American title to Fidel La Barba

1928 Won NBA recognition as flyweight champion

1929 Lost and regained NBA belt against Emile Pladner

1931 Lost championship to Young Perez in Paris

Died: New York, December 27, 1966, age 65

Career record: Fights 131, Won 98, Lost 22, Drawn 8, No Decisions 3

OLYMPIAN TURNED WORLD CHAMPION: GENARO WAS THE BEST FLYWEIGHT OF HIS GENERATION

SEE ALSO ◆ FIDEL LA BARBA 181 ◆ PANCHO VILLA 324

JOEY GIARDELLO

FACT FILE

1930	Born Carmine Orlando Tilelli, Brooklyn, New York
1948	Professional debut
1960	Drew NBA middleweight title fight with Gene Fullmer
1963	Outpointed Dick Tiger for world middleweight title
1964	Successful defense against Rubin "Hurricane" Carter
1965	Lost title back to Tiger

Career record: Fights 133, Won 100, Lost 25, Drawn 7, No Contest 1

Joey Giardello had a blunt answer to those who said he was a Mob fighter: "So how come it took so long to get me a title shot?".

Giardello was Italian, and so a lot of people assumed a lot of things, but he was studiously avoided in the days when the notorious Mob "fixer," Frankie Carbo, was operational.

He was 33 years old by the time he outsmarted the great Nigerian, Dick Tiger, over 15 rounds for the middleweight title in Atlantic City in December 1963.

A Flatbush streetfighter born Carmine Tilelli, he took the name Giardello when he joined the US Airborne Division at 15. After his real identity and age were discovered, he dug sewers in Philadelphia. Boxing seemed to be a good alternative.

Self-taught, he learned how to survive, ducking, diving, and developing an array of light but accurate, unorthodox punches. He could foul with the best too, as on the night he was allowed to box Gene Fullmer for the NBA title in Bozeman, Montana, in 1960. They butted each other silly for a 15-round draw, each angrily accusing the other of starting the trouble.

Giardello fought from 1948 until 1967. In 1952 in New York he needed a court ruling to uphold a split decision over Billy Graham when the commission changed the referee's card. He was jailed in 1955 for assault, lost his New York license, but battled on until in 1963 he beat the aging Ray Robinson.

Then came the triumph over Tiger, after which he successfully defended with a smart points victory over Rubin Carter in 1964, before losing a return with Tiger in New York in October 1965. In retirement he sold insurance and worked for a chemicals firm.

PERSISTENCE PERSONNIFIED: GIARDELLO WAS 33 WHEN HE BECAME A CHAMP

SEE ALSO ◆ **GENE FULLMER** 123 ◆ **BILLY GRAHAM** 139 ◆ **DICK TIGER** 307

TOMMY GIBBONS

One of the most knowledgable and intelligent ring technicians of all time, Tommy Gibbons is famous for his part in the fight that bankrupted the little town of Shelby, Montana.

When a group of local businessmen hit on the idea of putting Shelby on the map by staging a championship fight, Jack Dempsey asked for $300,000—and was promised it.

Finding most of the money eventually broke the town banks, but the fight went ahead in front of a small paying crowd with almost as many gatecrashers. Gibbons, who fought the world heavyweight champion for nothing but pride, boxed beautifully to take Dempsey 15 hard rounds. The champion, who had brought along the referee Jack Dougherty, was given the decision because he attacked more, but he admitted later: "Gibbons was a perfectionist, a fine defensive fighter. I couldn't corner him."

Gibbons learned the business alongside his brother Mike, one of the best middleweights never to win a world title, and who was known as the St. Paul Phantom. They knew every move in the book, but had no luck, no breaks.

Tommy twice had the better of no-decision bouts with the great middleweight Harry Greb and in 1917 outboxed reigning light-heavyweight champion Battling Levinsky when the title was protected by the no-decision rule.

Gibbons retired in 1925, after 14 years of fighting and at the age of 34, following the only knockout defeat of his career against Gene Tunney, who beat him in the 12th round in New York. He sold insurance and four times was elected sheriff of his home town, St. Paul, and remained one of the pillars of the community until his death.

FACT FILE

1891 Born St. Paul, Minnesota

1911 Professional debut

1915 Outboxed Harry Greb in a no-decision bout

1918 Beat former middleweight champ George Chip three times

1923 Lost 15-round decision to Jack Dempsey for world heavyweight title

1925 Retired after losing to Gene Tunney

Died: St. Paul, November 19, 1960

Career record: Fights 106, Won 57, Lost 4, Drawn 1, No Decisions 43

GIBBONS (LEFT) FOUGHT JACK DEMPSEY FOR NOTHING ON THE DAY THEY BROKE THE BANKS OF SHELBY, MONTANA

SEE ALSO ◆ JACK DEMPSEY 88 ◆ HARRY GREB 141 ◆ GENE TUNNEY 315

WILFREDO GOMEZ

Wilfredo Gomez was a gloriously skilled boxer with a heavy punch who was not only the best super-bantamweight in history, but also a three-weight champ who competed in a total of 23 world title fights.

Gomez burst on to the scene as a precocious 17-year-old in the 1974 World Amateur Championships in Havana when he won the bantamweight gold medal.

He won the WBC title in May 1977, when still only 20, by recovering from a first-round knockdown to stop Dong-kyun Yum of South Korea in the 12th round in Hato Rey, Puerto Rico. His finest defense was a tremendous fifth-round stoppage of WBC bantamweight champion Carlos Zarate in Hato Rey in 1978.

After 13 successive stoppage wins in title defenses he made an ill-advised attempt to move up to featherweight and dethrone the great Mexican, Salvador Sanchez. He was stopped in the eighth round in Las Vegas in August 1981.

Back at super-bantamweight, he made four more defenses, including a 14th-round stoppage of another reigning bantamweight champion, Lupe Pintor of Mexico. In 1983, Gomez at last gave up the struggle to stay at 122 lb., and moved up to featherweight. In March 1984 he outpunched compatriot Juan LaPorte over 12 rounds to become WBC 126 lb. champion, but was chillingly knocked out by Azumah Nelson in 11 rounds in San Juan in December 1984.

His answer was to move up another division to super-featherweight where against the odds he outpointed Rocky Lockridge over 15 rounds to win his third world title. But when he surprisingly lost it to Alfredo Layne of Panama in May 1986, he suddenly looked very much older than his 29 years. He boxed only twice more and retired in 1989.

GOMEZ MADE THE SUPER-BANTAMWEIGHT DIVISION HIS OWN, WINNING THE WBC TITLE IN 1977 AND KEEPING IT UNTIL HE MOVED UP TO FEATHERWEIGHT SIX YEARS LATER

SEE ALSO ◆ LUPE PINTOR 271 ◆ SALVADOR SANCHEZ 293 ◆ CARLOS ZARATE 348

BETULIO GONZALEZ

Betulio Gonzalez was a busy little man who traded on strength, durability and powerful punching. There were more skillful flyweights in history, but none more commited, and none snarled more defiantly and slammed back so fiercely when under pressure.

His love of a face-to-face brawl took him through 20 years in the business, from 1968 to 1988, and brought him 16 world-title fights. He held different versions of the world flyweight title three times.

Gonzalez was from Maracaibo, the teeming fight center of northeastern Venezuela. After failing against Masao Ohba of Japan and Erbito Salavarria of the Philippines in world-title bids, he was successful when he beat Socrates Batoto easily in four rounds for the vacant WBC belt in June 1972. His reign ended within three months when he was stopped in ten rounds in Bangkok by Venice Borkorsor.

His second reign was a little longer. He scored a close decision over arch-rival Miguel Canto in Caracas in August 1973, but after two defenses was outscored in Tokyo by Shoji Oguma in October 1974. He protested angrily about the decision, a reaction that was repeated after Canto beat him on a split decision in Monterrey in 1975.

Gonzalez was 28, an advanced age for a flyweight, when he won the WBA title by outscoring Mexican Guty Espadas in Maracay in August 1978. He was champion for 14 months, twice holding off old enemy Oguma and knocking out Martin Vargas in 12 rounds, before losing to Panamanian southpaw Luis Ibarra on a unanimous 15-round decision in Maracay.

Gonzalez twice lost WBA title challenges, and fought sporadically in the 1980s until he lost to future world champ Rodolfo Blanco in 1988 and retired at the age of 38.

FACT FILE

1949 Born Maracaibo, Venezuela

1972 Won and lost WBC flyweight title

1973 Regained WBC flyweight title against Miguel Canto

1974 Lost WBC title for second time to Shoji Oguma

1978 Won WBA flyweight title against Guty Espadas

1979 Lost WBA championship to Luis Ibarra

1988 Retired, age 38

Career record: Fights 92, Won 76, Lost 12, Drawn 4

STRONG AND ENDURING:
GONZALEZ, WHO HELD
VERSIONS OF THE FLYWEIGHT
TITLE THREE TIMES IN THE
1970S, TRADES WITH
JAPANESE SOUTHPAW
SHOJI OGUMA

HUMBERTO GONZALEZ

"Chiquita" Gonzalez began as a typical Mexican slugger, hunting men down with crashing left hooks, but developed into a cunning, deceptively clever boxer who was a world light-flyweight champion three times. "Sometimes you win with your fists," he said. "But sometimes you need your brains too."

Immensely popular, he modeled himself on 1970s welterweight Pipino Cuevas. One of ten children of a Mexico City butcher—"La Chiquita" was the name of the family shop—Gonzalez won the WBC title when he outpointed Yul-woo Lee in South Korea in 1989.

Honoring the options on his contract, he returned to hand out a 12-round drubbing to Korean legend Jung-koo Chang.

When he seemed a serious rival to Julio Cesar Chavez as Mexico's most celebrated active fighter, he lost the WBC belt on a sixth-round knockout to Rolando Pascua of the Philippines. It took time to restore his credibility, even though he regained the title the following year from Pascua's successor, Melchor Cob Castro. He defied a 15,000 crowd in Seoul to stop 1988 Olympic gold medalist Kwang-sun Kim, and regained his popularity. Then in 1993 he was the brink of a magnificent triumph against Michael Carbajal—the American had been down twice—when he was knocked out in the seventh.

They fought again in February 1994, and this time he abandoned his slugging style, counterpunching smartly and switching stance to outpoint Carbajal before a record crowd of 10,333 at the Great Western Forum in Los Angeles. In a "decider" in Mexico, Gonzalez won again, but responded to his wife's pleas and retired after a savage seventh-round defeat by Thailand's Saman Sorjatorung in 1995.

**"Chiquita" Gonzalez
storms into Michael
Carbajal. After being
knocked out in their first
fight, he won the next two**

SEE ALSO ◆ Michael Carbajal 55 ◆ Julio Cesar Chavez 67 ◆ Pipino Cuevas 81

BILLY GRAHAM

For a boy who was refused permission to box in the Golden Gloves because of a heart murmur, Billy Graham performed a medical miracle by surviving the roughhouse of the professional business for 14 years.

Graham, a fast, talented boxer with an iron chin, was also desperately unlucky not to win the world welterweight crown in 1951. Those who saw it say he decisively outscored Kid Gavilan in Madison Square Garden, but the split vote of the judges was for the Cuban-born champion.

The story ran that Graham's management refused to make pre-fight promises to underworld figure Frankie Carbo, who "ensured" the New Yorker was not awarded the title.

Because of the outrage at the time, Graham was given a rematch, but in Havana, Gavilan's territory. The decision was unanimous and Billy was never the same fighter again.

A product of New York's tough East Side, he turned professional at 18 and fought his way up through the smoky clubs of Elizabeth, Newark, White Plains, and Brooklyn. He was unbeaten in his first 58 fights before he was outscored by Tony Pellone in August 1946. After that he won most, but lost a decision here and there—one to Welshman Eddie Thomas in London, another to future lightweight champ Paddy DeMarco.

He won and lost in 10-rounders against Gavilan in 1950, and also battled away through hard fights with top-class fighters like Joey Giardello, Carmen Basilio, and Rocky Castellani. Against Basilio, one of the toughest welterweights in history, he won the first fight in 1952, lost the next and drew the third. He retired following successive points defeats by the popular Chico Vejar in 1955.

FACT FILE

1922 Born New York City
1941 Professional debut
1951 Lost disputed decision to world welterweight champ Kid Gavilan
1952 Outpointed in rematch to Gavilan in Cuba
Died: New York City, January 22, 1992, age 69
Career record: Fights 126, Won 102, Lost 15, Drawn 9

GRAHAM (RIGHT) THROWS A RIGHT HAND AGAINST KID GAVILAN IN 1951. HE WAS DESPERATELY UNLUCKY TO LOSE A SPLIT VOTE

SEE ALSO ◆ CARMEN BASILIO 28 ◆ KID GAVILAN 132 ◆ JOEY GIARDELLO 134

ROCKY GRAZIANO

FACT FILE

1922 Born Thomas Rocco Barbella, New York City

1942 Professional debut

1946 Lost savage battle with world middleweight champ Tony Zale

1947 Stopped Zale in six-round war in Chicago

1948 Lost decider to Zale in three rounds

1952 Beaten by Ray Robinson in last world-title bid

Died: New York City, May 22, 1990, age 67

Career record: Fights 83, Won 67, Lost 10, Drawn 6

If boxing ever saved anybody, it was Thomas Rocco Barbella. He was a juvenile delinquent: "We stole anything that began with A—A piece of fruit, A bicycle, A watch, Anything that wasn't nailed down." He was considered too unruly for the US Army, which threw him out after he did a year in jail for hitting an officer.

But when he became Rocky Graziano, borrowing the name of his sister's boyfriend when he walked into Stillman's Gym in New York, he found himself. Graziano wasn't skillful, but he had a heart as big as a ring and a punch to match.

His three world middleweight title scraps with Tony Zale from 1946 to 1948 were blood-curdling epics. Zale won the first in six rounds, but Graziano won the second, again in six rounds and took the ring microphone to holler: "Hey, ma, your bad boy done good!"

His reign didn't last. Banned for a year by the New York Commission for not reporting a bribe attempt, he lost to Zale in three rounds in Newark, New Jersey, in June 1948.

He was unbeaten in his next 21 fights and was given a shot at Ray Robinson for his old title in April 1952. He dropped Robinson in the third with a right, thrown like a stone out of a sling. Robinson got up and knocked him out.

He retired in September 1952 after a $50,000 payday against Chuck Davey and earned well in a TV slot alongside comedienne Martha Raye, moving into acting in commercials and movies. He also owned a pizza house and was much in demand on the after-dinner circuit. Paul Newman starred in the film of his book *Somebody Up There Likes Me.*

GRAZIANO SLAMS HIS RIGHT HAND INTO CHARLEY FUSARI'S FACE AT NEW YORK POLO GROUNDS IN 1949. FUSARI WAS AHEAD ON POINTS WHEN GRAZIANO CUT LOOSE AND STOPPED HIM IN ROUND TEN

SEE ALSO ◆ RAY ROBINSON 278 ◆ TONY ZALE 344

HARRY GREB

Harry Greb said famously: "Prize fighting ain't the noblest of arts, and I ain't its noblest artist."

Greb was magnificent. He had a flat nose, graveyard eyes, a great chin, and fists that never stopped working. He fought anybody, big or small, wherever and whenever.

Greb held nothing back, in or out of the ring. Apart from fighting, women were his greatest pleasure—and he was particularly delighted if he could entertain a couple in his dressing room before a fight. From 1921 he was blind in one eye—courtesy of an effective piece of gouging by Kid Norfolk. Rather than complain, Greb admired Norfolk's handiwork.

When he outpointed Gene Tunney for the American light-heavyweight title in 1922, he broke Tunney's nose and split open a four-inch gash over his eye. Tunney went to bed for a week, but outboxed him four times after that.

When Greb won the world middleweight title against south-paw Johnny Wilson in New York in August 1923, he mauled the champion for 15 long, very painful rounds.

His greatest night was when he outpointed Mickey Walker in a title defense before 60,000 people at New York Polo Grounds in July 1925. He hated referees and as well as battering Walker, twice floored the ref "by mistake" in clinches.

Eventually, with the sight in his good eye failing, he was twice beaten by Tiger Flowers. He retired, but when he underwent surgery to his nose following a car smash, he didn't awake from the anesthetic. Heart failure, said doctors. Never, said anybody who had ever seen him in a ring.

FACT FILE

1894 Born Pittsburgh, Pennsylvania

1913 Professional debut

1922 Beat Gene Tunney to win American light-heavyweight title

1923 Won world middleweight title against Johnny Wilson

1925 Beat Mickey Walker in classic battle

1926 Lost world title to Tiger Flowers

Died: Atlantic City, New Jersey, October 22, 1926, age 32

Career record: Fights 299, Won 264, Lost 23, Drawn 12

PERHAPS THE GREATEST OF THEM ALL: GREB AT THE HEIGHT OF HIS POWERS EVEN BEAT GENE TUNNEY

SEE ALSO ♦ TIGER FLOWERS 115 ♦ GENE TUNNEY 315 ♦ MICKEY WALKER 330 ♦ JOHNNY WILSON 337

THE GREAT FIGHTS

HARRY GREB
V.
MICKEY WALKER

POLO GROUNDS, NEW YORK CITY.
JULY 2, 1925.

Harry Greb and Mickey Walker were two of the most notorious hell-raisers in boxing history. Therefore, it was natural that the only time they fought each other in a ring, they put on a 15-round classic.

And some say the street brawl they staged later the same night was even better!

By 1925 Greb had been world middleweight champion for two years but had been fighting for a dozen. After more than 250 fights, he was a master of his craft. But that was emphatically not the traditionally "noble art." Walker was the young, brash welterweight champion, stepping up a division, unbeaten in his last 28 fights since he fouled Wildcat Nelson badly enough to be disqualified in Long Branch City in 1922.

Fist fights were being broken up by the police even as the announcements were made. Greb was horribly weight-drained and took a terrible beating in the early rounds. By the end of the fifth some even called for the massacre to be stopped, but he was still on his feet, still punching back.

In the sixth Greb turned the fight around with a magnificent display of counterpunching and then driving, relentless aggression. Walker's ear was torn, an eye swollen, and Greb was enjoying himself. Referee Eddie Purdy constantly nagged at him—and mysteriously found himself on the floor twice!

Walker rallied and they battered away down the stretch to the final bell. Greb was rocked twice in round 14, but then thumbed Walker in the eye. "You Dutch rat!" screamed the welterweight above the din, but he was knocked all over the ring in the 15th. Blood poured from Walker's cut mouth, and oozed from his ear. One eye was shut. He was out on his feet. Greb was unmarked... and still middleweight champion of the world.

Legend has it they met again later at a bar, had several drinks, fell out and had another war outside the famous Silver Slipper nightclub!

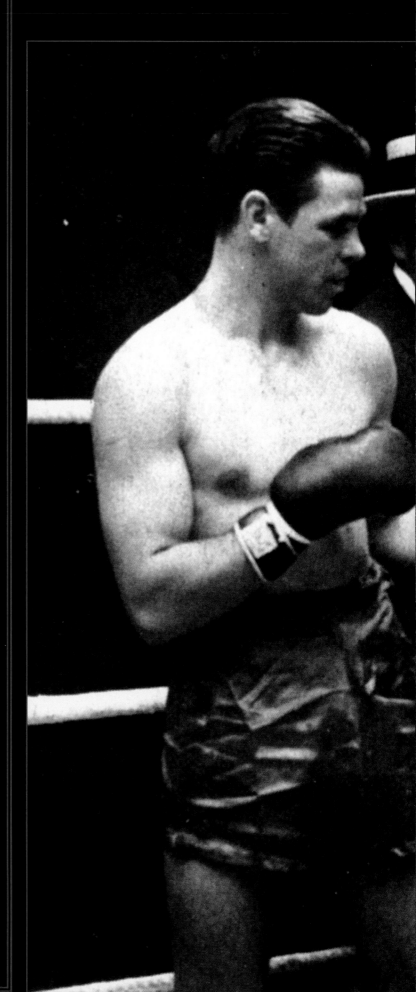

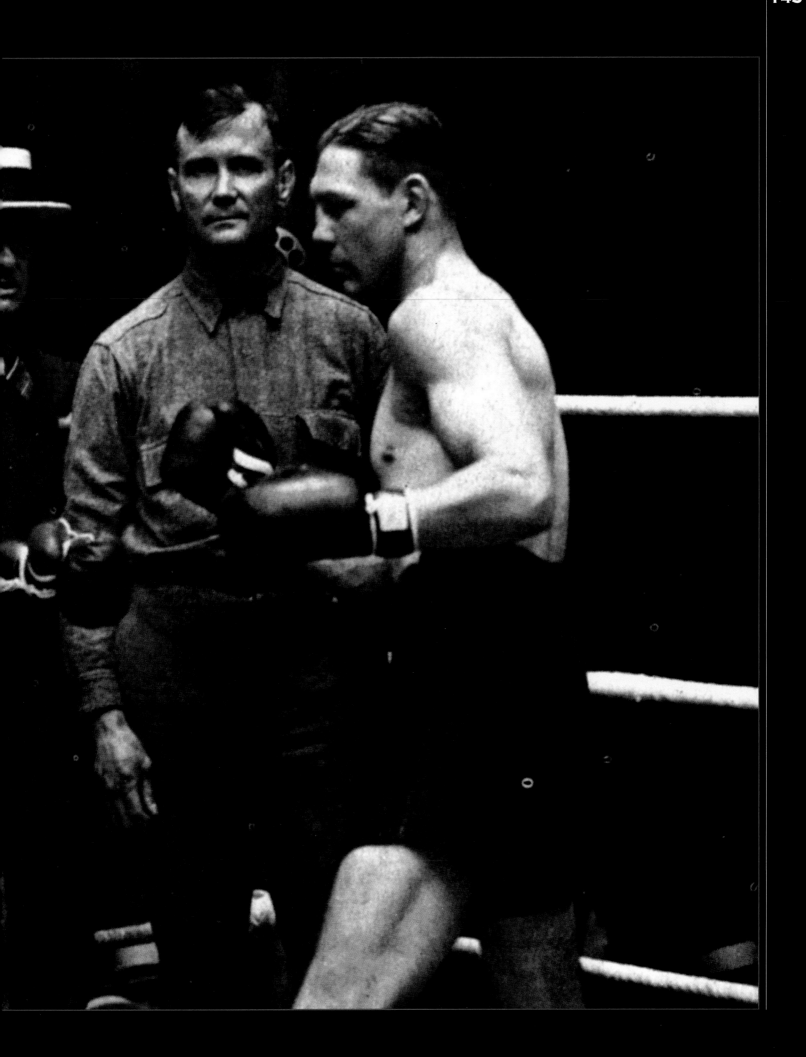

EMILE GRIFFITH

FACT FILE

1938 Born St. Thomas, Virgin Islands

1961 Won and lost against Benny Paret in world welterweight title fights

1962 Regain title in tragic fight with Paret

1963 Lost and regaiined welterweight crown against Luis Rodriguez

1966 Won world middleweight title by beating Dick Tiger

1967 Lost and regained title against Nino Benvenuti

Career record: Fights 112, Won 85, Lost 24, Drawn 2, No Contest 1

Emile Griffith's habit of doing just enough to win fights, even against boxers of the highest class, stemmed from the terrible night when his punches killed Benny Paret.

Paret taunted him because he worked designing hats for a New York milliner, and called him a homosexual, shortly before their third fight at Madison Square Garden on March 24, 1962. After one win each, they disliked each other anyway—and this heightened Griffith's anger.

In the 12th round of the fight he knocked Paret into a corner and smashed furiously at his head as the stricken Cuban eased almost gently down the ropes to the floor, his consciousness ebbing away. He died ten days later of brain injuries.

Shocked to his core by this, Griffith never lost control again, spending the next 15 years dealing with Paret's ghost, in the process almost teasing his opponents, and moving up the gears only when necessary, winning while inflicting as little pain as possible. He held the welterweight title three times and was also twice world middleweight champion, but by the late 1970s was a quality circuit opponent, losing to men who would barely have hit him in his prime. It was as if he still struggled to punish himself for Benny Paret's death.

Yet in his great days he won two out of three welterweight title fights with Luis Rodriguez of Cuba, won one out of three with Nino Benvenuti, outboxed Dick Tiger (to become middleweight champion in 1966) and beat top fighters like Dave Charnley, Bennie Briscoe, Joey Archer, Ralph Dupas, and Denny Moyer. When he retired he went on to become a highly respected trainer.

GRIFFITH IN LONDON IN 1964 WHEN HE BEAT BRIAN CURVIS AND ENDED THE CAREER OF DAVE CHARNLEY

SEE ALSO ◆ NINO BENVENUTI 34 ◆ BENNIE BRISCOE 40 ◆ DAVE CHARNLEY 66 ◆ LUIS RODRIGUEZ 279 ◆ DICK TIGER 307

YOUNG GRIFFO

Young Griffo was a genius, who rarely trained yet was virtually impossible to hit. He took very little seriously, especially his ability to box, which he saw as a delightful vehicle by which he might purloin his next drink.

Griffo was equally happy, whether he was making life a misery for a world champion inside a ring, or standing on a handkerchief in the middle of a bar betting customers they couldn't hit him on the head. He saw little difference between the activities, except that one paid better than the other.

His grasp of mathematics was shaky. Before he fought Kid Lavigne in October 1895, Griffo went to collect his $1,500 guarantee. But when the paymaster had counted out $500 the little Australian yelled: "Enough, sir, enough. What do you think I am, a bloomin' 'orse?" He didn't bother returning for the rest.

Another time when a promoter offered him twelve hundred for a fight, he declared he never fought for less than a thousand. They shook on it and Griffo boasted about the hard bargain he had struck.

Born on a ship bound for Sydney from England, Griffo was a bare-knuckler before moving into the gloved sport. He won the world featherweight title on September 2, 1890, stopping Torpedo Billy Murphy of New Zealand in 15 rounds in Sydney. Typically, he never pressed his claim.

In 1893 he sailed to California and fought the greatest little men of his time, including world champions George Dixon, Joe Gans, and Jack McAuliffe. But although he grossed around $100,000 from boxing, rather than spending money on a luxurious lifestyle, he lived his last 20 years in a basement room in New York. He died of a heart attack.

FACT FILE

1871	Born Albert Griffiths, "between England and Australia"
1889	Won Australian featherweight title
1890	Beat Torpedo Billy Murphy to claim world title
1893	Arrived in the United States
1911	Last fight, age 42
Died:	New York City, December 7, 1927, age 56

Career record: Fights 171, Won 65, Lost 12, Drawn 44, No Decisions 49, No Contest 1

FLAWED GENIUS: GRIFFO WAS A RING MARVEL WHO REFUSED TO TAKE THE BUSINESS SERIOUSLY

SEE ALSO ◆ JOE GANS 129 ◆ JACK MCAULIFFE 236

YOKO GUSHIKEN

FACT FILE

1955 Born Okinawa, Japan
1974 Professional debut
1976 Won WBA light-flyweight title against Juan Guzman
1981 Lost WBA light-flyweight title in 14th defense
Career record: Fights 24, Won 23, Lost 1

An exciting southpaw pressure fighter, Yoko Gushiken was that rarest of individuals—a man who knew to get out of boxing at the right time.

He could box behind an accurate right jab, but loved nothing better than wading forward and letting his punches go in bursts. He was known as "Kanmuriwashi," which translates as "Fierce Eagle" and he was one of the most popular Japanese fighters in history, repeatedly drawing sellout crowds.

From the island of Okinawa, Gushiken was an All-Japan High School champion who turned professional at 18. His progress was meteoric: in only his ninth paid bout he won the World Boxing Association light-flyweight crown with a seventh-round knockout of defending champion Juan Guzman of the Dominican Republic. From that night on October 10, 1976, Gushiken built up a marvelous record.

In four and a half years he made 13 successful title defenses, eight inside the distance. He twice beat former champion Jaime Rios of Panama, the first time on a split decision and then in the rematch on a 13th-round stoppage.

Yoko Gushiken was a particular scourge of world-class Panamanians. Apart from Rios, he also stopped Alfonso Lopez, who then went on to hold the WBA flyweight title, and he outpointed Rafael Pedroza, later a super-flyweight champion.

But when he struggled to outpoint Mexican Pedro Flores in Kanazawa in October 1980, there was a suspicion that he was fading. And when Flores stopped him in the 12th round of a rematch in Gushikawa, Okinawa, on March 8, 1981, it was described in Japan as "like the shattering of a gigantic mirror to the people." He announced his retirement five months later and never boxed again.

THE "FIERCE EAGLE" OF JAPAN: GUSHIKEN (RIGHT) ON HIS WAY TO VICTORY OVER YONG-HYUN KIM OF KOREA

MARVIN HAGLER

Marvin Hagler was driven by a bitter desire to prove himself. For years this brooding, sensitive man preached a chilling mantra of bad intent: "Destruct and Destroy."

After being persistently avoided and then held to a controversial draw in his first world title bid against Vito Antuofermo, Hagler arrived on a violent night at Wembley Arena in London in 1980. He cut up Britain's Alan Minter in three rounds to become champion, but his moment of triumph was buried beneath a cascade of bottles and general debris as the English crowd rioted.

Hagler was hurried away under police escort, but kept the belt for the next six and a half years. "The man was an artist," recalled one challenger, Tony Sibson. "I didn't know where

the next punch was coming from."

He was cold and ruthless, and won as the situation demanded. He outboxed a keyed-up Roberto Duran without taking undue risk, and butchered Thomas Hearns in a breathtaking battle in Las Vegas on April 15, 1985. When Hagler suffered an ugly gash over his eyes, it looked as if the fight must be stopped. Referee Richard Steele asked if he could see. Hagler muttered: "I ain't missing him, am I?" and proceeded to finish the fight in round three.

His career ended when he lost a fiercely disputed decision to Ray Leonard in Las Vegas in April 1987. Hagler brooded angrily on his first defeat in 11 years. His stable home life collapsed and he moved alone to Milan, where he built a new career in the film industry.

FACT FILE

1954	Born Newark, New Jersey
1973	Won US National AAU championship
1980	Stopped Alan Minter to win the world middleweight title
1987	Lost the title on disputed decision to Ray Leonard

Career record: Fights 67, Won 62, Lost 3, Drawn 2

MARVIN HAGLER POSES FOR THE CAMERA WHILE TRAINING

SEE ALSO ◆ ROBERTO DURAN 99 ◆ THOMAS HEARNS 153 ◆ RAY LEONARD 187

THE GREAT FIGHTS

MARVIN HAGLER
V.
THOMAS HEARNS

CAESARS PALACE, LAS VEGAS.
APRIL 15, 1985.

The middleweight collision between Marvelous Marvin Hagler and Thomas Hearns was the greatest fight of the decade.

They split more than $16 million in what at the time was the richest non-heavyweight fight in history, and the outdoor stadium at Caesars Palace was crammed to capacity.

Hagler knew victory would put him among the division's great fighters, and Ray Robinson, ailing with the first stages of Alzheimer's Disease, was ringside as if ready to offer him his membership card.

But Hearns had grown from the willowy welterweight who lost to Ray Leonard in this same ring in September 1981 into a light-middleweight good enough to flatten Roberto Duran in two rounds, and now into a middleweight scaling just ¼ lb. inside the 160 lb. limit.

There were plenty who believed Hearns's long-range boxing ability and tremendous power would bring him victory against Hagler's all-round southpaw skills.

But what none could expect was the savage intensity of the first round. Hagler was staggered and shaken, then Hearns rocked and reeled. The round, never mind the fight, swayed one way and then the other.

Just as Hearns seemed badly hurt, Hagler suffered a horrible vertical cut on the forehead, and another beneath his right eye. It seemed he couldn't possibly last. After round two, referee Richard Steele asked Hagler: "Can you see?" Hagler's grunted reply was magnificently precise. "I ain't missin' him, am I?"

Hearns knew he only had to stand up to win, and backed off in round three. The doctor inspected Hagler's injuries, and then Hagler found a right hook that took the life out of Hearns's legs. He staggered out of control like a skidding car, and Hagler bounced three more clubbing hooks off his head to send him down.

Hearns got up, but stared out of apparently sightless eyes as referee Steele waved it off.

Ray Robinson nodded in quiet appreciation of the newest member of the middleweight elite.

NASEEM HAMED

FACT FILE

1974	Born Sheffield, England
1992	Professional debut, age 18
1994	Won European bantamweight title
1995	Won WBO featherweight title against Steve Robinson
1997	Won IBF title

Career record: Fights 24, Won 24

HAMED CAME THROUGH ROUGH PATCHES TO STOP MANUEL MEDINA IN DUBLIN

One of boxing's great showmen, "Prince" Naseem Hamed proclaimed his extraordinary talent God given and repeatedly informed his mass audiences that they were witnessing the arrival of a legend.

A star of a generation brought up on laser technology and pounding musical extravaganzas, Hamed used all the available resources to conjure up a compelling stage presence. But beyond the gimmickry, he proved he could fight when he blasted apart World Boxing Organization featherweight champion Steve Robinson in eight one-sided rounds on a rain-soaked night in Cardiff in September 1995.

Hamed was only 21, but displayed astonishing verve and confidence to outclass a solid, steady champion who had held his belt for two and a half years.

Hamed was a brilliant schoolboy boxer, but turned professional at 18 because his extrovert behavior and darting, unorthodox style did not sit well with the staid, blazered amateur hierarchy. At 20, he comprehensively outboxed respected European bantamweight champion Vincenzo Belcastro over 12 rounds and won the WBC's International super-bantamweight title by stopping Freddy Cruz from the Dominican Republic in six. Cruz, asked by a puzzled cornerman why he wasn't punching back, said miserably: "I don't know where he is!"

As his management team tried to obtain a unification fight for Hamed, he showed one or two cracks in his make-up. He was floored by Daniel Alicea but got up to knock out the Puerto Rican in round two, and then was extended into the 11th by former WBC and IBF champ Manuel Medina. Nevertheless, by the end of 1996, the remarkably heavy punching Hamed had completed four WBO title defenses and in February 1997 he knocked out IBF Champion Tom Johnson in eight rounds.

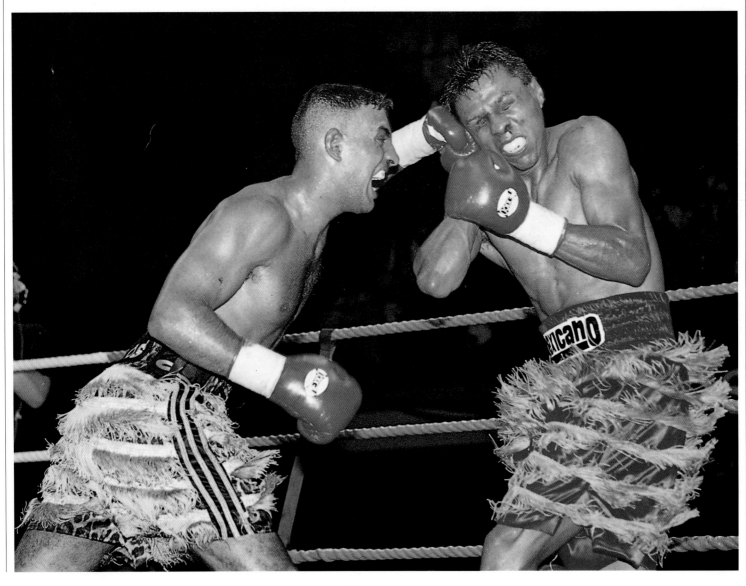

FIGHTING HARADA

By popular acclaim the greatest boxer ever produced in Japan, Masahiko "Fighting" Harada was a rough, aggressive fighting machine who traded on durability and pressure.

He was only 19 when he won the world flyweight championship by knocking out the respected Thai, Pone Kingpetch, in 11 rounds before an ecstatic capacity crowd of 10,000 at the Kokugikan Arena in Tokyo in October 1962. A rematch clause was written into the contract, and in the heat and humidity of Bangkok in January 1963, Harada lost a majority 15-round decision.

He grew into a bantamweight and became the first Japanese fighter to win a title in two divisions when he outhustled the brilliant, previously unbeaten Brazilian Eder Jofre for a 15-round decision in Nagoya in May 1965. In his first defense he drew a capacity 12,000 crowd to Budokan Hall in Tokyo, as he unanimously outpointed the courageous Liverpudlian Alan Rudkin.

Harada earned $30,000 for that battle, and picked up other lucrative paydays by defeating Jofre again, the Mexican Joe Medel, and Bernardo Caraballo of Colombia. The crowds, ticket prices, promotional profits and the purses steadily rose: Harada's reign sparked a boxing boom in Japan.

Weight-making became a nightmare for Fighting Harada. By 1967 he was training down from 147 lb. to fight at bantamweight, and in February 1968 he lost his title to the clever Australian Lionel Rose.

Inevitably, he moved up to featherweight and was unlucky to lose a 15-round decision to Johnny Famechon in a WBC title fight in Sydney, when he floored the Australian three times. They lured Famechon to Japan for the rematch, but this time Harada was stopped in 14 rounds and retired, still only 26.

FACT FILE

1943	Born Masahiko Harada, Tokyo, Japan
1962	Won world flyweight title against Pone Kingpetch
1963	Lost return with Kingpetch in Bangkok
1965	Won world bantamweight title against Eder Jofre
1968	Lost bantamweight title to Lionel Rose
1970	Retired after losing to featherweight champ Johnny Famechon

Career record: Fights 62, Won 55, Lost 7

FIGHTING HARADA—A HUMAN THRESHING MACHINE

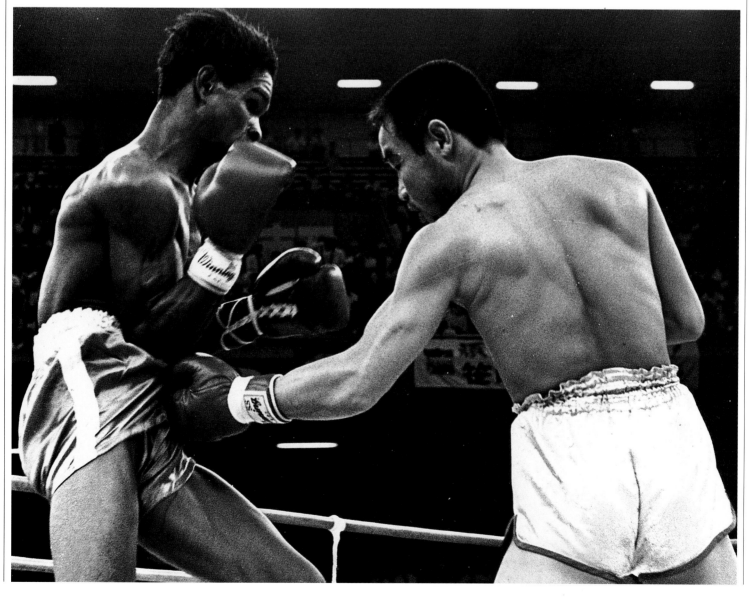

LEN HARVEY

Len Harvey, one of the most knowledgable and sportsmanlike stand-up stylists of the old British school, was the dominant figure in British boxing in the 1930s.

A Cornishman, he was only 12 when he first boxed for pay in Plymouth. By 1924 he was in London, and two years later he fought a draw with British welterweight champion Harry Mason. He was 18.

Harvey won the British middleweight title by knocking out Alex Ireland in seven rounds in 1929, won a Lonsdale Belt outright, and in 1932 lost a world championship fight with the brawling Frenchman Marcel Thil.

The following year he also lost his middleweight crown to Jock McAvoy, but made up for it by taking both the light-heavyweight and heavyweight belts, the latter with a 15-round decision over Jack Petersen. Once billed as Britain's "Wonder Boxer," he boxed beautifully to outpoint Larry Gains in a close one for the Empire title, but then was stopped in a rematch with Petersen.

His second world title bid, against the light-heavyweight champion John Henry Lewis at the Empire Pool, Wembley, in 1936 brought another points defeat, which was booed loudly by Harvey's loyal fans, but was reportedly fair.

Harvey continued to box, however, beating McAvoy twice and Gains once, as well as light-heavyweight Eddie Phillips, eventually claiming the world 175 lb. title before life was interrupted by World War II. He had not boxed for three years when he was knocked out in his final contest by Freddie Mills in 1942. He and his wife kept several London pubs, but Len's health was never the same after the death of their teenage son in 1947.

HARVEY KEEPS JOCK MCAVOY AT BAY WITH HIS MASTERFUL LEFT LEAD. THE CORNISHMAN WAS BRITAIN'S "WONDER BOXER" OF THE 1930S.

SEE ALSO ◆ LARRY GAINS 126 ◆ JOHN HENRY LEWIS 191 ◆ FREDDIE MILLS 217 ◆ JOCK MCAVOY 237 ◆ MARCEL THIL 306

THOMAS HEARNS

There was never a more spectacular boxing sight than The Motor City Cobra in full flow.

Thomas Hearns's right hand, thrown long and straight as an arrow but with the force of a cannon ball, didn't land or connect: It detonated. His clinical second-round dismissal of heavy-handed Pipino Cuevas in 1980, when he won his first world title at the age of 21, was a prime example of this.

Take, too, the phenomenal knockout of the great Roberto Duran, who was left face-down in what the old-timers used to call "blissful repose" after only four minutes, seven seconds at Caesars Palace, Las Vegas in 1984.

Part of Hearns's dramatic attraction was also an apparent vulnerability. So tall, so lean, he looked almost fragile, especially in his spindly, welterweight youth. Yet he was stopped only three times: by Marvin Hagler, Ray Leonard, and Iran Barkley.

The rare occasions when he failed were spectacular, too, although mostly the memory of Hearns is of a cold-eyed winner.

His achievements were remarkable, beginning with the triumph over Cuevas in 1980. Then he won the WBC light-middleweight title by outpointing Wilfred Benitez in 1982; the WBC light-heavyweight title with a six-knockdown, tenth-round stoppage of Dennis Andries, and the WBC middleweight belt by demolishing Juan Roldan in four rounds in 1987. The WBO super-middleweight title followed in 1988. Through one of the most exciting decades in boxing history, he was a major star.

Hearns continued to box sporadically, and ended an 18-month layoff with a win in December 1996.

FACT FILE

1958 Born Memphis, Tennessee

1980 Won WBA welterweight title against Pipino Cuevas

1981 Lost to Ray Leonard

1982 Won WBC light-middleweight title against Wilfred Benitez

1984 Knocked out Roberto Duran in two rounds

1985 Lost to Marvin Hagler

1987 Won WBC light-heavyweight and middleweight titles

1988 Won WBO super-middleweight title

1989 Drew rematch with Ray Leonard

1991 Won WBA light-heavyweight title against Virgil Hill

Career record: Fights 61, Won 56, Lost 4, Drawn 1

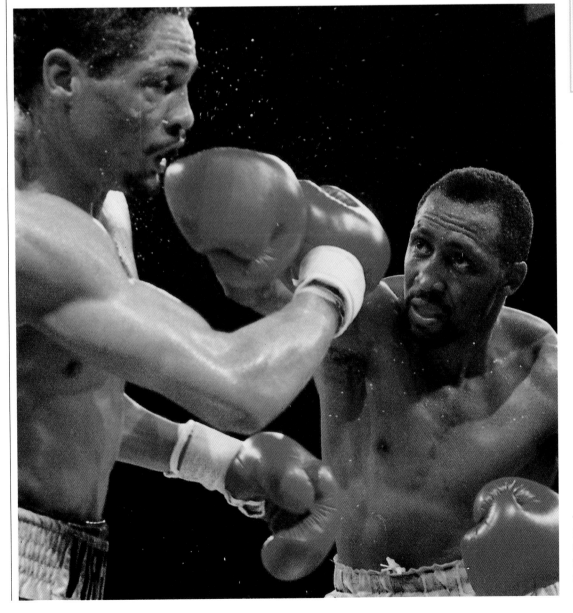

THE HIT MAN AT WORK: HEARNS CRASHES HOME A RIGHT HAND AGAINST VIRGIL HILL IN A WBA LIGHT-HEAVYWEIGHT TITLE FIGHT IN 1991

SEE ALSO ◆ WILFRED BENITEZ 32 ◆ PIPINO CUEVAS 80 ◆ ROBERTO DURAN 99 ◆ MARVIN HAGLER 147 ◆ VIRGIL HILL 157 ◆ RAY LEONARD 187

THE GREAT FIGHTS

RAY LEONARD

V.

THOMAS HEARNS

CAESARS PALACE, LAS VEGAS. SEPTEMBER 16, 1981.

This was the night when Ray Leonard proved how great he was. The quality of his mental dominance of Roberto Duran in their rematch was dimmed by the astonishing nature of the Panamanian's walkout. Duran lost, as much as, perhaps more than, Leonard won.

But when Leonard fought Thomas Hearns, the lean, almost gangling WBA welterweight champion, for the undisputed title in front of a crowd of 23,615 in Caesars Palace outdoor arena, he showed the quality of his character as well as the abundance of his artistry.

Leonard darted in and out, eyes staring, as Hearns, winner of all 32 of his fights, held the center of the ring, snaking out long, snappy, almost casual punches that raised a bump beneath Ray's left eye, which would worsen as the fight wore on.

It took until the sixth for Leonard to take decisive command, making all that had gone before seem irrelevant. Hearns took a pounding for two rounds until Leonard, pacing himself, gave up on the head in round eight and worked the body.

Amazingly, round nine saw the Hit Man revert to his jab, move, counter, amateur style—suddenly Leonard couldn't hit him! The boxer outboxed. The thinker out-thought.

Hearns was in front on points, and Angelo Dundee told Leonard succinctly: "You're blowin' it, kid."

Then in round 13, Leonard dug into the depths of his courage and persistence to find another level. Hearns, still shaking off the fog of the middle rounds, was badly hurt, reeled around the ring, went down through the ropes for what was ruled a slip by Davey Pearl, then down for an official knockdown.

He made it to round 14, still ahead, but was on the ropes, legs stiff and senses flapping like an unhinged gate, when Pearl waved it over as Leonard teed off.

It was a great fight, which had swayed one way and then the other, and an unforgettable moment of boxing history for all those who saw it.

PETE HERMAN

Pete Herman was a precise boxer especially clever at infighting, who held the world bantamweight title twice between 1917 and 1921.

Failing sight forced his early retirement, and he went blind, almost certainly as a result of damage suffered during his 144-fight, ten-year career.

A former shoeshine boy who was spotted in a street fight by a local promoter, Herman turned professional at 16 in his native New Orleans. He learned the hard way, losing several decisions early on, but in February 1916 Herman held the Danish-born world bantamweight champion Kid Williams to a 20-round draw for the title in New Orleans. A rematch was arranged for January 1917, and Herman scored a convincing points win.

His career was interrupted when he volunteered to serve in the US Navy in World War I. Although he was already almost blind in one eye he passed the medical.

Medical supervision of any sport, let alone boxing, was negligible at the time. Herman boxed 24 times in 1919 and lost his title to Joe Lynch in New York in December 1920. He had already signed to fight Welshman Jimmy Wilde in London the following month, but there was uproar when it was discovered that he was no longer world champion. He stopped Wilde in 17 rounds.

He ignored medical advice and boxed on, regaining the title from Lynch and then losing it to veteran Johnny Buff before the sight in his other eye began to fail. He retired in 1923 and ran a cafe in New Orleans.

HERMAN (LEFT) SHAKES HANDS WITH JOHNNY BUFF BEFORE THEIR 1921 WORLD TITLE FIGHT

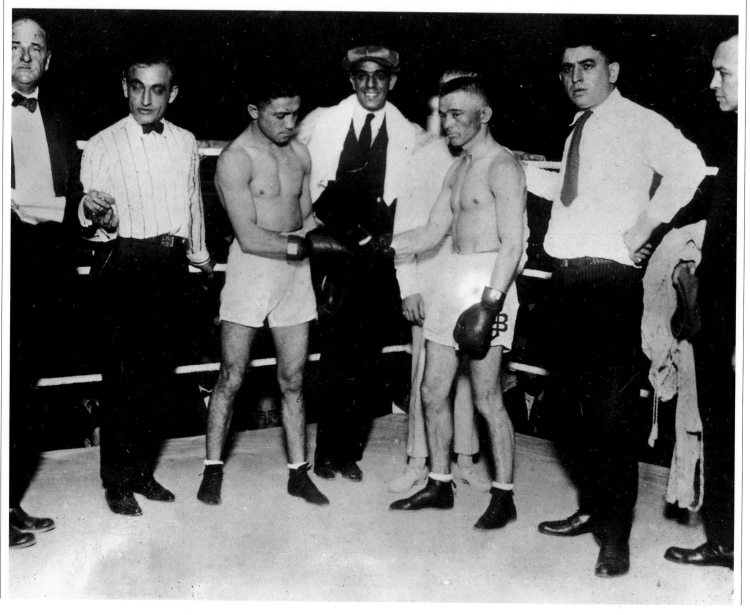

SEE ALSO ♦ JIMMY WILDE 335

VIRGIL HILL

Unfashionable but disciplined and determined, Virgil Hill was undervalued in his own land.

Hill attracted a fanatical following in his home base of North Dakota. The son of a plumber, he learned to box in a home-made gym after watching Muhammad Ali on television, and was an extremely successful amateur. Although mostly self-taught, he won 250 of 261 bouts, culminating in a silver medal in the Los Angeles Olympics in 1984.

When he challenged classy Trinidadian Leslie Stewart for the WBA light-heavyweight crown in September 1987, Hill was a 5-1 outsider, but won in four rounds.

Without ever commanding worldwide stardom, he built up tremendous support at home and turned back ten challenges, including former IBF champ Bobby Czyz. Then he gave a feeble performance in losing a decision to Thomas Hearns, which cost him the WBA belt, in Las Vegas in June 1991.

Serious personal problems had put him off the rails and in spite of having earned six-figure purses, he financed a "fresh start" move to Australia with a $20,000 loan from a Bismarck promoter, which he subsequently repaid from his purses.

He went to Australia, vowing to do nothing but eat, sleep, and breathe boxing, but returned after only one fight. He regained the WBA belt by winning a vacant title fight against his old Olympic teammate Frank Tate in September 1992, and went on to dominate the WBA light-heavyweight scene for a further four years, adding the IBF belt in 1996.

FACT FILE

1964	Born Clinton, Missouri
1984	Olympic Games middleweight silver medal
1987	Won WBA light-heavyweight title against Leslie Stewart
1991	Lost title in 11th defense to Thomas Hearns
1992	Regained WBA title by outpointing Frank Tate
1996	Won IBF belt from Henry Maske

Career record: Fights 44, Won 43, Lost 1

VIRGIL HILL LOOKING STRONG AGAINST DRAKE THADZI

SEE ALSO ◆ THOMAS HEARNS 153

LARRY HOLMES

FACT FILE

1949 Born Cuthbert, Georgia

1973 Professional debut

1978 Outpointed Ken Norton for WBC heavyweight title

1984 Left the WBC to continue as IBF champion

1985 Lost unbeaten record—and world title—to Michael Spinks

1988 Lost comeback fight to Mike Tyson

1992 Outpointed by Evander Holyfield

1995 Lost close decision to Oliver McCall in final world title bid

Career record: Fights 70, Won 65, Lost 5

Larry Holmes was one of the most highly skilled heavyweights in history, but his public image and marketability suffered from the fact that he was Muhammad Ali's heir.

A former truck driver, he cut his teeth as Ali's sparring partner in the early 1970s, and was consistently unapologetic about his motive for fighting: Money.

He invested heavily in property in his hometown of Easton, Pennsylvania, lost some in the financial depression of the early 1990s, but was still a substantially wealthy man in middle age.

Holmes won the WBC title with an epic 15-round points win over Ken Norton in June 1978, and went on to prove himself the best heavyweight of the generation.

His saddest night was when he systematically but halfheartedly outpunched a distressingly feeble Muhammad Ali in 1980. Two years later, however, he scored one of his most significant wins, beating heavily fancied Gerry Cooney in 13 rounds.

He lost his unbeaten record in his 49th fight on a controversial points decision to Michael Spinks. He stormed away from the game when Spinks was given another tight verdict in a return, but came back for the money against a peak Mike Tyson in 1988. Without a fight for almost two years, he was easily stopped in four rounds.

He came back in 1991 and fought his way to title fights against Evander Holyfield and Oliver McCall, but lost both on points. In 1996 he retired, then made a comeback when he accepted a final fight with Danish hope Brian Nielsen. "It's a chance to feather my nest a little more," he explained. He really was a businessman to the last.

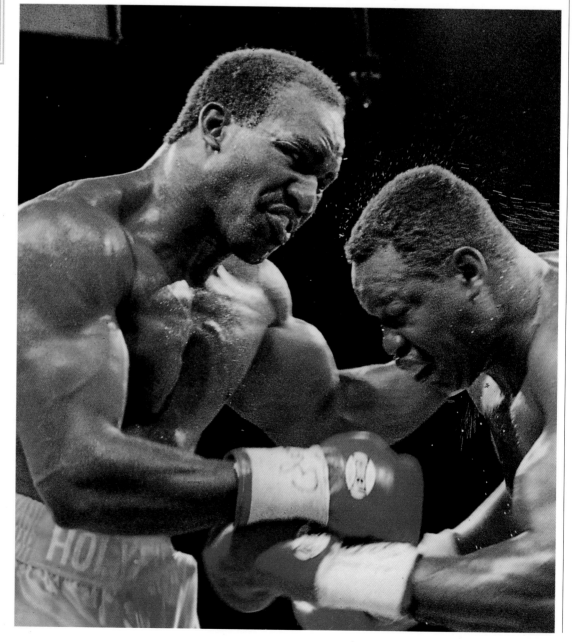

HOLMES (RIGHT) AS A 44-YEAR-OLD TOOK EVANDER HOLYFIELD 12 ROUNDS IN A TITLE FIGHT, 1992

SEE ALSO ◆ EVANDER HOLYFIELD 159 ◆ MICHAEL SPINKS 302 ◆ MIKE TYSON 319

EVANDER HOLYFIELD

Evander Holyfield's greatness was sealed on the night of November 9, 1996 when he destroyed the "Iron" Mike Tyson myth once and for all.

Before the fight Holyfield was considered a shot fighter, a man in steep physical decline, maybe so sick he should not be boxing at all.

Yet he cemented his place among the heavyweight elite by flooring Tyson in the sixth round and stopping him in the 11th at the MGM Grand Garden in Las Vegas.

Holyfield was a bronze medalist at the 1984 Olympics and won the WBA cruiserweight title with an epic, draining 15-round decision over Dwight Qawi in Atlanta in 1986. He unified the division by defeating rival champions Ricky Parkey and Carlos De Leon, then moved up in search of a showdown with Tyson.

The deal was made in 1990, but Buster Douglas wrecked it by upsetting Tyson in Tokyo. Holyfield trounced Douglas in three rounds to become undisputed champion in October 1990, but when the Tyson fight was made in 1991—and all tickets sold—it fell apart. Holyfield was injured, and then Tyson was jailed for rape.

Holyfield lost the title in a brutally exciting 12-rounder with Riddick Bowe, then beat Bowe in a rematch only to lose it to Michael Moorer, when apparently sick with a heart complaint. Bowe stopped him in another grueling fight in November 1995, but this intensely spiritual man rose from the ashes of his career and dethroned Tyson.

FACT FILE

1962	Born Atmore, Alabama
1984	Olympic Games light-heavyweight bronze medal
1986	Won WBA cruiserweight title against Dwight Qawi
1988	Unified cruiserweight title against Carlos De Leon
1990	Won undisputed heavyweight title against Buster Douglas
1992	Lost title to Riddick Bowe
1993	Regained WBA and IBF belts from Bowe
1994	Lost championships to Michael Moorer
1996	Regained WBA title by beating Mike Tyson

Career record: Fights 36, Won 33, Lost 3

BERT COOPER FEELS THE POWER BEHIND HOLYFIELD'S PUNCH

SEE ALSO ♦ RIDDICK BOWE 36 ♦ CARLOS DE LEON 86 ♦ BUSTER DOUGLAS 94 ♦ MICHAEL MOORER 230 ♦ DWIGHT QAWI 274 ♦ MIKE TYSON 319

THE GREAT FIGHTS

MIKE TYSON
V.
EVANDER HOLYFIELD

MGM GRAND GARDEN,
LAS VEGAS.
NOVEMBER 9, 1996.

Evander Holyfield, surely now secure among the greatest of heavyweight champions, encapsulated in one brief sentence why great fighters are special human beings.

"The prize," he said, after his astonishing 11th-round stoppage of Mike Tyson, "has to be greater than the pain."

But boxers have their own special definition of pain.

This modest, most Christian of men explained the psychological process that made him a three-time world heavyweight title holder.

"You have to go through what is necessary. Everybody hits hard. You know at any given time Mike Tyson can take you out. But I don't fear getting hit."

Since his release from jail in March 1995, Tyson had demolished four opponents in a total of eight rounds: Peter McNeeley, Buster Mathis, Frank Bruno, and Bruce Seldon. Everyone knew the real tests were to come, but nobody believed Holyfield had enough left at 34 to press the "New Tyson" too severely. For Evander, this all seemed five years too late. The fight should have happened in 1990, but Tyson lost to Buster Douglas. Then 1991 plans came to nothing, when Holyfield was injured and Tyson was jailed following the rape of Desiree Washington.

Now it was time, but Holyfield seemed to have faded too far. Boxing critics even feared his courage would merely prolong his suffering.

The worries proved groundless as Holyfield absorbed what Tyson could dish out, worked his way into the contest and floored him with a short, crisp left hook in round six.

By the end of the 10th Tyson was near exhaustion, and taking wrecking-ball right hands full on the head. After 37 seconds of round 11, referee Mitch Halpern hauled Holyfield away with Tyson slumped against the ropes.

Tyson, so often surly and cynical, went out with class and dignity, standing up at the press conference and telling Holyfield: "I just want to shake your hand. It's been so long. You fought a great fight." But seven months later, Tyson disgraced himself by biting off a chunk of Holyfield's ear. He was disqualified, and faced severe disciplinary action

LLOYD HONEYGHAN

Lloyd Honeyghan was a ruthless, alley-cat of a fighter who smashed his way to a sensational win over the supposedly supreme Donald Curry in Atlantic City in September 1986.

Curry, the undisputed world welterweight champion was talked of as the only credible opponent for middleweight titleholder Marvin Hagler, and Honeyghan's uncomplicated belligerence left some fearing for his welfare.

"I ain't scared of no man, I'll bash him up," he said. He wasn't and he did. Curry stayed on his stool after six rounds. His nose was broken, a jagged gash that needed 20 stitches ran by his left eye, and his lip was torn. He looked as if he had been mauled by a cornered beast.

Honeyghan outpointed another fine champion, Maurice Blocker, and needed only 45 seconds to stop Gene Hatcher in Marbella. A technical decision robbed him of his title against lucky Mexican Jorge Vaca in October 1987, after which he criticized manager Mickey Duff. Memorably, Duff retaliated: "There's nothing in our contract that says we have to like each other."

Honeyghan regained the WBC belt from Vaca with an all-out assault at Wembley in March 1988, but his reign ended with a nine-rounds defeat by the admirable Marlon Starling in Las Vegas in February 1989. He suffered a damaged nerve in his face early in the fight. "Every time he hit me it was like cutting me with a knife," he said.

Honeyghan's world title days ended with a third-round stoppage by Mark Breland in 1990, but he carried on fighting until 1995, winning the Commonwealth light-middleweight title. Before beating Curry his best win was a third-round knockout of Gianfranco Rosi in a European title fight in Italy.

RAGAMUFFIN MAN: HONEYGHAN IS TOO MUCH FOR MAURICE BLOCKER

SEE ALSO ◆ DON CURRY 82 ◆ GIANFRANCO ROSI 286 ◆ MARLON STARLING 303

BEAU JACK

Beau Jack learned to fight in battle royals—the terrible "entertainments" in which half a dozen blindfolded black kids punched each other until only one was left standing, in the hope of receiving small change from their white audience.

Jack, who also shone shoes at the Augusta National Golf Club, was eventually backed by some who saw him fight, including the great Bobby Jones, and left Georgia for Massachusetts to learn under trainer Syd Bell.

His real name was Sidney Walker but his grandmother called Beau Jack when he was a child. She also instilled his fighting spirit. When he came home crying after being robbed, she sent him back out: "Walkers fight until the blood runs in their shoes!"

He turned professional in 1940, and at 21 he knocked out Tippy Larkin with a right upper-cut in the third round to win New York recognition as world lightweight champion in December 1942.

The following year he twice beat the brutal welterweight champ Fritzie Zivic, unanimously outpointed the legendary Henry Armstrong, and fought two tremendous 15-rounders with Bob Montgomery for the title. He lost the first and won the second.

In 1944 he lost the "decider" with Montgomery on a split 15-round decision, and although he won a fourth fight the title was not at stake. Jack's aggressive, fast fighting style was a great draw—he topped the bill at Madison Square Garden 21 times. His championship days ended with a sixth-round defeat by Ike Williams in 1948, but he fought on for seven more years. In retirement he returned to shining shoes in a Miami hotel, and trained youngsters at the city's Fifth Street gym.

FACT FILE

1921 Born Sidney Walker, Augusta, Georgia

1940 Professional debut

1942 Beat Tippy Larkin for New York version of work lightweight title

1943 Lost and regained title against Bob Montgomery

1944 Lost third fight with Montgomery

1948 Beaten in title challenge by Ike Williams

1955 Retired, age 34

Career record: Fights 112, Won 83, Lost 24, Drawn 5

JACK DRIVES A RIGHT TO THE HEAD OF WILLIE JOYCE IN NEW YORK IN 1945

SEE ALSO ◆ **BOB MONTGOMERY 221** ◆ **IKE WILLIAMS 336** ◆ **FRITZIE ZIVIC 349**

The GREAT FIGHTS

DONALD CURRY
V.
LLOYD HONEYGHAN

CAESARS, ATLANTIC CITY.
SEPTEMBER 27, 1986.

America underestimated Lloyd Honeyghan. Sure, everyone knew Don Curry struggled to make 147 lb., but the party line was that he remained infinitely superior to any other welterweight in the world. The result was considered such a formality nobody bothered to produce souvenir programs, and the fight was hidden away in the relatively low-key Circus Maximus Theatre at Caesars on the Atlantic City boardwalk.

But Honeyghan entered the ring with the kind of belligerent determination that so many of his predecessors had lacked. He also backed himself with $25,000 at 5-1.

Curry, unbeaten since he was 16, cockily declared: "I'm not going to watch any more videos of him because I keep seeing flaws. He should wait till I move up a weight. I may ruin him."

Honeyghan bristled and said: "I ain't scared of Curry. I ain't scared of no one."

Curry, champion for three years, had a worried look in the first round as Honeyghan came straight at him, matching jabs, weaving forward, and throwing hard hooks, pushing him back. Curry looked casual, and paid for it early in round two when a right lead almost dropped him. He hung on, then ran. Rounds three and four saw the champion blast back, but in round five Honeyghan took over for good.

Curry's bottom lip was torn open by a thumping jab and overhand right and he was hurt by a left hook. In the sixth his left eye opened up and he was worked over. He pulled out at the end of the round, a forlorn figure who could not quite believe what had happened. His cut eye needed 20 stitches, and another went into his lip.

"Nobody thought I could beat him, but I knew I could," yelled an excited Honeyghan, who returned to a hero's welcome in South London. Curry, who before the fight was considered the only marketable challenger for Marvin Hagler's middleweight title and had boiled down from 168 lb. to make welterweight, was never the same again.

JULIAN JACKSON

Some said Julian Jackson's eyesight was so bad he needed a white stick. Tell that to the 47 men he knocked out.

Jackson had a history of retina surgery when he disputed the vacant WBC middleweight title with Herol Graham in Spain in 1990. He had swellings around the eyes and, fears for his long-term safety seemed justified. He was on the brink of being pulled out of the fight, when he found a split-second opening in the fourth round. Graham was unconscious before he hit the floor.

Jackson, a father of six from St. Thomas in the Virgin Islands, dedicated his life to God after losing his first world title bid in two rounds to Mike McCallum in 1986. A modest, unassuming man, he came back from the McCallum setback, to win the WBA title by stopping In-chul Baek of South Korea in three rounds in Las Vegas in November 1987. He defended the 154 lb. belt three times. His eye problems interrupted his career, but he returned to beat Graham and reigned as WBC middleweight champion for three years.

He was dethroned in a marvelous battle in Las Vegas in 1993 when Gerald McClellan stopped him in the fifth round. In a return McClellan beat him in one, but Jackson regained the title by taking out Italy's Agostino Cardamone in two rounds in March 1995—typically, after being in trouble in the opening session. By now, however, he was slowing markedly, and Texan southpaw Quincy Taylor stopped him in six rounds to end his championship days in August 1995.

THE HAWK AT WORK: JACKSON ATTACKS THOMAS TATE

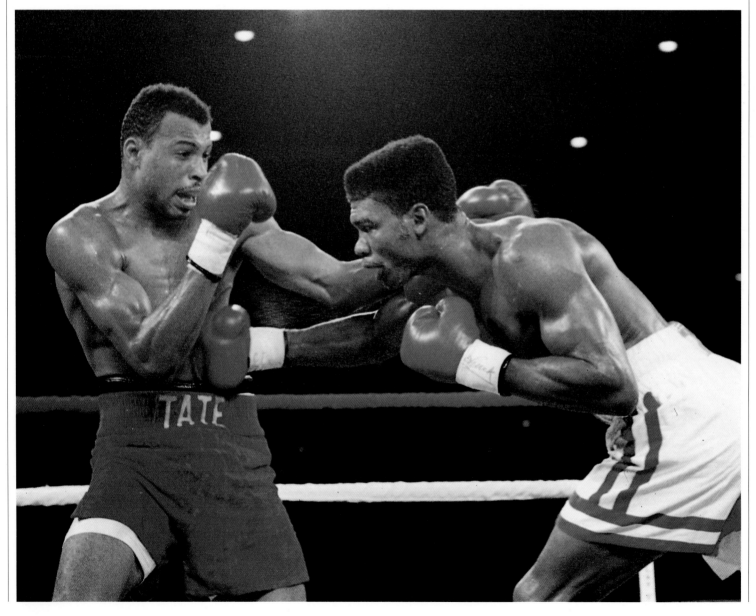

SEE ALSO ◆ MIKE McCALLUM 238

PETER JACKSON

Writing near the end of his life, James J. Corbett called Peter Jackson "the greatest fighter I have ever seen." A year before he became world heavyweight champion by knocking out John L. Sullivan in 1892, Corbett fought an incredible three-hour battle with Jackson that was called off in the 61st round because they were both exhausted.

Those who saw the 6 ft., 1in., 196-lb. West Indian say he would have beaten Sullivan easily, but the champion blustered: "I have never fought a negro, and I never shall."

Jackson was taken to Australia as a boy when his father sailed to join in the Gold Rush of 1863. He grew up to be a champion swimmer, oarsman, and, eventually, boxer. He won the Australian heavyweight title in 1886 and two years later sailed to America to chase Sullivan and the world championship, but had to be content with knocking out George Godfrey of Boston instead. The California Athletic Club pressed for a championship fight, but Sullivan would have none of it.

Although Corbett gave Jackson his chance in 1891, once "Gentleman Jim" had the world title, he avoided a rematch. Jackson won two British Empire title fights in London, most memorably against Frank Slavin at the National Sporting Club, but made his living on the stage and by teaching boxing. He was ill with tuberculosis when he lost in three rounds to James J. Jeffries in 1898. He returned to Australia to die, and was buried in Brisbane beneath a monument that read boldly: "This Was A Man."

FACT FILE

1861	Born Christiansted, St. Croix, Virgin Islands
1886	Won Australian heavyweight title
1888	Arrived in the United States, knocked out George Godfrey
1891	Fought a 61-round slog with James J. Corbett
1892	Won British Empire heavyweight title in London
Died:	Roma, Queensland, Australia, July 13, 1901, age 40

Career record: Fights 33, Won 23, Lost 3, Drawn 5, No Decision 1, No Contest 1

PIONEERING SPIRIT: JACKSON FOUGHT JIM CORBETT TO A 61-ROUND DRAW

SEE ALSO ◆ JAMES J. CORBETT 80 ◆ JAMES J. JEFFRIES 168

JAMES J. JEFFRIES

FACT FILE

1875 Born Carroll, Ohio, April 15, 1875

1896 Professional debut

1899 Knocked out Bob Fitzsimmons to win world heavyweight title

1905 Announced retirement as undefeated champion

1910 Came back to lose to Jack Johnson

died: Burbank, California, March 3, 1953, age 77

Career record: Fights 21, Won 18, Lost 1, Drawn 2

One of the strongest men to hold the heavyweight title, James J. Jeffries earned the respect and affection of ordinary people with his honest, steady ways, and in retirement his exploits became the stuff of legend. Sadly, his reputation demanded he return to fight the hated Jack Johnson at the age of 35. Johnson battered him in 15 one-sided rounds in Reno, Nevada, in 1910.

The son of an itinerant preacher who moved from Ohio to California in the late 1870s, Jeffries had little education, but at 15 was wielding a sledgehammer making iron boilers. He moved on to copper mining, and so into boxing, where he worked as a sparring partner for world champion James J. Corbett and was once described as "a Californian grizzly bear" because of his hairy shoulders and slow, mauling style.

He was ringside when Corbett lost the title to Bob Fitzsimmons in 1897, and two years later, with his awkward, crouching technique devised by welterweight champion Tommy Ryan, knocked out Fitzsimmons in 11 rounds. He ended the century with a 25-round decision over "Sailor" Tom Sharkey.

He was outboxed systematically by Corbett in May 1900, but caught up with him and knocked him out in the 23rd —a triumph for substance over style, for workaday values over pomp and ceremony.

He beat Fitzsimmons and Corbett again, also knocked out Jack Finnegan and Gus Ruhlin, and in 1904 intimidated a good fighter named Jack Munroe, who folded in the second round.

Jeffries retired to life as a California farmer in 1905—and no doubt wished he had not been tempted to fight Johnson in 1910.

JEFFRIES IN HIS GLORY DAYS AS HEAVYWEIGHT CHAMPION OF THE WORLD AT THE TURN OF THE CENTURY

SEE ALSO ◆ BOB FITZSIMMONS 114 ◆ JACK JOHNSON 171

EDER JOFRE

An intelligent, independent thinker, Eder Jofre did things his way. For example, in a sport dominated by traditionalists who believed fighters performed best on a diet of raw steak, Jofre was a vegetarian. He also ignored advice to fight in the United States, insisting he would fight best if he remained with his people in Brazil.

Jofre was from fighting stock—and that included his mother, Olga, who was a professional wrestler. He crowned a long amateur career by reaching the 1956 Olympic quarterfinals, and went on to win NBA recognition as bantamweight champion with a sixth-round knockout of Eloy Sanchez in Los Angeles in November 1960—one of only three appearances he made in the States. When he returned to Sao Paulo, a throng of 100,000 people lined the roads from the airport. He insisted his parade take him to the poverty-stricken area of Parque Peruche, where he grew up.

He unified the championship before 18,000 fans in São Paulo, stopping Ireland's Johnny Caldwell in ten rounds. For the next three years he fought a draining battle against increasing weight, until in 1965 in Japan he was outworked—he said outfouled—by "Fighting" Harada. In a rematch Harada beat him again and he retired for three years.

In Brasilia in May 1973, he outboxed Jose Legra to win the WBC featherweight championship. He dedicated his first defense, a fourth-round knockout of Vicente Saldivar, to his dying father. He was stripped of his title the following year and retired in 1976 following the sudden death of his brother. He became a politician in São Paulo, working tirelessly for the betterment of his people.

FACT FILE

1936	Born São Paulo, Brazil
1956	Olympic Games representative
1960	Won NBA bantamweight title
1962	Beat Johnny Caldwell for undisputed world bantamweight title
1965	Lost bantamweight title to Fighting Harada
1973	Beat Jose Legra for WBC featherweight title, age 37
1974	Stripped of WBC championship
1976	Retired, age 40

Career record: Fights 78, Won 72, Lost 2, Drawn 4

UNDER PRESSURE (LEFT) AGAINST FIGHTING HARADA: JOFRE ALWAYS SAID HE WAS FOULED OUT OF THE TITLE

SEE ALSO ◆ JOHNNY CALDWELL 50 ◆ FIGHTING HARADA 151

INGEMAR JOHANSSON

1932 Born Gothenburg, Sweden

1952 Olympic heavyweight finalist

1956 Won European heavyweight title

1959 Won world heavyweight title by stopping Floyd Patterson

1960 Lost title in return with Patterson

1961 Lost decider to Patterson

1963 Retired, age 30

Career record: Fights 28, Won 26, Lost 2

Ingemar Johansson's place in boxing history was secure the moment his "Hammer of Thor" right hand connected with the chin of world heavyweight champion Floyd Patterson in the third round at Yankee Stadium, New York, on June 26, 1959.

Patterson crashed to the canvas for the first of seven knockdowns in the round before referee Ruby Goldstein stopped the slaughter.

It was a moment of immense personal redemption for Johansson, who had been disqualified for not trying in the 1952 Olympic heavyweight final against Ed Sanders of the United States. Johansson had been developed well in Sweden and knew his business. He knocked out Franco Cavicchi in 13 rounds in Bologna in 1956 to win the European title, and defended it by knocking out Britons Henry Cooper and Joe Erskine. Then he clinched his world title shot by blasting out top contender Eddie Machen in the first round in Gothenburg in September 1958.

Patterson's manager Cus D'Amato had studiously avoided the most dangerous contenders of the time, but made a huge blunder in accepting Johansson.

Nevertheless after winning the title, Ingemar could not capitalize on it. He was knocked out in the fifth round of the inevitable rematch in June 1960, and then knocked out in six in a third meeting in Miami in March 1961. He was prompted to retire in 1963 when Brian London flattened him with the last punch of their 12-rounder in Stockholm. Johansson won the decision, but knew it was time to go.

In retirement he invested his money, competed in marathons, and in the 1980s and 1990s was a regular broadcaster and boxing analyst for Scandinavian television.

JOHANSSON TRADES WITH FLOYD PATTERSON IN THEIR THIRD AND "DECIDING" FIGHT IN 1961

SEE ALSO ♦ HENRY COOPER 79 ♦ FLOYD PATTERSON 265

JACK JOHNSON

No sporting champion has been hated more than the first black heavy-weight champion Jack Johnson, who held the world title for a full seven years.

Johnson's victories altered the balance of the relationship between black and white in America. As 1908 drew to a close, some even felt a Johnson win over the Canadian world heavyweight champion Tommy Burns would spark a racist revolution.

Of course, it didn't. When Johnson out-classed Burns in 14 rounds at Rushcutter's Bay, near Sydney, the "revolution" consisted of a band of wealthy Chicago blacks hiring white servants for a banquet!

However, when Johnson trounced James J. Jeffries in Reno, Nevada, in July 1910, the mood was far uglier. Before the fight, a white band played a merry little ditty called "All Coons Look Alike To Me." Afterward the casualty list was horrific. Black workers were killed in Georgia, a white man had his throat slashed in Houston, two blacks were killed in a street car in Little Rock, lynchings took place in Virginia, Delaware, Texas, and Louisiana and across America murders and riots spread like fire. All because a black man had beaten a white man in a boxing contest.

Johnson flaunted his enjoyment of white women to the point where he was forced to leave the country, but held on to his title until 1915 when a big, raw-boned cowboy, Jess Willard, knocked him out in the 26th round in Havana, Cuba. He returned to serve an outstanding jail sentence in 1920, and died in a car crash in 1946 while on his way to watch the next black champion, Joe Louis, defend his title against Billy Conn.

FACT FILE

1878 Born Galveston, Texas

1897 Professional debut

1908 Won the world championship by stopping Tommy Burns

1910 Defeated James J. Jeffries in Reno, Nevada

1915 Lost world title to Jess Willard in Havana

1928 Last professional fight, age 50

Died: Raleigh, North Carolina, June 10, 1946, age 68

Career record: Fights 108, Won 86, Lost 10, Drawn 11, No Contest 1

PROUD AND FIERCELY INDEPENDENT: JOHNSON ENJOYED HIMSELF IMMENSELY OUTSIDE THE RING, BUT INSIDE IT WAS ABSOLUTELY SERIOUS

SEE ALSO ◆ TOMMY BURNS 49 ◆ JAMES J. JEFFRIES 168

THE GREAT FIGHTS

JACK JOHNSON
v.
JAMES J. JEFFRIES

RENO, NEVADA.
JULY 4, 1910.

Because Jack Johnson, a black Texan, won the heavyweight championship of the world by trouncing Tommy Burns in 1908, racial tension in the United States of America hit a terrible peak.

Pressure had mounted for James J. Jeffries, who had retired as unbeaten champion in 1905, to return and restore the title to white America. By 1910, he could stand it no more, and came from his Californian alfalfa farm to meet his destiny in Reno, Nevada.

The town was awash with humanity for days before the fight, and while 15,760 paid to get into the arena, another 15,000 were locked out, unable to get tickets. Boxes were provided at the back for ladies.

Before the fight, Jeffries gave a stirring statement. "I'll lick this black man so badly that he'll never want to see a boxing glove again.... I've had to do a lot of training to put myself in shape and I've had to give up a lot of pleasure. It's no fun for a man of my inclinations to have to deny himself everything, to knuckle down and work his blamed head off just on account of a coon."

Johnson, used to the treatment, said: "I only wish I was as sure of getting a million dollars as I am that I'll whip Mister Jeffries."

The fight itself, refereed by the promoter, Tex Rickard, was one of the easiest of Johnson's life. He cut Jeffries cheek in the sixth, bloodied his nose and half-closed one eye. Jeffries chewed gum, but dispensed with it when the blood in his mouth ran too freely.

In the 15th Jeffries wearily crumbled, going down three times before Rickard stopped it.

The next day, 19 people died and 251 were seriously injured in race riots across America. "Most of the casualties were negroes," reported one foreign newspaper.

ROY JONES

A smooth, classical boxer who oozed self-confidence, Roy Jones was considered the leading candidate for the best pound-for-pound fighter in the world during the mid-1990s.

Jones hit the headlines in the 1988 Olympics in Seoul when, as a 19-year-old light-middleweight, he "lost" a scandalous decision in the final to Si-hun Park of South Korea. The Best Boxer of the Tournament trophy was little consolation. The decision almost led to boxing being thrown out of the Olympics—and led to the introduction of the controversial computer-scoring system.

Jones put the heartbreak behind him by turning professional, guided by his father Roy Snr. He was brought along cautiously without mishap, and in 1993 won the vacant IBF middleweight title by outpointing the dangerous Bernard "The Executioner" Hopkins. It was a safety-first performance designed to achieve a result rather than win friends, but Jones followed up with an explosive second-round win over the normally solid Thomas Tate, and then moved up to super-middleweight to dethrone a sluggish, weight-weakened James Toney on a wide decision in Las Vegas in November 1994.

Jones outclassed his challengers, including Vinny Pazienza and Tony Thornton, but failed to attract the unification fight for which he has publicly pressed. He seemed bored by the political machinations of those who controlled the sport, and drew criticism in June 1996 when he played basketball on the day that he stopped Canadian challenger Eric Lucas in 11 rounds. A move up to light-heavyweight to outpoint veteran Mike McCallum sparked more interest in him but in March 1997 he lost on a disqualification to Montell Griffin.

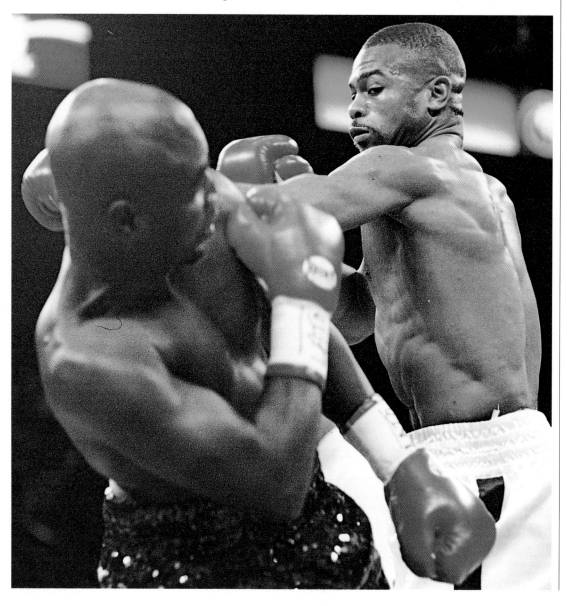

JONES (RIGHT), ARGUABLY THE BEST POUND-FOR-POUND FIGHTER OF THE MID-90S

SEE ALSO ◆ MIKE MCCALLUM 238 ◆ JAMES TONEY 310

PETER KANE

ven when he was the flyweight champion of the world, Peter Kane continued working for 18 shillings ($4.50) a week as a blacksmith in the small Lancashire town of Golborne where he grew up.

Kane was a very down-to-earth, solid Lancastrian who fought for love, not money—even though he collected plenty in the course of 102 professional contests in 14 years, only seven of which he lost.

Kane's first world title fight, and the one for which most probably still remember him, was when as a relatively raw 19-year-old he fought the great Benny Lynch before 40,000 people at the Shawfield Stadium in Glasgow. Lynch dropped him in the first round, but he plowed his way back and gave the Scot a classic struggle before losing in the 13th.

In a rematch at Anfield Stadium in Liverpool, the city where Kane trained throughout his career, Lynch insisted on a non-title fight at 118 lb. to protect his title. They fought a 12-round draw.

When Lynch finally blew the flyweight title on the scales, Kane outpointed American Jackie Jurich for the vacant championship at Anfield in September 1938. He relinquished his world title because of weight problems in August 1939, and during World War II joined the RAF.

He lost to Jackie Paterson in one round in a world flyweight title fight in Glasgow in 1943, and the following year was caught in the eye by the lapel of a coat in a freak accident and suffered serious damage. He lost the sight in it altogether, but after the War held the European bantamweight title briefly before retiring.

KANE IS THE WORLD FLYWEIGHT CHAMPION AFTER OUTPOINTING JACKIE JURICH

SEE ALSO ◆ BENNY LYNCH 205

STANLEY KETCHEL

FACT FILE

1886 Born Stanislaus Kiecel, Grand Rapids, Michigan

1904 Professional debut in Montana, age 18

1908 Won world middleweight title against Jack Sullivan, lost it to Billy Papke, regained it

1909 Lost to heavyweight champ Jack Johnson

Died: Conway, Missouri, October 15, 1910, age 24

Career record: Fights 64, Won 55, Lost 4, Drawn 5

Stanley Ketchel lived on the edge of sanity, an unruly child who drifted from home when maybe as young as 12 to learn how to ride rails, and survive in hobo jungles and mining camps. As a boy he drank, whored, and fought as the mood took him.

Ketchel, who was called "The Michigan Assassin," was an icy storm of a fighter who would walk in and throw his unbelievably hard punches from whatever angle presented itself. A superstitious, tempestuous man, who once shot his trainer for waking him up too soon, he was also capable of immense generosity.

He was 21 when he won the world middleweight title by knocking out Jack "Twin" Sullivan in 20 rounds in Colma near San Francisco in May 1908. He lost and regained the championship in fierce struggles with Billy Papke, and then in October 1909 he had the audacity to drop heavyweight champ Jack Johnson with a big right hand in the 12th round in Colma. Johnson, 35 lb. heavier, jumped up and knocked Ketchel cold with an uppercut. Ketchel's front teeth were embedded in Johnson's glove.

By 1910 Ketchel was burning out, thanks to the arrival of reprobate manager Wilson Mizner, who introduced him to opium and merrily shared his women. He was at a friend's farm in Conway, Missouri, when he was shot dead by a drifting laborer, Walter Dipley, who said Ketchel had slept with his girlfriend. After his funeral, a lady described as Ketchel's fiancée, Miss Jewell Bovine, was so distraught she attempted to kill herself by drinking carbolic acid.

KETCHEL POSES WITH JACK JOHNSON BEFORE THEIR 1909 EPIC

SEE ALSO ◆ JACK JOHNSON 171 ◆ BILLY PAPKE 263

JOHNNY KILBANE

Johnny Kilbane knew if he fought world featherweight champion Abe Attell on the inside he would lose, not because Attell was a better infighter than he was, but because the champ had coated his back with chloroform!

Every time they got in a clinch with Kilbane's head, over Attell's shoulder he caught a strong whiff of the stuff and felt dizzy... a charge that Attell, who was known as a stroke-puller of the first order, vigorously denied.

Kilbane, who had lost a 10-round decision to Attell in his first attempt in 1910, used his superior youth, skill, and speed to stay at long range and won the title.

Kilbane was a clever boxer, but not a big puncher, and the great majority of his fights went the distance. He was good enough to keep the championship for 11 years, which even allowing for World War I, was a tremendous achievement. He outpointed the great lightweight champion Benny Leonard in 1915, before Leonard won the title, but was knocked out by him in three rounds two years later. As a featherweight he was perfectly capable of holding on to his title, and turned back challenges from Jimmy Walsh, Johhny Dundee, Jimmy Fox, George KO Chaney, Eddie Wallace, Alvie Miller, and, finally, in 1921 Danny Frush.

He more or less retired after that, but was tempted to defend once more for a reported $75,000 against French war veteran Eugene Criqui. He was knocked out in six rounds. Kilbane returned to Cleveland after his career ended and served in the Ohio State senate. He stayed in touch with boxing by running a gym and refereeing fights.

FACT FILE

1889 Born Cleveland, Ohio
1907 Professional debut at 18
1910 Lost first world title challenge to Abe Attell
1912 Beat Attell over 20 rounds for world featherweight title
1923 Lost world title in last fight to Eugene Criqui, age 34
Died: Cleveland, May 31, 1957, age 68
Career record: Fights 142, Won 114, Lost 14, Drawn 12, No Contests 2

KILBANE WAS WORLD FEATHERWEIGHT CHAMPION FOR 11 YEARS, FROM 1912 UNTIL 1923

SEE ALSO ◆ ABE ATTELL 25 ◆ BENNY LEONARD 186

PONE KINGPETCH

FACT FILE

1936 Born Hua Hin,
Thailand, February
12, 1936

1960 Beat Pascual Perez
to win world flyweight
title

1962 Lost title to Fighting
Harada in Tokyo

1963 Regained title from
Harada in Bangkok,
lost it to Hiroyuki
Ebihara

1964 Became three-time
champ by beating
Ebihara

1965 Lost belt to Salvatore
Burruni in Rome

Died: Ramanthi, Bangkok,
May 31, 1982, age 46

Career record: Fights 40,
Won 33, Lost 7

Pone Kingpetch, a tall, skinny stylist from the Thai seaport of Hua Hin, held the world flyweight title three times between 1960 and 1965. The first Thai to win a world championship, he was a pharmaceutical laboratory worker when he beat the long-time champion Pascual Perez in a split decision in Bangkok in April 1960.

Kingpetch was around 8 in. taller, younger, faster, and was roared on by a sellout 30,000 crowd in the Lumpinee Stadium, which included the Thai king and queen. Not surprisingly, Kingpetch staged an inspired display to dethrone a man who held held the world title for nearly six years.

One of nine children, Kingpetch had only three amateur bouts, and his professional progress was hampered when he broke his jaw in an automobile accident. But he beat Perez a second time, stopping him in eight rounds at the Olympic Auditorioum, Los Angeles, in September 1960—the first time he had traveled outside Thailand. Pickings were not rich: he grossed a miserable $2,900, the same as his challenger.

He outboxed Mitsunori Seki in his second defense in Tokyo, which because of some bizarre scoring by the Japanese judge was officially a split decision. And this time the pay was better—$50,000 plus TV rights. His reign ended with an 11th-round knockout inflicted by Fighting Harada in Tokyo in 1962, but he went on to outscore Harada in a return in Bangkok in 1963.

Hiroyuki Ebihara took only 127 seconds to relieve him of the title in September 1963, but once again when he brought the Japanese to Bangkok, he won the decision. But in April 1965 he was outpointed by Salvatore Burrini in Rome—and retired 12 months later. He died of pneumonia when he was 46.

KINGPETCH (RIGHT)
DETHRONED A GREAT CHAMP,
PASCUAL PEREZ, TO BEGIN
THE FIRST OF THREE REIGNS

SEE ALSO ◆ FIGHTING HARADA 151 ◆ PASCUAL PEREZ 270

HIROSHI KOBAYASHI

One of the most skillful boxers ever produced in Japan, Hiroshi Kobayashi held the WBA 130 lb. title for four years and a quarter of a century later was still running his own boxing school.

Kobayashi turned professional at 17 and survived several hard lessons early in his career. He once lost four in a row, but won the Japanese featherweight title in 1964, and was eventually sent on an educational mission to Venezuela, Ecuador, Mexico, and Los Angeles.

He lost two of his six fights on the tour but learned well, and in December 1967 he won the WBA super-featherweight title with a comprehensive 12th-round knockout of compatriot Yoshiaki Numata in Tokyo. Numata, who had beaten the great Filipino Flash Elorde for the title earlier in the year, was floored four times during the fight.

Kobayashi had a shaky first defense when he could only draw with Rene Barrientos in Tokyo, and was twice beaten by Californian lightweights, Mando Ramos and Ruben Navarro, in non-title fights. But once he settled down, he proved a determined and long-lasting champion who was well respected for his boxing skills.

He rebuffed challenges from Jaime Valladares, Antonio Amaya (twice), Carlos Canete, and, most impressively, the talented Mexican Ricardo Arredondo. He seemed to be boxing his way to another points win when he ran out of stamina and was stopped in ten rounds by Alfredo Marcano of Venezuela in July 1971. In his next fight he lost to 20-year-old Roberto Duran and retired.

FACT FILE

1944 Born Isesaki, Gunma, Japan
1962 Professional debut
1967 Beat Yoshiaki Numata for WBA super-featherweight title
1971 Lost title at seventh defense to Alfredo Marcano

Career record: Fights 74, Won 60, Lost 10, Drawn 4

KOBAYASHI FLATTENS YOSHIAKI NUMATA TO BECOME WBA SUPER-FEATHERWEIGHT CHAMP IN 1967

SEE ALSO ◆ RICARDO ARRENDONDO 24 ◆ ROBERTO DURAN 99

DAVID KOTEY

FACT FILE

1950	Born Accra, Ghana
1966	Professional debut, age 15
1974	Won African and Commonwealth featherweight titles
1975	Beat Ruben Olivares for the WBC title
1976	Lost title to Danny Lopez in Accra

Career record: Fights 45, Won 38, Lost 6, Drawn 1

KOTEY (RIGHT) DETHRONES RUBEN OLIVARES IN 1975

David Kotey inspired an entire nation when he traveled to Los Angeles and dethroned Mexican hero Ruben Olivares in September 1975.

"Poison" Kotey, the first world champion to come from Ghana, floored Olivares in the first round and withstood a late rounds surge to win a split decision. Strangely, as if the 8,000 crowd already knew the result, chairs and bottles flew and fights broke out at ringside the moment the final bell sounded. Kotey was hustled away to his dressing room, robbed of the joy of hearing his name announced as the new champion of the world.

Whereas Olivares admitted he paid for "training on beer," Kotey, who had waited for this night from the moment he turned professional at 15, fought to his absolute limit. Backstage, he could hardly talk, he was so exhausted.

Kotey, who had previously won the African and Commonwealth titles, enjoyed a marvelous homecoming in a non-title win in Accra in December 1975, and then defended the championship there in March 1976 with a 12th-round stoppage of Japanese champion Harugi "Flipper" Uehara. Then he traveled to Tokyo to stop Shige Fukuyama in three rounds, earning a career-best payday of $75,000.

But when it seemed set for a long and lucrative reign, he was upset by Danny "Little Red" Lopez. Fighting in 90-degree heat in Accra, Kotey took an unexpected pounding and long before the end his fans were streaming out of the stadium.

In a rematch in Las Vegas in February 1978, on the undercard of the first Muhammad Ali–Leon Spinks fight, Kotey was overpowered by Lopez in six rounds. He never fought in world class again.

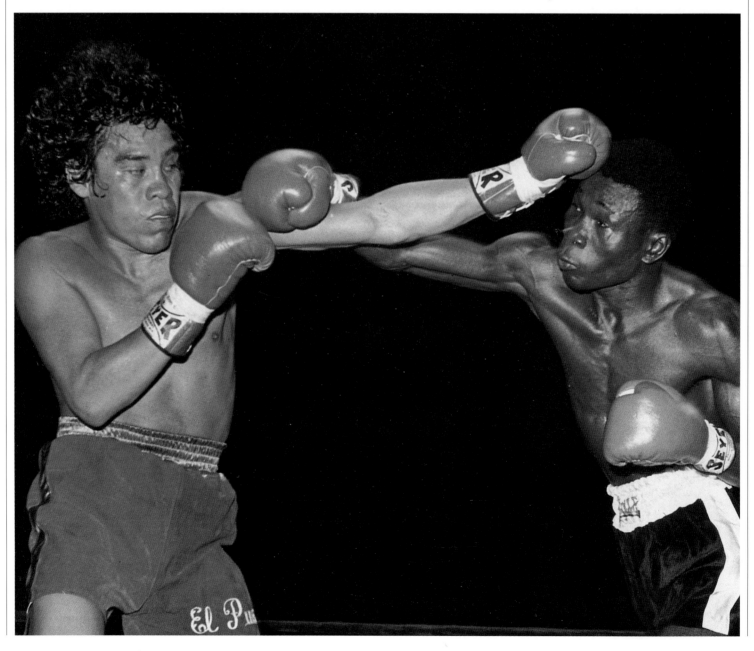

SEE ALSO ◆ DANNY LOPEZ 201 ◆ RUBEN OLIVARES 257

FIDEL LA BARBA

Fidel La Barba is the only man who has given up a world title in favor of a college degree!

La Barba had won the 1924 Olympic Games flyweight gold medal in Paris, and then went on to become world flyweight champion in January 1927 with a 12-round decision over Scotland's Elky Clark in Madison Square Garden, New York.

But seven months later he stunned the boxing world by announcing his retirement because he wanted to concentrate on his forthcoming studies at Stanford University.

Even more strangely, he returned to the ring after one year, not because he couldn't cope with the course, but because his lecturers and professors thought he was crazy to give up the riches of the ring for a life of academia!

"They'd say 'La Barba, what did you give up your title for? What are you, nuts or something? You could have made yourself another hundred thousand dollars," he remembered.

La Barba, born in New York but raised in Los Angeles, duly returned to boxing but outgrew the flyweight division rapidly and never regained a championship. Although he beat the great Cuban, Kid Chocolate in 1930, he was outpointed for the featherweight title by Battling Battalino in 1931 and then by Chocolate for the New York version the following year, when he injured an eye while he was training.

He lost a fortune in the Wall Street Crash, eventually lost the sight of the eye he hurt in the build-up to the Chocolate fight, and after retiring from the ring in 1933 worked both as a newspaperman and movie script writer in Hollywood.

FACT FILE

1905	Born New York City
1924	Olympic flyweight gold medal
1927	Beat Elky Clark for vacant world flyweight title and retired
1928	Made comeback
1933	Retired, age 27
Died:	Los Angeles, October 3, 1981, age 76

Career record: Fights 95, Won 73, Lost 15, Drawn 7

AN ACADEMIC AS WELL AS A FIGHTER: WORLD CHAMP LA BARBA BRIEFLY RETIRED TO CONCENTRATE ON HIS UNIVERSITY STUDIES

SEE ALSO ◆ KID CHOCOLATE 72

JAKE LA MOTTA

FACT FILE

1922	Born Giacobe La Motta, Bronx, New York
1941	Professional debut
1943	Beat Ray Robinson in Detroit
1949	Stopped Marcel Cerdan to win world middleweight title
1951	Lost middleweight title to Robinson
1954	Retired, age 31

Career record: Fights 106, Won 83, Lost 19, Drawn 4

LA MOTTA (RIGHT) DEFENDS AGAINST TIBERIO MITRI IN 1950

Jake La Motta had two careers: one as the middleweight champion of the world; the other as a celebrity, after the release of the film of his book, *Raging Bull.*

Roberto De Niro played a bleak La Motta: a guy with a grim wit and self-destructive streak, fueled by the belief that as a teenager he had murdered a bookmaker for his day's takings. He hadn't. The "ghost" turned up to congratulate him in the crowded dressing room on the night he stopped Marcel Cerdan for the championship in 1949. La Motta admitted he spent his career taking unnecessary punches to punish himself for his sin.

La Motta was the first man to beat Sugar Ray Robinson, in Detroit in 1943, and Robinson beat him four times after that. "We fought so often it's a wonder I don't have diabetes."

In title defenses he outscored Tiberio Mitri, then knocked out Laurent Dauthuille of France with 13 seconds left in the fight. He was trailing on points. He lost the title to Robinson in 13 rounds in February 1951. When the referee stopped it, Jake was still on his feet, stubbornly muttering: "You can't put me down."

When he retired in 1955 he ran a Miami nightclub, did time in prison on a chain gang, and was divorced for the third time. In 1961 he testified that he had taken a dive on mob instructions against Billy Fox in 1947 in order to get his title shot against Cerdan. He was ostracized, but eventually moved into acting, worked as a nightclub host in New York, and then co-wrote the book *Raging Bull,* which changed his life.

SEE ALSO ◆ MARCEL CERDAN 60 ◆ RAY ROBINSON 278

ISMAEL LAGUNA

A tough, skilled craftsman with a sturdy chin, Ismael Laguna had two short reigns as world lightweight champion. He was also a true gentleman.

From a family of ten children born in a Panama fishing village, Laguna was a professional fighter at 17, and champion of the world at 21, after an upset 15-round majority points win over established champion Carlos Ortiz in Panama City in April 1965. He lost the championship back to Ortiz on a unanimous verdict in San Juan seven months later.

Laguna avoided nobody, drawing with the superb Argentine Nicolino Loche and losing a decision to Filipino veteran Flash Elorde in a brutal fight in Manila. When he fought Ortiz a third time, the Puerto Rican outpointed him in Shea Stadium, New York, in August 1967.

Fourteen wins in his next 15 fights earned him a chance against young Californian Mando Ramos before 15,000 fans in the UCLA Arena in Los Angeles, and he scored a stunning upset by forcing Ramos to retire after the ninth round in March 1970. Ramos was cut over both eyes.

In Panama City, Laguna beat Ishimatsu Suzuki of Japan in 13 rounds, but then lost a shock split decision to Ken Buchanan in San Juan on September 26, 1970. Buchanan beat him in a return in Madison Square Garden, after which Laguna retired.

He kept his money, lived in a good district outside Panama City where he also promoted fights briefly, but his health was affected by sickle-cell anaemia.

ISMAEL LAGUNA BEATS CUBAN ANGEL GARCIA IN TEN ROUNDS

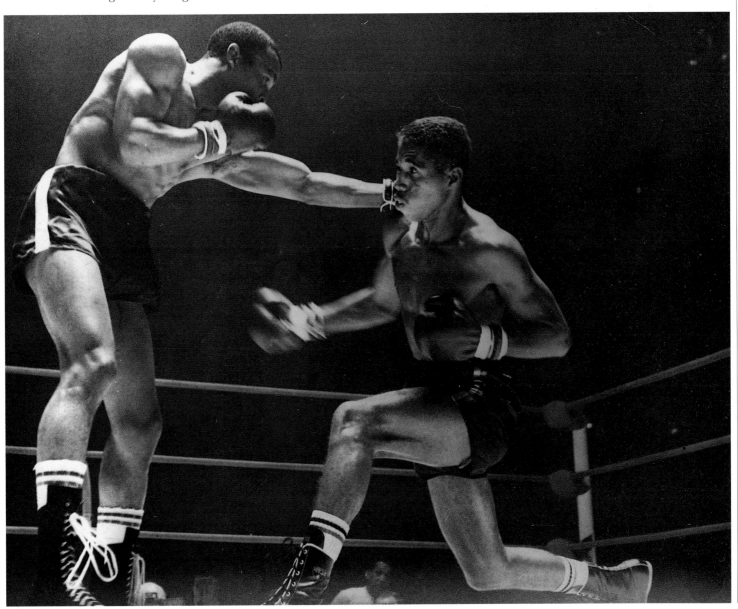

SAM LANGFORD

FACT FILE

1880 Born Weymouth, Nova Scotia

1902 Professional debut in Boston

1906 Lost 15-round decision to Jack Johnson

1909 Knocked out British champ Iron Hague in London

1926 Last fight in Oklahoma

Died: Cambridge, Massachusetts, January 12, 1956, age 75

Career record: Fights 291, Won 187, Lost 50, Drawn 47, No Decisions 4, No Contests 3

Sam Langford had short arms, stood only 5 ft., 7 in. and weighed less than 168 lb., yet was acknowledged as one of the best fighters who ever lived. Langford didn't worry who he fought, where, or for how much. He knocked out fully blown heavyweights like "Fireman" Jim Flynn, Gunboat Smith, and Harry Wills. But, even though as black fighters had to do at the time, he lost some fights by not trying, he was too good for his own good. Nobody would let him fight for a championship, either at middleweight, light-heavyweight, or heavyweight.

Known as the Boston Tar Baby, he was born in Canada but moved south to turn professional. His age varied from time to time, and he once admitted he didn't even know when he was born.

He lost a 15-round decision to Jack Johnson in Chelsea, Massachusetts, in 1906, but although he was about 30 lb. lighter than the big Texan he was never given a return for the heavyweight title after Jack had beaten Tommy Burns. Instead, Langford was condemned to the fringes. He twice knocked out Jim Flynn, who fought both Burns and Johnson in title fights. He knocked out British heavyweight champion Iron Hague in four rounds at the National Sporting Club in London, but mostly fought other tough black heavyweights like Sam McVey, Joe Jeannette, and Harry Wills.

He was in his 40s when he finally retired. A contented, ready smiling man, his old age was made easier by a public subscription fund after a sportswriter tracked him in Harlem. He had been blind for many years.

IN HIS PEAK YEARS LANGFORD WAS ONE OF THE MOST FORMIDABLE HEAVYWEIGHTS OF HIS OR ANY OTHER AGE, YET RARELY WEIGHED MORE THAN MIDDLEWEIGHT

SEE ALSO ◆ TOMMY BURNS 48 ◆ JACK JOHNSON 171

JOSE LEGRA

A flashy, exuberant Cuban who began working life as a shoeshine boy, Jose Legra was once labeled "a pocket Cassius Clay." He tried to live up to the image, grinning broadly as he once told reporters in Spanish: "I am the greatest!"

Legra left his mother, father, and seven brothers and sisters behind when Fidel Castro outlawed professional boxing, but regularly sent money home to help support them. He eventually settled in Spain where he became a naturalized citizen.

His record in Cuba was obscure, but he was 20 years old when he arrived in Spain, fought on average once every three weeks, and in 1967 won the vacant European title by outclassing Yves Desmarets of France in three rounds in Madrid.

In July 1968 Legra won the WBC feather-weight title in Porthcawl, south Wales, when he stopped Howard Winstone in five rounds, despite never having been a devastating puncher. Six months later, he was outpointed over 15 rounds by Australian counter-puncher Johnny Famechon at the Albert Hall in London, although some felt Legra, who broke his right thumb in the fight, had been unlucky.

Legra lost ground when he was outpointed in Los Angeles by Vicente Saldivar, but regained the European title—and then in December 1972 traveled to Mexico to fight Clemente Sanchez for the WBC title in Monterrey. Sanchez failed to make the weight, but Legra won the championship by knocking him down 12 times for a 10th-round stoppage.

As before, his reign was short. In Brazil in May 1973, veteran Eder Jofre outpointed him. He retired the same year after a quick defeat by Alexis Arguello.

FACT FILE

1943	Born Baracoa Beach, Oriente, Cuba
1958	Claimed professional debut
1963	Settled in Spain
1967	Won European featherweight title
1968	Stopped Howard Winstone to win WBC featherweight title
1969	Lost title to Johnny Famechon in London
1972	Regained world title against Clemente Sanchez
1973	Lost title to Eder Jofre in Brazil

Career record: Fights 148, Won 132, Lost 12, Drawn 4

A NIGHT OF FRUSTRATION: LEGRA SPENT 15 ROUNDS CHASING THE ELUSIVE AUSTRALIAN, JOHNNY FAMECHON, BEFORE LOSING HIS WORLD TITLE. FAMECHON SLIPPED OVER REPEATEDLY

SEE ALSO ◆ JOHNNY FAMECHON 107 ◆ EDER JOFRE 169 ◆ HOWARD WINSTONE 338

BENNY LEONARD

FACT FILE

1896 Born Benjamin Leiner, New York City

1917 Won World lightweight title by stopping Freddie Welsh

1922 Lost world welterweight title fight with Jack Britton on a foul

1925 Announced retirement as undefeated lightweight champion

1931 Returned to the ring

1932 Retired after losing to Jimmy McLarnin, age 36

Died: New York City, April 18, 1947, age 51

Career record: Fights 213, Won 180, Lost 21, Drawn 6, No Decisions 6

Benny Leonard was a master boxer, a genius who completed his art and yet still went on reinventing it, who's simple message was: "Think. Learn how to think."

It was a sermon he practiced himself, most notably when he came from the brink to win lightweight title defenses against big hitters Charlie White and Richie Mitchell.

To Leonard, who was world lightweight champion from 1917 until he announced his retirement in January 1925, boxing was a way of life, to be enjoyed and appreciated from morning until night.

He was born Benjamin Leiner to immigrant Jewish parents on the Lower East Side of New York in 1896, and by the age of 15 was fighting professionally, adapting his name to stop his mother finding out!

Leonard was world champion for almost eight years, winning it by stopping Freddie Welsh in nine rounds in Manhattan in May 1917, and turning back challenges from White, Joe Welling, Mitchell, Rocky Kansas, and Lew Tendler. He lost on a 13th-round foul when he tried to win the world welterweight title against Jack Britton, a result that smelled of a fix. He boxed lethargically, and when he put Britton down with a low punch, yet saw the referee pick up the count, he walked over and hit Britton while he was still on the canvas.

He retired as undefeated lightweight champion in 1925, but lost his life savings overnight in the Wall Street Crash. He made an unsuccessful comeback, but was working a contest as a referee in April 1947 when he died of a heart attack.

LEONARD LOST HIS SAVINGS IN THE WALL STREET CRASH AND WAS FORCED TO RETURN TO THE RING IN 1931

SEE ALSO ◆ JACK BRITTON 42

RAY LEONARD

Ray Leonard was a skillful boxer with dazzling footwork, a solid punch, and a self-confidence bordering on arrogance. A media man's dream, he also happened to hold world titles at five separate weights.

He won the 1976 Olympic light-welterweight gold medal with a picture of his fiancee and infant son taped to his sock, and grossed $40,000 for his debut—and his marketability has never waned in the 20 years since.

Leonard won the WBC welterweight title in November 1979 when he stopped defending champ Wilfred Benitez in the 15th round in Las Vegas. The following year was dominated by his fights with Roberto Duran. Leonard lost the first when he was outbrawled in Montreal, but won the second when Duran turned away, snarled "No Mas," and walked out of the fight in round eight.

Leonard took a sideways step to annex the WBA light-middleweight crown by stopping Ayub Kalule of Uganda in nine, but then won a classic battle for the undisputed welterweight title against Thomas Hearns in the 14th round at Caesars Palace in 1981.

Eye surgery forced his retirement, but he came back briefly in 1984, and then again, astonishingly, in April 1987 when he took a close 12-round decision over Marvin Hagler for the world middleweight title. He retired, then returned to win the WBC light-heavyweight belt by stopping Canadian Donnie Lalonde in nine in 1988. The victory also gave him the vacant WBC super-middleweight title.

In faded replicas of his old classics, he drew with Hearns and easily outscored Duran in 1989, but showed a champion's heart and class in losing a 12-round decision to WBC light-middleweight champ Terry Norris in Madison Square Garden in 1991. A return in 1997 against Hector Camacho brought a five-round defeat.

FACT FILE

1956 Born Wilmington, South Carolina

1976 Olympic light-welterweight gold medalist

1979 Won WBC welterweight title against Wilfred Benitez

1980 Lost and regained title against Roberto Duran

1981 Won undisputed welterweight title against Thomas Hearns

1987 Outpointed Marvin Hagler for middleweight title

1988 Beat Donnie Lalonde for WBC light-heavyweight crown

1989 Drew with Hearns, beat Duran in super-middleweight fights

1991 Lost to WBC light-middleweight champ Terry Norris

Career record: Fights 39, Won 36, Lost 2, Drawn 1

LEONARD'S LAST MOMENT OF GREATNESS: HE OUTPOINTS MARVIN HAGLER IN LAS VEGAS IN 1987

SEE ALSO ◆ WILDRED BENITEZ 32 ◆ ROBERTO DURAN 99 ◆ MARVIN HAGLER 147 ◆ THOMAS HEARNS 153 ◆ TERRY NORRIS 255

THE
GREAT FIGHTS

MARVIN HAGLER
V.
RAY LEONARD

CAESARS PALACE, LAS VEGAS.
APRIL 6, 1987.

Some said this fight should not happen, that Ray Leonard could not fight once in five years and then step up in weight to face a middleweight champion as great as Marvin Hagler. Some went so far as to say his health was in danger.

Yet the fears were erased as Leonard, a 4-1 outsider, fought a shrewd tactical battle to win a bitterly disputed, highly controversial 12-round decision.

Leonard set out, in his own words, to mess up Hagler's mind and his life. In saying that, the former welter and light-middleweight champ demonstrated the mean streak that lay beneath the articulate voice and handsome face. And in the fight itself, not for the first time, Leonard demonstrated what a hard, durable man he was.

Hagler, finally proven by the Newark public records office to be 32 not 34, was so confident he agreed with Leonard's proposal to confine the bout to 12 rounds—a crucial error.

Hagler began cautiously and by the time he opened up, Leonard had built a solid lead. He survived a torrid fifth and then bluffed his way through with bursts of eye-catching, but harmless arm punches as Hagler walked him down. Leonard traded with him in the ninth, but all the time the champion was eating away at the deficit. Leonard countered, but often hit arms and gloves, and the tension increased with the realisation that not only was the fight going 12 rounds, it was incredibly close.

At the final bell Leonard was near exhaustion, but victory rejuvenated him. "I had fun tonight," he beamed. "This is what I said I would do and I did it. It wasn't for the title. Beating Marvin Hagler was enough."

Hagler's contempt was total. "Leonard fought like a girl," he said. "His punches meant nothing. I fought my heart out. I kept my belt. I can't believe they took it away from me."

GUS LESNEVICH

FACT FILE

1915 Born Cliffside Park, New Jersey

1939 Lost first world light-heavyweight title bid against Billy Conn

1941 Won recognition as undisputed champion against Tami Mauriello

1946 Stopped Freddie Mills in London

1948 Lost rematch with Mills on points

1949 Retired after losing to NBA heavyweight champ Ezzard Charles

Died: Cliffside Park, New Jersey, February 28, 1964, age 49

Career record: Fights 79, Won 60, Lost 14, Drawn 5

A solid, down-to-earth crafts-man, Gus Lesnevich was called "The Russian Lion" because of his strength and heart. He grew up working in his mother's New Jersey restaurant, at one time had a job selling candy apples at a local fairground, and went on to top the light-heavyweight division for seven years.

He won a Golden Gloves title before turning professional, managed by Joe Vella in 1934. Together they went to the top. Lesnevich failed in two title challenges against Billy Conn, and once contemplated retiring, but outpointed Anton Christoforidis to win NBA recognition as world champion in May 1941.

His claim was cemented three months later with a hotly disputed split decision over Tami Mauriello in Madison Square Garden. A rematch was essential—and in November 1941 Lesnevich proved his superiority by taking a unanimous 15-round verdict.

Wartime duties with the US Coast Guard restricted his ring activity and when, upon his return in 1946, he was stopped by heavyweight Lee Oma, his chances of remaining champion seemed rather bleak.

But in May 1946 at Harringay Arena in north London, he won a torrid struggle with Britain's Freddie Mills in the 10th round. Then came two stoppage wins over "Blackjack" Billy Fox, the second in only one minute, 58 seconds, before he returned to London to face Mills a second time at the White City Stadium in 1948. This time Mills, who remembered Lesnevich as a quiet, gentlemanly, and intelligent man with a keen sense of humor, outpointed him.

Lesnevich finally retired in 1949 after losing to Joey Maxim and, for the NBA heavyweight title, to Ezzard Charles in seven rounds. He died of cancer 15 years later in Cliffside Park, New Jersey.

LESNEVICH NAILS "BLACKJACK" BILLY FOX WITH A LEFT HOOK IN 1948. LESNEVICH STOPPED HIM TWICE

SEE ALSO ♦ EZZARD CHARLES 65 ♦ BILLY CONN 75 ♦ FREDDIE MILLS 217

JOHN HENRY LEWIS

John Henry Lewis was only 24 when the doctor examined him. It was March 1939 and he was ready to defend his world light-heavyweight title against Dave Clark in Detroit. Lewis had conned medics before, the kind promoters bought on the cheap. But this one knew what he was doing—and quickly discovered that the boxer could no longer distinguish light from dark, nor detect the number of fingers held up just 18 inches away. To all intents and purposes, the man was blind!

Lewis had held the light-heavyweight title since 1935, when he handed out a 15-round drubbing to Bob Olin in St. Louis. The son of a physical trainer at the University of Southern California, Lewis was a beautifully conditioned athlete and an extremely talented boxer. It was said he was also a descendent of bare-knuckle legend Tom Molyneaux.

On the way up he beat future heavyweight champ James J. Braddock, but when he beat Olin he fought for expenses only because only a small crowd turned out. He boxed regularly, usually in non-title fights, but also turned back a number of challenges from Jock McAvoy, Harvey, Olin, Emilio Martinez, and Al Gainer.

Eventually, with his eyesight failing, he was given a shot at Joe Louis for the heavyweight title in January 1939 before a sellout crowd at Madison Square Garden. Unknown to him, John Henry's father traveled by bus to sit in the crowd and watch his son challenge for the greatest prize in sport. It lasted two minutes, 29 seconds. Louis said he made it quick, so that Lewis, whom he considered a friend, should not suffer.

FACT FILE

1914 Born Los Angeles
1928 Professional debut, age 14
1935 Won world light-heavyweight title against Bob Olin
1939 Lost to heavyweight champion Joe Louis, retired
Died: Berkeley, California, April 18, 1974, age 59
Career record: Fights 117, Won 103, Lost 8, Drawn 6

LEWIS WITH THE WORLD CHAMPIONSHIP TROPHY AFTER HIS 15-ROUND DECISION OVER LEN HARVEY

SEE ALSO ◆ JAMES J. BRADDOCK 36 ◆ JOE LOUIS 204

THE GREAT FIGHTS

GUS LESNEVICH
V.
FREDDIE MILLS

HARRINGAY ARENA, LONDON.
MAY 14, 1946.

Jack Solomons built the postwar British boxing boom on this amazing fight. He tempted world light-heavyweight champion Gus Lesnevich to London to defend against Freddie Mills, whom Britain had claimed was the best 175 lb. man in the world since his 1942 win over Len Harvey, and 11,000 fans crammed into the oval-shaped Harringay Arena in north London.

The ring appearances of both men had been severely restricted by World War II, but while Lesnevich had boxed twice since, Mills went into this fight without a warm-up. He had been out of the ring for 15 months, and had not long returned from service in India.

Britain's fight-starved fans saw a classic confrontation between boxer and slugger, and as big-hearted a performance as anybody could wish to see. Yet it looked all over in round two when Mills ran on to a stiff jab and devastating right hand that put him down for six. Lesnevich dropped him twice more and handed out such severe punishment that the fight should have been stopped. Yet Mills not only came up for the third, but tucked his chin into his shoulder and outjabbed the champion.

Lesnevich, his nose broken and an eye almost shut, seemed all but finished. After the ninth he shook his head at his cornermen, yet turned it around dramatically in the tenth, saving his title by flooring Mills three more times.

What followed was a cruel indictment of the way things used to be. Mills was ill in the dressing room and twice vomited on the way from the arena. For a week his speech was slurred, he suffered throbbing headaches, and slept unusually heavily. Three weeks after losing to Lesnevich, he fought British heavyweight champion Bruce Woodcock and went down on points after 12 hard rounds.

Two years later Lesnevich returned to London and lost the championship title to Mills on points over 15 rounds at White City Stadium.

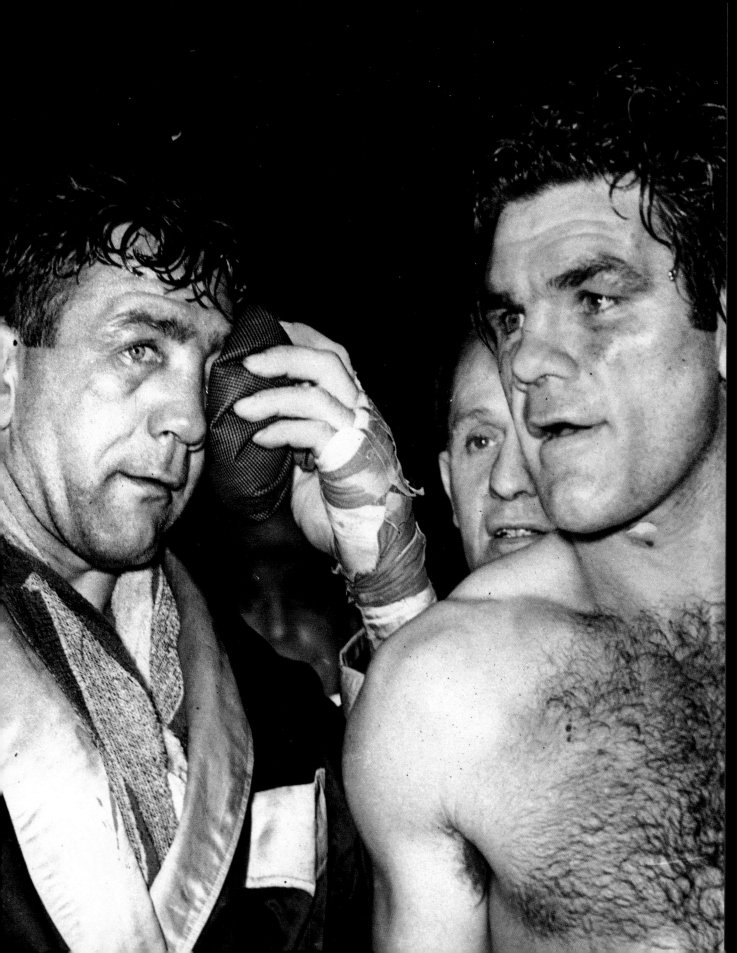

LENNOX LEWIS

LEWIS IN HIS BIZARRE WIN OVER OLIVER MCCALL

A smart boxer with a heavy right hand, Lennox Lewis was a giant of a man at 6 ft., 4¾ in. and nearly 240 lb. When the World Boxing Council sent him a letter saying they recognized him as their champion at the end of 1992, he became the first British-born boxer of the 20th century to hold the heavyweight championship.

Lewis was born in London, but his mother Violet took him to Kitchener, Ontario, where he grew up—and learned to box. Under the Canadian flag he reached the 1984 Olympic Games quarter-final, and in Seoul in 1988 he stopped Riddick Bowe in the super-heavyweight final to win the gold medal.

Lewis returned to Britain to turn pro under London manager Frank Maloney, won the British, Commonwealth, and European titles and then won a WBC final eliminator by knocking out Razor Ruddock in two rounds.

A calm, classy man who ducked nobody, Lewis was awarded the WBC championship when Bowe reneged on a contract to defend against him. Lewis earned a huge £6 million ($9 million) payday for outpointing Tony Tucker in Las Vegas, labored to a seventh-round stoppage of Frank Bruno at a rain-soaked Cardiff Arms Park, and then outclassed Phil Jackson in eight rounds in Miami.

He seemed set for a showdown with Bowe, but lost the WBC title when Oliver McCall stopped him in two rounds at Wembley in September 1994. Lewis regained the title from McCall, but big money fights with Bowe, Evander Holyfield, and Mike Tyson continued to pass him by.

SEE ALSO ◆ RIDDICK BOWE 36 ◆ FRANK BRUNO 44 ◆ EVANDER HOLYFIELD 159 ◆ MIKE TYSON 319

TED KID LEWIS

There was never anybody like Ted Kid Lewis, the best British boxer of them all.

He was a European champion from featherweight up to middleweight and twice held the world welterweight title in a four-year spell. They called him "Crashing, Bashing, and Dashing," and he did his best to live up to the billing. Fearlessly aggressive, he worried about no man, no matter what he weighed or how good he was supposed to be.

Born Gershon Mendeloff into a poor Jewish family in London's East End, Lewis was a professional fighter at 15. He won the British and European featherweight titles, but quickly outgrew the division after seeking his fortune in the United States. By August 1915 he was big enough to floor and outpoint Jack Britton for the world welterweight title in Boston. Theirs was an intense rivalry: Britton took away Lewis's title with a 20-round points win in New Orleans in April 1916, but The Kid reversed that one with a 20-round decision in Dayton, Ohio, in June 1917.

In 1918 he stayed champion, and also had the better of the great lightweight champion Benny Leonard in an eight-round no-decision bout, but lost the belt back to Britton in 1919.

Lewis returned home in 1920 to win the British and European titles, lost once more to Britton in New York for the world championship, and then moved up to middleweight, where again he conquered Britain and Europe. But in May 1922 a challenge to world light-heavyweight champ Georges Carpentier ended when, outweighed by 18 lb., he turned to complain to the referee and was knocked out in 135 seconds.

He fought on until 1929, and in retirement refereed fights, did some bit part acting, and somehow took four years off his age in order to join the RAF in World War II. He lived on to be a much-loved elder statesman of the British boxing scene.

LEWIS WON MORE THAN 200 RING BATTLES AND TWICE HELD THE WORLD WELTERWEIGHT TITLE

FACT FILE

1893 Born Gershon Mendeloff, London

1915 Won world welterweight title against Jack Britton

1916 Lost title back to Britton

1917 Regained title from Britton

1919 Britton beat him in nine rounds to end his second reign

1922 Lost to Georges Carpentier for world light-heavyweight title

Died: London, October 20, 1970, age 76

Career record: Fights 283, Won 215, Lost 44, Drawn 24

SEE ALSO ♦ JACK BRITTON 41 ♦ GEORGES CARPENTIER 59

SONNY LISTON

FACT FILE

1932 Born Charles Liston, St. Francis County, Arkansas

1953 Professional debut in St. Louis

1962 Knocked out Floyd Patterson to win world heavyweight title

1964 Lost in strange circumstances to Cassius Clay

1970 Won last fight with Chuck Wepner

Died: Las Vegas, Nevada, December 30, 1970, age 38

Career record: Fights 54, Won 50, Lost 4

ife gave few breaks to Sonny Liston, the most menacing and misunderstood of men.

Perhaps it's understandable, given the fact that Charles was the 24th of her 25 children, that his mother couldn't exactly remember when he was born. Liston's age was a matter of cruel conjecture for years. Cynics called the birth certificate he produced a fake. Certainly, when he fought Cassius Clay in 1964, the supposedly 31-year-old heavyweight champion had a daughter of 17. In the end what did years matter?

Liston was a child when he caught a bus from the Arkansas cotton fields to St. Louis to follow his mother. He ran with street gangs and was jailed for armed robbery. In prison he learned to box, encouraged by a priest who would later sit ringside at his fights, and when he came out, he went straight.

Apart from one night when a joker named Marty Marshall made him laugh and broke his jaw, Liston beat everybody. Unfortunately, in 1956 the list of victims was extended to include a police officer. He was jailed for nine months.

It took until 1962 to get a world title chance. And when he destroyed Floyd Patterson in 126 seconds, he thought people would be pleased he'd made something of himself. They weren't. Even when he demolished Patterson a second time, he was slammed as a bad example to American youth.

After twice losing in mysterious circumstances to Cassius Clay (Muhammad Ali), Liston was never again entertained as a world title candidate. When he was found dead in the bedroom of his Las Vegas home, the coroner ruled death by natural causes. Few people believed him.

FEARSOME LISTON SMASHES THE WORLD HEAVYWEIGHT TITLE LOOSE FROM FLOYD PATTERSON. LISTON WON BOTH OF THEIR FIGHTS INSIDE A ROUND

SEE ALSO ◆ MUHAMMAD ALI 12 ◆ FLOYD PATTERSON 265

NICOLINO LOCHE

icolino Loche was a brilliant tactician, a crafty, skilled, and, by the time he became the WBA light-welterweight champion, veteran campaigner with more than 100 fights behind him.

Loche was a light puncher—103 of his 117 wins were on points—but somehow managed to combine a tight defense with a pressing, aggressive style.

He won the WBA title in Tokyo in December 1968 when he forced defending champion Paul Fujii, a Hawaiian-born Japanese who served in the US Marines, to retire at the end of nine rounds. Fujii's surrender after being completely outboxed did not draw sympathy from the Japanese fans, who tossed fruit and other debris into the ring!

For Loche, who had turned professional ten years earlier in his home state of Mendoza, it was his first fight outside Argentina.

The excursion over, Loche took the title home, defended it in Buenos Aires in May 1969 with a clear 15-round decision over Carlos Hernandez, in which both men were on the floor, and then turned back challenges from Joao Henrique of Brazil and the tough American Adolph Pruitt. In 1971 Domingo Barrera of Spain and the rising star of the division, Venezuelan Antonio "Kid Pambele" Cervantes, were both of them outpointed.

After the Barrera fight, which he won on a split decision, Loche retired for six months, then changed his mind. He lost the belt on a 15-round decision to Alfonzo Frazier in Panama City in March 1972, and then in March 1973 challenged the much-improved Cervantes in Venezuela. Loche was 33 years old, and Cervantes stopped him at the end of the ninth round. This was the only time he lost inside the distance. Loche quit the ring for good in 1976.

FACT FILE

1939 Born Tunuyan, Mendoza, Argentina

1958 Professional debut, age 19

1968 Won WBA light-welterweight title against Paul Fujii in Tokyo

1972 Lost WBA titloe to Alfonzo Frazer in Panama

1976 Last fight, a points win, age 36

Career record: Fights 136, Won 117, Lost 4, Drawn 14, No Contest 1

LOCHE SLAMS A LEFT HOOK INTO THE HEAD OF PAUL "TAKESHI" FUJII IN TOKYO IN DECEMBER 1968. LOCHE WON IN 10 ROUNDS

SEE ALSO ◆ ANTONIO CEVANTES 62

The
GREAT
FIGHTS

FLOYD PATTERSON
V.
SONNY LISTON

COMISKEY PARK, CHICAGO.
SEPTEMBER 25, 1962.

Sonny Liston was the most avoided heavyweight of his time... and with good reason.

Floyd Patterson became the youngest champion in heavyweight history when he knocked out Archie Moore in 1956. But his mentor, Cus D'Amato, knew that 21-year-old Floyd was still very much a developing fighter, mentally as well as physically.

He steered him clear of the most dangerous contenders. Nino Valdes, Eddie Machen, Zora Folley, Cleveland Williams, and, above all, Charles "Sonny" Liston, should have been given a chance ahead of those who were chosen.

Finally, by 1962, after Patterson had lost and regained the championship against Ingemar Johansson, and against D'Amato's advice, let his pride rule his business brain: Liston was selected.

A menacing character who had mixed with hoodlums and gangsters, Liston had turned to boxing while in jail. His professional career had once been interrupted by another spell behind bars for assaulting a policeman.

Liston's chance came in the open air at Comiskey Park, Chicago, before a crowd of 18,894. Pre-fight opinion was divided—those who picked Patterson included Ring editor Nat Fleischer, and former champs Johansson, Rocky Marciano, and James J. Braddock.

Liston needed only 126 seconds to prove them horribly wrong. He thumped away inside, but took Patterson out with two tremendous left hooks to the head. The new champion said enthusiastically: "I'll fight anyone who deserves a shot at the title. I won't make a challenger wait the way Patterson made me wait. The public owns the title and I brought it back to the public."

Sadly, the American public would reject him as a bad example to youth and would crush his hopes of becoming an acceptable face in society. He would brood on the whys and wherefores for the rest of his short life.

Patterson sat in his dressing room and wept, and left the arena in a false beard, driving 800 miles home to be with his wife.

In Las Vegas 10 months later, Patterson came out of seclusion, enforced the rematch clause—and was knocked out in 130 seconds.

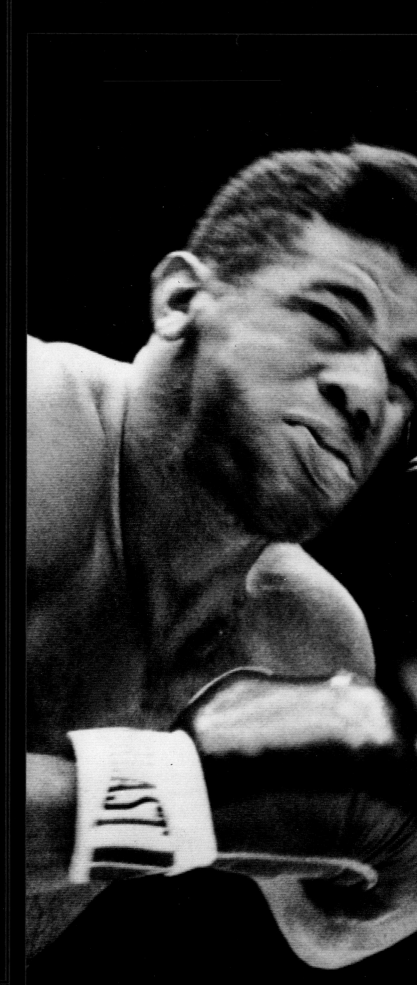

DIULIO LOI

FACT FILE

1929 Born Trieste, Italy
1948 Professional debut, age 19
1954 Won European lightweight title
1959 Won European welterweight title
1960 Won world light-welterweight title against Carlos Ortiz
1962 Lost and regained world light-welter crown against Eddie Perkins

Career record: Fights 126, Won 115, Lost 3, Drawn 8

Short and strong, Diulio Loi was a remarkable fighter from the Italian port of Trieste, who fought out of Milan. A converted southpaw, Loi employed a bobbing, weaving style to get to close range, where he worked away relentlessly.

Loi lost three fights in his life. The first was a European lightweight championship match in Copenhagen in August 1952, when Jorgen Johansen outpointed him.

The second was on a split decision in his first world light-welterweight title bid against Carlos Ortiz in San Francisco in June 1960, and the third was when he lost his world title to Eddie Perkins in Milan in 1962. All three of them were avenged.

He took the world title from Ortiz on a majority verdict in Milan in September 1960 when roared on by more than 65,000 fans, and when they fought a third time in the San Siro stadium in Milan in May 1961, another huge crowd of more than 60,000 turned out to see Loi drop Ortiz in the sixth round and win again clearly.

When Loi could only draw with Perkins in Milan, a rematch was inevitable, and they fought again at the 20,000-capacity Vigorelli Stadium in Milan in September 1962. Perkins, who claimed bitterly that he was robbed in the first fight, won beyond dispute with a hard left jab. Loi, the hero so many times, was booed from the ring.

He knew he was near the end at 33, but dug deep and produced one final hour of inspiration, outpointing Perkins in Milan in December 1962. A month later, he announced his retirement.

ONE OF ITALY'S SPORTING FAVORITES: LOI IN HIS WORLD TITLE WINNING PERFORMANCE AGAINST CARLOS ORTIZ IN MILAN

SEE ALSO ♦ CARLOS ORTIZ 258

DANNY LOPEZ

anny Lopez was alarmingly easy to hit, but could himself knock a man cold with one shot.

Known as "Little Red" because big brother Ernie was plain "Red," Lopez was one of the biggest single punchers in the history of the featherweight division. On his night, he could have lived with any one of them.

Typical Lopez fare was served up on September 15, 1978 when 63,000 fans packed the New Orleans Superdome to see the Muhammad Ali–Leon Spinks return. In a companion title fight, Lopez defended his WBC belt against Juan Malvarez of Argentina.

After half a minute Lopez was on the floor. He got up, but looked ready to fall again, until midway through round two he planted his feet and uncorked a terrific right to the point of the chin. Malvarez was out cold.

Lopez, who was originally from Utah but fought out of Los Angeles, knocked out his first 21 professional opponents. A tough 1974, when he was stopped by Bobby Chacon and Shige Fukuyama, set him back, but he knocked out Ruben Olivares and stopped Sean O'Grady to get back on track.

Very few visitors win a championship in Africa, but Lopez did. In November 1976 he punished WBC champ David Kotey so badly the local fans streamed from the stadium before the final bell.

Lopez won all eight of his successful defenses inside the distance, before the great Mexican Salvador Sanchez twice counterpunched him to defeat, in 13 and 14 rounds respectively. "Little Red" had the good sense to stop then, his reputation as one of the most exciting fighters in history intact. Ironically, in retirement he took a job in demolition.

FACT FILE

1952	Born Fort Duchesme, Utah
1971	Professional debut, age 18
1976	Beat David Kotey in Ghana for WBC featherweight title
1980	Lost title to Salvador Sanchez in ninth defense

Career record: Fights 47, Won 42, Lost 5

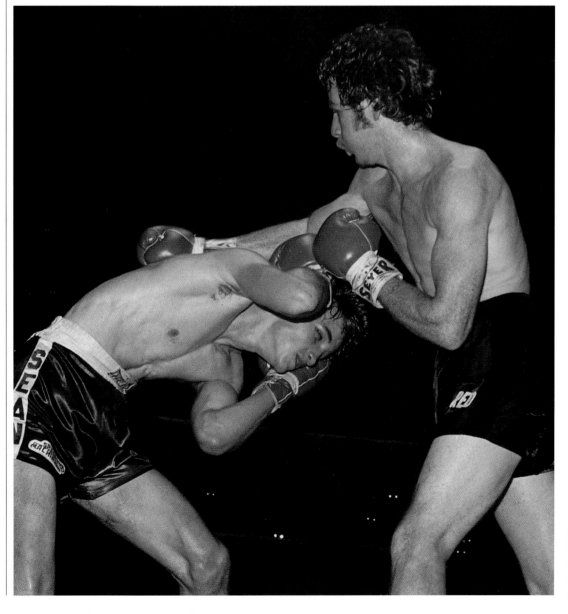

LOPEZ (RIGHT) HIT TOO HARD FOR YOUNG SEAN O'GRADY IN LOS ANGELES IN 1976. "LITTLE RED" WON IN THE FOURTH

SEE ALSO ◆ DAVID KOTEY 180 ◆ SALVADOR SANCHEZ 293

RICARDO LOPEZ

FACT FILE

1966 Born Mexico City
1985 Professional debut
1990 Won WBC
strawweight title by
knocking out
Hideyuki Ohashi
Career record: Fights 44,
Won 44

A calculated, clinical boxer, Ricardo "Finito" Lopez was close to perfection in a boxing ring.

The greatest star of boxing's lightest division, the disciplined, organized man from Mexico City proved himself a class above all of his contenders for six years. Lopez yearned for the chance to prove himself against his major rivals for attention in the lower weight categories, light-flyweights Humberto Gonzalez and Michael Carbajal. But Gonzalez retired without facing him, and by the end of 1996 talk of a fight with Carbajal had amounted to just that... talk.

Lopez, a hyperactive child who pressed his father Magdaleno to take him to a boxing gym, won ten amateur titles including the 1984 Mexican Golden Gloves. By 18 years of age, he was a professional fighter.

He won the WBC strawweight (105 lb.) belt by knocking out Hideyuki Ohashi of Japan in five rounds in Tokyo in October 1990. Six years on, he was still champion, having disposed of 18 consecutive challengers from all parts of the globe. The most impressive result was a second-round stoppage of Thailand's Saman Sorjatorung in 1993. Saman went on to beat Humberto Gonzalez for the light-flyweight title. In March 1996, Lopez came back from hand surgery to outclass his No. 1 contender Ala Villamor of the Philippines.

A regular on Don King's promotional extravaganzas, Lopez cut a strangely quiet, dignified figure among the hustle and bustle. He seemed a man at peace with his job, away from which he said he was perfectly content to relax with his fiancée Enriqueta, reading, listening to salsa music, and watching his favorite old movies.

THEY CALLED HIM "FINITO":
LOPEZ LIVED UP TO THE
CHILLING BILLING, BUT THE
BIG FIGHTS REPEATEDLY
ELUDED HIM

SEE ALSO ◆ MICHAEL CARBAJAL 55 ◆ HUMBERTO GONZALEZ 138

TOMMY LOUGHRAN

Tommy Loughran was a dancing master with a dream of a left hand. He more than made up in skill for the handicap that had hampered him since he suffered a seriously broken right hand early in his career, which inevitably meant a loss of punching power.

He was an accomplished light-heavyweight champion, who beat Irishman Mike McTigue over 15 rounds in New York in October 1927 to take the title. Jimmy Slattery, Leo Lomski, Pete Latzo, Mickey Walker, and James J. Braddock tried to dethrone him, but he outboxed every one of them.

Early in his career, he was a middleweight—and six times fought the great Harry Greb, beating him once, on points in Boston in 1923.

When Gene Tunney retired, Loughran moved up to heavyweight in search of the biggest prize of all, but in spite of beating Max Baer and Jack Sharkey, he had a chastening experience when he fought Primo Carnera for the championship in Miami in March 1934.

Loughran conceded an incredible 86 lb. to the 270 lb. Italian. Knowing he had to keep the giant at long range, he plastered his hair with the foulest smelling grease possible. Whenever they clinched, Carnera's eyes watered, he spluttered and broke free. But the lumbering champ still managed to tread on Loughran's foot and crush his toe! Loughran slowed as the fight wore on and lost on points.

He fought until 1937, joined the US Marines and earned a fortune as a Wall Street broker.

FACT FILE

1902 Born Philadelphia
1927 Won world light-heavyweight title against Mike McTigue
1929 Defeated Mickey Walker and James J. Braddock, gave up title
1934 Lost to Primo Carnera for the world heavyweight title
1937 Last fight in Philadelphia, age 34
Died: Altoona, Pennsylvania, July 7, 1982, age 79
Career record: Fights 174, Won 123, Lost 30, Drawn 13, No Decisions 7, No Contest 1

SMART IN AND OUT OF THE RING: LOUGHRAN WAS LIGHT-HEAVYWEIGHT CHAMP, BUT TOO LIGHT TO HANDLE THE GIANT PRIMO CARNERA

SEE ALSO ◆ MAX BAER 26 ◆ JAMES J. BRADDOCK 37 ◆ PRIMO CARNERA 58 ◆ MIKE MCTIGUE 250 ◆ JACK SHARKEY 296 ◆ MICKEY WALKER 330

JOE LOUIS

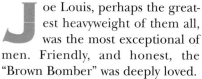

Joe Louis, perhaps the greatest heavyweight of them all, was the most exceptional of men. Friendly, and honest, the "Brown Bomber" was deeply loved.

Louis had a way of gliding into range and unleashing combinations of astonishing speed and accuracy. He had perfect balance, and instinctively knew when to fire his punches, when to wait. He was economical, never wild, always engrossed by the moment.

His sheer ability could frighten a man. King Levinsky pleaded with the referee: "Please, don't let him hit me again!" And one writer described Johnny Paychek as "a ghost walking."

Louis lost only to the German, Max Schmeling, in his first 15 years of fighting. And that defeat, caused by a combination of a young man's overconfidence and Schmeling's experience and eye for detail, was avenged by a chilling first-round triumph in 1938 in a fight played out to an overtly political backcloth which anticipated the forthcoming war.

Louis won the heavyweight championship by knocking out James J. Braddock in eight rounds in 1937. In 12 years he made 25 successful defences, donating several of his purses to the war effort.

America didn't thank him for it. When he should have retired, he was forced to box again because he had not paid tax on those purses and was charged interest on the non-payment. Old and tired, he lost to the new champion Ezzard Charles in 1950, and Rocky Marciano finished him off by knocking him out the following year.

He damaged his heart earning peanuts in wrestling matches, suffered mental illness but, before his final decline, spent happy years as a greeter at Caesars Palace, Las Vegas.

SEE ALSO ◆ JAMES J. BRADDOCK 37 ◆ EZZARD CHARLES 65 ◆ ROCKY MARCIANO 209 ◆ MAX SCHMELING 294

BENNY LYNCH

ALCOHOLISM destroyed Benny Lynch even as he was celebrating his most brilliant victories.

The little man from the Gorbals tenements was a sensational flyweight champion of the world, an all-action crowd pleaser whose life took on an extra dimension when he laced on a pair of gloves.

Lynch could box and punch, was fast, developed into a hard puncher, and had a strong chin. He was Scotland's first world champion and proud of it.

Yet even as he was beating the best flyweights the world could serve up, he was falling apart. Torn between his love for boxing, his anxiety to provide for his wife and family, and the disease that pulled him toward the next dram, the next hit, he was crumbling inside.

He annihilated Jackie Brown in two rounds at Manchester's Belle Vue arena in September 1935 to win the world title—and even the United States was convinced when he outpointed Small Montana, who was an American-based Filipino, at Wembley in January 1937.

Lynch won a classic and memorable battle with England's Peter Kane in front of a total of 40,000 fans at Shawfield Stadium in Glasgow in October 1937, but by the time they drew a non-title fight the following March, he had aged dramatically.

But Lynch lost the flyweight title on the scales when he weighed in 6½ lb. too heavy for a defense against American Jackie Jurich at Paisley in June 1938. He beat Jurich, but it was all over. Four months later he heard them yell "drunk" and "bum" as he lost to a Romanian named Aurel Toma. A hopeless alcoholic, he died of pneumonia in a Glasgow hospital eight years later.

FACT FILE

1913 Born Glasgow, Scotland

1931 Professional debut, age 18

1935 Won world flyweight title by stopping Jackie Brown in Manchester, England

1937 Outpointed Small Montana in London for undisputed title

1938 Lost championship on scales

Died: Glasgow, August 6, 1946, age 33

Career record: Fights 122, Won 90, Lost 15, Drawn 17

HOW MOST BOXING FANS WOULD LIKE TO REMEMBER LYNCH: YOUNG AND BRIGHT-EYED AT THE TOP OF HIS TRADE

SEE ALSO ◆ PETER KANE 175

THE GREAT FIGHTS

BENNY LYNCH

V.

PETER KANE

SHAWFIELD PARK, GLASGOW.
OCTOBER 13, 1937.

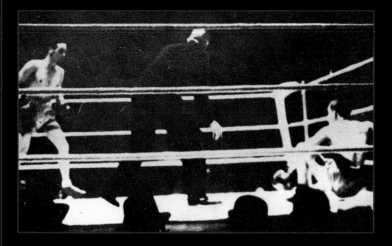

Benny Lynch, a beautiful boxer with a sharp punch, had been world flyweight champion for two years. At 24, he was at his peak. Peter Kane, a heavy punching blacksmith from Lancashire, was only 19 but sold out arenas wherever he fought.

Critics said the teenager was being pitched in too soon, but Glasgow promoter George Dingley paid Lynch £4,000 ($20,000) and Kane £1,500 ($7,500), and then had the satisfaction of seeing a crowd of 33,000 pay to watch an epic confrontation at Shawfield Park.

Kane was a fast, perpetual motion fighter, whereas Lynch was more methodical but when he wanted he could be just as quick.

In the opening round Lynch floored Kane with a left hook to the body and a perfect right to the chin. He got up at three, and said later he knew nothing of the fight after that.

Yet he battled back as Lynch, for once, was overanxious to finish it. In round two Lynch was badly shaken by a right hand, and boxed more economically from then on, blocking patiently and chipping away with precise counters and body punches as Kane, in his youthful exuberance, thought about nothing beyond the desire to throw punches.

By the ninth Kane was tiring and Lynch calmly raised his pace. Kane tried to stay with him, but his punches gradually lost their sting and accuracy. In the 12th Kane was shaken by a left hook to the jaw, and late in the round walked on to another left that dropped him. He refused to quit, hauling himself up at a count of three and, ignoring the blood in his nose and mouth, fighting back. But this gamest of challengers had nothing left but his heart. Two more knockdowns in the 13th put him out cold, draped over the bottom rope. Five months later they fought a 12-round draw in Liverpool, and within eight months Lynch had forfeited his title on the scales. His tragedy had begun. Kane succeeded him as champion in September 1938.

RAY MANCINI

FACT FILE

1961 Born Youngstown, Ohio

1981 Fought Alexis Arguello for WBC lightweight title

1982 Won WBA lightweight title from Arturo Frias

1984 Lost WBA lightweight title to Livingstone Bramble

1992 Lost last fight to Greg Haugen

Career record: Fights 34, Won 29, Lost 5

MANCINI: ONE OF THE BRAVEST, WHO ALWAYS PUT EVERYTHING ON THE LINE

You knew where you were with Ray Mancini. He walked out, dipped low, and threw punches until the time came to stop. No half measures, no excuses, just effort and plenty of it.

Some criticized him for taking too many shots himself, others rose to his honesty, his willingness to lay everything on the line.

Mancini's father Lenny was a top-class fighter in the 1940s, and Ray inherited his dreams as well as his "Boom Boom" nickname. Naturally, it was a moment of immense pride when he won the WBA lightweight title with a first-round stoppage of Arturo Frias at the Aladdin Hotel, Las Vegas, in May 1982. "This is the greatest present our son could give us," said his father at the time.

Ray's previous world title attempt had been a characteristically brave effort against Alexis Arguello for the WBC title in October 1981, when he was stopped in the 14th round in Atlantic City, but emerged with his reputation enhanced.

A committed Christian, Mancini admitted he relied on his faith to get him through the death of challenger Duk-koo Kim in Las Vegas in November 1982. Kim was stopped in the 14th round and suffered a blood clot on the brain.

Mancini continued fighting, successfuly defending his title a total of four times until Livingstone Bramble outboxed and outpunched him for a 14th-round stoppage in Buffalo in June 1984. Mancini retired when he lost the return on points, came back to lose a disputed split decision to Hector Camacho, but when he returned again in 1992, the fire had gone and he lost in seven to Greg Haugen.

SEE ALSO ♦ **ALEXIS ARGUELLO 20** ♦ **HECTOR CAMACHO 51**

ROCKY MARCIANO

Rocky Marciano was impossible to discourage, and seemed impervious to pain. Archie Moore, Ezzard Charles, and Jersey Joe Walcott all forgot more about boxing technique than Marciano ever learned. Yet "The Rock" knocked them all out.

Against Walcott, on the night he won the world heavyweight title in Philadelphia in September 1952, he was floored and outboxed. Then in round 13, Rocky's right hand, the punch he called his "Suzy-Q," transformed a world-class athlete into a discarded rag doll in a fraction of a second. Walcott slid gently down the ropes, one arm trapped in them, completely out.

Marciano's wade-in, swarming style was modified by trainer Charley Goldman. He couldn't stop Rocky getting hit or cut, but he taught him how to get close enough to hurt. Marciano had a warrior's heart and a pitiless instinct—as he showed when he finished Joe Louis's career in 1951. When outboxed by college graduate Roland LaStarza in a 1953 defense, Marciano smashed away at his arms, knowing he couldn't hit the chin. Eventually, LaStarza couldn't hold his arms up because of the pain and was stopped in round 11.

Charles stayed the distance with Marciano first time around and sliced his nose open in the rematch, but was knocked out in round eight. Moore, the reigning light-heavyweight champ, dropped "The Rock" in round two, but couldn't keep him down and was knocked out in the ninth.

Marciano retired in 1956, after 49 wins and six title defenses, and resisted all offers to return. He died in a plane crash age 45.

"THE ROCK" CRUSHES ROLAND LA STARZA IN 1953

FACT FILE

1923 Born Rocco Marchegiano, Brockton, Massachusetts
1947 Professional debut
1951 Knocked out Joe Louis in Madison Square Garden
1952 Knocked out Jersey Joe Walcott to win world title
1955 Last fight against Archie Moore
Died: Newton, Iowa, August 31, 1969, age 45
Career record: Fights 49, Won 49

SEE ALSO ♦ EZZARD CHARLES 65 ♦ JOE LOUIS 204 ♦ ARCHIE MOORE 226 ♦ JOE WALCOTT 328

THE GREAT FIGHTS

ROCKY MARCIANO
V.
JERSEY JOE WALCOTT

MUNICIPAL STADIUM, PHILADELPHIA.
SEPTEMBER 23, 1952.

Jersey Joe Walcott won the world heavyweight title with one of the best left hooks anyone could wish to see... and lost it to one of the best right hands in championship history.

Walcott was already 37 when he knocked out Ezzard Charles in the seventh round at Pittsburgh in July 1951 to become champion at the fifth attempt.

After outpointing Charles in a rematch, he took on Rocky Marciano, the latest sensation to hit the heavyweight division. Whereas Walcott was a smooth, educated boxer with beautiful, almost balletic footwork, Marciano was boxing's equivalent of a runaway truck. He slammed forward and punched. Hard.

Walcott sneered at Marciano's raw, crude, slugging style. "Marciano is an amateur," he said. "He wouldn't even have qualified for Joe Louis's Bum of the Month tour. If I lose I deserve to have my name taken out of the record books."

One of his followers answered a journalist's question about what would happen if Marciano lost. "Fifty thousand Italians are going to commit suicide!"

The odds in Marciano's favor looked crazy in the opening round when the old champion dropped Marciano for a count of three with a left hook. Rocky yelled out: "You son of a bitch, I'll get you!" as he clambered up, but proceeded to absorb a boxing lesson. He steamed in, but his rushes made no impression on a ring technician who had seen all this countless times before.

Sheer pressure and swarming workrate kept Marciano in the fight, and Walcott's left eye dripped blood. After 12 rounds, however, the champion was well in front on the scorecards.

Then just over half a minute into round 13, Walcott threw a jab. As he followed with another, Marciano stepped inside it and exploded a clean right to the jaw. Walcott, out cold, slid gently to the canvas, suspended long enough with his arm trapped in the ropes for Marciano to add a cuffing left hook. Marciano, 29-year-old Rocco Francis Marchegiano to be precise, was the world heavyweight champion.

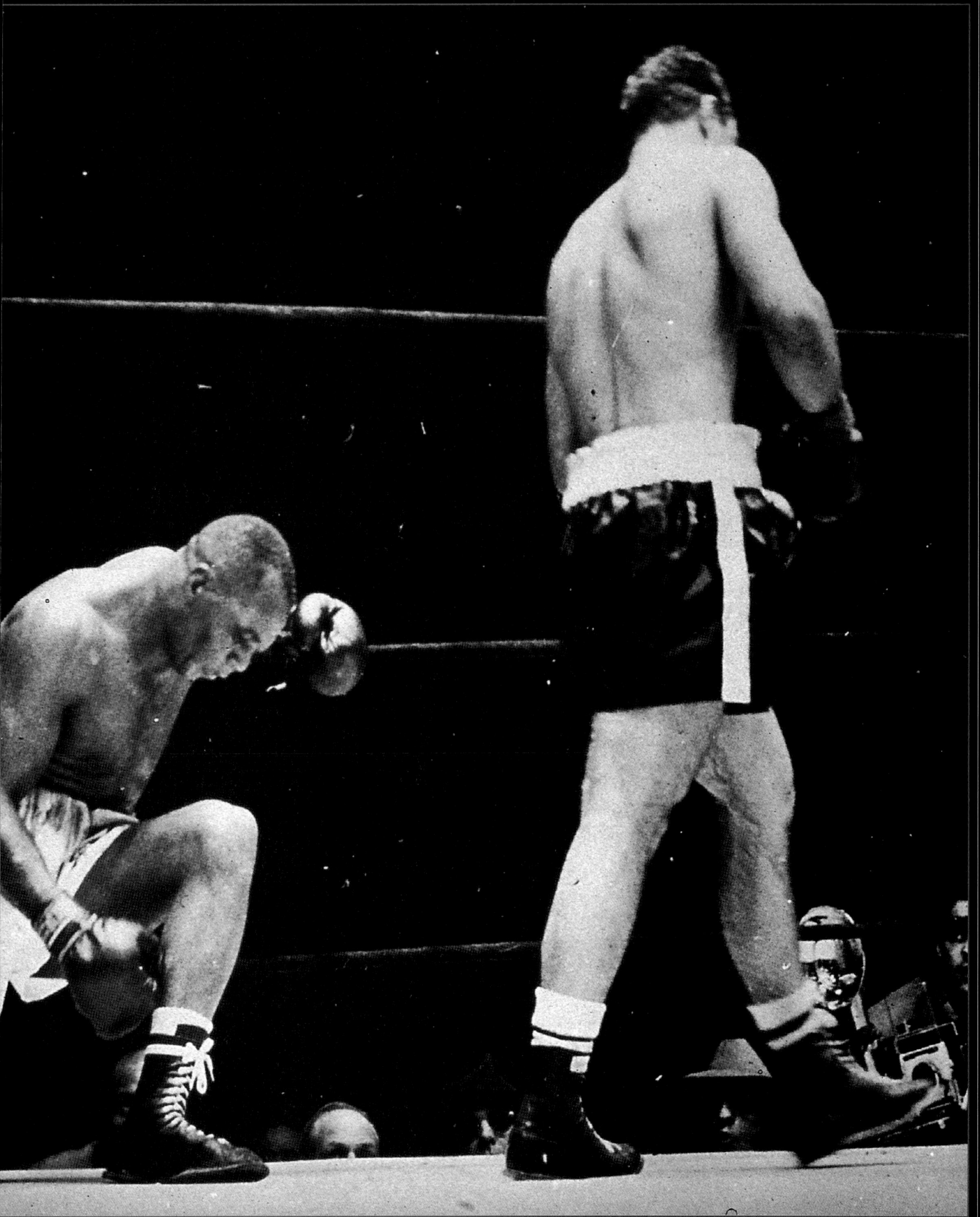

DADO MARINO

Dado Marino, Hawaiian-born of Filipino parents, was a fast, precise little fighter who matured late to win the world flyweight title, age 33.

Marino was considered an outsider against world champion Terry Allen, even with home advantage. But this level-headed man boxed beautifully, cutting Allen over the left eye in the second round, dropping him in the fifth and finishing a unanimous points winner. Often described as the first grandfather to win a championship, this was by marriage only, but at least it focused on how old Dado was, remarkably so for a flyweight.

Marino did not turn professional until he was 24 and in 1947 traveled to England to fight world champ Jackie Paterson, only for the Scot to be stripped for failing to make the weight. In a non-title fight Marino beat substitute Rinty Monaghan on a disqualification, then lost a 10-round decision to former champion Peter Kane in front of 7,000 fans in Manchester.

He also lost on points to Monaghan for the vacant title in London in October 1947—a dreadful fight in which neither man did himself justice. Marino said later he had never grown used to the British climate, but in 1949 in Honolulu was clearly outpointed in a world bantamweight title fight by the classy Californian Manuel Ortiz.

Just when it seemed he would be one of boxing's multitude of nearly men, he dethroned Allen in August 1950. After outscoring the London barrow-boy in a rematch, he was knocked out in a non-title fight by Yoshio Shirai of Japan. In 1952 Shirai outpointed Marino for the championship in Tokyo, and won a rematch, after which the Hawaiian veteran retired. He was 36.

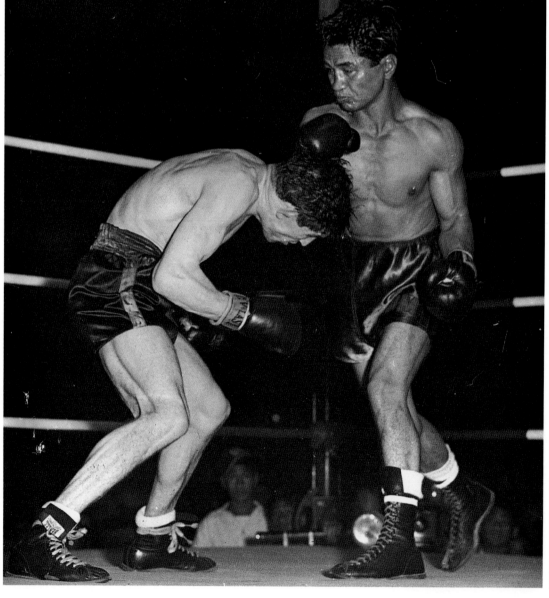

MARINO TURNS BACK THE WORLD FLYWEIGHT CHALLENGE OF TERRY ALLEN IN THEIR REMATCH IN HONOLULU

SEE ALSO ◆ TERRY ALLEN 13 ◆ PETER KANE 175 ◆ RINTY MONAGHAN 220 ◆ MANUEL ORTIZ 259

JOEY MAXIM

For a man the record books say couldn't punch, Joey Maxim did a comprehensive job on defending world light-heavyweight champion Freddie Mills. When he put Mills down for the count in the 10th round at Earls Court, London, on January 24, 1950, he also knocked out three of his teeth!

Maxim, who was managed by the veteran Jack "Doc" Kearns, was a tall boxer with a methodical style and a good left hand. As an amateur he won a Golden Gloves title, at 18 he turned professional and during the war he served as a physical training instructor in the US Army.

He won the American light-heavyweight title with a decision over Gus Lesnevich in 1949, and then demolished Mills to become world champ at the age of 27. An attempt to win the NBA heavyweight title against Ezzard Charles brought him only a one-sided points defeat, but he earned well from the light-heavyweight belt.

He outpointed knockout specialist "Irish" Bob Murphy in New York, and then outlasted Ray Robinson rather fortunately on a stifling summer's night before a 48,000 crowd in Yankee Stadium in June 1952. Robinson, the reigning middleweight champ, retired with heat exhaustion after the 13th round.

Six months later Maxim was guaranteed $100,000 to defend against Archie Moore in St. Louis. Kearns, who realized Moore would probably win, stuck to his demand even though it meant the challenger fought 15 hard rounds for nothing.

Twice beaten by Moore in rematches, Maxim outboxed the young Floyd Patterson, then drifted into life as a journeyman and lost eight of his last nine fights.

FACT FILE

1922	Born Giuseppe Berardinelli, Cleveland, Ohio
1949	Won American light-heavyweight title against Gus Lesnevich
1950	Knocked out Freddie Mills for world title in London
1951	Lost world heavyweight title bid against Ezzard Charles
1952	Lost light-heavyweight belt to Archie Moore
1958	Retired, age 36

Career record: Fights 115, Won 82, Lost 29, Drawn 4

MAXIM'S UNDER PRESSURE HERE, BUT EVENTUALLY KNOCKED OUT FREDDIE MILLS TO WIN THE WORLD LIGHT-HEAVYWEIGHT CROWN

THE GREAT FIGHTS

JOEY MAXIM
V.
RAY ROBINSON

YANKEE STADIUM, NEW YORK.
JUNE 25, 1952.

Heat—unbearable, humid, throat-parching heat —robbed Ray Robinson of the world light-heavyweight title before 48,000 sweltering spectators in Yankee Stadium.

Robinson challenged Joey Maxim for the world 175 lb. belt on a summer's night which New York weather officers said was the hottest June 25 since the last century.

Maxim, bigger, stronger and heavier at 173 lb., had an economical, unflustered style, while Robinson, the reigning middleweight champion and only 157½ lb., relied on speed and his exuberant talents.

For five rounds Robinson outboxed Maxim easily, but burned up too much energy. Gradually he slowed as his strength was sapped. Maxim plodded on, chipping away, walking in and drilling his left jab at Robinson's head. He rode a seventh round right hand—and then after nine Robinson flopped on to his stool, his mouth open with tiredness. He wanted to sleep.

In the 10th it became too much for referee Ruby Goldstein, who had to be helped from the ring. A replacement, Ray Miller, stepped up.

At the end of the 11th Robinson was confused enough to weave his way to the wrong corner, and in the 12th and 13th could barely control his legs. Once he fell on his face after missing wildly, and when the bell rang to end the 13th he didn't know where he was. His seconds crammed ice against his neck and waved smelling salts under his nose, but it was no good.

Across the ring Maxim watched as a New York commission doctor informed referee Miller that Robinson could not go on. Maxim grinned broadly as he was lifted high by his seconds, but looked drained as the official announcement was made.

After cooling down gradually in his dressing room, but still speaking incoherently, Robinson was sent home and put to bed.

Six months later, without boxing again, he announced his first retirement, 24 hours after Maxim had earned $100,000 but lost the title to Archie Moore in St. Louis.

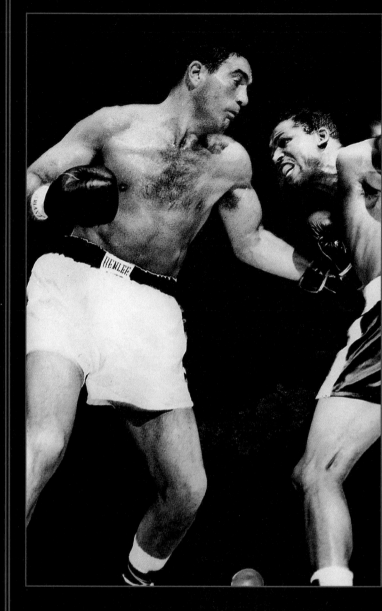

SANDRO MAZZINGHI

An immensely strong, fiery, and sometimes crude fighter, Sandro Mazzinghi twice held the world light-middleweight title and, in a career that eventually spanned 17 years and 69 fights, only two men officially beat him.

His first defeat was in a relatively insignificant eight-rounder against Giampaolo Melis in Rome in 1962, and the great Nino Benvenuti beat him twice in world title fights in 1965.

Mazzinghi stopped Ralph Dupas of New Orleans in nine rounds in Milan in September 1963. Dupas, a veteran of more than 100 fights, did a little better in the rematch in Sydney in December 1963, but was eventually rescued after three knockdowns in round 13. Mazzinghi was forced to pay a third of his purse to the Australian government before he left the country, and only rarely ventured outside Italy again after his return there.

After two more successful defenses, Mazzinghi found Benvenuti too smart for him in 1965, losing their first fight in six rounds and then, before a sellout crowd at the Milan Sports Palace, going down on points in the rematch. Mazzinghi grumbled that he was worth at least a draw.

He regained the world title by outpointing Korean southpaw Ki-soo Kim before a 50,000 crowd in Milan in May 1968, but could not go on after eight rounds because of severe cuts against classy American Freddie Little in Rome in October 1968. Amazingly, a No Contest was ruled, but this was overturned and Mazzinghi was stripped of the championship.

He retired in 1970, at 32, but came back in November 1977, won three more fights, and then retired for good.

MAZZINGHI BEARS THE CUTS AND BRUISES OF BATTLE, BUT LIKE MANY A STAR BEFORE AND SINCE, FINDS CAMERAS ARE READY TO CLICK AT THE LEAST CONVENIENT MOMENTS!

SEE ALSO ◆ NINO BENVENUTI 34

FREDDIE MILLS

They came no braver than Freddie Mills.

Cheerful, honest, and generous to a fault as a man, Mills was a fearless fighter who made up for what he lacked in subtlety and skill with indomitable spirit and solid punching.

He arrived in world class by knocking out an admittedly washed-up Len Harvey in two rounds at White Hart Lane stadium, London, in 1942, but then his career was on hold during his war service in the RAF. Mills fought world light-heavyweight champion Gus Lesnevich in a torrid struggle at Harringay Arena in London in 1946. He was given a terrible battering early on, fought back on instinct but was stopped in the 10th round.

The brutal standards of the day allowed him to be back in the ring three weeks later in a losing 12-rounder against British heavyweight champion Bruce Woodcock, even though he was vomiting after the Lesnevich fight, suffered severe headaches, and could only complete a few loosening up runs in between. Later that year he also took a terrible pounding from American heavyweight Joe Baksi.

Yet in July 1948, the 28-year-old former milk delivery boy from Bournemouth staged the boxing display of his life to outpoint Lesnevich and take the world title before an ecstatic crowd at White City Stadium.

Mills lost a return for the British and Empire heavyweight titles with Woodcock, and then lost his world title to Joey Maxim in January 1950 and retired.

He ran a restaurant and nightclub in London, but his business fell apart rapidly. He died of gunshot wounds while resting in his car in July 1965. The coroner ruled suicide, a verdict friends believed unjust.

FACT FILE

1919 Born Bournemouth, England

1936 Professional debut at 16

1946 Lost in 10 rounds to world light-heavyweight champ Gus Lesnevich

1948 Outpointed Lesnevich to win title

1950 Lost light-heavyweight title to Joey Maxim, retired

Died: London, July 25, 1965, age 46

Career record: Fights 97, Won 74, Lost 17, Drawn 6

MILLS TOSSES A RIGHT HAND OVER THE JAB OF JOEY MAXIM IN THEIR 1950 WORLD TITLE BOUT. MILLS LOST . . . AND ANNOUNCED HIS RETIREMENT

SEE ALSO ◆ GUS LESNEVICH 190 ◆ JOEY MAXIM 213

BRIAN MITCHELL

With good reason, they called Brian Mitchell the ultimate road warrior. Only two weeks after Mitchell's 10th-round stoppage of Alfredo Layne in Sun City in September 1986 the World Boxing Association decreed that they would sanction no more bouts in South Africa.

In making their anti-apartheid stand, the WBA stood their ground boldly against an appalling regime—and at the same time condemned Mitchell to a life of fighting against the odds, of defending his title before hostile fans, and of wondering if each payday would be his last.

Mitchell obviously felt at a disadvantage. "I'm not a politician, I'm a sportsman," he said. "You cannot choose your birthplace. I've thought about quitting. But I don't fight for the WBA, or the WBC, or the South African Government. I fight for my wife and two boys."

It was no secret that if Mitchell had lost the super-featherweight title, he would not have been given another chance. But he didn't lose. This admirable man retained his belt in Puerto Rico, Panama, France, Italy, Spain, England and the USA, in the process moving his family to San Diego. In London when he outpointed Jim McDonnell, 200 protesters opposed the decision to allow him to box.

Ironically, Mitchell had done most of his early fighting in the black townships, where he was extremely popular. He lost only once—a 10-round decision against Jacob Morake in a Transvaal title fight in 1982, only nine months into his 49-fight, 14-year career.

After beating Layne he defended the WBA belt 12 times in five years, before switching to the IBF and defeating Tony Lopez in Sacramento in 1991. He retired, came back briefly and then took up managing fighters.

JUAN MOLINA

Juan Molina was a fighter's fighter, an all-round, hard-working technician who could do a little bit of everything. An accurate, crisp puncher with a tough chin and full of heart, he was a handful for anybody. He also won 11 of his 14 world title fights over a seven-year span.

Molina was a brilliant amateur, winning a world junior title in 1983, boxing in the 1984 Olympics in Los Angeles and winning gold medals in the North American Championships and 1985 World Cup, when he stopped American Kelcie Banks in the final. The Duva family's Main Events organization reportedly paid him a $100,000 signing-on fee before his professional debut in 1986.

Molina, who was known as "John-John," lost his first IBF title attempt when Tony "The Tiger" Lopez outpointed him in Sacramento in 1988. Six months later he won the WBO belt by outpointing veteran Juan LaPorte, then dumped that when he stopped Lopez in the 10th round of a rematch. The Sacramento crowd rioted.

When they fought a decider in Reno, Nevada, in May 1990, Molina boxed badly and lost a split decision.

After two years in the wilderness, Molina won the vacant IBF title by outclassing South African Jackie Gunguluza in four rounds in 1992, and this time dominated his weight division. He turned back seven challengers, including top-quality Mexicans Manuel Medina and Goyo Vargas, and Welsh southpaw Floyd Havard.

Eventually Molina gave up the title because of weight-making problems, but lost a hard-fought 12-rounder with Oscar De La Hoya having moved up for the WBO lightweight crown in February 1995.

FACT FILE

1965	Born Fajardo, Puerto Rico, July 3, 1965
1983	World Junior champion
1984	Boxed in Los Angeles Olympics
1989	Won WBO and IBF super-featherweight titles
1990	Lost to Tony Lopez
1992	Regained IBF title against Jackie Gunguluza
1995	Moved up to lightweight, lost decision to Oscar De La Hoya

Career record: Fights 43, Won 39, Lost 4

MOLINA (RIGHT) HAD TWO SPELLS AS IBF SUPER-FEATHERWEIGHT CHAMPION, DISMISSING CHALLENGES FROM TOP MEXICANS MANUEL MEDINA AND GOYO VARGAS

SEE ALSO ◆ OSCAR DE LA HOYA 85

RINTY MONAGHAN

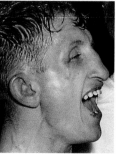

Rinty Monaghan was an entertainer by heart, a boxer by choice. A tough little scrapper whose nickname was an abbreviation of "Rin Tin Tin," which his grandmother called him, he loved to treat his crowds to a post-fight rendition of "When Irish Eyes Are Smiling."

He was a professional at 14, but had been scuffling for pennies in special exhibitions for years before that. Many of his early bouts were unrecorded, and he once estimated that the total should be around 100.

As far as records can show, he lost only twice before World War II put his career on hold. He had an eventful war—shipwrecked in the British Merchant Navy, an ambulance driver in Belfast, and finally a job as an British armed forces entertainer with a group called The Three Hillbillies!

He resumed his boxing career in 1945, and won NBA and European recognition as world flyweight champion by outpointing Dado Marino in a dull fight in London in October 1947. He had previously been disqualified in a non-title fight with Marino in Glasgow, when he had been a late substitute for the match.

Scotland's Jackie Paterson objected to being stripped of the world title for failing to make the weight against Marino, but Monaghan put him in his place with a spectacular seventh-round knockout in the atmospheric King's Hall in Belfast, Ireland in March 1948.

Monaghan held off challenges from Maurice Sandeyron and Terry Allen, although he could only draw with the latter, before retiring in 1950 as undefeated champion because of chronic bronchitis.

He made a living as an entertainer in the Belfast area, and was a regular face at big fights in Ireland, until his death from cancer in 1984.

PARTY PIECE: AFTER HIS FIGHTS, MONAGHAN SERENADED FANS WITH "WHEN IRISH EYES ARE SMILIN"

SEE ALSO ◆ TERRY ALLEN 13 ◆ DADO MARINO 212

Bob Montgomery, known as The Bobcat, was one of the toughest in an era that overflowed with great lightweights. Along with Beau Jack and Ike Williams, he dominated the division in the 1940s.

Born in South Carolina, he hitchhiked to Philadelphia when he was 15 and stayed. He was fighting in world class by the time he was 21, mixing with former champions like Lew Jenkins and Sammy Angott.

A smooth, relentlessly aggressive fighter, he won New York recognition as lightweight titleholder when he outpointed Jack on a unanimous 15-round decision in Madison Square Garden in May 1943. He was a 1-4 favorite to retain his belt against Jack six months later, but in spite of flooring him twice he was outfought and lost the decision.

Montgomery knocked out Williams in the 12th round in Philadelphia after gambling more than $1,000 on himself, but was flattened in one round by the erratic but dangerous Al "Bummy" Davis. Two weeks later came the third fight with Jack—and Montgomery won a split decision as 19,066 fans packed the Garden. In 1945 he was called up to the Army, but spent most of his time boxing exhibitions in aid of the war effort or to entertain troops.

By 1946 he was back, retaining his lightweight title by stopping Allie Stolz and Wesley Mouzon, who fought him with a detached retina. Then in August 1947, Montgomery earned a career-best $47,000 but was knocked out in six rounds by Ike Williams at Philadelphia's Municipal Stadium. When he retired in 1950, he owned property in Philadelphia, but lost everything because of a gambling habit, worked as a salesman and in the 1970s was hired to help control Philadelphia's street gangs.

FACT FILE

1919 Born Sumter, South Carolina

1943 Won and lost against Beau Jack for New York world lightweight title

1944 Regained New York title from Beau Jack

1947 Lost to Ike Williams for undisputed lightweight title

1950 Retired, age 31

Career record: Fights 97, Won 75, Lost 19, Drawn 3

MONTGOMERY POUNDS THE HEAVY BAG AT A PUBLIC WORKOUT IN NEW JERSEY IN 1947

SEE ALSO ◆ BEAU JACK 163 ◆ IKE WILLIAMS 336

CARLOS MONZON

In the ring Carlos Monzon was grim, expressionless, cold, his personality understated. Out of it, he was the archetypcal "machismo" hero, whose life was violent, chaotic, and ultimately very tragic.

Monzon was deceptively cunning. If you saw him once, he looked ordinary, even beatable, with his upright style and laconic way of working behind his thudding, straight punches. You might think him one-paced.

Yet in a 101-fight career which lasted 14 years, he lost only three times, all on points when he was a relative novice. From November 1970 when he destroyed proven Italian, Nino Benvenuti, in 12 rounds in Rome, until his retirement after his 14th defense in 1977, he was the world middleweight champion. Admiring from afar, legendary trainer Angelo Dundee called him "the complete fighter."

Monzon avoided nobody. He knocked out Benvenuti in three rounds of a return, beat Emile Griffith twice, and then Denny Moyer, Jean-Claude Bouttier twice, Tom Bogs, Bennie Briscoe, Jose Napoles, Tony Mundine, Tony Licata, Gratien Tonna, and in an impressive grand finale, Rodrigo Valdez of Colombia twice.

Out of the ring he was a disaster area. His youth was wild, often beyond the law. His first wife signaled the end of their volatile relationship by shooting him. One bullet stayed in his back for the rest of his life.

And in 1989 he was jailed for 11 years for the murder of his lover Alicia Muniz, who fell mysteriously from the balcony of Monzon's home. He was driving on a country road, returning from permitted temporary home leave to Las Flores prison, when his car overturned. He and a friend were killed.

RUTHLESSLY EFFECTIVE: MONZON LETS FLY WITH A RIGHT HAND AGAINST OUTGUNNED TONY MUNDINE

SEE ALSO ◆ NINO BENVENUTI 34 ◆ RODRIGO VALDEZ 322

SUNG-KIL MOON

An exciting, wade-forward slugger, Sung-kil Moon was a Korean national hero long before he became a two-weight world professional champion.

Labeled "Hands of Stone" after Roberto Duran, he lost on cuts in the 1984 Olympic Games quarter-final and won the World Amateur Championships bantamweight gold medal in Reno, Nevada, in 1986.

When he signed professional terms, amateur dignitaries were outraged that he had turned his back on what they saw as a certain gold medal in the Seoul Olympics in 1988, but his promoter, Mrs. Yoen-ja Shim, promised he would win a world championship before the Games took place. He did, when he was given a sixth-round technical decision over an angry Khaokor Galaxy of Thailand for the WBA bantamweight title in Seoul in August 1988.

Moon was prone to bad cuts, and the modern rules, whereby in the event of an accidental injury the fight went to scorecards, bailed him out of difficulties more than once.

In a rematch with Galaxy in Bangkok in July 1989, Moon lost on points, but then dropped down a weight and won the WBC super-flyweight championship—again, on a hotly disputed technical decision.

He did impress in stopping former champion Gilberto Roman on an eighth-round retirement, then won another technical decision in an exciting brawl with Japan's Kenji Matsumara. Again, it was Moon who was cut. Moon overpowered Konadu in a return in Spain, and went on to make six successful defenses of the 115 lb. belt. In November 1993 he lost the title to clever Mexican Jose Luis Bueno on a split decision in Pohang.

FACT FILE

1963	Born Yeoung-Am, South Korea
1986	World Amateur champion
1988	Won WBA bantamweight title against Khaokor Galaxy
1989	Lost WBA bantamweight title to Galaxy
1990	Won WBC super-flyweight title against Nana Konadu
1993	Lost WBC super-flyweight title to Jose Luis Bueno

Career record: Fights 22, Won 20, Lost 2

MOON (RIGHT) IN A BRUISING ENCOUNTER WITH GREG "THE FLEA" RICHARDSON

THE GREAT FIGHTS

CARLOS MONZON
V.
RODRIGO VALDEZ

LOUIS II STADIUM,
MONTE CARLO.
JUNE 26, 1976.

By 1976 Carlos Monzon had one boxing argument left to settle. If he wanted to be remembered beyond all dispute as the best middleweight of his generation, he had to fight Rodrigo Valdez.

The Colombian had recognition as WBC champion, and was a smart, tough fighter. He had knocked out "Bad" Bennie Briscoe, a result that raised eyebrows around the world, and had beaten 57 of his 64 opponents. But this was Monzon's 100th bout—and he had not lost for 12 years.

Italian promoter Rodolfo Sabbatini lured the two fighters to Monaco—Monzon accepted $250,000, Valdez $200,000. Some respected experts tipped Valdez to be too quick and even hit too hard for a champion who at approaching 34 was concentrating increasingly often on outside interests. For example, the Argentine was shortly to make a movie with current girlfriend Suzanna Gimenez, and his ringside guests included actors Omar Sharif and Alain Delon.

Maybe it was because Monzon wound him up by calling him "Chico"—Little Boy—or because a brother was killed a week earlier, but for whatever reason Valdez did not live up to his billing.

Monzon controlled him in the early stages with his long range jabbing and straight right hands. Monzon also backed to the ropes as Ali had done against Foreman, letting Valdez throw punches as he covered up.

In the eighth Valdez did shake Monzon with a ferocious right hand, but by the 10th his left eye was closed as the Argentine opened up again.

The Colombian continued to press forward, fighting as hard as he could, but in the 14th ran on to a right hand that dropped him for eight. At the final bell the scores were surprisingly close: the two judges scored for Monzon by only two points, and the referee, Raymond Baldeyrou, by four.

Valdez was not satisfied, and boxed Monzon again the following year. This time he managed to score a knockdown, but was again outpointed. Monzon then retired, leaving Valdez to win the vacant title.

ARCHIE MOORE

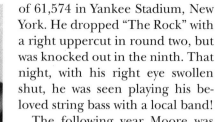

"Ancient" Archie Moore was one of a legion of quality black fighters who were exploited, avoided, and confined to the club circuits in the 1930s and 1940s. Unlike most, Moore persisted, and eventually held the world light-heavyweight title for almost 10 years.

"I geared my way of living and my boxing style to last," he said. Nevertheless, in 1950 he fought twice and in his own words, "made a living hustling with my pool cue".

By the time he fought Joey Maxim for the championship, he was 39 years old and a veteran of almost 170 bouts... and Maxim's manager Jack Kearns bled the promotion deal so dry that Moore boxed for $800 minus expenses—which meant for nothing.

In 1955 he challenged heavyweight champion Rocky Marciano before a massive crowd of 61,574 in Yankee Stadium, New York. He dropped "The Rock" with a right uppercut in round two, but was knocked out in the ninth. That night, with his right eye swollen shut, he was seen playing his beloved string bass with a local band!

The following year Moore was knocked out in five rounds by Floyd Patterson, who at 21 was literally half his age, for the vacant heavyweight crown. But he stayed light-heavyweight champion until he was in his late 40s, turning back a total of nine challengers, including one ferocious effort from Canadian Yvon Durelle in 1958. Durelle put Moore down three times in the first round, but Archie got up, fought back, and won in the 11th. His last world-class fight was when Cassius Clay knocked him out in four rounds in 1962. He was 48 years old and went on to train fighters for many years.

A BULKY MOORE WORKS THE SPEEDBALL AT THE TOBY GYM IN BERMONDSEY, LONDON, IN MAY 1956 BEFORE HIS FIGHT WITH YOLANDE POMPEY

SEE ALSO ◆ ROCKY MARCIANO 209 ◆ JOEY MAXIM 213 ◆ FLOYD PATTERSON 265

DAVEY MOORE

History remembers Davey Moore as a man whose desire and ability to fight cost him his life.

On March 21, 1963, Moore was beaten in 10 rounds by Cuban exile Ultiminio "Sugar" Ramos in Los Angeles and collapsed with brain injuries. He died four days later. Bob Dylan wrote a song about it. "Who killed Davey Moore?" he asked. "Not I," replied everybody connected with the sport.

Moore was one of nine children of a preacher from Lexington, Kentucky, and in the ring was a crafty, short-armed counter-puncher who won a national amateur title, reached the 1952 Olympic Games quarter-finals and turned professional at 19.

Six years later, in March 1959, in the Olympic Auditorium, Los Angeles, he forced defending featherweight champion Hogan Bassey of Nigeria to retire after 13 rounds. In a rematch he beat Bassey in 10, handing over 10 percent of his purse to help his father build a new church.

When he fought Ramos, he had been world champion for four years and had lost only once in his last 38 fights. He was on top of his sport, a master of his trade. The road had been hard—in 1956 he had retired to work as a truck driver because boxing did not support his wife and three children—but by 1963, he was able to look forward and plan a comfortable future for them all.

The end came terribly in Dodger Stadium in Los Angeles. He was retired by his corner after the 10th round, spoke to reporters in the dressing room—"I've beaten them all, big ones, little ones, but tonight just wasn't my night," he said. An hour later he was in a coma.

FACT FILE

1933 Born Lexington, Kentucky, November 1, 1933

1952 Reached Olympic Games quarter-finals

1959 Beat Hogan Bassey for world featherweight title

1963 Lost title in tragic fight with Sugar Ramos in Los Angeles

Died: Los Angeles, March 25, 1963, age 29

Career record: Fights 67, Won 59, Lost 7, Drawn 1

MOORE IN LONDON IN 1959 WHEN HE FOUGHT BOBBY NEILL

SEE ALSO ◆ HOGAN BASSEY 30

THE GREAT FIGHTS

ARCHIE MOORE
V.
YVON DURELLE

MONTREAL FORUM, CANADA.
DECEMBER 10, 1958.

Ancient Archie Moore was a couple of days short of his 45th birthday when he put his world light-heavyweight title on the line against Canadian fisherman Yvon Durelle at Montreal Forum.

Moore had been champion for the past six years, had twice failed in heavyweight title attempts against Rocky Marciano and Floyd Patterson, but was established as an eccentric but extremely able light-heavyweight king.

Durelle, from the town of Moncton in New Brunswick, was strong, brave, and not afraid to commit himself... and literally caught Moore cold, knocking him down three times in the first round.

Moore said the Forum arena, normally used by the Montreal Canadians hockey team, was too chilly and he was too stiff and slow. Referee Jack Sharkey, the former heavyweight champion, might have stopped the fight, but gave the champion the benefit and allowed him to go on.

Moore had one of the most remarkable minds of any fighter in history. He enjoyed the situation. "Much of the fun in winning fights is not losing," he wrote a couple of years later. By contrast, Durelle said he had lost his edge because he thought he had won the fight—he forgot the three-knockdown rule which was usually applied in Canada was not in use now.

Moore's veteran manager Jack Kearns told him not to worry, and slowly he boxed his way back, throwing hooks and quick combinations behind an accurate left jab. Afterwards he said he was in a daze until the sixth, by which time he had been down again - flat on his back this time in round five.

But then Moore took over. Durelle was down for three in the seventh, and saved by the bell when floored at the end of the 10th. Two more knockdowns in the 11th finished one of the most astonishing world title fights of them all.

They boxed again in Montreal eight months later. This time Moore won in three rounds.

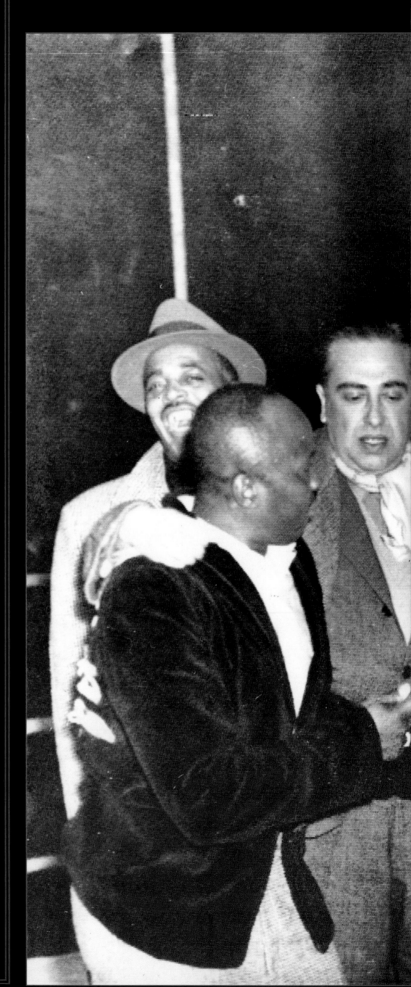

MICHAEL MOORER

FACT FILE

1967 Born Brooklyn, New York

1988 Professional debut and won WBO light-heavyweight title

1992 Won WBO heavyweight title against Bert Cooper

1994 Won WBA and IBF titles against Evander Holyfield, lost to George Foreman

1996 Beat Axel Schulz to regain IBF title

Career record: Fights 40, Won 39, Lost 1

Michael Moorer was a moody fighter who suffered few fools, and whose talents often seemed to be masked by a strange, almost detached reluctance to communicate.

Yet he was a knowledgable, thoughtful boxer with a solid boxing background who won both light-heavyweight and heavyweight world championships. He was the first southpaw to hold a version of the heavyweight title.

Born in Brooklyn, raised in Pennsylvania, Moorer developed as a boxer under Emanuel Steward in Detroit's Kronk Gym. An amateur international, he won the WBO light-heavyweight championship nine months after turning professional, stopping Ramzi Hassan in four rounds in December 1988.

Moorer made nine defenses at light-heavyweight, finishing all of his challengers inside the distance. In 1992 he stopped Smokin' Bert Cooper for the WBO heavyweight belt, but gave it back soon afterward.

He liked to portray a brooding, violent picture of himself, but retained a grim sense of humor, as he showed when wearing a "U Have The Right To Remain Violent" T-shirt before his 1994 challenge to Evander Holyfield at Caesars Palace, Las Vegas. That fight, which Moorer won on points, was a triumph for his inspirational trainer, Teddy Atlas, who at one point reeled off a straight-from-the-heart exhortation that would have done Abraham Lincoln justice at Gettysburg!

Some said Moorer won the fight almost in spite of himself, and when his stunning 10th-round defeat by 45-year-old George Foreman in November 1994 cost him his title he also lost a huge chunk of credibility.

Yet Moorer showed character and determination to resurrect his career and regain the IBF version of the title by outpointing Axel Schulz in Germany in June 1996, retaining it against Frans Botha in November.

FINEST HOUR: MOORER OUTBOXES EVANDER HOLYFIELD FOR THE WBA AND IBF HEAVYWEIGHT BELTS AT CAESARS PALACE, LAS VEGAS

SEE ALSO ◆ GEORGE FOREMAN 118 ◆ EVANDER HOLYFIELD 159

OWEN MORAN

Truculent Owen Moran would fight absolutely anybody... and was particularly partial to managers!

One drunken brawl with the renowned Jimmy Johnston left Moran recovering in hospital nursing a sore head, broken hand, and broken jaw.

But when sober, and against boxers, the battling Brummie was one of the best of his day and should have been the world featherweight champion.

At 16, Moran was a professional in Birmingham. He claimed the British bantamweight title in 1905 and the world championship two years later, following a 20-round points win over Al Delmont at the National Sporting Club in London.

He was desperately unlucky not to beat world featherweight champion Abe Attell—both of their 1908 title fights ended in draws, the first over 25 rounds on New Year's Day, the second over 23 rounds in September, both in San Francisco. Both times Moran seemed to have won clearly.

He was probably at his peak when he knocked out Battling Nelson in 11 rounds in San Francisco in November 1910, but was foiled in a lightweight title bid in July 1911 against Ad Wolgast, whom he had previously beaten in a non-title bout. Wolgast was on top in the 13th round when he hit Moran low and the Englishman was counted out while still writhing on the canvas.

In January 1913, Moran fought bitter rival Jim Driscoll for the British and European titles in London, with the winner also receiving limited recognition as world champ. Yet again, Moran was foiled by a draw. Driscoll won the early rounds, but Moran almost knocked him out in the closing stages. Moran retired in 1916, and kept a pub in Birmingham, England for many years.

FACT FILE

1884	Born Birmingham, England
1907	Claimed world bantamweight title
1908	Twice drew world featherweight title fights with Abe Attell
1911	Lost in 13 rounds to world lightweight champ Ad Wolgast
1913	Drew 20-rounder with Jim Driscoll
Died:	Birmingham, England, March 17, 1949, age 64

Career record: Fights 108, Won 81, Lost 19, Drawn 8

BATTLING NELSON FLOORED BY OWEN MORAN IN 1910

SEE ALSO ◆ ABE ATTELL 25 ◆ JIM DRISCOLL 95 ◆ AD WOLGAST 340

The GREAT FIGHTS

MATTHEW SAAD MUHAMMAD
V.
JOHN CONTEH

RESORTS HOTEL, ATLANTA CITY.
AUGUST 18, 1979.

This was the last great performance from John Conteh, one of the best British boxers of all time. Conteh had been stripped of the WBC light-heavyweight title for refusing to go through with a defense against Miguel Cuello in Monte Carlo, and then failed to regain it when controversially outscored by Mate Parlov in Belgrade.

Since then the WBC belt had passed from Parlov to Marvin Johnson and on to Matthew Saad Muhammad, previously known as Matthew Franklin, and one of the most exciting, give-and-take fighters of the day.

Franklin was not hard to hit, but he was impossible to discourage. Conteh, with a far more fragile temperament, was by far the more gifted but had a history of bad hands as well as backroom disruption.

Although only 28, Conteh was considered a sliding fighter, while Saad Muhammad, two weeks after his 25th birthday, was at his peak.

Yet Conteh boxed brilliantly, providing Saad Muhammad with few opportunities to unload his big punches. In round five Conteh seemed poised for a wonderful victory when a dreadful cut appeared above the champion's left eyebrow. But the American corner jammed it with a cement-like substance which was later proven illegal. Saad Muhammad boxed on, under heavy fire, but gradually clawed his way back.

Down the stretch, it was close and tantalizingly balanced. But in round 13 Conteh took a hammering. In the 14th he went down twice, and in the last he was also cut as Saad Muhammad finished to claim a unanimous points win.

The controversy over the white substance used to block up his cut allowed a British protest to succeed. They fought again in Atlantic City in March 1980, but Conteh seemed dispirited and out of sorts before the first bell. He was stopped easily in four rounds.

Saad Muhammad retained his championship until December 1981 when he was stopped by Dwight Muhammad Qawi.

MATTHEW SAAD MUHAMMAD

FACT FILE

1954 Born Maxwell Antonio
Loach, Philadelphia
1979 Won WBC light-
heavyweight title by
stopping Marvin
Johnson
1981 Lost WBC light-
heavyweight title to
Dwight Muhammad
Qawi
1992 Last fight, age 37
Career record: Fights 58,
Won 39, Lost 16, Drawn 3

Matthew Saad Muhammad could be forgiven if he spent his youth searching for himself.

As a child he was found abandoned on the Benjamin Franklin Parkway in Philadelphia. He was raised by nuns who called him Matthew... and Franklin after the road where he was found.

Matt Franklin grew into one of the bravest, hardest-hitting light-heavyweights of his day. His trademark was to take punches, appear on the verge of defeat, then battle through the pain and win a battle of wills. He had enormous strength of mind for a man who had already come through so much.

One of his most ferocious wars was with Marvin Johnson, an Indianapolis southpaw, even before he became world champion. In July 1977 Franklin came back from the precipice to knock out Johnson in the 12th round to win the North American title.

When they fought again, Johnson was WBC champion... and in another tremendous struggle, Franklin won in round eight.

Still seeking so much truth in his life, Matthew changed his name to Saad Muhammad as a mark of his Muslim faith. A typical late rally saved his title on a 15-round points win against an equally inspired John Conteh in August 1979, but he overwhelmed the Englishman in the rematch in four rounds.

Another titanic battle saw him stop Alvaro "Yaqui" Lopez in 14 rounds in July 1980, and each time it seemed the wars must take their toll sooner rather than later. In fact, he made eight successful defenses before he lost in 10 rounds to Dwight Muhammad Qawi in Atlantic City in December 1981. Qawi beat him a second time, but Saad Muhammad fought on until 1992.

SAAD MUHAMMAD, WHEN HE
WAS PLAIN MATT FRANKLIN,
WORKS THE BAG IN A
PHILADELPHIA GYM

SEE ALSO ◆ DWIGHT MUHAMMAD QAWI 274 ◆ EVANDER HOLYFIELD 159

DAVE McAULEY

ave McAuley was a stiffpunching flyweight who was an enduring International Boxing Federation champion. He is remembered best, however, for a fight he lost—a breathtaking war with the Colombian, Fidel Bassa, in 1987.

McAuley, a chef in the family restaurant in the Irish coastal town of Larne, took on Bassa at the King's Hall in Belfast in only the 14th fight of his career. It was one of the fights of the decade, with Bassa down three times and adrift on all three scorecards, only for McAuley to punch himself out and lose in the 13th round. A matter of months later the WBA reduced its championship distance to 12 rounds.

A rematch was a disappointment with Bassa winning a points decision in a fight that never really caught fire, but in June 1989 McAuley switched to the IBF and outfought Duke McKenzie over 12 rounds at Wembley to become a champion at the third attempt.

Once he had the belt strapped around his waist, he kept a solid grip on it. He was a good champion, outpointing Dodie Penalosa of the Philippines, American veteran Louis Curtis, Rodolfo Blanco of Colombia, and Pedro Feliciano of Puerto Rico and then knocking out Baby Jake Matlala of South Africa in the 10th round.

His championship reign—and his professional career—ended in January 1992 when Blanco won a close, bitterly disputed decision in Bilbao, northern Spain. Of his 23 fights, nine were for world titles.

He continued to work in the family business in retirement, emerging from time to time to provide lucid and intelligent boxing analyst work on both TV and radio.

FACT FILE

1961 Born Larne, Northern Ireland

1987 Lost WBA flyweight title epic with Fidel Bassa

1989 Outpointed Duke McKenzie to win IBF flyweight title

1992 Lost IBF title to Rodolfo Blanco in Spain

Career record: Fights 23, Won 18, Lost 3, Drawn 2

MCAULEY LOST A CLASSIC WITH FIDEL BASSA IN HIS FIRST WORLD TITLE BID, BUT BECAME CHAMPION AT THE THIRD ATTEMPT BY BEATING DUKE MCKENZIE

SEE ALSO ◆ DUKE MCKENZIE 243

JACK McAULIFFE

FACT FILE

1866 Born Meelin, County Cork, Ireland

1884 Professional debut in New York

1886 Claimed world lightweight title

1887 Fought 74-round draw with Jem Carney

1897 Last fight, age 31

Died: Forest Hills, New York, November 5, 1937, age 71

Career record: Fights 37, Won 31, Drawn 5, No Decision 1

Jack McAuliffe was a great lightweight, although historians argue over his rightful status simply because of the chaotic nature of the sport when he was claiming to be the champion of the world.

Some say he should only be recognized as American champion, others that his 28th-round knockout of Englishman Harry Gilmore in a gloved fight in January 1887 earned him the right to be called world champ.

Whatever the theories, nobody denies that McAuliffe was extraordinarily talented. Quick-thinking, sharp-punching, and an expert ring general, he called himself "The Little Napoleon of the Ring".

He was born in County Cork and his father emigrated to America before Jack was born. He took his family with him and settled in Brooklyn, New York, where Jack first boxed as a teenager.

He had more than the 37 fights on his official record, boxing on tour in nightly shows against all-comers. He beat American lightweight champion "Professor" Billy Frazier in 21 rounds in Boston, but a marathon with English champion Jem Carney ended in a riot during the 74th round with Carney well on top. As order could not be restored the referee ruled a draw, which saved McAuliffe's reputation, even though he was ill with a stomach complaint.

At the festival of boxing in New Orleans in September 1892, which saw James J. Corbett win the heavyweight crown from John L. Sullivan, McAuliffe knocked out Billy Myer in 15 rounds.

Out of shape increasingly often, he received a generous decision against young Australian Young Griffo in 1894, and retired permanently after outscoring Philadelphia Tommy Ryan in September 1897.

McAULIFFE WAS ONE OF THE PIONEERS OF THE LIGHTWEIGHT DIVISION. HE NEVER OFFICIALLY LOST A FIGHT

SEE ALSO ◆ YOUNG GRIFFO 145

JOCK MCAVOY

ock McAvoy, otherwise known as "The Rochdale Thunderbolt," was that rarity—a devastating puncher who could take one himself.

An exciting, ruthless fighter who had an unnerving habit of gnawing at his gloves in his corner before a fight, he was denied a shot at the world middleweight title in the 1930s because he was too dangerous.

When he went to New York in search of a championship chance in late 1935, he stunned the boxing world by knocking out the mob-controlled world middleweight champion Eddie "Babe" Risko in the first round of an over-the-weight match. After that, he was not allowed a rematch for the championship.

When he was offered a world title fight in March 1936, it was against John Henry Lewis, the light-heavyweight champion. McAvoy beefed himself up to just over 168 lb., but Lewis was too big and too capable a boxer, winning a unanimous decision in Madison Square Garden.

At home McAvoy had won the British middleweight title at the second attempt by outpointing Len Harvey, but missed out in a European title attempt when Marcel Thil outpointed him. He did win the British light-heavyweight title on a 14th-round knockout of Eddie Phillips in 1937.

Harvey outpointed him in July 1939 in a British and Empire light-heavyweight bout which also had British recognition as a world title fight, and he faded then. A back injury effectively ended his career in the first round of a fight with the rising star, Freddie Mills, in 1942 although he came back for a few fights just after the War ended.

Two years later he contracted polio, which disabled him for the rest of his life.

THE ROCHDALE THUNDERBOLT: TOO DANGEROUS TO BE GIVEN A WORLD MIDDLEWEIGHT TITLE BOUT

SEE ALSO ♦ LEN HARVEY 152 ♦ JOHN HENRY LEWIS 195 ♦ FREDDIE MILLS 217 ♦ MARCEL THIL 306

MIKE MCCALLUM

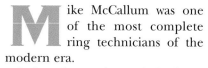

FACT FILE

1956 Born Kingston, Jamaica

1978 Commonwealth Games welterweight gold medalist

1984 Won WBA light-middleweight title against Sean Mannion

1989 Won WBA middleweight title against Herol Graham

1994 Won WBC light-heavyweight championship against Jeff Harding

Career record: Fights 54, Won 49, Lost 4, Drawn 1

Mike McCallum was one of the most complete ring technicians of the modern era.

A Jamaican who switched his fighting base to the United States to turn professional in 1981, McCallum remained a fiercely independent voice, refusing to bow to the demands of a single promoter and changing backroom teams frequently.

Known as "The Body Snatcher" because of his expertise at working the belly and ribs, McCallum also had a vicious left hook to the chin, as he showed when flattening Donald Curry with a single shot in Las Vegas in 1987.

McCallum was a world-class amateur, but took time to blossom as a pro—he was already 27 when he outclassed the stubborn Irishman Sean Mannion over 15 horribly one-sided rounds in New York for the WBA light-middleweight title in 1984.

McCallum was a great light-middleweight, reigning for three years and trouncing other top-quality fighters in Julian Jackson, Milton McCrory, and Curry. He moved up to middleweight in 1988, but lost his first fight at the weight to Sumbu Kalambay for the WBA belt in Italy. It took him 14 months to get another chance, and this time outpointed Herol Graham in London for the vacant WBA championship.

He beat Steve Collins, Michael Watson, and Kalambay again, before moving up to super-middle, and twice missed out in controversial decisions against IBF champ James Toney. The first fight was a draw, Toney won the second on a decision that surprised many neutrals.

McCallum became a three-weight world champ in 1994 when he outpointed Jeff Harding, but lost the championship the following year to Fabrice Tiozzo of France.

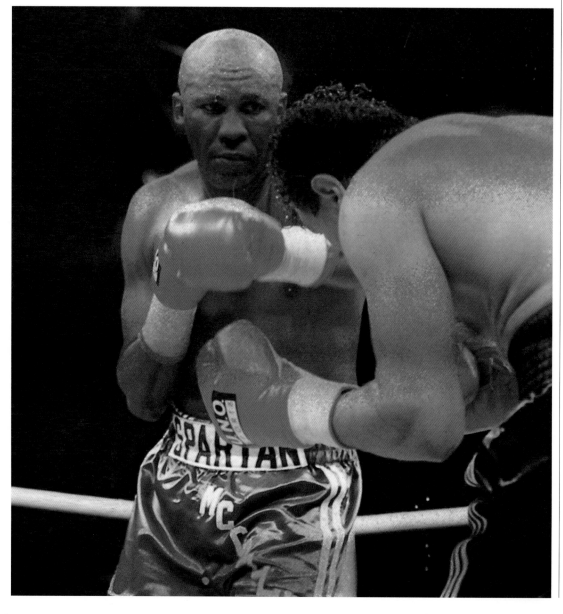

THE BODY SNATCHER: MCCALLUM WAS A MASTER CRAFTSMAN WHO WON WORLD TITLES AT THREE WEIGHTS

SEE ALSO ◆ STEVE COLLINS 74 ◆ DONALD CURRY 82 ◆ JAMES TONEY 310

CHARLES "KID" McCOY

Norman Selby, a strangely charming man given to bouts of depression throughout his uneven life, walked away from his Indiana home while still a boy. His father was a fanatically religious storekeeper, his mother and sister were both psychologically disturbed.

He rode the rails and became Kid McCoy, borrowing the name from a burglar in a popular novel. Lean and at times almost affectedly elegant, he made a living where he could, learning to box along the way. There were fights as far north as St. Paul, Minnesota, and as far south as New Orleans.

He had a natural talent, and a cunning, devious mind. He had been a sparring partner for world welterweight champion Tommy Ryan, and when the latter claimed the middleweight belt, McCoy pleaded for a title shot, saying he was suffering from consumption and needed the money. Ryan took pity on him, and to his horror, was knocked out in the 15th round by a perfectly fit athlete.

McCoy was also known to take dives from time to time, prompting one writer to wonder whether or not he had just seen "The Real McCoy." The phrase passed into the language. He once knocked out a heavyweight by pointing to his feet, and when the giant looked down, clouted him on his unprotected chin.

He was married ten times, to eight women, and found his way into silent movies, but in 1924 killed his wife, Theresa Mors, and robbed six people. Convicted of manslaughter, he then served seven years in San Quentin. He was in Detroit, working quietly as a gardener, when he committed suicide, explaining in his farewell note he could endure the world's madness no more.

FACT FILE

1872	Born Norman Selby, Moscow, Indiana
1896	Claimed world middleweight title after beating Tommy Ryan
1903	Outpointed by Jack Root in world light-heavyweight title fight
1916	Last official fight, age 43
Died:	Detroit, Michigan, April 18, 1940, age 67

Career record: Fights 108, Won 92, Lost 7, Drawn 7, No Contests 2

KID McCOY: A STRANGE, COMPLEX MAN WHO MET A TRAGIC END

TERRY MCGOVERN

FACT FILE

1880 Born Johnstown, Pennsylvania, March 9, 1880

1899 Won world bantamweight title against Pedlar Palmer

1900 Won world featherweight title against George Dixon

1901 Lost featherweight crown to Young Corbett

1908 Last fight, age 28

Died: Brooklyn, New York, February 26, 1918, age 37

Career record: Fights 78, Won 66, Lost 6, Drawn 6

"Terrible" Terry McGovern, otherwise known as "The Brooklyn Terror," was a former streetfighter who shot to fame at the turn of the century.

Raised in the Irish district of South Brooklyn, he was a phenomenal talent. He was only 19 when he won the world bantamweight title by flattening Englishman Pedlar Palmer in the first round in an outdoor arena at Tuckahoe, New York. His wife Grace watched from a nearby house with their two-month old son, Joey.

McGovern was a sensational puncher. In times where fights tended to be stopped later rather than earlier, the Palmer massacre was just one of 11 consecutive fights that year which he won inside three rounds.

In January 1900, McGovern demolished the brilliant stylist George Dixon in eight rounds the Broadway Athletic Club to become world featherweight champion. He took out a string of challengers, none of whom lasted beyond round seven, before his notoriously short temper snapped against Young Corbett at Hartford, Connecticut, in November 1901. On his way to the ring, Corbett banged on McGovern's dressing room door and yelled: "Come out you Irish rat and take the licking of your life." McGovern emerged in a rage, made stupid errors, and was knocked out in two rounds.

McGovern lost in 11 rounds to Corbett in a return fight, but he was never the same man after the deaths of his two daughters, ages three and one, in 1903 and 1904. By the following year he was losing his mind and was treated for "complete exhaustion" in a sanitorium. He carried on boxing until Englishman Spike Robson toyed with him in 1908. McGovern died of pneumonia in 1918.

McGovern won a world title at 19, but burned out early

SEE ALSO ◆ George Dixon 93 ◆ Pedlar Palmer 261

WALTER MCGOWAN

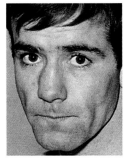

A stylish, quick-thinking boxer, Walter McGowan was a joy to watch.

The youngest of five brothers, he was trained and molded by his father Thomas, who had boxed under the name of Joe Gans. "I had two fists and a heart," said the father. "But Walter's a genius. I see no fault in him."

McGowan lost only twice in 124 amateur contests and won the ABA flyweight title before turning professional in 1961.

Three years on, and by then the British and Empire champion, McGowan was outpointed in a European title fight in Rome by the vastly experienced Salvatore Burruni. He returned the following year to fight for the European bantamweight title against Tommaso Galli. McGowan was clearly superior, the draw decision scandalous. Another setback was when he was stopped by world-class Mexican bantamweight Joe Medel, but he then boxed magnificently to deservedly win the WBC flyweight championship by outpointing Burruni at Wembley in June 1966.

Three months later he outpointed Alan Rudkin over 15 rounds for the British and Empire bantamweight titles, but on 30 December 1966 in front of 16,000 Thais in the Kittikachorn Stadium, Bangkok, a hideous gash on the outside, and damage inside the nose cost him his world championship against Chartchai Chionoi when the fight was evenly poised.

In a rematch at Wembley in September 1967, McGowan was magnificent, winning the first six rounds, only to be stopped because of a cut left eye in round seven.

Two years later, after losing a return with Rudkin but on a run of six wins, McGowan carried out his promise to "go out of boxing when I wanted to, not when I had to". He was still only 27.

FACT FILE

1942 Born Burnbank, Lanarkshire, England

1961 Won ABA flyweight title

1963 Won British and Empire flyweight titles

1966 Beat Salvatore Burruni for WBC title, lost it to Chartchai Chionoi

1967 Lost rematch with Chionoi, again on cuts

1969 Last fight, age 27

Career record: Fights 40, Won 32, Lost 7, Drawn 1

McGowan (right) takes a jab to the body from Salvatore Burruni on the way to the world flyweight title in 1966

BARRY MCGUIGAN

FACT FILE

1961 Born Clones, Ireland
1978 Commonwealth Games gold medal
1985 Won WBA featherweight title against Eusebio Pedroza in London
1986 Lost WBA title to Steve Cruz in Las Vegas
1989 Lost last fight on cuts to Jim McDonnell, age 28

Career record: Fights 35, Won 32, Lost 3

Barry McGuigan had a magnetism that could generate jubilant, partisan support. His finest hour was when 10,000 Irishmen traveled to the open-air Loftus Road soccer stadium to watch him outpoint long-serving WBA featherweight champion Eusebio Pedroza over 15 heart-stopping rounds on a summer's night in 1985.

But as wonderful as that was, McGuigan's fighting home was in the atmospheric King's Hall in Belfast which was reopened after a break of almost 20 years because of his immense popularity.

Whenever McGuigan was boxing there, a packed house was guaranteed. His appearances on the way up against men like Charm Chiteule, Jose Caba and Juan LaPorte were unforgettable, and after beating Pedroza he returned to the King's Hall in his first defence, wearing down the American Bernard Taylor for an eighth round stoppage.

An aggressive, hard-hitting fighter who was utterly dedicated to his craft, McGuigan's was a fairytale that deserved a happy ending. He grabbed the nation's hearts when as a 17-year-old bantamweight he broke down in tears on the winner's rostrum at the 1978 Commonwealth Games in Canada.

From Clones, in Monaghan, he had a solid, forward-thinking team led by wealthy businessman Barney Eastwood, but slowly cracks appeared, and after he lost his WBA title on a split decision to Steve Cruz on a searingly hot Las Vegas afternoon in June 1986, the partnership disintegrated bitterly.

McGuigan resurfaced under Frank Warren's promotional banner, but in 1989 he retired after losing on a cut eye to Jim McDonnell. He carved out a new career for himself as a TV boxing analyst, and also honored the pledge he had made to put something back into the sport by helping to form the Professional Boxers Association.

McGuigan's finest hour: his 15-round points win over Eusebio Pedroza in London

SEE ALSO ◆ EUSEBIO PEDROZA 267

DUKE McKENZIE

The only British boxer this century to win a world title at three separate weights, Duke McKenzie was a gritty text-book boxer with an excellent left jab and a solid technique.

McKenzie was a capable but not outstanding amateur who blossomed with increasing confidence as a professional. He was from a family of boxers, the most successful of whom, elder brother Clinton boxed in the 1976 Olympics and won British and European light-welterweight titles.

Duke, one of the gentlemen of the sport, ended the career of former world champ Charlie Magri with a five rounds win in 1986, and moved from British and European titles to knock out Filipino Rolando Bohol in 11 rounds to win the IBF flyweight championship in 1988. In his second defense he was outfought by Dave McAuley and lost on points,

but immediately moved up to bantamweight, and in 1991 turned in probably the finest boxing display of his career to outclass Texan Gaby Canizales for the WBO bantamweight title in London.

After two emphatic defenses, he was surprisingly beaten in one round by Rafael Del Valle of Puerto Rico, but his response was to move up to super-bantamweight and within five months he was the WBO champion in the 122 lb. division. This followed a close points triumph over Texan southpaw Jesse Benavides. He was unlucky, after time out with illness, to lose a majority verdict at home to Daniel Jimenez of Puerto Rico, in June 1993.

At featherweight he was beaten by a single body punch from Steve Robinson in the ninth round of a WBO title bid, and in 1996 was still attempting to find a path to another world championship at the age of 33.

FACT FILE

1963	Born London, England
1986	Beat Charlie Magri for British and European flyweight titles
1988	Knocked out Rolando Bohol to become IBF flyweight champion
1989	Lost IBF flyweight title to Dave McAuley
1991	Outpointed Gaby Canizales for WBO bantamweight title
1992	Lost WBO bantamweight belt, won super-bantamweight title
1993	Lost WBO sujper-bantamweight title to Daniel Jimenez

Career record: Fights 43, Won 37, Lost 6

McKENZIE, WHO WAS KNOWN AS "THE LITTLE MAN", WAS THE FIRST BRITISH-BORN, THREE-WEIGHT WORLD CHAMP SINCE BOB FITZSIMMONS

SEE ALSO ◆ DAVE McAULEY 235

THE GREAT FIGHTS

EUSEBIO PEDROZA
V.
BARRY MCGUIGAN

LOFTUS ROAD FOOTBALL GROUND, LONDON. JUNE 8, 1985.

This was the moment generations met, when a great and honored champion was forced to bow to the energy and ferocious desire of youth. Eusebio Pedroza, in his 20th WBA featherweight title fight, met a peak-form Barry McGuigan who fought like a man who knew this was his rightful hour, the one moment in all of his fighting life when everything would—and had to—come right.

McGuigan had drawn together the whole of his terribly divided people, had become the most popular Irish sportsman in memory, with a series of phenomenally exciting performances in Belfast's King's Hall. The world title fight was staged at the Loftus Road soccer stadium in London... and drew a singing, cheering, celebrating, partisan crowd of 27,000.

Pedroza knew boxing from back to front, from start to finish. He could box like a classical stylist, could hit sharply, and could rumble with the toughest. More than one opponent had called him a dirty fighter.

He was 32 years old, and in his 45th fight, but by no means washed up. Four months earlier he had soundly outpointed an excellent fighter, Jorge Lujan, before 15,000 fans in Panama City.

Yet this night belonged to Ireland and to McGuigan, whose father Pat set the tone by singing "Danny Boy" in the slot normally reserved for national anthems.

He swamped Pedroza from the first bell, steaming in and throwing a tidal wave of punches that lasted 15 rounds. He missed with plenty, but kept throwing them, absorbing counterpunches like a man driven by an obsession. Pedroza's elegant skills kept him in the fight for the first six rounds, but in the seventh McGuigan floored him with a right hand. From then on, it was his fight. Pedroza refused to quit, kept his defenses together and landed some stinging counters, but at the final bell was still well beaten.

As McGuigan made two successful defenses, then lost to Steve Cruz in Las Vegas, bitterness, anguish, and anger replaced the joy. But this night, above all others, belonged to him.

JIMMY McLARNIN

Jimmy McLarnin was one of millions who sailed from Ireland for a new life across the Atlantic—and one of the few who made his fortune.

McLarnin was a child of three when his family emigrated to Canada. In old age McLarnin, who moved on to California as a young man, would say he had his first fight for $1 and his last for $60,000. By the age of 19, he had $100,000 in the bank.

He enjoyed a lifelong friendship with manager Pop Foster, who guided him to the world welterweight title from his first days in a boxing gym. "Baby Face" McLarnin had a dynamic right, which was too often held in check because it was fragile. But Barney Ross, who fought three epic welterweight title struggles with the Irishman, said it was hard enough to

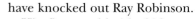

have knocked out Ray Robinson.

His first world title bid was a losing 15-rounder against Sammy Mandell for the lightweight title in New York in 1928, but a 1932 win over one of his boyhood heroes, the by-then aging Benny Leonard, earned him enough notice for him to be given a world welterweight title shot against Young Corbett III in Los Angeles in May 1933. He won the fight in the first round.

His three fights with Ross were epic affairs. Ross won the first and third, McLarnin the middle one, but there was very little between them at any stage in the 45 rounds. He retired on a high note in 1936, following points wins over Tony Canzoneri and Lou Ambers. He was a successful businessman, settling in Glendale, California, with his wife and four children.

WINNING EXIT: McLARNIN LEFT BOXING ON A HIGH NOTE IN 1936 WITH A POINTS WIN OVR LOU AMBERS

SEE ALSO ◆ TONY CANZONERI 54 ◆ BENNY LEONARD 186 ◆ RAY ROBINSON 278 ◆ BARNEY ROSS 287

MIKE McTIGUE

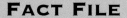

The Irish Civil War was temporarily suspended in and around La Scala Theatre in Dublin on St. Patrick's Night, 1923, as Mike McTigue took the world light-heavyweight title from Battling Siki.

Inside the building, 1,500 McTigue fans roared him home and outside thousands more milled around waiting for the result. Some say the streets were echoing to the sound of bombs and bullets. Certainly, there was an explosion nearby shortly before the fight began.

It must have been unnerving even for the eccentric Siki, but equally weird for McTigue, who had returned to box in Ireland for the first time after nine years as a professional in the United States.

A farmer's son from County Clare, McTigue emigrated to New York when he was 16, made his professional debut in 1914, and fought Harry Greb twice, Battling Levinsky, and Tommy Loughran.

After beating Siki on points over 20 rounds with a controlled display of boxing on the move, he fought greats of the day such as Young Stribling, Loughran, and Mickey Walker, but then lost the championship when Paul Berlanbach outpointed him in Yankee Stadium, New York, in May 1925.

McTigue was good enough to beat top-class operators like Tiger Flowers, Johnny Risko, and Berlanbach in a return, but Loughran outboxed him for the vacant light-heavyweight title in October 1927. Three years later he suffered the humiliation of having his license withdrawn because of poor form. He kept a bar for some time on Long Island, but was hospitalized for the last ten years of his life, his memory shattered, probably by the punches he took in his long-ago youth.

FACT FILE

1892 Born Kilnamona, Ennis, County Clare, Ireland

1923 Won world light-heavyweight title against Battling Siki in Dublin

1925 Lost world title to Paul Berlanbach in New York

1927 Lost vacant title fight to Tommy Loughran

1930 Last fight, age 37

Died: Jamaica, Queens, New York, August 12, 1966, age 73

Career record: Fights 166, Won 104, Lost 45, Drawn 10, No Decisions 6, No Contest 1

McTigue is chaired by his fans after his St Patrick's Night triumph over Battling Siki in Dublin

THE GREAT FIGHTS

SALVADOR SANCHEZ
V.
AZUMAH NELSON

MADISON SQUARE GARDEN, NEW YORK.
JULY 21, 1982.

The great Salvador Sanchez boxed for the last time in his short career against a little-known substitute from Ghana, Azumah Nelson, before a disappointing crowd of 5,575 fans at Madison Square Garden.

The low house was not surprising. For all his wonderful skills, Sanchez was by no means a household name. He was revered by the trade, but the public at large were more concerned with the exploits of Leonard, Duran, Hagler, Hearns, and Holmes.

Yet this relatively low-key occasion turned out to be a magnificent fight and a significant moment in boxing history: the passing of one great champion, the first sight of another.

Nelson was given no chance, mostly because American fight people had never heard of him. Yet the 24-year-old African champion attacked Sanchez as if he were a mediocre journeyman, sometimes almost leaping forward, prodding out jabs and hooking hard with both hands. "I feel weak," Sanchez complained at the end of round four.

Sanchez, a man driven to seek out greatness whose eventual ambition was to become a doctor, thought the problems through, counter-punched, established himself, and then floored Nelson with a left hook in round seven.

Gradually, almost imperceptibly, he took over, learning to read Nelson's rushes. At the end of the ninth Nelson walked to Sanchez's corner in a daze. The champ tapped him on the shoulder and pointed him in the right direction.

By the 15th one judge had Nelson in front, the other two saw it for Sanchez. Nelson tore into the champion, but was knocked down by a left hook. "Come on," he said to Sanchez, who did, and Nelson hit the "wall" marathon runners know so well. He was being propped up by the force of the punches and by the ropes against his back as referee Tony Perez stopped it 71 seconds short of the final bell.

Nelson returned to become one of the greatest champions in history—and Sanchez was killed in an automobile crash 22 days later. He was 23.

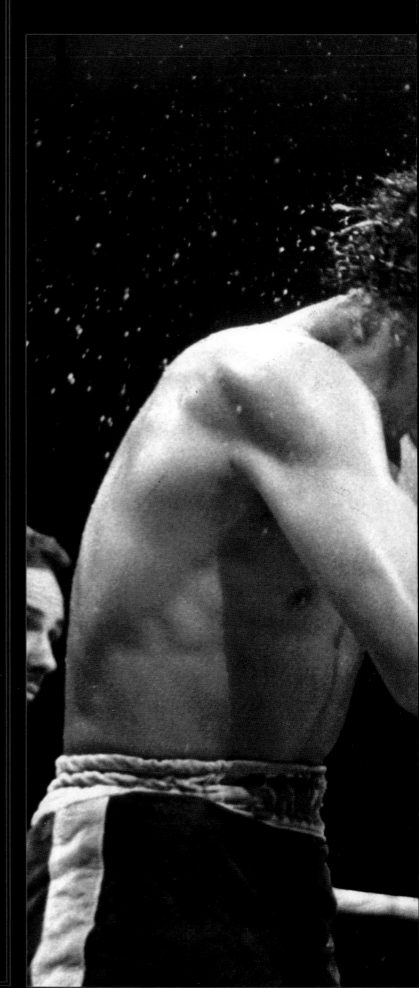

JOSE NAPOLES

Jose Napoles was a beautiful, rhythmic boxer with a chilling ability to finish a fight once he sensed a man was in trouble. A brilliant amateur in his native Cuba, he had to wait for his professional chance until April 1969, when he stopped defending champion Curtis Cokes after 13 rounds at Inglewood Forum in Los Angeles. It was a clinical, systematic destruction of a good champion.

Only 10 weeks later, Napoles forced Cokes to retire after the 10th round on a chilly, rainy night in Mexico City when 25,000 fans turned out to welcome him to the home he had adopted when he walked away from Fidel Castro's regime in 1962.

Napoles outpointed Emile Griffith and stopped Ernie "Red" Lopez in the 15th round, but then lost the title on cuts to unheralded Billy Backus in Syracuse, New York —close to Backus's hometown of Canastota. In a rematch in Los Angeles in June 1971, Napoles won easily to resume where he left off as champion.

Six more defenses followed, as he demonstrated why he was one of the best welterweights in history, but when he attempt to bridge the gap between 147 lb. and 160 lb., he was given a six-round battering by world middleweight champion Carlos Monzon.

At welterweight, he was still good enough to stave off four more challenges, though he was lucky to benefit from the new-fangled technical decision rule when badly cut against Armando Muniz. In December 1975, however, he was stopped in six rounds by Englishman John H. Stracey in Mexico City and retired.

NAPOLES AT THE HEIGHT OF HIS POWERS: HE KNOCKS OUT ENGLAND'S RALPH CHARLES AT WEMBLEY

SEE ALSO ◆ EMILE GRIFFITH 144 ◆ CARLOS MONZON 222 ◆ JOHN H. STRACEY 305

AZUMAH NELSON

Azumah Nelson was the greatest of all African fighters. Called variously "The Lion of Africa," "The Terrible Warrior," and "The Professor," Nelson had a perfect temperament, a disciplined, organized ring brain, a tremendous punch, and the stoutest of chins.

Nelson made his name in world class against WBC featherweight champion Salvador Sanchez in Madison Square Garden in 1982, when he came in as a substitute and pushed the Mexican into the 15th round before running out of gas.

He flattened Puerto Rican hero Wilfredo Gomez in 11 rounds to become WBC champion in San Juan in December 1994. Of his six successful defenses, the most impressive was a first-round knockout of Britain's Pat Cowdell in Birmingham.

In 1988 he outgrew the featherweight division and won the WBC super-featherweight belt by outpointing Mario Martinez in Los Angeles. He was still grieving after the death of his wife when he challenged Pernell Whitaker for the lightweight title in 1990. Not surprisingly, he lost the decision to one of the cleverest performers of the era.

If some felt him lucky to draw against Australian Jeff Fenech in Las Vegas in June 1991, he was at his ruthless best when he traveled to Melbourne and outclassed Fenech in eight rounds nine months later. His later claim was that he had been suffering from the after-effects of malaria when he agreed to the first fight.

In May 1994 he looked old as he was outpointed by James Leija, but in December 1995 regained the championship by knocking out Leija's successor, Gabriel Ruelas, in five rounds. Then he stopped Leija to reestablish himself as the best super-featherweight in the world at the age of 37.

FACT FILE

1958 Born Accra, Ghana
1978 Commonwealth Games featherweight gold medal
1984 Knocked out Wilfredo Gomez for WBC featherweight title
1988 Beat Mario Martinez for WBC super-featherweight title
1994 Lost WBC super-featherweight title to James Leija
1995 Regained WBC super-featherweight title from Gabriel Ruelas

Career record: Fights 44, Won 39, Lost 3, Drawn 2

AFRICA'S GREATEST: NELSON'S CHAMPIONSHIP REIGNS SPANNED 13 YEARS

SEE ALSO ◆ JEFF FENECH 110 ◆ WILFREDO GOMEZ 136 ◆ SALVADOR SANCHEZ 293

THE
GREAT
FIGHTS

AZUMAH NELSON
V.
JEFF FENECH

PRINCES PARK, MELBOURNE, AUSTRALIA.
MARCH 1, 1992.

Ten years on from his first world title fight against the legendary Salvador Sanchez, Azumah Nelson confirmed his right to be counted among the best boxers of his age.

If anyone doubted Nelson's quality, the evidence was in his clinical eighth round dismissal of Australian favorite Jeff Fenech on a rain-swept afternoon in front of 38,000 hostile fans in Melbourne.

Fenech had complained angrily after a controversial draw for Nelson's WBC super-featherweight crown in Las Vegas the previous year, but Nelson had suffered malaria 10 days before the fight as well as an elbow injury. His poor performance led most critics to believe Fenech would clinch his fourth world championship and end the career of the 33-year-old Ghanaian.

In fact, it was Fenech's career that was wrecked as Nelson produced a majestic combination of ringcraft and destructive punching.

Fenech was floored in the opening round by a clean right hand to the chin, and got up at five, looking shocked and hurt. He was down again in the second and Nelson controlled the pace of the fight after that. He tucked up and drew the sting from the Australian by letting him bull forward and punch, blocking most of the blows on the arms and gloves. Whenever Nelson opened up, his command was undeniable. Strangely, he was only level on two official scorecards, and ahead by three points on the third scorecard.

Fenech plugged away, but was rocked in the fifth, then wobbled dramatically at the end of round seven. The finish came in the eighth, when Nelson sent him sprawling with three left hooks and a right hand. Referee Arthur Mercante let it go on, then waved it over with Fenech in distress.

"He's truly a great fighter," acknowledged the beaten Australian.

Nelson, grimly satisfied, his point proven, said: "No one can fight me twice and win. I said I would knock him out and I did."

BATTLING NELSON

FACT FILE

1882 Born Oscar Nielson, Copenhagen, Denmark

1896 Professional at 14 in Indiana

1905 Won world lightweight title by knocking out Jimmy Britt

1906 Lost championship on 42nd-round foul to Joe Gans

1908 Regained title by knocking out Gans in 17 rounds

1910 Lost title to Ad Wolgast on 40th-round knockout

1917 Lost last fight to Freddie Welsh

Died: Chicago, Illinois, February 7, 1954, age 71

Career record: Fights 130, Won 67 Lost 30, Drawn 25, No Decisions 7, No Contest 1

Battling Nelson was grotesquely tough. When he stepped between the ropes, dirty fighting took a new meaning. His thumbs were inquisitive when it came to eyes, his knees often seemed to have a reflex jerk towards testicles, his forehead tended to take aim independently...

Legends grew up around "The Durable Dane." Some even said his skull was three times thicker than that of a normal man, such was his refusal to acknowledge pain. And he is said to have ruined the lemonade at the Jack Dempsey–Jess Willard fight in 1919 by honoring the occasion with a rare bath before anyone else arrived at the arena!

Nelson, born in Denmark but raised in Chicago, knocked out Jimmy Britt in 18 rounds to become champion in San Francisco in September 1905. He lost the title in 1906 in Goldfield, Nevada, when he smacked Joe Gans appallingly low in the 42nd round.

In 1908 Nelson twice knocked out the rapidly declining Gans but his second championship reign ended when Ad Wolgast beat him in one of the most brutal fights ever witnessed. Nelson's eyes were closed and he was vomiting blood when the fight was stopped in round 40, but he was furious and growled angrily: "I woulda had him in another round!"

For more than 20 years he fought the toughest opponents, asking no favors and certainly granting none, and for all his crudities of style paid great detail to fitness and conditioning. Out of the ring, he could be sensitive and gentle. He loved children, never drank or smoked, and said the hardest blow he ever had to take was when his marriage collapsed. When he was nearly 70 he was attacked by two hoodlums with blackjacks and suffered serious head injuries. He later died, his mind and money gone, in a Chicago hospital.

NELSON (LEFT, WITH A SPARRING PARTNER) WAS NICKNAMED "THE DURABLE DANE" . . . WITH GOOD REASON

SEE ALSO ◆ JOE GANS 129 ◆ FREDDIE WELSH 333 ◆ AD WOLGAST 339

TERRY NORRIS

A slick, confident boxer with a stiff punch, Terry Norris was a three-time light-middleweight champion of the world in the 1990s.

He left his home town of Lubbock, Texas, when, following his part in a brawl during a baseball game, he was stabbed by a masked man in a night club, and shot at. "If I'd stayed, I'd probably be in a pine box," he said.

He left for the KO Corral boxing ranch in California, run by Joe Sayatovich, to be with elder brother Orlin, who would later be a WBC cruiserweight champion. Terry was the more naturally talented of the two, but he had an occasional tendency to lose discipline—he was disqualified three times, twice in world title bouts against Luis Santana—and he was knocked out by Julian Jackson and then by Simon Brown.

The 1989 defeat by Jackson rudely curtailed his first world title shot, but in March 1990 he knocked out Ugandan dangerman John Mugabi in one sensational round in Tampa, Florida, to become WBC champion.

He floored Ray Leonard twice and outpointed him in Madison Square Garden and beat other champions Don Curry, Meldrick Taylor, and Maurice Blocker. A huge money match with Julio Cesar Chavez went to waste when Norris lost in four rounds to Simon Brown in Mexico in December 1993, but he outpointed Brown with a brilliant display to regain the belt.

The disqualifications against Santana cost him money, but Norris easily stopped him the third time to become WBC champ again in August 1995, and added the IBF belt with a landslide decision over Paul Vaden.

FACT FILE

1967	Born Lubbock, Texas
1990	Defeated John Mugabi in one round for WBC light-middleweight title
1991	Ended the career of Ray Leonard
1993	Knocked out by Simon Brown to lose title in 11th defense
1994	Regained title against Brown, lost it on a foul to Luis Santana
1995	Beat Santana at third attempt to become champion again

Career record: Fights 50, Won 44, Lost 6

THE CLEANEST OF PUNCHERS: NORRIS DISLODGES CARL DANIELS' MOUTHPIECE IN A 1992 LIGHT-MIDDLEWEIGHT DEFENCE

SEE ALSO ◆ JULIO CESAR CHAVEZ 67

PHILADELPHIA JACK O'BRIEN

Historians have credited Philadelphia Jack O'Brien with the light-heavyweight world championship because of a 13-rounds win over Bob Fitzsimmons in San Francisco in December 1905. Whatever the merits of that, and some do argue about the billing of the contest, there is no doubt that O'Brien was one of the quickest and most skillful boxers of his day.

O'Brien twice disputed the heavyweight title with champion Tommy Burns in Los Angeles, the first fight in November 1906 ending in a draw which was said to have been prearranged, and the second in May 1907 in a points win for Burns. After the second fight O'Brien accused Burns of double-crossing him—he said he had paid the champion $3,500 to take a dive! He also claimed many of his other fights had been fixed, but that is impossible to establish.

In a 10-round no-decision bout with ferocious middleweight Stanley Ketchel, O'Brien outboxed the "Michigan Assassin" until the last seconds of the bout when a Ketchel haymaker knocked him cold. The final bell rang with the count at eight, denying Ketchel the knockout. In a return Ketchel won in three rounds.

Early in his career O'Brien boxed tough campaigners like Joe Choynski, Peter Maher, and the future world champ Marvin Hart, as well as champions from the lighter weights like Joe Walcott, Kid McCoy, and Tommy Ryan. He also got the better of both Fitzsimmons and Burns in no-decision six-round bouts, and once crammed as many as 46 fights into less than 18 months.

On his retirement in 1912, the year after he had lost decisively to Sam Langford, he developed a successful engineering business.

PHILADELPHIA JACK: 180 FIGHTS IN 16 YEARS

SEE ALSO ◆ TOMMY BURNS 49 ◆ BOB FITZSIMMONS 114 ◆ STANLEY KETCHELL 176 ◆ KID McCOY 239 ◆ JOE WALCOTT 329

RUBEN OLIVARES

They came no more colorful, nor more dynamic than Ruben Olivares, for years the most popular fighter in Mexico.

Olivares was a happy, carefree character who sometimes failed to find the discipline required of a great champion, but whose punching power and exciting style gave him a public appeal long after the sharpness of youth had faded.

He held the world bantamweight title twice, and two versions of the featherweight championship. When he knocked out Lionel Rose of Australia with a left hook to the body and right cross to the chin in the fifth round before 18,549 jubilant fans at the Inglewood Forum, Los Angeles in August 1969, it was his 51st knockout win in 53 fights.

Olivares, whose father owned a construction company, was privately educated in an attempt to steer him away from street fights. Instead he found his way into the ring... and the hearts of his people.

He demolished Britain's Alan Rudkin in two rounds, outpointed compatriot Chucho Castillo, but lost on a 14th-round cut in a rematch. A third fight saw Olivares regain the belt on points in April 1971, but after two more defenses he lost in eight rounds to Rafael Herrera in March 1972.

Olivares won the WBA championship by flattening Zensuke Otagawa of Japan in seven rounds in 1974. The Nicaraguan, Alexis Arguello, beat him in 13 rounds, but Olivares rebounded with a two-round win over Bobby Chacon to become WBC champion in June 1975. Three months later he lost a split decision in Los Angeles to David Kotey.

A last world title fling ended with a 12th-round stoppage by WBA champion Eusebio Pedroza in Texas in 1979.

FACT FILE

1947 Born Mexico City
1969 Won world Bantamweight title by knocking out Lionel Rose
1970 Lost title on cuts to Chucho Castillo
1971 Regained championship from Castillo
1972 Lost title on 8th-round knockout to Rafael Herrera
1974 Won WBA featherweight title against Zensuke Qtagawa, lost it to Alexis Arguello
1975 Won WBC title against Bobby Chacon, lost it to David Kotey
1988 Last fight in Mexico, age 41

Career record: Fights 104, Won 88, Lost 13, Drawn 3

KO KING: OLIVARES KNOCKS OUT ALAN RUDKIN DURING HIS BANTAMWEIGHT HEYDAY

SEE ALSO ◆ ALEXIS ARGUELLO 20 ◆ DAVID KOTEY 180 ◆ EUSEBIO PEDROZA 267

CARLOS ORTIZ

arlos Ortiz always had a sound business head. By the time he outboxed Joe "Old Bones" Brown for the world lightweight title, the Puerto Rican-born New Yorker already owned his house, a Cadillac, had stocks carefully invested, life insurance policies in place, and trust funds for each of his three children.

Ortiz came from a tough, honest background—his father earned less than $90 a month as a cook and porter—and after learning to box at a Police Athletic League gym in New York, he was skillful enough to turn professional at 18. He developed into a brilliant, innovative boxer, who outthought as much as outfought opponents.

Because he was unable to get a shot at Brown, his promoter "rediscovered" the defunct junior-welterweight division, and he stopped Kenny Lane in two rounds to win the vacant title in New York in June 1959. Eventually, he lost it to Diulio Loi in Milan, but soon made amends by outpointing Brown in Las Vegas in April 1962 to become the new world lightweight champion.

He made the title work for him for the next six years. He lost it to Ismael Laguna in 1965, but beat Laguna twice in rematches, and also defeated good fighters in Flash Elorde, Doug Vaillant, Sugar Ramos, and Johnny Bizzarro.

Finally, he was outpointed in June 1968 in Santo Domingo by local hero Carlos "Teo" Cruz. He quit boxing, but enjoyed a comeback until Ken Buchanan became the only man to stop him, in six rounds in New York, in September 1972. In retirement he owned a nightclub, a liquor store, several apartment buildings in New York, and other companies in Puerto Rico.

ORTIZ (RIGHT) FLOORED AND OUTPOINTED MAURICE CULLEN IN A NON-TITLE FIGHT IN LONDON IN 1963

SEE ALSO ♦ JOE BROWN 43 ♦ KEN BUCHANAN 45 ♦ ISMAEL LAGUNA 183 ♦ DIULIO LOI 200

MANUEL ORTIZ

Manuel Ortiz, a chunky, aggressive pressure fighter with an iron chin and a very genuine love of life, dominated the bantamweight division for most of the 1940s.

His was a story from a movie script. A truck driver who went to watch an amateur show, he was persuaded to fill in as a substitute when a fighter did not turn up, loved it and changed his life on the spot.

In 1937 he traveled to Boston to win the National AAU flyweight crown and turned professional at 21, learning his trade in the rings around Los Angeles, losing almost as many as he won. Gradually, his hard-hitting, big-hearted displays earned him a sizable reputation throughout the United States.

Eventually, at the Hollywood Bowl in August 1942, the 5 ft. 4 in. slugger from Corona outpointed Lou Salica over 12 rounds to win the world bantamweight title. Ortiz was a phenomenal success, defending his championship an incredible eight times in 1943 alone, and 15 times altogether, before he was outpointed by Chicago's light-hitting but crafty Harold Dade, a 12-1 underdog, in San Francisco in January 1947.

Poor Dade was champion for two months. In March 1947, Ortiz outpointed him in Los Angeles, and carried on where he left off, defiantly turning back four more challenges before the ambitious, determined South African, Vic Toweel, outpointed him in Johannesburg in May 1950. Ortiz, close to 34 years old and in his 23rd world title fight, simply didn't have it any more.

He went on fighting until 1955, and retired to his 600-acre farm in California, and owned a ranch and nightclub. Unfortunately, he spent his money and was living a hand-to-mouth existence before his death from liver disease at the age of 53.

FACT FILE

1916	Born Corona, California
1937	National AAU flyweight champion
1942	Beat Lou Salica for world bantamweight title
1947	Lost and regained world title against Harold Dade
1950	Lost world bantamweight title to Vic Toweel
1955	Retired from boxing after 17-year career
Died:	San Diego, California, May 31, 1970, age 53

Career record: Fights 127, Won 95, Lost 29, Drawn 3

THE DOMINANT BANTAMWEIGHT OF THE 1940S, ORTIZ WORKS OUT IN BRIGHTON IN 1949 BEFORE HIS MEETING WITH BRITAIN'S RONNIE CLAYTON

JORGE PAEZ

CLOWN PRINCE: PAEZ DREW HUGE TV RATINGS WHEN IBF FEATHERWEIGHT CHAMPION

Jorge Paez was one of boxing's great showmen... as one might have expected from a man who spent his early years in a circus.

Paez's grandmother owned the Big Top in Mexicali and Jorge worked as a juggler, acrobat and clown. However much boxing purists protested, he was adored by his fans. At his peak in the late 1980s, he drew huge TV ratings.

Moonwalking, breakdancing, and walking on his hands were part of the routine. He would kiss ringcard girls between rounds, and celebrated one victory with a handstand on a cornerpost. In support of a Safe Sex campaign, he tossed condoms into the crowd. He used his head as an advertising board for a "No Drugs" message. Once, in a famous moment of provocation, he boxed before WBC president Jose Sulaiman with a haircut that read "IBF"!

But beyond all that, this seemingly perpetually happy man could fight. At his best he was a tough, determined featherweight champion who defended his IBF title eight times.

He floored defending champ Calvin Grove three times in the 15th round to win a unanimous decision in Mexicali in August 1988. He stopped Grove in a return, drew with Louie Espinoza, beat Steve Cruz, Jose Lopez, Lupe Gutierrez, and, controversially when he lost three pounds in five hours before the weigh-in, Troy Dorsey. In a fight that also involved the WBO title, he outpointed Espinoza, and drew with Dorsey, before finally accepting he could no longer make the weight.

He was less effective in the higher divisions, but remained one of boxing's great entertainers into the mid-1990s.

SEE ALSO ◆ **PERNELL WHITAKER 334**

PEDLAR PALMER

Known as "Box O' Tricks", Pedlar Palmer was from fighting stock. His father was a bare-knuckle champion of Essex, and his mother could handle any woman in London's East End!

He was an elusive, extremely clever boxer who developed into an extravagant showman, with moves learned in a boyhood stage act with his brother.

He won bouts advertised as for the world 100 lb. title in 1893 against Walter Croot and Mike Small, and was acknowledged as world bantamweight champion in 1895 when he beat Billy Plimmer of Birmingham on a 14th-round foul. He boxed a draw with world feather-weight champion George Dixon in New York in 1896, and kept his bantamweight title through five defenses against Johnny Murphy, Ernie Stanton, Dave Sullivan of Cork, Plimmer, and Billy Rochford.

Palmer lost his title in Tuckahoe, New York, in September 1899 when he claimed he was blinded by the ring lights and "Terrible" Terry McGovern knocked him out in the first round. He was still only 22 years old.

Life remained a source of adventure for Palmer even though his skills faded as his liking for a drink took its toll. He lost the British bantamweight title to Harry Ware in November 1900, and although he won two out of three fights with Dixon and beat Digger Stanley, another world champ, he was twice beaten in British featherweight title fights by Ben Jordan and Joe Bowker.

In 1907 he killed a man on a train to Epsom Races, and served four years for manslaughter. On his release, he boxed again, but the great days were over. For the last 20 years of his life, he was a bookmaker in Brighton.

FACT FILE

1876	Born Thomas Palmer, Canning Town, London
1893	Won world 100 lb. title by stopping Walter Croot
1895	Won British and world bantamweight titles against Billy Plimmer
1899	Lost world title to Terry McGovern
1900	Lost British title to Harry Ware
1919	Last fight against Jim Driscoll
Died:	London, February 13, 1949, age 72

Career record: Fights 64, Won 47, Lost 13, Drawn 4

PALMER IN HIS BRILLIANT, SWAGGERING YOUTH WHEN HE WAS ACKNOWLEDGED AS WORLD BANTAMWEIGHT CHAMPION

SEE ALSO ♦ GEORGE DIXON 93 ♦ JIM DRISCOLL 95 ♦ TERRY MCGOVERN 240 ♦ BILLY PLIMMER 272

CARLOS PALOMINO

An intelligent, workmanlike world welterweight champion, Carlos Palomino knew his business well. He also combined boxing with an education at Long Beach State College, graduating even as he held the world title.

From a middle-class background, he worked his way up through the preliminary bouts in Los Angeles, but fairly swiftly moved into top class. When he traveled to London in June 1976 to challenge home favorite John H. Stracey, he was unimpressive in sparring and given little chance. But he rose to the occasion magnificently, mixed up ferocious shots to the head and body, stopping a desperately disappointed champion in the 12th round.

He stopped Californian rival Armando Muniz with 36 seconds left in the 15th round in the Olympic Auditorium, Los Angeles, in January 1977, and then returned to London to knock out big-hearted English challenger Dave Green with a superb left hook in round 11.

Five more defenses followed against Everaldo Costa Acevedo, Jose Palacios, Ryu Sorimachi, Mimoun Mohotar, and Muniz again, before he lost the title on a split decision in San Juan by Wilfred Benitez in January 1979. After he was outpointed in a 10-round non-title fight by Roberto Duran in New York in June 1979, he retired at the age of 29, having grossed around $1.5 million in the previous three years.

He worked as a film and TV actor, and stayed in touch with boxing as a member of the California State Athletic Commission. In late 1996, following the death of his father, he was contemplating a limited comeback for old times' sake at the age of 47.

PALOMINO: UNDER-RATED WELTERWEIGHT CHAMPION, AND A SMART, INTELLIGENT FIGHTER

SEE ALSO ◆ WILFRED BENITEZ 32 ◆ JOHN H. STRACEY 305

BILLY PAPKE

Only one middleweight ever beat the legendary Stanley Ketchel in his great years... that was William Herman Papke, a reticent, suspicious former miner from Illinois.

Papke and Ketchel were bitter rivals from the time they fought a 10-rounder in Milwaukee in June 1908. Ketchel won the decision, but the fair-haired, deceptively boyish Papke complained angrily that he had not recovered after Ketchel had knocked him down at the beginning of their fight instead of touching gloves as was the tradition.

Three months later he repaid Ketchel in a title fight in Vernon, California, walking across to shake hands and smiling broadly during the preliminaries. When the bell rang, Ketchel offered his glove and was stunned by a right hand, then battered in a brutal fight. By the ninth Ketchel's eyes were virtually shut, and in the 11th the crowd yelled for the slaughter to be stopped. Two more knockdowns in round 12 gave Papke the world middleweight title.

He was champion for only two months. Ketchel beat him in 11 rounds in Colma, San Francisco, and then outpointed him in a grueling 20-round struggle which Papke's fans felt he won on a blazing summer's day in Colma in July 1909. Their wars gave them a grudging mutual respect, and after Ketchel's death in 1910, Papke claimed the championship. He boxed in Australia and Europe, where he defeated 20-year-old French prospect Georges Carpentier on a foul, but lost his claim when he was disqualified against Frank Klaus in Paris in 1913.

Papke owned property and a citrus grove in Altadena, but in November 1936 after drinking all day in Los Angeles, he drove to the house of his estranged wife, shot her dead and then turned the gun on himself.

FACT FILE

1886 Born Spring Valley, Illinois

1908 Won and lost world middleweight title against Stanley Ketchel

1909 Lost 20-round decision to Ketchel

1912 Beat Georges Carpentier in Paris

1913 Lost on a foul to Frank Klaus for world midleweight title

Died: Newport, California, November 26, 1936, age 50

Career record: Fights 62, Won 42, Lost 13, Drawn 7

PAPKE HAD FOUR LEGENDARY BATTLES WITH STANLEY KETCHEL. BOTH MET TRAGIC ENDS

SEE ALSO ◆ STANLEY KETCHELL 176

LASZLO PAPP

A cagey southpaw with a heavy left hook, Laszlo Papp confused his government as much as his opponents.

Papp's amateur achievements were magnificent. He won the middleweight gold medal at the 1948 Olympic Games in London, and dropped down to light-middleweight to collect golds in Helsinki in 1952 and Melbourne in 1956.

The 1956 Hungarian uprising threw the country into turmoil, and in the wake of it came an attempt at a more liberal attitude. In May 1957, at the age of 31, Papp was allowed to box professionally from a base in Vienna, although there remained deep suspicion and opposition in his own country.

By then his hands had become fragile, and he spent time out of the ring with injuries. Eventually, however, in May 1962 he stopped Chris Christensen of Denmark in the seventh round in Vienna to become European middleweight champion. He was two weeks short of his 36th birthday.

He proved his superiority over his European rivals by defending his title six times. Only Mick Leahy managed to stay the 15-round distance in 1964.

Papp was long overdue a world championship opportunity, and seemed perfectly capable of beating titleholder Joey Giardello, but the Hungarian Government prevaricated, uncomfortable at the wealth the greatest sportsman in their history was accumulating.

In November 1964, they finally called him home, and revoked his permit to travel abroad. As there was no professional boxing in Hungary itself, this in effect retired him.

Papp turned his attention to the amateur code and coached Hungary's national team for many years.

PAPP FLOORS BRITAIN'S JOHNNY WRIGHT IN THE 1948 OLYMPICS

FLOYD PATTERSON

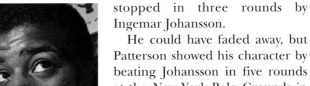

For all his wonderful achievements in the ring, Floyd Patterson's autobiography Victory Over Myself summed up his greatest fight.

An introverted, lonely teenager, Patterson overcame his inferiority complex to win the 1952 Olympic middleweight gold medal. Four years later he became the youngest heavyweight champion in history by knocking out Archie Moore in the fifth round in Chicago for the vacant title. He was 21.

Patterson's manager, Cus D'Amato, refused to cooperate with the all-powerful International Boxing Club, which "moved the pieces" at the time. Instead he steered an individual course, acutely aware that Floyd was still developing as a fighter and a man: they avoided the dangermen of the time in favor of softer defenses against Tommy Jackson, Pete Rademacher, Roy Harris, and Brian London.

In June 1959 D'Amato made a mistake: Patterson was dropped seven times and stopped in three rounds by Ingemar Johansson.

He could have faded away, but Patterson showed his character by beating Johansson in five rounds at the New York Polo Grounds in June 1960 to become the first man to regain the heavyweight championship.

But in Chicago in September 1962 Patterson—proudly, foolishly ignoring D'Amato's advice—fought Sonny Liston, and was smashed aside in 126 seconds. Patterson left by a back door, wearing dark glasses and a false beard.

He spent the rest of his career as a contender. Liston annihilated him again, Muhammad Ali stopped him nonchalantly in 12 rounds in Las Vegas in 1965, and he lost a WBA title fight to Jimmy Ellis in Stockholm in 1968. He retired in 1972, managed his adopted son Tracy Harris Patterson to a world title, and became chairman of the New York State Athletic Commission.

FACT FILE

1935	Born Waco, North Carolina
1952	Olympic middleweight gold medal, age 17
1956	Became youngest world heavyweight champ at 21
1959	Lost heavyweight title to Ingemar Johansson
1960	Regained heavyweight title by knocking out Johansson
1962	Knocked out by Sonny Liston in one round
1965	Lost to Muhammad Ali in attempt to become 3-time champ

Career record: Fights 64, Won 55, Lost 8, Drawn 1

PATTERSON DRIVES JIMMY ELLIS ON TO THE BACK FOOT IN THEIR WBA TITLE FIGHT IN STOCKHOLM

SEE ALSO ◆ MUHAMMAD ALI 12 ◆ SONNY LISTON 196 ◆ INGEMAR JOHANSSON 170

SAMART PAYAKARUN

FACT FILE

1962 Born Chacherngsao, Thailand

1982 Professional debut, beat former world champ Netrnoi Vorasingh

1986 Knocked out Lupe Pintor to win WBC super-bantamweight title

1987 Lost WBC title to Jeff Fenech in Australia

1994 Lost WBA featherweight title fight to Eloy Rojas

Career record: Fights 23, Won 21, Lost 2

Samart Payakarun was a brilliant southpaw with a fast, hard left hand, who was an outstanding kick-boxer before turning to the international code in 1982. He went on to win a world championship, before squandering his vast talent.

Matched with former WBC light-flyweight champion Netrnoi Vorasingh in his debut, Samart justified the confidence of his backers by winning a wide 10-round decision.

In Bangkok on January 18, 1986, in only his 11th fight, he outclassed defending WBC super-bantamweight champion Lupe Pintor of Mexico. A ready-smiling young man with film star looks, Payakarun was popular, and consolidated his reputation by stopping Juan "Kid" Meza of Mexico in the 12th round in his first defense in Bangkok in December 1986.

Thais gambled heavily on his retaining the title again when he traveled to Sydney to fight unbeaten Australian Jeff Fenech, but his countrymen did not know that Samart had barely trained. He landed a hard right hand to drop Fenech for the first time in his life, but the Aussie climbed all over him and knocked him out in the fourth round.

When Samart returned, with revelations of his overconfidence now made public, he retreated to a monastery, officially in a socially acceptable display of penitence, unofficially until those who had lost large amounts of money calmed down!

When he emerged he found instant fortune and fame as a Thai pop star, with a string of hit records. Nagging at the back of his mind, however, was the wasted ring career. He returned and fought his way back to top level, only to be knocked out in a WBA featherweight title fight by Eloy Rojas of Venezuela in September 1994.

PAYAKARUN LEANS NONCHALANTLY ON THE ROPES AS LUPE PINTOR GOES DOWN. THE POPULAR THAI IS SECONDS AWAY FROM BEING CROWNED WORLD CHAMPION

SEE ALSO ◆ JEFF FENECH 110 ◆ LUPE PINTOR 271

EUSEBIO PEDROZA

Eusebio Pedroza, an angular, educated boxer, was among the best featherweights of all time.

He combined a brilliant ring brain with a ruthless streak—"I never fought a dirtier fighter," said Puerto Rican Juan LaPorte—Pedroza held the WBA belt for an astonishing seven years.

Yet his world title experience began unfavorably with a stunning two-round knockout defeat by WBA bantamweight champion Alfonso Zamora in Mexicali in April 1976. He was overmatched—and probably weight-drained as well.

Two years later, on April 15, 1978, Pedroza delighted a 12,000 crowd in Panama City as he wore down Spanish southpaw Cecilio Lastra to win the WBA featherweight title in 13 rounds.

He went on to make 19 successful defenses, although the dream fight with his rival WBC champion, Salvador Sanchez, never materialized. He needed all his experience to take a split decision over previously unbeaten Rocky Lockridge in McAfee, New Jersey, in 1980. He repeatedly hit Juan LaPorte low in their 1982 battle in Atlantic City, but won a unanimous verdict and grimly accused the Puerto Rican of "crying."

He drew with Bernard Taylor, outpointed Lockridge in a rematch, and went on until June 1985 when he was floored and outscored by Barry McGuigan at his peak.

In retirement he was a controversial, somewhat shadowy figure in the government congress of the infamous General Noriega. When Noriega fell in 1989 Pedroza was temporarily imprisoned by the American forces and his assets, said to be considerable, were frozen. He returned to the ring for a brief, unsuccessful comeback in the early 1990s.

FACT FILE

1953 Born Panama City, Panama

1973 Professional debut, age 20

1976 Lost WBA bantamweight title fight with Alfonso Zamora

1978 Won WBA featherweight title against Cecilio Lastra

1985 Lost WBA featherweight title to Barry McGuigan in 20th defense

1992 Last fight, age 39

Career record: Fights 49, Won 42, Lost 6, Drawn 1

Pedroza's 20th defence was his last, but he still went 15 rounds with Barry McGuigan in London

SEE ALSO ◆ Barry McGuigan 242 ◆ Alfonso Zamora 343

PAUL PENDER

PENDER (LEFT) WON TWO OUT OF THREE AGAINST BRITAIN'S TERRY DOWNES

Long before Chris Eubank called boxing barbaric, another middleweight champion with a social conscience, Paul Pender, wondered whether it deserved his attention.

"Boxing is rotten clear through, infested by gangsters and thieves," he said, shortly before he won partial recognition as world champ with a split decision over Ray Robinson in 1960. "The public has lost all confidence in it. I have too." They called him before the Massachusetts Commission for that, and he withdrew his smear.

Ring editor of the time Nat Fleischer called Pender "a queer mixture; part bitter, part tough, part kind."

He retired four times in the 1950s because of brittle hands, returning because it was what he did best—and he needed to put food on the family table. He was a smart, knowledgable boxer with confidence and a big heart, as he showed when he took a pounding from Gene Fullmer in 1955 but lasted the 10 rounds.

He turned professional at 18, as early ambitions in physical education and politics came to nothing. Eventually he became a fireman. When he beat Robinson, he scorned ideas of going on to become a great champion.

"All I want is to take home a bundle and call it quits," he said.

Pender beat Robinson on a second split decision in Boston in June 1960, stopped Terry Downes in seven because of a cut nose and outpointed 34-year-old Carmen Basilio.

In July 1961 he lost the title on cuts to Downes in London, but regained it by outpointing the Englishman in Boston in April 1962, then drifted away to get on with the rest of his life.

SEE ALSO ◆ CARMEN BASILIO 29 ◆ GENE FULLMER 123 ◆ RAY ROBINSON 278

WILLIE PEP

Willie Pep was a ring artist, so beautiful to watch one writer called him "a tap dancer with gloves on."

Never a very heavy hitter, he teased opponents, toyed with them, and beat them psychologically as much as physically.

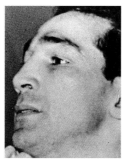

Once he set out to prove in one fight that he could win a round without throwing a punch, and did so, effortlessly keeping his opponent off balance, demoralizing and bewildering him to the point where he had completely dictated the session.

He won the world featherweight title by outpointing Albert "Chalky" Wright in New York in November 1942. It was his 55th consecutive win. He lost only one of his first 138 fights—a 10-round decision to former lightweight champ Sammy Angott in New York in 1943.

He outpointed NBA champion Phil Terranova in February 1945, and defied doctors in 1947 by recovering from serious injuries suffered in a plane crash to box again six months later.

His run came to an end in October 1948 when Sandy Saddler beat him with surprising ease in four rounds to begin a series of great fights. Pep won the second on points four months later, but Saddler beat him in September 1950 when Pep retired with a shoulder injury after seven rounds.

Their final battle, won in nine rounds by Saddler, was a disgraceful brawl—and Pep did not box for a title again. He boxed to the end of the 1950s, then had a six-year break before another largely successful 12-month comeback when he was in his early 40s and still good enough to outbox men half his age.

FACT FILE

1922	Born Guglielmo Papaleo, Middletown, Connecticut
1940	Professional debut, age 17
1942	Outpointed Chalky Wright for world featherweight title
1947	Severely injured in plane crash
1948	Lost world title to Sandy Saddler
1949	Regained world title against Sandy Saddler
1950	Lost title back to Saddler
1966	Last fight, age 43

Career record: Fights 242, Won 230, Lost 11, Drawn 1

PEP'S IMMACULATE LEFT HAND KEEPS RAY FAMECHON OCCUPIED AT MADISON SQUARE GARDEN IN 1950

SEE ALSO ◆ SANDY SADDLER 289

PASCUAL PEREZ

The only serious rival to Carlos Monzon as Argentina's greatest fighter, flyweight Pascual Perez was a boxing terrier, a tiny man with a heavy, jolting punch in either hand.

He became a national hero when he won the flyweight gold medal in the 1948 Olympic Games in London, and Argentine dictator Juan Peron persuaded him to continue as an amateur, offering him a large house as compensation for his loss of earnings.

Eventually Peron agreed Pascual should exchange life as a civil service janitor for that of a professional boxer. The fighter never forgot his mentor, visiting Peron in exile, for which he was heavily criticized in Argentina.

He won the world flyweight title in November 1954 by outpointing the six inches taller Yoshio Shirai in Tokyo, and kept the championship for the rest of the decade. He knocked out Shirai in seven rounds in a return, and dealt with whoever was put in front of him, most emphatically the clever Welshman Dai Dower, who was knocked out in one round in Buenos Aires in 1957.

He also beat Leo Espinosa, Oscar Suarez, Young Martin, Ramon Arias, Dommy Ursua, Kenji Yonekura, and Sadao Yaoita, who had become the first man to beat him—in a non-title 10-rounder in Tokyo in January 1959. In the return for the title in Osaka 10 months later, Perez stopped Yaoita in 13 rounds.

Perez lost the title in Bangkok to Pone Kingpetch in April 1960, and was stopped in the eighth round of a rematch, but instead of retiring, was forced to go on because of a costly divorce. He finally retired in 1964, aged 38. He died from liver failure 13 years later.

PEREZ: THE FINEST FLYWEIGHT IN THE WORLD FOR SIX YEARS

SEE ALSO ◆ PONE KINGPETCH 178

LUPE PINTOR

A tough, all-action brawler with a fast left hook, Lupe Pintor fought his way out of poverty to win two world titles.

He loved to work the body and became a big favorite in Mexico and the West Coast, where he sometimes rode his luck but always gave big-hearted performances.

In Britain he is remembered for his tragic fight with Johnny Owen in Los Angeles in September 1980. He knocked out Owen in the 12th round, and the Welshman died 45 days later after undergoing two brain operations. Pintor kept in touch with Owen's family, who sent him a "Good Luck" telegram before his ring return against Alberto Davila. Pintor went on to win a 15-round thriller on a majority decision at Caesars Palace, Las Vegas.

Pintor was lucky to win a 15-round decision over the great Carlos Zarate in June 1979, but went on to prove himself an excellent cham-

pion. He was cut-prone, and struggled dreadfully to make the weight, usually taking neither food nor liquid for two days before a weigh-in, but made eight defences.

After losing in 14 rounds to WBC super-bantamweight champion Wilfredo Gomez in December 1982, he relinquished the bantamweight title.

This battle-hardened little man, who learned to box in order to protect his pitch as an ice cream seller, won the WBC 122 lb. belt in August 1985 when he outpointed compatriot Juan Meza in Mexico City, but was then knocked out in five by the brilliant Thai southpaw Samart Payakarun in Bangkok in January 1986.

He retired for eight years, made a comeback as a light-welterweight in 1994, which was inexpressibly sad for anyone who saw him in his prime.

FACT FILE

1955 Born Cuajimalpa, Mexico

1974 Professional debut, age 18

1979 Beat Carlos Zarate to win WBC bantamweight title

1982 Lost to Wilfredo Gomez for WBC super-bantamweight title

1983 Relinquished bantamweight crown after eight defenses

1985 Won WBC super-bantamweight title against Juan Meza

1986 Lost title in five rounds to Samart Payakarun

Career record: Fights 72, Won 56, Lost 14, Drawn 2

PINTOR, RUGGED AND HARD-HITTING, REIGNED AS BANTAMWEIGHT CHAMPION FOR FOUR YEARS

SEE ALSO ◆ WILFREDO GOMEZ 136 ◆ SAMART PAYAKARUN 266 ◆ CARLOS ZARATE 348

BILLY PLIMMER

A game, scientific boxer of the old British school, Billy Plimmer could also hit extremely hard for a man who in his prime rarely weighed even 112 lb.

Plimmer, from Birmingham, was a well-schooled boxer who learned his trade on the booths and made excellent professional progress with victories over well respected English fighters like Chappie Moran and Arthur Westley.

When he stopped Jem Stevens in the 15th round of a British bantamweight title fight at the National Sporting Club, London, in April 1891, Plimmer gambled everything he owned on the result. That summer he took off for the United States, where he made an immediate impression.

In May 1892 at the West End Casino, Coney Island, New York, 10,000 fans paid up to $100 a head to see Plimmer win the world bantamweight champion by knocking out the renowned "Harlem Spider," Tommy Kelly, in the 10th round.

Plimmer defended his title by stopping Joe McGrath in eight rounds, then drew over 25 with Johnny Murphy in New Orleans. In one of numerous non-title outings, he outscored world featherweight champion George Dixon over four rounds.

In May 1895 he returned home and knocked out George Corfield of Sheffield in seven rounds for a £300 ($1,500) purse at the NSC, but he was passing his peak, and his weight was increasing. He lost his title to Pedlar Palmer on a 14th-round foul in November 1895, and fought rarely after that. Palmer knocked him out in 17 rounds in 1898, and his last fight was a 20-round draw with old rival Corfield in September 1900. He lived an obscure, meagre life in retirement, most of his ring earnings having long gone.

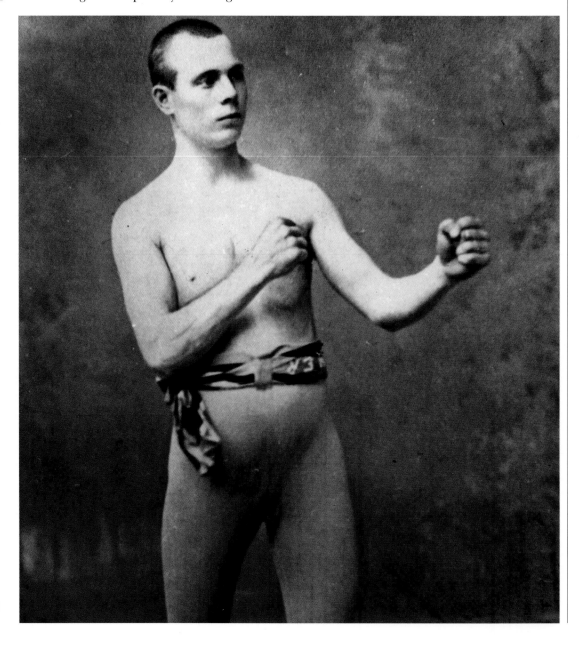

A MASTER BOXER: PLIMMER IN HIS PRIME IN THE 1890S

SEE ALSO ♦ GEORGE DIXON 93

Aaron Pryor

It was Aaron Pryor's fate to be one of the greatest and most wayward of fighters, a history-maker who found it impossible to use the platform of his fame to build a future.

In 1990 it was also the fate of the sadly declined "Cincinnati Hawk" to break new grounds in political correctness, when he was permitted to box in Wisconsin although legally blind in his left eye. The reason? Because to deny him the right would be to discriminate against the handicapped!

The promoter involved, one Diana Lewis, pointed out that Pryor still had another eye, and her point was proved as he knocked out his opponent in three rounds. Fortunately, he saw enough for himself to know that retirement was his only serious option.

Pryor lost in the 1976 Olympic trials final to Howard Davis. Consequently, he labored as an odd-job man, while boxing part-time for a fraction of the purses afforded the returning heroes of Montreal.

But in 1980 he overpowered Venezuelan Antonio Cervantes in four rounds for the WBA light-welterweight title. It was the beginning of a thrilling era. Pryor fought like a crazy man, with a perpetual motion style, yet knew precisely what he was doing. He made eight successful WBA title defenses in four years, twice knocking out the great Alexis Arguello and stopping Kronk Gym hope Dujuan Johnson in seven rounds.

In 1984 he switched allegiance to the IBF and made two more defenses, but by this stage he had a serious cocaine habit and he drifted away. His only defeat was in a 1987 comeback when he was already fighting from memory.

FACT FILE

1955	Born Cincinnati, Ohio
1973	National AAU lightweight champion
1980	Stopped Antonio Cervantes to win WBA light-welterweight title
1982	Beat Alexis Arguello in 14th round
1983	Relinquished WBA title after beating Arguello a second time
1984	Proclaimed IBF light-welterweight champion
1985	Vacated IBF title after two defenses

Career record: Fights 40, Won 39, Lost 1

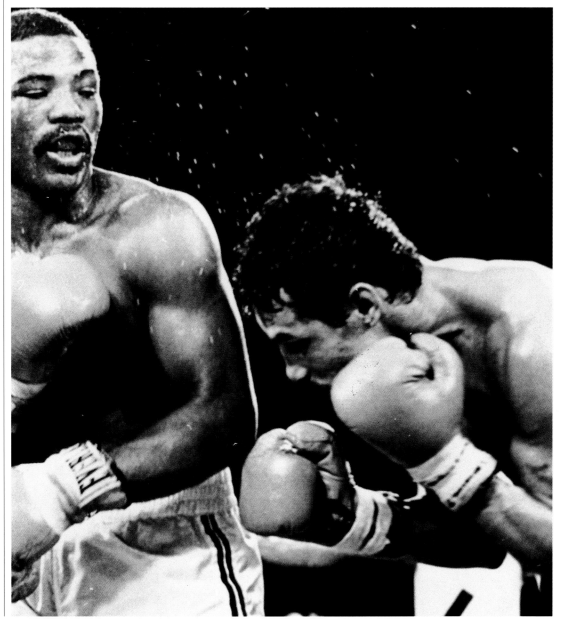

PRYOR'S TWO VICTORIES OVER ALEXIS ARGUELLO WERE PERHAPS THE TRUE MARKS OF HIS GREATNESS

SEE ALSO ◆ ALEXIS ARGUELLO 20 ◆ ANTONIO CERVANTES 62

DWIGHT MUHAMMAD QAWI

FACT FILE

1953 Born Dwight Braxton, Baltimore, Maryland

1978 Professional debut

1981 Stopped Matthew Saad Muhammad to win WBC light-heavyweight title

1983 Lost unification fight with WBA champion Michael Spinks

1985 Beat Piet Crous in South Africa to become WBA cruiserweight champ

1985 Lost to Marvin Hagler

1986 Lost WBA title on split decision to Evander Holyfield

1992 Retired after defeat by Nate Miller, age 39

Career record: Fights 50, Won 39, Lost 10, Drawn 1

Deceptively quick, hard to hit because of his crouching style, and immensely strong, Dwight Muhammad Qawi looked as if he were armor-plated. Closer inspection revealed the "armor" to be solid slabs of muscle built by lifting 300 lb. blocks in his job on a demolition site.

Qawi was born Dwight Braxton in Baltimore, and life on the tough city streets led him to Rahway State Penitentiary. He had no amateur experience, but learned the business in the best schools of all, the gyms of Philadelphia after he was released from Rahway in 1977.

He returned to jail once, in September 1981—to outpoint inmate James Scott, who dreamed of winning the world light-heavyweight title while behind bars. Braxton, who changed his name when he converted to Islam, beat Scott comfortably to line up a shot at WBC champion Matthew Saad Muhammad.

"How come that little short-to-the-ground crab beat me?" inquired the incredulous Saad Muhammad after he was stopped in the 10th round in Atlantic City in December 1981.

Qawi, who became a model citizen in Camden and backed a "Stay In School" program for kids, beat Saad again. He also turned back challenges from Jerry Martin and Eddie Davis, before Michael Spinks used an eight-inch height advantage to outpoint him in a unification fight.

Qawi moved up to cruiserweight and won the WBA belt by stopping South African Piet Crous in 11 rounds Sun City in July 1985. A sixth-round stoppage of Leon Spinks followed, before he lost a 15-round war with Evander Holyfield on a split decision in Atlanta in July 1986. Two further attempts to regain the title failed, but he was not deterred, and boxed on until 1992.

QAWI LEARNED HIS TRADE IN
THE GYMS OF PHILADELPHIA
. . . AND WENT ON TO WIN TWO
WORLD TITLES

SEE ALSO ◆ EVANDER HOLYFIELD 159 ◆ MATTHEW SAAD MUHAMMAD 234

WILLIE RITCHIE

As a boy in San Francisco, Willie Ritchie climbed the fence to see Battling Nelson knock out his hero Jimmy Britt for the lightweight title. Seven years later, on November 28, 1912, Ritchie won that same championship by thrashing the great Ad Wolgast in the very same Mission Street Arena in Colma.

Ritchie outboxed Wolgast and dropped him with a right hand, and the outgoing champ deliberately landed two low blows to get himself disqualified in the 16th round.

Ritchie was a marvelous counterpuncher, with a steely discipline and will. He made up for his relatively light hitting—only nine knockout wins in 75 fights—with exceptional skills and a bravery that enabled him to survive the roughest of wars.

After beating Wolgast, Ritchie knocked out "Mexican" Joe Rivers in 11 rounds in San Francisco on July 4, 1913. In no-decision bouts he "beat" Leach Cross in a bloodbath in New York and Wolgast in Milwaukee, and outpointed Harlem Tommy Murphy in a 20-round championship battle in San Francisco.

He lost the title to Freddie Welsh on a disputed 20-round decision at the Olympia Sporting Club in London on July 7, 1914. "I thought I outpointed him very easily," said Ritchie. "I felt shock. I felt hurt."

Ritchie beat Welsh in a no-decision bout the following year in New York. He won and lost against Benny Leonard in 1919, boxed rarely after that, retiring for good in 1927.

In retirement he refereed and promoted fights, then served as California State Commission chief inspector for 25 years. He was still playing golf into his 80s.

FACT FILE

1891	Born Gerhard Steffen, San Francisco, California
1907	Stopped in professional debut, age 15
1912	Won world lightweight title against Ad Wolgast
1914	Lost world title in London to Freddie Welsh
1919	Won and lost against Benny Leonard
1927	Last fight in Los Angeles, age 36
Died:	Millbrae, California, March 24, 1975, age 84

Career record: Fights 75, Won 49, Lost 11, Drawn 15

RITCHIE: LIGHT PUNCHER BUT NOTORIOUSLY DIFFICULT TO BEAT

SEE ALSO ◆ **BENNY LEONARD 186** ◆ **FREDDIE WELSH 333** ◆ **AD WOLGAST 340**

THE GREAT FIGHTS

DWIGHT MUHAMMAD QAWI V. EVANDER HOLYFIELD

OMNI COLISEUM, ATLANTA, GEORGIA.
JULY 12, 1986.

In front of a roaring, cheering, sometimes screaming crowd at a searingly hot Omni arena in his home town of Atlanta, Evander Holyfield pushed himself to the limits to beat tanklike Dwight Muhammad Qawi on a split decision for the WBA cruiserweight title.

Holyfield, an unlucky bronze medalist in the 1984 Olympic Games, was the first of that wonderful USA boxing team to collect a professional world championship.

And he did so with a combination of stamina and style in a battle of deep-felt intensity which at times didn't seem as if it could possibly go the full 15 rounds.

Qawi was a proud champion who had learned to fight in the gyms of Philadelphia after a stint in Rahway Penitentiary. He had won the WBC light-heavyweight title against Matthew Saad Muhammad, and was now champion in his second weight division. Short, stumpy, and fighting out of a crouch which earned him the nickname of the Camden Buzz-saw he refused to give Holyfield room to use his height or boxing skills.

But Holyfield had prepared for the fight with high-tech workouts in Houston, where eventually he would employ a dietician, ballet teacher, and body conditioner as he went on to hold the heavyweight crown three times.

He was fit enough to outfight the fighter, swamped the shorter man with combinations and mauled him inside. Qawi taunted him, weaving and punching in sudden, electrifying bursts. Holyfield seemed to flag in the middle rounds, but dug deep and produced the better finish to take the verdict by strangely differing scores of 144-140, 147-138 (for Holyfield) and 143-141 (Qawi).

Afterwards Holyfield was taken ill at home and rushed to hospital with kidney problems brought on by dehydration. Doctors said but for the quick thinking of his wife he could have been on a dialysis machine for the rest of his life.

RAY ROBINSON

FACT FILE

1921 Born Walker Smith, Detroit, Michigan

1946 Won world welterweight title against Tommy Bell

1951 Won, lost, and regained middleweight title in fights with Jake La Motta and Randolph Turpin

1952 Announced retirement

1955 Regained middleweight crown by knocking out Carl Olson

1957 Lost, regained, and lost title against Gene Fullmer and Carmen Basilio

1958 Regained title from Basilio

1960 Lost title for last time on split decision to Paul Pender

1965 Announced retirement after 25 years of boxing

Died: Los Angeles, April 12, 1989, age 67

Career record: Fights 202, Won 175, Lost 19, Drawn 6, No Contests 2

Ray Robinson, the original Sugar Ray, was a flawless, graceful fighter who carried the old art form to fresh planes of achievement.

His old adversary Jake La Motta, whom he fought five times, called him the greatest of them all, an opinion reiterated whenever a magazine or TV show runs an all-time great poll. Robinson tops every time.

He was the uncrowned welterweight champion for four years before he won the title in December 1946 by outpointing talented, stubborn Tommy Bell over 15 rounds in Madison Square Garden.

He was champion until 1951 when he moved up to middleweight and beat La Motta, the Bronx Bull, in the 13th round for the title in Chicago Stadium on February 14, 1951. They called it the Valentine's Day Massacre.

Sugar Ray lost shockingly to Randolph Turpin in London in July 1951, but 64 days later stopped Turpin at the New York Polo Grounds. In December 1952 he announced his retirement, six months after heat exhaustion led to his 13-round retirement against light-heavyweight champ Joey Maxim on a sweltering night in New York.

Robinson knocked out Carl "Bobo" Olson in two rounds to begin his third reign in 1955, lost the title to Gene Fullmer, regained it with one of the greatest punches in championship history, a perfect left hook, and then lost it to Carmen Basilio, all in 1957. He outpointed Basilio to become champ for the fifth time, but lost the title to Paul Pender on a split decision in Boston in 1960. He fought on for another five years, and in retirement in Los Angeles developed his successful Sugar Ray Youth Foundation. He was ill with Alzheimer's Disease for several years before his death.

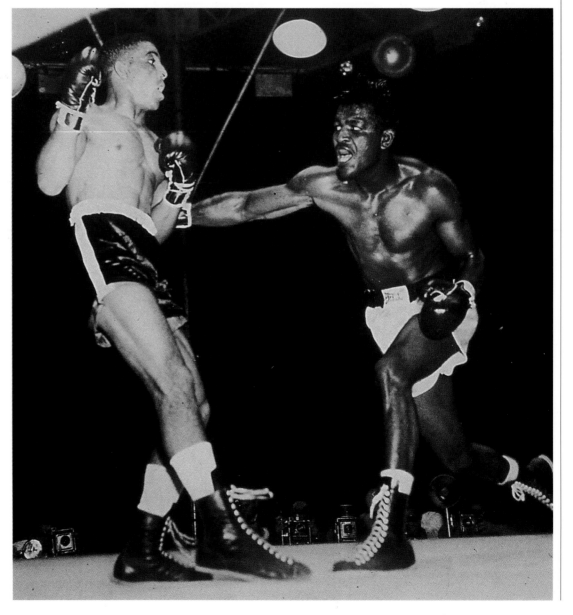

ROBINSON REGAINS THE WORLD MIDDLEWEIGHT TITLE FROM RANDOLPH TURPIN AT NEW YORK POLO GROUNDS IN 1951

SEE ALSO ♦ CARMEN BASILIO 29 ♦ GENE FULLMER 123 ♦ JAKE LA MOTTA 182 ♦ RANDOLPH TURPIN 318

LUIS RODRIGUEZ

Luis Rodriguez, unkindly nicknamed El Feo, or The Ugly, had a chugging, swarming, accelerating kind of style that took him from Fidel Castro's Cuba to the welterweight championship of the world.

He reigned only briefly—79 days in 1963—but was unlucky to be a contemporary of Emile Griffith, who beat him on split decisions in three of their four fights.

Griffith won a 10-rounder in New York in December 1960, but when they fought for the welterweight title in the Dodger Stadium, Los Angeles, in March 1963, Rodriguez won an upset 15-round verdict. The flat-nosed new champ did a war-dance to celebrate, while Griffith pranced around, shouting: "I was robbed."

They fought again in Madison Square Garden on June 8, 1963 and this time Griffith took the verdict. Both said they won easily.

Rodriguez's trainer, Angelo Dundee, said: "Luis dominated the fight."

In June 1964, they fought again, and again Griffith got it, this time in an unusually rough fight in Las Vegas. Rodriguez was furious. After losing a WBA eliminator to Curtis Cokes, he moved up to middleweight. He fought Nino Benvenuti for the world title in Rome in November 1969, but was knocked out by him in 11 rounds.

He was a shot fighter by the time he retired in 1972. "I could have lasted another 10 years," he said. "But I liked women..."

In his great days, he beat Rubin "Hurricane" Carter twice, Bennie Briscoe, Denny Moyer, George Benton, Tony Mundine, Curtis Cokes, and Virgil Akins. His overenthusiasm for a good time and, especially, a drink, left him with severe kidney disease, from which he died.

FACT FILE

1937 Born Camaguey, Cuba

1956 Professional debut in Havana

1963 Won and lost world welterweight title against Emile Griffith

1964 Lost disputed decision to Griffith in third fight

1969 Lost to Nino Benvenuti in world middleweight title bid

1972 Announced retirement

Died: Miami, Florida, July 8, 1996, age 59

Career record: Fights 121, Won 107, Lost 13, No Contest 1

RODRIGUEZ: A MARVELOUS FIGHTER WHO RARELY HAD LUCK ON HIS SIDE WHEN IT MATTERED

SEE ALSO ♦ NINO BENVENUTI 34 ♦ BENNIE BRISCOE 40 ♦ EMILE GRIFFITH 144

THE GREAT FIGHTS

JAKE LA MOTTA V. RAY ROBINSON

CHICAGO STADIUM. FEBRUARY 14, 1951.

They called Jake La Motta's world middleweight title defense against Ray Robinson the "St. Valentine's Day Massacre." They weren't far wrong.

La Motta was the only man to have beaten Robinson—on points over 10 rounds in Detroit in 1943—in 124 professional fights. Robinson had also outpointed him four times, but this meeting was the most eagerly anticipated of all.

Robinson was 29, La Motta 28. Robinson had held the welterweight title for five years, and now had Pennsylvania Commission recognition as middleweight champion. La Motta had been champion anywhere but in Pennsylvania since he battered the title away from Frenchman Marcel Cerdan in nine rounds in Detroit in June 1949.

La Motta, the child of the streets, became a grade one thug...and eventually, a great fighter. His friend Rocky Graziano called him "Hammerhead" but mostly he was known as the "Bronx Bull." He was one of the toughest, most absorbent fighters of all time. Robinson was just Robinson. Walking class.

La Motta struggled terribly as he took off 16 lb. too quickly to make 160 lb., but for the first six rounds he held his own and bloodied Robinson's mouth and nose. Then gradually, the classical skills of Sugar Ray began to impose themselves, even though after eight rounds two of the judges still had La Motta ahead. Jake had a bruised and swollen right eye by the 10th and in the next he tried a ferocious barrage, but although he hurt Robinson, he couldn't bring him down. He was all in after that, and was punched around the ring in the 12th.

He swore at Robinson and shouted: "You can't do it, you can't put me on the deck." Maybe not, but Sugar Ray handed out a savage beating as La Motta set himself on his tree-trunk legs and stood waiting until referee Frank Sikora stopped it in the 13th.

Robinson danced happily, but La Motta's courage had won the hearts of the crowd. They sang, cheered and shouted in a genuine salute as he trudged wearily to his dressing room.

GILBERTO ROMAN

FACT FILE

1961 Born Pueblo Nuevo, Mexico, November 29, 1961

1981 Professional debut, age 19

1986 Outpointed Jiro Watanabe to win WBC super-flyweight title

1987 Lost title to Santos Laciar in 7th defense

1988 Regained WBC title from Sugar Baby Rojas

1989 Lost championship to Nana Yaw Konadu

1990 Lost to WBC champion Sung-kil Moon

Died: Near Chilpancingo, Mexico, June 27, 1990, age 28

Career record: Fights 61, Won 54, Lost 6, Drawn 1

A superb technician, Gilberto Roman understood the depths of boxing's art. He was a precise fighter who had a good defense and an instinct for discovering an opponent's weaknesses. Although most of his 16 world title fights went the distance, he could hit sharply enough when he chose.

A gregarious man from the border town of Mexicali, he boxed brilliantly to take the WBC super-flyweight championship from Jiro Watanabe in Osaka in March 1986. Sometimes he cut it fine, as when he beat first challenger Edgar Montserrat in Paris on a split vote, and in a draw with rock-hard Argentine Santos Laciar in August 1986. But he defended successfully six times before a cut eye deprived him of the belt in the 11th round in a rematch with Laciar in France in May 1987.

Roman regained the championship with an April 1988 points decision over Miami-based Colombian Sugar Baby Rojas, and this time made five defenses, including decisions over Rojas and Laciar.

A showdown with the great WBA champion Khaosai Galaxy would have been a wonderful blend of boxer and slugger, but instead, Roman surprisingly lost to Nana Yaw Konadu, a big-hitting Ghanaian who floored him five times for a 12-round decision in Mexico City in November 1989.

His discipline had faded, and he was underprepared when he challenged Korean star Sung-kil Moon in June 1990. He retired after eight rounds.

Gilberto Roman was killed instantly when his car was struck in the rear by a truck, forcing it to career into the path of a tractor on the road from Mexico City to Acapulco. He died a wealthy man.

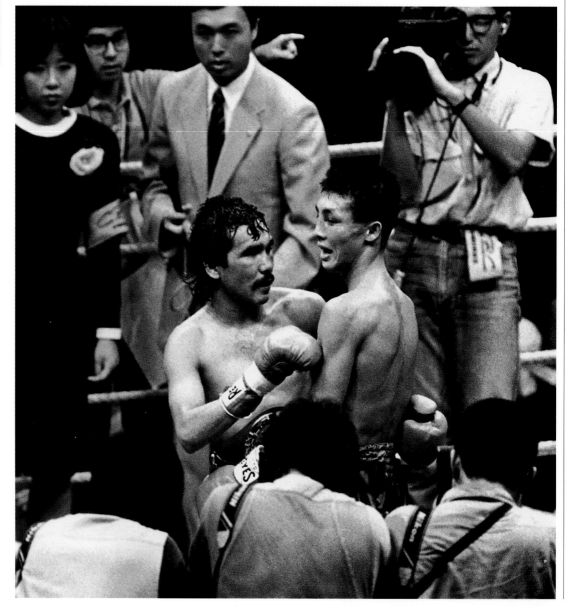

ROMAN WAS A POPULAR FIGHTER IN JAPAN WHERE HE WAS UNBEATEN IN THREE SUPER-FLYWEIGHT TITLE FIGHTS, INCLUDING THIS ONE AGAINST KIYOSHI HATANAKA

SEE ALSO ◆ SUNG-KIL MOON 223

EDWIN ROSARIO

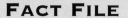

At his best Edwin "Chapo" Rosario was one of the heaviest hitting, most exciting of lightweight champions. He was also erratic and suffered from brittle hands, as well as being unfortunate enough to meet Julio Cesar Chavez on arguably the Mexican's peak night.

Rosario was born in Santurce, San Juan, and raised in Toa Baja. A family man who married his childhood sweetheart, he was only 20 when he outpointed Mexican southpaw Jose Luis Ramirez for the WBC lightweight title in 1983. Guided by Jim Jacobs and Bill Cayton, Rosario turned back challenges from Roberto Elizondo and 1976 Olympic gold medalist Howard Davis before surprisingly losing a rematch wtih Ramirez in four rounds.

Backroom reshuffling and four non-title wins, including a tough 10-round points win over Frankie Randall in London, rebuilt his career. He was extremely unlucky to lose a 12-round decision against Hector Camacho in a grueling WBC title fight in New York in June 1986, but landed his big right hand on the chin of WBA champ Livingstone Bramble to claim that belt in two rounds in Miami in September 1986.

Chavez, a super-featherweight champion for three years, moved up to dethrone Rosario in the 11th round of a wonderful fight in Las Vegas in November 1987.

Rosario held the WBA title again for nine months in 1989–1990, stopping southpaw Anthony "Baby Face" Jones in six rounds, but surprisingly losing to compatriot Juan Nazario.

He seemed on the way out, but rallied to hold the WBA light-welterweight belt from June 1991, when he knocked out home town hero Loreto Garza in three rounds in Sacramento, until April 1992 when he lost in one round to Akinobu Hiranaka in Mexico. He retired but returned to the ring in 1997.

FACT FILE

1963 Born Santurce, Puerto Rico

1983 Beat Jose Ramirez for WBC lightweight title

1984 Lost title in return with Ramirez

1986 Won WBA championship by knocking out Livingstone Bramble

1987 Lost in 11 rounds to Julio Cesar Chavez

1989 Regained WBA lightweight title against Anthony Jones

1990 Third lightweight title reign ends against Juan Nazario

1991 Won WBA light-welterweight title against Loreto Garza

1992 Dethroned by Akinobu Hiranaka in Mexico

Career record: Fights 44, Won 38, Lost 6

ROSARIO: HEAVY PUNCHER WITH FRAGILE HANDS, WHOSE CHAMPIONSHIP DAYS SPANNED NINE YEARS

SEE ALSO ◆ HECTOR CAMACHO 51 ◆ JULIO CESAR CHAVEZ 67

LIONEL ROSE

FACT FILE

1948 Born Drouin, Victoria, Australia

1964 Professional debut, age 16

1967 Knocked out Rocky Gattelari for Australian bantamweight title

1968 Beat Fighting Harada in Tokyo to win world title

1969 Lost world bantamweight title to Ruben Olivares in Los Angeles

1971 Failed in WBC super-feather title bid against Yoshiaki Numata

1976 Last fight, age 28

Career record: Fights 53, Won 42, Lost 11

When Lionel Rose, an engaging, ready-smiling, teenaged Aborigine who smoked a pipe, fought Chucho Castillo in Los Angeles, legend has it that Elvis Presley sat at ringside in false beard and dark glasses—and when fans rioted after Rose was given the decision, Kirk Douglas had his car blown up!

Rose was a sensational bantamweight who won the world title at 19, blew a fortune on wine and women, suffered a heart attack, and battled back from the brink by working with the Department of Aboriginal Affairs.

He was born in a one-room home in a four-family Aboriginal settlement. A beautiful, quick boxer, Rose learned from his father, who died shortly before his first amateur bout, from Frank Oakes, whose daughter he married, and from Jack Rennie, who managed his professional career. It was Rennie who persuaded him to compromise his heavy cigarette smoking by using a pipe, although when he challenged world bantamweight champ Fighting Harada in Tokyo in February 1968, they convinced the Japanese media his habit was an ancient Aboriginal training aid!

Rose gave Harada a boxing lesson, then returned five months later to outpoint Takao Sakurai, the 1964 Olympic gold medalist. In Los Angeles he outscored Castillo, after which Rennie was cracked on the head by a bottle as the Mexicans threatened to tear the place down. In Australia, where 250,000 had lined the Melbourne streets to welcome him back from the Harada triumph, he outpointed Alan Rudkin, but lost his championship in August 1969 when Ruben Olivares knocked him out in five rounds.

His weight ballooned as he lost discipline, and he was never as good again. He retired, at the second attempt, in 1976.

ROSE (BACK TO THE CAMERA) DEALS WITH JESUS "CHUCHO" CASTILLO OF MEXICO IN LOS ANGELES. ROSE WON ON POINTS.

SEE ALSO ◆ FIGHTING HARADA 151 ◆ RUBEN OLIVARES 257

MAXIE ROSENBLOOM

Maxie Rosenbloom, labeled Slapsie Maxie by his critics, didn't give a damn what anybody thought about his eccentric fighting style. It worked, that's all that mattered. And it not only took him to the light-heavyweight championship of the world, but funded admirably the lifestyle he chose.

Rosenbloom worked hard, and played hard... not to mention late, and often. He didn't drink, but saw no point in ignoring New York's wonderful nightlife when he had the time, the youth, and the money to give it the kind of attention it deserved.

Maxie boxed 299 times in 16 years—and because he couldn't punch, he rattled up something like 3,000 competitive rounds! He stopped only 19 opponents, but was in turn terribly hard to fathom, and consequently difficult to beat. "I like to fight everybody," he said. "But I don't like to hurt anybody."

He lost a 10-round decision to Jimmy Slattery for the NBA title in 1927 but fought the great names of the day: Ted Kid Lewis, Harry Greb, Tiger Flowers, Jack Delaney, Young Stribling, John Henry Lewis, and Johnny Wilson.

He won the world title in Buffalo in June 1930 when he outpointed Slattery over 15 rounds, and confounded experts by keeping it for four years. He stopped Abie Bain and Bob Godwin, outpointed Slattery again, Lou Scozza, Adolf Heuser, and Mickey Walker, and drew with Joe Knight, before fellow New Yorker Bob Olin outpointed him on a controversial split decision in Madison Square Garden in November 1934.

Rosenbloom retired in 1939, acted in movies and on the stage (once at the Dunes in Las Vegas with Betty Grable) and ran nightspots. He was in a psychiatric hospital when he died, age 71 years.

FACT FILE

1904	Born Leonard's Bridge, Connecticut
1927	Lost NBA light-heavyweight title fight against Jimmy Slattery
1930	Won undisputed recognition as champ by beating Slattery again
1934	Lost world title to Bob Olin
1939	Last fight, at 34, after 16-year career
Died:	South Pasadena, California, March 6, 1976, age 71

Career record: Fights 299, Won 210, Lost 38, Drawn 26, No Contests 2, No Decisions 23

SLAPSIE MAXIE: ROSENBLOOM HAD A STRANGE TRAIT FOR A BOXER. HE ADMITTED HE DIDN'T LIKE HURTING PEOPLE!

GIANFRANCO ROSI

FACT FILE

1957 Born Assisi, Italy

1984 Won European welterweight title against Perico Fernandez

1985 Lost European title to Lloyd Honeyghan

1987 Won European and WBC light-middleweight titles

1988 Lost WBC title to Donald Curry

1989 Won IBF light-middleweight title against Darrin Van Horn

1994 Lost IBF title to Vincent Pettway

1995 Won WBO light-middleweight title against Verno Phillips

Career record: Fights 64, Won 59, Lost 4, Drawn 1

Giangfranco Rosi was a clever and long-lasting world light-middleweight champion. Though never fashionable outside Italy, he won three versions of the title and boxed in 17 championship contests.

In an 18-year career, three of his four defeats were to world champions—Lloyd Honeyghan, Don Curry, and Vincent Pettway—and the fourth was a meaningless cut eye setback when he was still a preliminary fighter.

He was a disciplined, organized boxer who had a thoroughly professional outlook. Even when he boxed in Italy, he kept himself isolated from the crowd and concentrated firmly on the job. He was a perfect example of a man who made the most of his talents.

He held European titles at welterweight and light-middle, losing the former on a stunning three rounds knockout to Honeyghan in 1985, but winning the latter on a deserved points decision against Chris Pyatt.

He won the WBC 154 lb. crown by upsetting Californian Lupe Aquino in October 1987, stopped Duane Thomas of Detroit in seven rounds, but was then outclassed by Don Curry in nine rounds in July 1988. The following year, he switched to the IBF, trounced Darrin Van Horn on points in Atlantic City, and kept the title for five years. He made 11 successful defenses.

Rosi lost the IBF crown when he was 37, knocked out in four by Pettway, and then won the WBO version by upsetting Verno Phillips on points over 12 rounds in May 1995, only to fail a dope test, about which he vehemently protested. The title was declared vacant, and Rosi, too old for an Italian license, took one out in Serbia, insisting he was not yet finished with the sport.

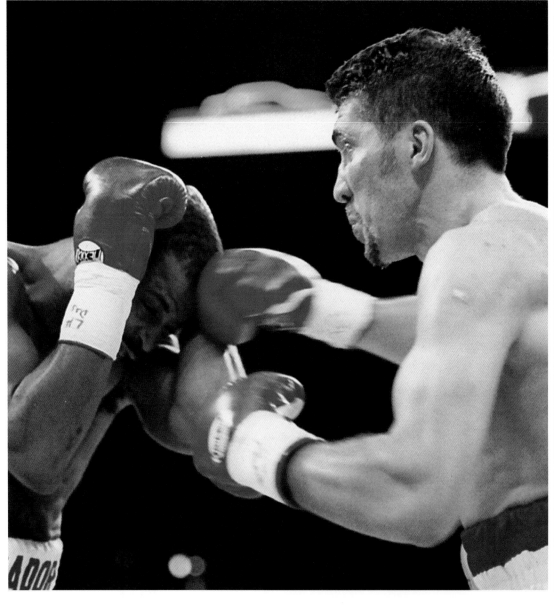

ENDURING CHAMP: GIANFRANCO ROSI WAS NEVER FASHIONABLE OUTSIDE ITALY, BUT HE HAD 17 WORLD TITLE FIGHTS

SEE ALSO ◆ DONALD CURRY 82 ◆ LLOYD HONEYGHAN 162

BARNEY ROSS

Nobody had a bigger heart than Barney Ross, in or out of a ring.

Ross took one of the worst poundings a fighter ever absorbed when he lasted 15 rounds with Henry Armstrong before 35,000 fans in the Long Island Bowl in May 1938.

Long before the end referee Arthur Donovan wanted to stop it, but Ross wouldn't let him. "Let me finish," he said. "This is the last favor I'll ever ask of you. I'll never fight again."

For the last three rounds even his own corner couldn't watch, but all of them respected Ross's right to go out the way he wanted.

Whatever the medical niceties of the 1990s, in the Thirties it was, as Ross said through a torn mouth to a reporter, "Champ's privilege."

Ross was from an orthodox Jewish family in the Chicago ghetto, whose shopkeeper father was murdered. He fought his way up to hold three world titles. He won the lightweight and light-welterweight titles at the same time by outpointing Tony Canzoneri in Chicago in June 1933. He kept both until 1935.

He also fought a magnificent three-fight series with Jimmy McLarnin for the welterweight championship. Ross won the first in May 1934, lost the second four months later, and won the third in May 1935. All three were fought at an incredible pace, yet lasted the full 15 rounds.

He enlisted in the US Marines in World War II, was seriously wounded, and became addicted to morphine as a result of attempts to control his pain. He eventually conquered the addiction, testified to a Senate investigation on narcotics, and wrote an autobiography. He died of cancer at 57.

FACT FILE

1909 Born Beryl David Rosofsky, New York City

1929 Professional debut, age 19

1933 Beat Tony Canzoneri for world light and light-welter titles

1934 Won and lost world welterweight title against Jimmy McLarnin

1935 Regained welterweight title from McLarnin, reliquished world light and light-welter titles

1938 Lost world welterweight title to Henry Armstrong

Died: Chicago, January 17, 1967, age 57

Career record: Fights 81, Won 74, Lost 4, Drawn 3

NOBODY BRAVER: ROSS WAS ALSO ONE OF THE MOST SKILFUL CHAMPIONS IN HISTORY, WHO HELD TITLES AT THREE WEIGHTS

SEE ALSO ◆ HENRY ARMSTRONG 21 ◆ TONY CANZONERI 54 ◆ JIMMY MCLARNIN 246

TOMMY RYAN

FACT FILE

1870 Born Joseph Youngs, Redwood, New York

1891 Claimed world welterweight title after 76-round win over Danny Needham

1894 Outpointed Mysterious Billy Smith for world welterweight title

1896 Claimed middleweight title, lost to Kid McCoy

1898 Continued to claim world middleweight title, beat Tommy West and Jack Bonner

1907 Last fight against Hugo Kelly in New York

Died: Van Nuys, California, August 3, 1948, age 78

Career record: Fights 104, Won 86, Lost 4, Drawn 6, No Decisions 2, No Contests 6

As well as claiming the world welter and middleweight titles, Tommy Ryan was a brilliant boxing theorist and coach.

It was Ryan who devised the crouching technique that served world heavyweight champ James J. Jeffries so well. He also worked with "Gentleman" Jim Corbett.

Ryan was from Redwood, New York, but ran away from home and changed his name to avoid being retrieved. He worked in lumber camps, developing tremendous stamina to go with his ringcraft. He was quite at home in long contests: he fought 57 rounds with Jimmy Murphy, without a result, at Grand Rapids, Michigan, in 1889 and laid an early claim to the welterweight title when he beat Danny Needham in 76 rounds in Minneapolis in 1891.

Ryan also had a long series with Mysterious Billy Smith. They drew twice, before Tommy won a fight that was interrupted by police in the 20th round. They also boxed 18 rounds without a result in 1895, and the following year Ryan won on a ninth-round foul.

He received a shock against former sparring partner, Kid McCoy, in 1896. McCoy, who said he needed the money because he was mortally sick, turned out to be extremely fit and beat an underprepared Ryan in 15 rounds.

Ryan's claim to the middleweight title was fairly haphazard, but after he outpointed Jack Bonner in 1898, he was largely accepted as the top man. He beat Frank Craig, known as "The Harlem Coffee Cooler", and Tommy West, and in his last five years, only Philadelphia Jack O'Brien got the better of him. In retirement Ryan opened a gym in Syracuse, managing boxers until he moved to California.

BRILLIANT THEORIST: RYAN KNEW THE BOXING BUSINESS INSIDE-OUT AND WAS A RESPECTED COACH AS WELL AS WORLD CHAMPION FIGHTER

SEE ALSO ◆ KID MCCOY 239 ◆ MYSTERIOUS BILLY SMITH 299

SANDY SADDLER

Sandy Saddler was an exceptional fighter, who knew how to use his 70-in. reach by boxing at long range, yet could brawl on the inside with the roughest if the need arose.

Proof of his quality is easy to establish: he won three out of four world championship battles with Willie Pep and, that rivalry aside, dominated the division for nine years.

Saddler was boxing in world class by the time he was 20. He knocked out Joe Brown in New Orleans in May 1947 and the following month drew a 10-rounder with another future light-weight champion, Jimmy Carter. At the time he claimed Scottish ancestry and entered the ring wearing a kilt!

It was neither his blood-line nor his ring garb that made his name, but the fights with Pep. He outclassed the "Will O' The Wisp" in four rounds in the first fight in October 1948, only for Pep to upset him on a 15-round decision in the rematch in February 1949. They shifted the third fight outside from Madison Square Garden to Yankee Stadium in September 1950, when 38,781 fans saw Pep retire after seven rounds because of a dislocated shoulder. Fourth time around in September 1951, Saddler won a brawl when Pep quit after nine brutal, bloody rounds at the Polo Grounds.

In the midst of all that, Saddler also held a local version of the world junior-lightweight title, following a 10-round decision against Orlando Zulueta in Cleveland in December 1949. After a couple of successful defenses, he let the relatively minor championship drift to some extent, but remained featherweight champion until 1957. He retired, still undefeated, because of an eye injury he had suffered in a car crash.

FACT FILE

1926	Born Boston, Massachusetts
1944	Professional debut, age 17
1948	Knocked out Willie Pep to win world featherweight title
1949	Lost rematch with Pep, claimed world junior-lightweight title
1950	Regained featherweight crown by beating Pep
1957	Announced retirement, still undefeated featherweight champion

Career record: Fights 162, Won 144, Lost 16, Drawn 2

RUTHLESS AND UNCOMPROMISING: SADDLER BEAT WILLIE PEP THREE TIMES OUT OF FOUR

SEE ALSO ◆ JOE BROWN 43

THE GREAT FIGHTS

WILLIE PEP
V.
SANDY SADDLER

YANKEE STADIUM NEW YORK.
SEPTEMBER 8, 1950.

Willie Pep was one of the quickest, most elusive boxers the world has ever seen—and Sandy Saddler was one of the most complete. Between them, these great featherweights served up an astonishing four-fight series.

Saddler won the first, handing Pep a brutally one-sided four-rounds knockout in Madison Square Garden in October 1948. The return clause, almost a routine affair in those days, ensured Pep had a rematch the February. And against the odds, he produced a marvelous boxing exhibition to win a unanimous 15-round points verdict.

The stage was perfectly set for a third fight, but Pep kept Saddler waiting for 19 months, and put a high price on his title—$92,408. Saddler had to be bitterly content with a third of that, which also happened to be his biggest payday so far, even though the gate was $262,150.

Pep boxed beautifully, but Saddler had the power, as he showed in round three when a long left hook dropped the champion for a count of nine. Pep got up and worked neatly, outboxing Saddler until Sandy began to break him up with prolonged body attacks and rough him up on the inside in round seven.

Pep was in front on all three cards, but retired in his corner, claiming a dislocated shoulder as a result of foul tactics by Saddler. However, they filed no protest at the verdict which returned the championship to the man from Boston, who muttered grimly: "Dislocated shoulder? Nuts. It was my kidney punches!"

Pep said later: "All of a sudden my shoulder snapped and it hurt bad. I couldn't lift my arm and there was no way I could continue unless I wanted to fight Sandy with one hand... I couldn't continue."

Speculation that Pep quit was widespread—and he had more criticism after their fourth fight in September 1951, when he retired after the eighth of a foul-filled brawl at the Polo Grounds. Saddler's superiority was complete.

VICENTE SALDIVAR

FACT FILE

1943 Born Mexico City

1961 Professional debut, age 17

1964 Won world featherweight title against Sugar Ramos in Mexico City

1965 Outpointed Howard Winstone in London

1967 Retired after winning third fight with Winstone

1969 Returned to the ring, defeating Jose Legra in comeback fight

1970 Regained featherweight title from Johnny Famechon, lost it to Kuniaki Shibata

1973 Last fight against Eder Jofre in Brazil

Died: Mexico City, July 1985, age 42

Career record: Fights 41, Won 38, Lost 3

Vicente Saldivar was a sawn-off Marciano, a non-stop attacker who traded on heart, stamina, and sheer southpaw persistence.

Points deficits meant nothing to the tireless little man from Mexico City. An extraordinarily low pulse rate meant he could slam away without slowing. Sooner or later, he tracked down even the slickest of boxers.

Saldivar was a professional fighter at 17, and a world champion at 21. He earned his title shot by outpointing brilliant lightweight Ismael Laguna, and then took the world feather-weight title by stopping Sugar Ramos, the Mexican-based Cuban, in the 12th round of a thriller in Mexico City in September 1964.

He made eight defenses, three of them classics against Welsh stylist Howard Winstone. He won the first fight in London, the second, controversially, in Cardiff, and the third in 12 rounds in Mexico City.

Saldivar also beat Mitsunori Seki of Japan twice, but retired after his third win over Winstone, who visited him during the 1968 Olympics. "One night we went out drinking—four world champions, Saldivar, me, Raul Rojas, and Sugar Ramos! That was some night!"

Retirement lasted only 21 months. Saldivar came back to outpoint Jose Legra in Los Angeles, and then regained his old belt by outpointing Australian counterpuncher Johnny Famechon over 15 rounds in Rome. A marvellous achievement.

Success was short-lived, as Kuniaki Shibata of Japan dethroned him with a 13th-round win in Tijuana. He came out of another retirement to fight Eder Jofre for the championship in Brazil in 1973, but lost in four rounds. The spark had gone forever. Saldivar died of heart disease at the age of 42.

SALDIVAR IN LONDON BEFORE HIS FIRST MEETING WITH HOWARD WINSTONE

SEE ALSO ◆ JOHNNY FAMECHON 107 ◆ EDER JOFRE 169 ◆ JOSE LEGRA 185 ◆ HOWARD WINSTONE 338

SALVADOR SANCHEZ

Salvador Sanchez was one of the finest craftsmen boxing has ever seen. Smart and articulate outside the ring, he was a sharp intelligent boxer with a solid punch, great stamina, and a big heart. Perhaps greatest of all was his ability to adapt his technique during a contest.

Both Pat Cowdell and Azumah Nelson, two of his last three challengers, caused him early problems. He floored Cowdell in the final round to win a split decision in Houston, and then stopped Nelson in the 15th at Madison Square Garden.

Sanchez lost only once—in a Mexican bantamweight title fight when he was 18, a 12-round decision against Antonio Becerra. There was also a draw in Los Angeles against Juan Escobar when he made his American debut at 19.

After that he was unstoppable. He counter-punched WBC champ Danny Lopez to conclusive defeat twice: in 13 rounds to win the title in Phoenix in February 1980, when a week past his 21st birthday; and in 14 rounds in Las Vegas four months later. In between he outpointed Ruben Castillo in Tucson.

He also outpointed the granite-like Juan LaPorte in El Paso, and hammered reigning super-bantamweight champ Wilfredo Gomez in eight rounds in Las Vegas.

He said after his ring career he wanted to study to be a doctor. "I'm only 23, I have all the time in the world..."

On 12 August 1982, he was driving to his training camp in his white Porsche, when he accelerated and passed a truck. Another truck hit him head on. He was identified by papers in his wallet.

FACT FILE

1959 Born Santiago Tianuistencio, Mexico

1975 Professional debut, age 16

1980 Stopped Danny Lopez to win WBC featherweight title, age 21

1982 Defended WBC title for ninth time against Azumah Nelson

Died: Near San Luis de Potosi, Mexico, August 12, 1982, aged 23

Career record: Fights 46, Won 44, Lost 1, Drawn 1

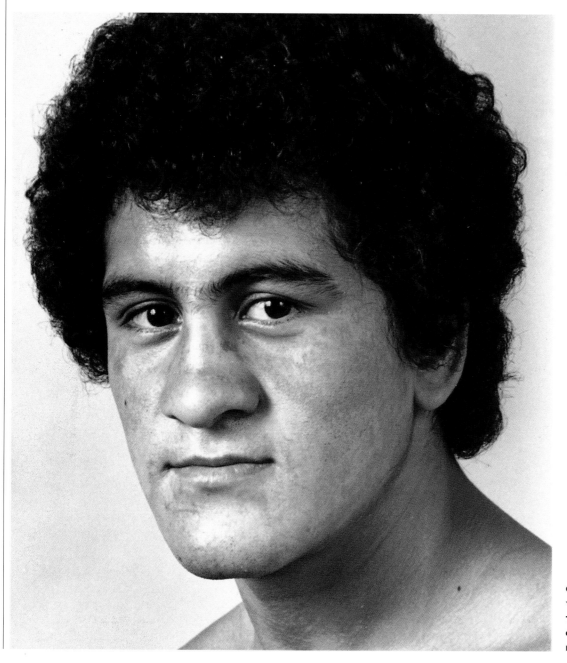

GREAT CHAMP WHO DIED YOUNG: SANCHEZ STILL HELD THE WBC FEATHERWEIGHT CROWN WHEN HE LOST HIS LIFE

SEE ALSO ♦ **DANNY LOPEZ 202** ♦ **AZUMAH NELSON 251**

MAX SCHMELING

A thoughtful, clever tactician with a solid punch, Max Schmeling is remembered more for his two fights with Joe Louis than for the fact that he held the world heavyweight title for two years.

Schmeling was "fed" to Louis in New York in June 1936, on the grounds that he was a former champion supposedly on the way down. But after telling reporters he had spotted a weakness in Louis's defense, the 30-year-old German knocked him out in the 12th round with a timely barrage of right hands. It was an astonishing upset.

When they met for the title two years later, Adolf Hitler was gathering his resources before the start of World War II, and Schmeling became a compulsory puppet for the Third Reich. Schmeling was not a Nazi—and continued to employ his Jewish manager, Joe Jacobs, in the face of Hitler's opposition.

Nevertheless, he represented his people. The pressure on both him andd Louis was immense. "The Brown Bomber" suddenly found himself elevated from black American to the walking, talking champion of freedom and democracy. It was no longer just a fight. As Louis knocked out Schmeling in 124 seconds, Germany's radio link to the United States was mysteriously cut.

Schmeling lost his money because of the Second World War, and was forced to return to the ring in 1947, 17 years after he had beaten Jack Sharkey on a fourth-round low punch to become heavyweight champion, and 15 years after Sharkey had controversially outpointed him in the return.

The comeback was short, but Schmeling made a second fortune when he won the franchise to distribute Coca-Cola in Germany. In his early 90s, he is still living at his Hamburg home.

MAX SCHMELING – THE ONLY MAN TO WIN THE WORLD HEAVYWEIGHT TITLE ON A FOUL.

SEE ALSO ◆ JOE LOUIS 204 ◆ JACK SHARKEY 296

SAMMY SERRANO

Sammy Serrano was a cool-headed, quick-footed boxer who was never fashionable, even in Puerto Rico, but whose achievements in the ring are hard to ignore.

Even Puerto Rican critics called him the "Artful Dodger" or "Marathon Man" and constantly compared him to bigger-punching, more exciting national heroes.

Yet this dour man held the WBA junior-lightweight title in two spells for more than six years and took part in 18 world championship contests. In 1977 he was voted the WBA boxer of the year.

He was tall with a good reach, and controlled fights with an unerring, frustrating left jab. He held and spoiled inside, but was deceptively strong and like most top-class fighters—especially those who are not naturally big hitters—was very capable of intense, prolonged concentration.

Serrano began as a 16-year-old in San Juan,

twice held the Puerto Rican featherweight title, but his career took off when he moved up to the 130 lb. division. Unlucky to draw with WBA champ Ben Villaflor in Honolulu in April 1976, he won the rematch six months later on a unanimous decision in San Juan. Over the next four years, because he did not draw big crowds at home, his defenses also included trips to Ecuador, Venezuela, Japan, and South Africa, where 12,000 fans saw him knock out Nkosana "Happy Boy" Mgxaji.

He lost the title to a stumpy Japanese slugger, Yasutsune Uehara, when knocked out by a single right hand in the sixth round in the Joe Louis Arena in Detroit, but clearly outboxed Uehara in the return in Japan in April 1981. This time he was champion until January 1983, when he was knocked out in eight rounds by Roger Mayweather. He retired in 1984, served a prison term for drug offences, and made a brief, unsuccessful comeback as a welterweight in 1996.

SERRANO (RIGHT) LOST AND REGAINED THE SUPER-FEATHERWEIGHT TITLE AGAINST YASUTSUNE "FLIPPER" UEHARA

SEE ALSO ◆ JOE LOUIS 204

JACK SHARKEY

As a fighter, Jack Sharkey was controversial, unpredictable and emotional, prone to weeping tears of frustration and rage. But when it came to banking his money, he was as level-headed as any Wall Street broker.

In his major fights he insisted on being paid in advance. As soon as he collected the check, he paid it into the nearest bank. By the time he arrived home, the check had cleared.

Sharkey won the world heavyweight championship with a controversial points win over Max Schmeling in June 1932, and lost it on a sixth-round knockout to Primo Carnera 12 months later. For the rest of his long life he was accused of taking a dive against the mob-controlled Italian. He always emphatically denied it.

Sharkey beat most of the best of his time—Harry Wills, George Godfrey, Tommy Loughran, Carnera (in 1931), Jimmy Maloney, and Young Stribling. His biggest night came when 72,283 fans paid to see him fight Jack Dempsey in Yankee Stadium—the first non-championship fight to gross $1 million—in July 1927. He lost in seven rounds, knocked out while complaining to the referee about being hit low.

After the retirement of Gene Tunney, Sharkey and Schmeling were matched for the vacant title in 1930. Sharkey was disqualified for a low blow in round four, and pocketed another $175,000.

He was never the same fighter after he lost to Carnera, and in August 1936 bowed out, following a three-round defeat—and a $36,000 payday—against Joe Louis.

In retirement he took up fly fishing. Typically, he became one of the best in the business.

TEMPERAMENTAL TALENT: SHARKEY WAS THE ONLY MAN TO FIGHT BOTH JACK DEMPSEY AND JOE LOUIS

SEE ALSO ◆ PRIMO CARNERA 58 ◆ JACK DEMPSEY 89 ◆ TOMMY LOUGHRAN 203 ◆ JOE LOUIS 204 ◆ MAX SCHMELING 294 ◆ GENE TUNNEY 315

Yoshio Shirai

Yoshio Shirai stood side by side with an American marine biologist, Dr Alvin R. Cahn, and wept openly as 45,000 fans in the Korakuen Hall in Tokyo acclaimed the first Japanese world boxing champion.

Shirai, who had just outpointed Hawaiian-Filipino Dado Marino over 15 hard rounds, publicly acknowledged his debt to the man who had inspired and worked with him for the past three years.

Cahn was a theorist and a motivator, who believed psychology was as vital a part of training a boxer as roadwork or sparring. He came across Shirai in a Tokyo gym and "cured" rheumatism in his right arm, which he had suffered since he was a naval aviation mechanic in the Japanese forces in World War II.

After that Cahn gave Shirai a strict routine and within a year the tough, wiry man had won the Japanese flyweight and bantamweight titles. He lost a 10-round decision to Marino in a non-title fight in Tokyo in May 1951, but in a return in Honolulu—supposedly safe enough for the champion, who was earning as much as possible in between title defences—Shirai won in seven rounds. Their third meeting made 28-year-old Shirai a national sporting icon.

He outpointed Marino again in November 1952, turned back challenges from Tanny Campo of the Philippines and Britain's Terry Allen in 1953, and outpointed Leo Espinosa, another Filipino, in May 1954.

A good non-title payday in Buenos Aires against 1948 Olympic gold medalist Pascual Perez saw him go home with a draw, but when he gave Perez a title shot in Tokyo in November 1954, the little Argentine outpointed him over 15 rounds. Shirai boxed once more, losing in five rounds to Perez in Tokyo in May 1955.

FACT FILE

1923	Born Tokyo, Japan
1943	Professional debut, age 20
1949	Won Japanese flyweight and bantamweight titles
1952	Won world flyweight title against Dado Marino
1954	Lost world title to Pascual Perez
1955	Last fight, failed to regain title from Pascual Perez, age 31

Career record: Fights 57, Won 47, Lost 8, Drawn 2

Shirai drops Dado Marino on the way to a points win for the world flyweight title in 1952

SEE ALSO ◆ Dado Marino 22 ◆ Pascual Perez 270

BATTLING SIKI

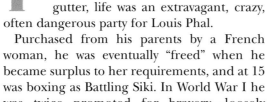

FACT FILE

1897 Born Louis Phal, St. Louis, Senegal

1912 First professional fight in France

1922 Knocked out Georges Carpentier to win world light-heavyweight title

1923 Lost world title to Mike McTigue in Dublin

1925 Last fight, lost 12-round decision to Lee Anderson in Baltimore

Died: New York City, December 15, 1925, age 28

Career record: Fights 94, Won 64, Lost 25, Drawn 5

From his birth in Senegal to his death 28 years later in a New York City gutter, life was an extravagant, crazy, often dangerous party for Louis Phal.

Purchased from his parents by a French woman, he was eventually "freed" when he became surplus to her requirements, and at 15 was boxing as Battling Siki. In World War I he was twice promoted for bravery—loosely termed, as one incident involved massacring nine defenseless German prisoners —and twice bumped back to private for indiscipline.

Siki could fight. From 1919, when he picked up his career, until the end of 1922, he was unbeaten in 45 contests, a detail which historians conveniently ignore when they intimate that he was a second-rater who was the beneficiary of an extraordinary piece of luck.

His break came on September 24, 1922, when he was employed as the challenger for Georges Carpentier's world light-heavyweight title in Paris. His role was to survive long enough for the film to be worth selling. Then he would take a dive.

Unfortunately for the scriptwriters, Siki was hurt by a right hand, lost his temper, and knocked out Carpentier in round six. Blatant attempts to disqualify him for "tripping" were howled down, and like it or not France had a new world champion.

Six months later Siki was silly enough to defend against an Irishman, Mike McTigue, on St. Patrick's Night in Dublin. He lost the 20-round decision, then took off for New York, where he lived in Hell's Kitchen and enjoyed a two-year drunken party, which was intermittently interrupted by frenetic bursts of ring activity. Early on December 15, 1925, however, his reckless journey was ended for him when he was shot dead in 41st Street.

A RARE SERIOUS MOMENT FROM SIKI, ONE OF THE CRAZIEST CHARACTERS IN BOXING'S BIZARRE HISTORY

SEE ALSO ◆ GEORGES CARPENTIER 59 ◆ MIKE McTIGUE 247

MYSTERIOUS BILLY SMITH

Mysterious" Billy Smith didn't concern himself with fancy footwork or flashy boxing: he was happy to be acknowledged as one of the roughest fighters of his extremely tough era.

Smith, who didn't like his real name Amos and so adopted Billy, held the world welterweight title twice in the 1890s. He was labeled "Mysterious Billy" by a sportswriter after letters from fans asking who he was. The name stuck.

Smith was born in Nova Scotia, but was in San Francisco when he lodged a claim to the welterweight championship after a 14th-round knockout of Danny Needham in 1892.

His most serious rival was the clever, scientific Tommy Ryan. They shared two six-round draws before meeting for what was in effect the undisputed title in Minneapolis in July 1894. Ryan won decisively on points over 20 rounds. When they fought again in Brooklyn in May 1895, police interrupted the fight in the 18th of the scheduled 45 rounds. Smith lost to Ryan again on a foul —a habitual problem for him, he was disqualified 10 times in his career!—but claimed the title again after a pair of 25-round verdicts over George Green and Matty Matthews in 1898.

Smith fought the West Indian, Joe Walcott, six times, and their rivalry was so intense that once "Mysterious Billy" had to sign a contract promising to fight within the rules!

He was a busy fighter, putting together a run of 17 fights without defeat when he was champion. His reign ended when Matthews knocked him out in 19 rounds in New York on 17 April 1900. His last fight was in 1911—aptly enough, a disqualification in San Francisco.

His wife divorced him because of his heavy drinking, but in 1911 she was walking with Billy in Portland, Oregon, when her new husband saw them together and shot him. "Billy Smith fatally shot," ran the next day's headlines, but he survived to live another 26 years.

FACT FILE

1871 Amos Smith, Little River, Digby County, Nova Scotia, Canada

1892 Knocked out Danny Needham to claim world welterweight title

1894 Outpointed by Tommy Ryan for world title

1898 Outpointed Matty Matthews over 25 rounds to regain world title

1900 Lost world title in 18 rounds to Matty Matthews

1911 Last fight in San Francisco

Died: Portland, Oregon, October 15, 1937, age 66

Career record: Fights 85, Won 29, Lost 19, Drawn 28, No Decisions 7, No Contests 2

NOTORIOUSLY ROUGH: SMITH PAID LITTLE ATTENTION TO PERIPHERAL NICETIES LIKE RULES!

SEE ALSO ◆ JOE WALCOTT 329

THE GREAT FIGHTS

GEORGES CARPENTIER
V.
BATTLING SIKI

PARIS, FRANCE.
SEPTEMBER 24, 1922.

The script was straightforward. Georges Carpentier, the most glamorous sportsman in French history, would appear on film, retaining his world light-heavyweight title with elegant ease against a brave but outclassed challenger, Battling Siki.

The crowd at the Velodrome Buffalo in Paris would rise to applaud as Carpentier, the celebrated Orchid Man who could make women swoon with the radiance of his smile, scored a dramatic knockout.

And the movie would sell out cinemas all over France.

Carpentier, a professional since he was 14, was at the stage where he was cashing in on the years of hard work. His challenge for Jack Dempsey's world heavyweight title in Jersey City had lasted only four rounds, but had increased his bank balance by $200,000. Since then, enterprising manager Francois Descamps had kept public interest high by talking up a rematch with Dempsey, claiming that but for a thumb broken in the second round, Carpentier could have won.

The Siki fight was part of the hard sell.

Siki, who may or may not have understood the script, seemed frightened in the first round, dropping when tapped by a right hand. But in the second after he was floored for six, he furiously steamed into a startled Carpentier flinging heavy swings and hooks.

Carpentier was hit on the chin, sagged down for a count of two and only just survived the round. In the third he dropped Siki momentarily with a hard right, but twice fouled him blatantly—and surprisingly the crowd turned on him, booing and jeering.

The out-of-shape champion absorbed a hiding. By the sixth one eye was closed, the other swollen, and his face was covered in blood. Siki knocked him out, but the fans' mood became menacing when referee Henri Bernstein disqualified Siki for tripping!

Carpentier needed an armed guard to reach his dressing room in the ensuing riot. Almost an hour later, the referee was overruled. Siki was the new light-heavyweight champion of the world.

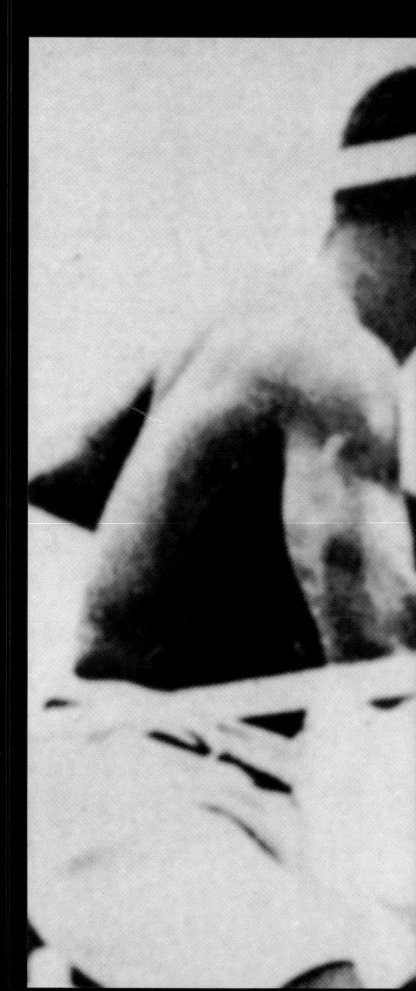

MICHAEL SPINKS

FACT FILE

1956 Born St. Louis, Missouri

1976 Olympic middleweight gold medal

1981 Won WBA light-heavyweight title by outpointing Eddie Mustafa Muhammad

1983 Unified world title by beating WBC champion Dwight Muhammad Qawi

1985 Beat Larry Holmes to win the IBF world heavyweight title

1987 Stopped Gerry Cooney in five rounds, stripped of IBF belt

1988 Lost in one round to Mike Tyson for undisputed title, retired

Career record: Fights 32, Won 31, Lost 1

Michael Spinks was a calm, organized man who provided a marked contrast to his "wild child" elder brother Leon.

While Leon shot to fame by defeating Muhammad Ali for the heavyweight championship in his eighth pro fight, and then rapidly disintegrated as a fighter, Michael's success was more measured and methodical, and eventually even more distinguished.

Both brothers won Olympic gold medals in Montreal in 1976, Leon at light-heavyweight, Michael at middle. Michael built his pro career steadily and won the WBA title with a 15-round decision over Eddie Mustafa Muhammad in Las Vegas in July 1981. He made five defenses before unifying the title with a points win over WBC champ Dwight Muhammad Qawi in Atlantic City in March 1983.

Michael, a clever, powerful, and quick fighter with a lethal right hand nicknamed "The Spinks Jinx," stayed light-heavyweight champ until 1985, when he accepted an offer to challenge for Larry Holmes's IBF heavyweight belt. Holmes was closing on Rocky Marciano's record of 49 straight wins, but Spinks, given little chance, pulled off a remarkable unanimous points triumph at the Riviera Hotel in Las Vegas in September 1985.

Holmes complained bitterly—and yelled even louder after the rematch at the Las Vegas Hilton in April 1986 when Spinks was given a split decision. Spinks was stripped by the IBF for taking a big money showdown against Gerry Cooney, which he won easily. But when he challenged Mike Tyson in what at the time was the richest fight in heavyweight history, in Atlantic City in June 1988, he lost in just 91 seconds.

He had invested wisely the fortune he had amassed in his 15 world championship fights—and never boxed again.

SPINKS WENT FROM OLYMPIC GOLD MEDALIST TO DOUBLE WORLD CHAMPION

SEE ALSO ◆ LARRY HOLMES 302 ◆ DWIGHT MUHAMMAD QAWI 274 ◆ MIKE TYSON 319

arlon Starling was a down-to-earth man who suffered few fools. He also knew the boxing business from the bottom to the top.

Starling was cast in the role of unfashionable, workaday pro from Connecticut when he challenged Mark Breland for the WBA welterweight title in 1987. Breland was the "Golden Boy", returning to his ancestral home in South Carolina to show off the skills that had brought him to the brink of his million-dollar dream. A unification fight with Lloyd Honeyghan was already planned. But Starling, the fall guy, blew the script when he overcame a wide points deficit by flattening Breland in the 11th round.

Starling was a solid man, who brought up his son in Hartford as a single parent, and who knew the meaning of sacrifice. He paid his dues in the boxing world, working for every chunk of recognition he received. On the way up he had given Don Curry two hard fights over 12 and 15 rounds, the latter for the undisputed title in 1984.

After two defenses against Fujio Ozaki and Breland (a draw), Starling was knocked out by a punch after the bell to end round six from Tomas Molinares in Atlantic City in 1988. Molinares kept the title, though he later retired with psychological problems, and the WBA, rather too late, altered the verdict to a No Decision.

Starling switched to the WBC and stopped Lloyd Honeyghan in a nine rounds masterclass in Las Vegas in February 1989, but retired the following year after a points defeat by middleweight champ Michael Nunn, followed by a defeat for the WBC welter crown, by Maurice Blocker. The future for himself, and his son, was secure.

FACT FILE

1958	Born Hartford, Connecticut
1984	Lost first world welterweight title bid to Don Curry
1987	Knocked out Mark Breland to win WBA belt in 11th round
1988	Lost belt in controversial finish with Tomas Molinares
1989	Won WBC title by stopping Lloyd Honeyghan in Las Vegas
1990	Lost title fights with Maurice Blocker and middleweight champ Michael Nunn

Career record: Fights 53, Won 45, Lost 6, Drawn 1, No Decision 1

STARLING (RIGHT) POSES WITH MICHAEL NUNN BEFORE THEIR MIDDLEWEIGHT TITLE FIGHT IN 1990

SEE ALSO ◆ DON CURRY 82 ◆ LLOYD HONEYGHAN 162

TEOFILO STEVENSON

Teofilo Stevenson could have named his price as a professional fighter. Promoters would have gladly shelled out millions of dollars for his signature.

But the 6 ft., 4 in., 225 lb. Cuban was not a man for the moving. "I don't believe in professionalism," he said bluntly after the first of his three Olympic gold medals in Munich in 1972. "I believe in the Revolution."

If he ever felt any temptation to walk away from Fidel Castro's Communist regime, it didn't show. Stevenson was an obviously proud figurehead as Cuba rose to dominate the world amateur scene in the 1970s.

After Munich, when he destroyed American sailor Duane Bobick in his second bout and coasted to the gold medal, he returned to life as a university student.

He won the gold medal in the 1974 World Championships in Havana, outpointing a tough American named Marvin Stinson in the final, and then claimed his second Olympic gold at Montreal in 1976. This time his American victim was John Tate, who would go on to win the WBA heavyweight crown as a professional. Stevenson chopped him down with brutal precision in the semi-final, and then went on to stop Mircea Simon of Romania in the final.

In the 1978 World Championships in Belgrade, he took another gold, and then, looking bored and short of top form, won the 1980 Olympic final in Moscow with a 4-1 split decision over Pyotr Zaev of the Soviet Union. Stevenson's career was in doubt when a stove blew up in his face, and he seemed to be fading when in the 1982 Worlds Italy's Francesco Damiani beat him. But at 34 he capped a magnificent career with the 1986 world super-heavyweight gold in Reno.

STEVENSON'S IDEOLOGICAL PRINCIPLES PREVENTED HIM FROM TRYING HIS LUCK IN THE PROFESSIONAL BUSINESS

JOHN H. STRACEY

If ever John H. Stracey needed his fighting heart, it was in the first round of his world welterweight title bid against the great Jose Napoles in Mexico City in December 1975.

The 25-year-old from London's East End had hardly settled into the fight when he was sent crashing to the canvas. For Stracey, given little chance even in Britain, it must have been his worst nightmare, but he was on his feet at eight and grittily withstood the champion's attempts to finish him off.

Gradually, his left hand skills and the speed of youth brought him back, and from round three the truth of Napoles' physical decline was glaringly obvious. Stracey took him apart, drilling home the punches until the fight was stopped in round six with 35-year-old Napoles soaking up punishment on the ropes.

Stracey celebrated with a classy 10th-round stoppage of Hedgemon Lewis on an emotional night at Wembley, and then took on Carlos Palomino in June. But just as the Londoner had been woefully underestimated in Mexico, so was Mexican-born Palomino in London. Stracey was beaten in 12 rounds.

As a 17-year-old Stracey had been the baby of Britain's 1968 Olympic team, and had gone on to win British and European titles in a solid career that brought him world class wins over Roger Menetrey and Ernie Lopez.

After rising so methodically, Stracey's career disintegrated with astonishing speed. He was roughed up and stopped on an eye injury by Dave Green, parted from his management team, and retired after one more fight at the age of 27.

FACT FILE

1950 Born Bethnal Green, London

1968 Boxed in Mexico Olympics

1969 ABA light-welterweight champion

1973 Won British welterweight title against Bobby Arthur

1974 Stopped Roger Menetrey to win European welterweight title

1975 Beat Jose Napoles to win the WBC welterweight crown

1976 Lost WBC title to Carlos Palomino

1978 Last fight against Georges Warusfel, age 27

Career record: Fights 51, Won 45, Lost 5, Drawn 1

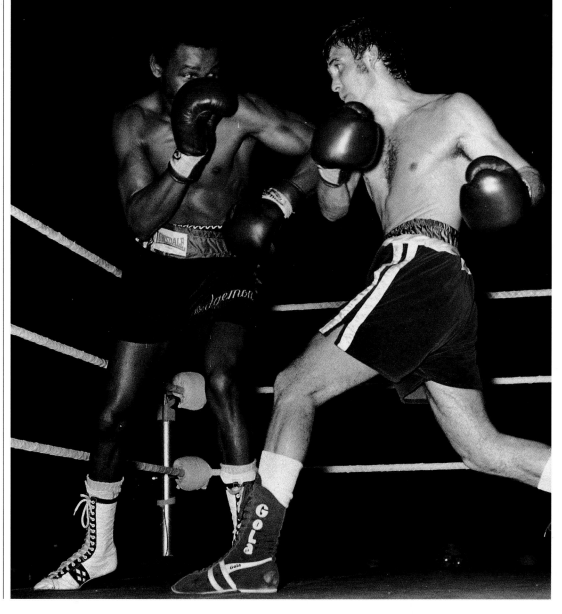

JOHN H. STRACEY IN HIS FIGHT AGAINST HEDGEMON LEWIS

SEE ALSO ◆ **JOSE NAPOLES 250** ◆ **CARLOS PALOMINO 262**

MARCEL THIL

Strong as a horse, Marcel Thil had a straightforward fighting style. He walked out and had a brawl. Bald, with a hairy back and chest, his caveman type of approach fitted his looks.

Yet he was crafty—he was one of the first fighters to coat his body in oil to make himself more difficult to pull around in clinches—and hard-hitting, with tremendous resilience to pain, as well as great stamina. In short, Thil could fight.

From Saint Dizier, just outside Paris, he was fighting professionally at 16, and worked his way up through French and European titles to earn International Boxing Union recognition as world middleweight champion in Paris in June 1932 when he beat the American, William "Gorilla" Jones in 11 rounds. Jones was trailing when he deliberately hit Thil low and was then disqualified.

A month later Thil gave Britain's immaculate defensive boxer, Len Harvey, a 15-round mauling in London even though one eye was shut tight by the third round, and kept his title in spite of a variety of American claimants, until September 1937 when he was stopped in the 10th round of an over-the-weight match by Fred Apostoli in New York. Thil, who was running out of ambition, gave up the championship and retired the following year, without boxing again. He had previously beaten the Canadian Lou Brouillard three times, as well as Britain's Jock McAvoy.

Formidably brave, he fought for the French resistance in the War, and survived in spite of being tortured by the Gestapo. His health declined rapidly following two separate automobile accidents in 1967. He died in Cannes the next year.

THIL: AN AWKWARD, DURABLE AND VERY EFFECTIVE WORLD MIDDLEWEIGHT CHAMPION

SEE ALSO ◆ LEN HARVEY 152 ◆ JOCK MCAVOY 237

DICK TIGER

A frugal, dignified man, Dick Tiger was a sophisticated ambassador for African boxing. His rise to world championship reigns at middleweight and light-heavyweight was a tribute to his patience, sense of purpose, and self-belief.

Tiger was politically committed. From the Ibo tribe which broke away from Nigeria in the late 1960s to form the Biafran nation, he saw his people slaughtered in the subsequent war.

He moved from Nigeria to England in 1955 and combined life as a boxing journeyman with a job in a paint factory. After five years, which included a win over future middleweight champ Terry Downes and two spells as British Empire titleholder, Tiger switched his base to New York City.

"America made me a better fighter," he said, and in October 1962 he won the WBA middleweight title by outpointing Gene Fullmer in San Francisco. Recognition from the rest of the world was quickly granted, but in December 1963, after successfully holding off Fullmer in two rematches, he was outpointed by tricky Joey Giardello in Atlantic City.

Tiger campaigned loudly for a return, beat Rubin "Hurricane" Carter, and finally outpointed Giardello in Madison Square Garden in October 1965 to regain the championship.

The lighter, younger Emile Griffith outsped him to deprive him of the title again in April 1966, but at 37, Tiger moved up and outpointed Jose Torres to win the world light-heavyweight crown. After defenses against Torres and Roger Rouse, he lost it when Bob Foster knocked him out in just four rounds in May 1968.

Tiger was working at a New York museum in 1971 when advanced liver cancer was diagnosed. He went home to his stricken land to die.

FACT FILE

1929 Born Richard Ihetu, Amaigbo, Nigeria

1958 Won British Empire middleweight title against Pat McAteer

1960 Lost and regained Empire title against Wilf Greaves

1962 Outpointed Gene Fullmer to win world title

1963 Lost world middleweight title to Joey Giardello

1965 Regained middleweight title against Giardello

1966 Lost middleweight title to Emile Griffith, beat Jose Torres for light-heavyweight championship

1968 Lost world light-heavyweight title to Bob Foster

Died: Nigeria, December 14, 1971, age 42

Career record: Fights 81, Won 61, Lost 17, Drawn 3

DICK TIGER DEFENDS HIS TITLE AGAINST ROGER ROUSE

SEE ALSO ♦ BOB FOSTER 119 ♦ GENE FULLMER 123 ♦ JOEY GIARDELLO 134 ♦ EMILE GRIFFITH 144 ♦ JOSE TORRES 311

THE GREAT FIGHTS

BOB FOSTER
V.
DICK TIGER

MADISON SQUARE GARDEN, NEW YORK.
MAY 24, 1968.

For several years Bob Foster was the world light-heavyweight champion in waiting.

The 6ft., 3in. former US airman was avoided, kept out of the picture as the title passed from glove to glove, until finally the Nigerian veteran Dick Tiger asked for, and was paid, $100,000 to defend against him in Madison Square Garden. That left virtually nothing for Foster, whose backers lost more than $20,000 on the show.

But Foster repaid the gamble in style. Tiger knew only one way to fight: he chugged forward in his methodical, slow-you-down, wear-you-out fashion, working the body and looking, especially, for left hooks to the head.

But this time he was in with a man who not only had immense physical benefits—Foster was seven inches taller and five pounds heavier—but could box well and hit with formidable power.

Tiger, officially a lieutenant in the Biafran Army in the civil war that was tearing apart his native Nigeria, slammed forward and won the opening round, getting inside and scoring with left hooks to the head.

In the second Foster's jab began to come into play, but Tiger's aggression made it close. But Foster's left hand, combined with some hard short rights brought him on.

Just as the fight seemed set for a long, grueling tussle, Foster produced one of the great finishes in championship history, a chilling left hook that dropped Tiger on to his back for the full count from referee Mark Conn. He tried to get up at nine, but his legs gave way.

At ringside Jack Dempsey called Foster's jab the best since Joe Louis.

Foster said, as he celebrated with his wife Pearl and mother Bertha: "Now I'll have plenty of money to provide for my family. I want to turn my title into money... I will accept any challenger my manager chooses."

He was to reign for the next six years and become one of the greatest light-heavyweight champions of all.

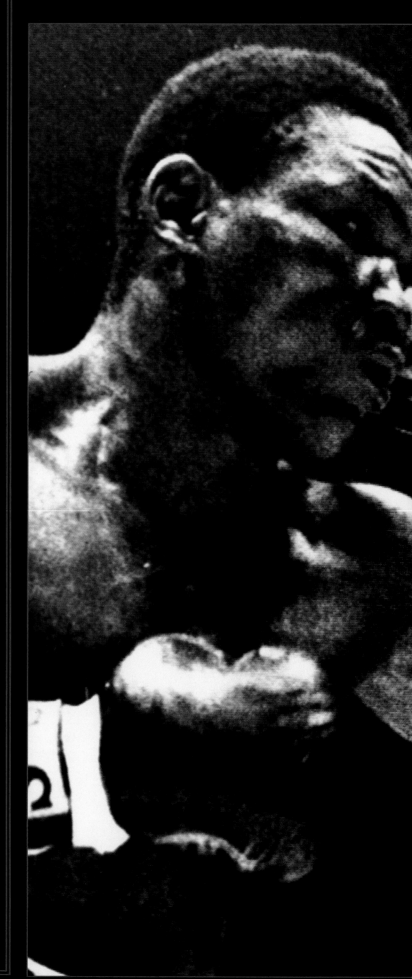

JAMES TONEY

TONEY PROMISED A "REIGN OF TERROR" WHEN HE BECAME CHAMP.

A visit to superstar Thomas Hearns was all the inspiration James Toney needed for a successful career.

He saw Hearns's five championship belts in a showcase, his Rolls-Royce, his sunken swimming pool with the words "Five-Time World Champion" on the bottom, his gym ... and not forgetting his parrot and his monkey!

Toney, a sometimes truculent, outspoken character, went on to win world title belts of his own and was a star of the early 1990s.

Raised by his mother Sherry after his father walked out when he was seven months old, Toney was a street kid in Ann Arbor, Michigan, whose first manager Johnny "Ace" Smith was gunned down in Detroit. He moved on to Jackie Kallen, and won the IBF middleweight title by upsetting Michael Nunn, coming from behind to knock him out in round 11, in Nunn's home town of Davenport, Iowa, on May 10, 1991.

Toney sneered: "I'm looking to kick everyone's ass in the middleweight division. This is the beginning of my reign of terror."

A controversial figure who came through several tight decisions, he made six defenses of the middleweight belt, including decisions over Reggie Johnson and Mike McCallum (after they had drawn first time around). Then he moved up to super-middleweight and trounced Iran Barkley in nine rounds, knocked out "Prince" Charles Williams in the 12th round, eventually losing the belt in his fourth defence on a wide decision to Roy Jones, when weight-drained.

He left Kallen, moved up to light-heavyweight and in 1996 became champion according to the newest of the world sanctioning bodies, the World Boxing Union.

SEE ALSO ♦ IRAN BARKLEY 27 ♦ ROY JONES 174

JOSE TORRES

An extrovert, articulate man, Jose "Chegui" Torres also had talent enough to win an Olympic silver medal and the world light-heavyweight title

Torres, the second of a family of seven from Puerto Rico, took up boxing when he joined the US army as an 18-year-old. Two years later he held the marvelous Hungarian south-paw Laszlo Papp to a close decision in the Olympic light-middleweight final in Melbourne.

Offers poured in for his professional signature, but he settled on Cus D'Amato, who had already guided Floyd Patterson to the world heavyweight title.

Torres, a sharp-punching, smooth, and stylish boxer, won the world light-heavyweight title by forcing Willie Pastrano to retire after nine rounds in Madison Square Garden on March 30, 1965.

Critics asked how much he wanted to fight when he spent his first year as champion cultivating his public image by playing guitar and singing on TV shows, and contenting himself to one non-title outing, a points win over heavyweight Tom McNeeley.

But in 1966 he rattled up wins over Wayne Thornton of Canada, Eddie Cotton and Scotland's Chic Calderwood, the latter in just two rounds. He lost his heavyweight title on a unanimous 15-round decision to Nigerian Dick Tiger in December 1966, and Tiger put him out of the picture again the following year when he beat him on a split decision.

Torres retired in 1969, wrote a successful book on Muhammad Ali entitled *Sting Like A Bee* in 1971, became chairman of the New York Boxing Commission, wrote a biography of Mike Tyson *Fire And Fear*, and then joined the World Boxing Organization.

FACT FILE

1936 Born Playa Ponce, Puerto Rico

1956 Olympic light-middleweight silver medal

1965 Beat Willie Pastrano for world light-heavyweight title

1966 Lost world title to Dick Tiger in fourth defense

1969 Last fight, knocked out Charlie Green, age 33

Career record: Fights 45, Won 41, Lost 3, Drawn 1

TORRES SHOWED HIS IMMACULATE LEFT HAND AGAINST DICK TIGER

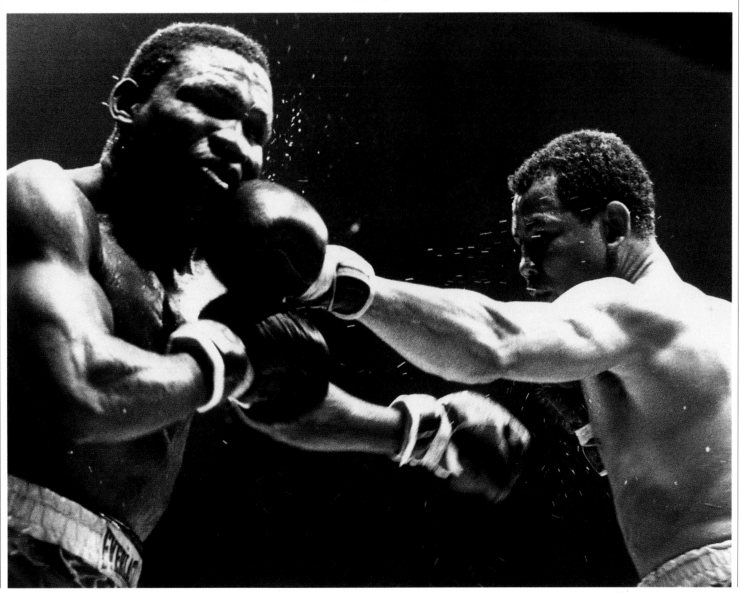

SEE ALSO ◆ LASLO PAPP 264 ◆ DICK TIGER 307

THE GREAT FIGHTS

GENE TUNNEY
V.
JACK DEMPSEY

SOLDIER FIELD, CHICAGO.
SEPTEMBER 22, 1927.

Gene Tunney, one of the most disciplined, stylish heavyweights of all, had ended the seven-year reign of Jack Dempsey on a rainy night in Philadelphia's Sesquicentennial Stadium in September 1926. They had drawn an enormous crowd—120,757—which had paid record receipts of $1,895,733.

Now 12 months on, came the return. Dempsey had knocked out Jack Sharkey in seven rounds in the interim, Tunney had rested. This time at Soldier Field, 104,943 fans shelled out an incredible $2,658,660.

Referee Dave Barry explained the new rule, whereby in the event of a knockdown the standing boxer must retreat to the farthest neutral corner. This was strange stuff to Dempsey, who liked to stand over a man and hit him as soon as his gloves left the canvas.

It seemed irrelevant as they began, Dempsey rushing, and Tunney countering beautifully, and spearing him with left leads. Dempsey slowed, absorbing the jabs and right crosses, but still prowling forward.

After six rounds Tunney was well in front, but then in the seventh Dempsey swarmed forward, knocked the champion into the ropes, landing two heavy right hands and a left hook as he fell in a glassy-eyed heap. But Dempsey chose that moment to forget the new rule - "What the hell is a neutral corner anyway?" he said later - and Barry spent precious seconds persuading him to leave the nearest corner to the fallen Tunney and cross the ring. Some say five seconds elapsed before Barry began counting at "one."

Tunney, who had one of the finest ring brains of any heavyweight, used the full nine, rose and retreated as quickly as he could until his senses unscrambled and the spring was fully restored to his legs. Dempsey's chance had gone, and in the eighth he went down momentarily from a straight right. Tunney controlled the rest of the fight to win the decision, but arguments raged for years about the "Battle of the Long Count".

Afterward Tunney gave promoter Tex Rickard $9,554.46 —his purse had come to $990,445.54, and Rickard wrote him a check for $1 million.

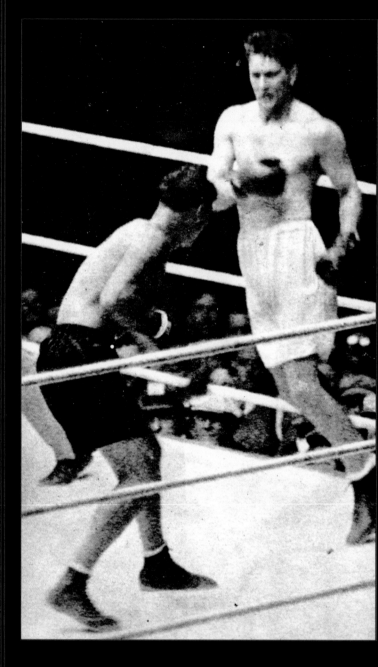

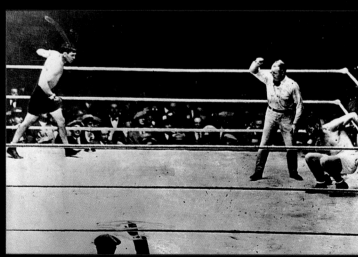

VIC TOWEEL

Vic Toweel gave South African sport its finest hour when he outpointed Californian Manuel Ortiz over 15 rounds to win the world bantamweight championship on May 31— Union Day—1950.

Toweel turned on a dazzling display in front of 28,000 fans at Wembley Stadium, Johannesburg, and clearly beat a man who had held the world championship, apart from a nine-week interlude in 1947, for the previous eight years.

He later gave a graphic description of how hard was. "My speed was my only trump card... the punches felt like bricks thrown in my face... my nose was knocked completely out of shape, my head was singing... I wanted to give up because the pain was too much." Yet after the ninth round, he took over and fought his way to a wonderful points win.

In Cape Town, the South African Parliament was in the thick of a night debate when news arrived that Toweel had won. Proceedings were interrupted so that Minister of the Interior could make a formal announcement of the result!

Weight-making was always hell for Toweel, even though he stood only 5 ft., 3 in. tall, and family wrangles distracted him. He also began to suffer blurred vision.

He turned back challenges from Danny O'Sullivan, Luis Romero, and Peter Keenan, at the same time holding the South African featherweight title, but the fairy story came to an end in Johannesburg on November 15, 1952, when he dried out for four days before the fight to make 118 lb. for a defense against Australian southpaw Jimmy Carruthers. He was stopped in 139 seconds.

A rematch ended with Toweel beaten in round 10, and by 1954 he had retired.

TOWEEL FLOORS CHALLENGER PETER KEENAN

SEE ALSO ◆ JIMMY CARRUTHERS 60 ◆ MANUEL ORTIZ 259

GENE TUNNEY

Gene Tunney was an extraordinary man. He was intellectually able—he read widely from Shakespeare to Samuel Butler and enjoyed the company of George Bernard Shaw. He was socially sophisticated enough to woo and win the hand of fabulously wealthy heiress Polly Lauder. And he was a shrewd businessman—every one of his companies thrived.

But for all these successes, the world remembers him as the man who beat the immortal "Manassa Mauler," Jack Dempsey, first in 1926 and again in 1927.

Tunney was extremely tough, physically and mentally. His only defeat in 13 years was when Harry Greb battered him for 15 rounds in 1922. Tunney was cut over both eyes, his nose was smashed, and he could barely see. Yet he stayed the distance, and lay in bed for a week thinking of one thing: Revenge.

His courage was remarkable, and he had the better of Greb, a great middleweight champion, in three of their four fights after that. One was close enough for the newspaper decision to be a draw, but Tunney was superior in the others.

He took the world heavyweight title by outboxing Dempsey on a rainy night before an amazing crowd of 120,757 in the Sesqui-centennial Stadium, Philadelphia, in September 1926.

The rematch a year later was the famous "Battle of the Long Count" in which Dempsey floored Tunney heavily in round seven, but forgot the new rule of going to a neutral corner when a knockdown occurred. This gave Tunney precious extra seconds before the count began, and he got up at nine, dropped Dempsey in the next round and won on points again.

After stopping Tom "Hard Rock" Heeney in 11 rounds, Tunney retired.

FACT FILE

1897 Born New York City

1922 Beat Battling Levinsky for American light-heavyweight title, lost it to Harry Greb

1923 Regained American title from Harry Greb

1926 Outpointed Jack Dempsey to win world heavyweight title

1927 Beat Dempsey in famous "Battle of the Long Count"

1928 Last fight against Tom Heeney, an 11th round win

1929 Announced retirement

Died: Greenwich, Connecticut, November 7, 1978, age 81

Career record: Fights 83, Won 62, Lost 1, No Contest 1, No Decisions 19

TUNNEY HAS THE CROUCHING JACK DEMPSEY UNDER CONTROL IN THEIR FIRST FIGHT IN 1926

SEE ALSO ◆ JACK DEMPSEY 89 ◆ HARRY GREB 141

THE GREAT FIGHTS

RAY ROBINSON V. RANDOLPH TURPIN

EARLS COURT, LONDON.
JULY 10, 1951.

When Sugar Ray Robinson was persuaded to interrupt his European Tour for a $100,000 payday against a modest, humble Englishman named Randolph Turpin, the fight was viewed as little more than a diversion.

Turpin was dismissed as just another dreamer, who would try but be found wanting against arguably the most talented fighter of all time. Turpin was well liked, and might have been tipped to beat an ordinary champion. But the great Sugar Ray ?

Robinson had traveled Europe in style, complete with his pink Cadillac, his personal hairdresser and doctor, as well as a dwarf and several others whose job details were sketchy. He hadn't lost in eight years. Not surprisingly, all 18,000 tickets were snapped up within hours of going on sale.

Turpin was not fazed by his task. When Sugar Ray stepped grandly through the ropes, Turpin's cornermen huddled around him to shield him, to help him concentrate on his own job. He asked them to step aside. He wanted to soak everything in.

From the first bell, Turpin outfought and outjabbed Robinson, who simply couldn't get set to throw his dazzling, trademark combinations. As rounds drifted by and Turpin's lead developed, the crowd's excitement rose.

In the seventh Robinson's left eyebrow was cut, and he continued to struggle. He rallied in the later stages, winning the 12th and 13th but Turpin was well in front and knew it. He outjabbed a desperate Robinson over the final round to clinch a deserved decision from referee Eugene Henderson. When his arm was raised at the final bell, the crowd burst into a chorus of "For He's A Jolly Good Fellow.".

Turpin was welcomed home to Leamington Spa to a civic reception, but his heroics were brought to an end 64 days later when Robinson overcame a terrible cut over the left eye to regain the title in the 10th round at the Polo Grounds in New York.

Nevetheless, he had given British boxing a night of celebration unrivaled before or since.

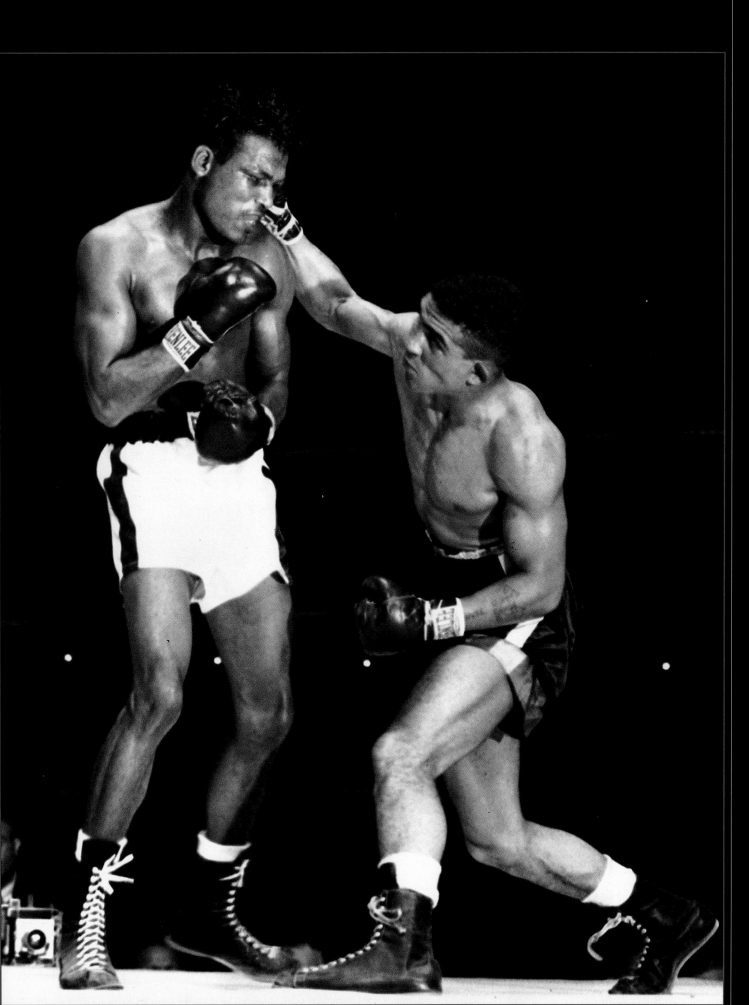

RANDOLPH TURPIN

FACT FILE

1928 Born Leamington Spa, England

1950 Won British middleweight title against Albert Finch

1951 Won European title by defeating Luc Van Dam in one round, won and lost world middleweight title against Ray Robinson

1952 Won Empire middle and light-heavyweight titles

1953 Lost world middleweight title fight with Carl Olson

1954 Lost European title to Tiberio Mitri

1955 Won British light-heavyweight title against Alex Buxton

Died: Leamington Spa, England, May 17, 1966, age 37

Career record: Fights 75, Won 66, Lost 8, Drawn 1

At Earls Court, London, on a heady night in July 1951, Randolph Turpin, the most tragic of British boxing heroes, pulled off a magnificent 15-round points win over Sugar Ray Robinson.

Robinson, the reigning world middleweight champion, had lost only once in 132 fights, but Turpin, an open, humble, and friendly man from the small Warwickshire town of Leamington Spa, outjabbed the boxing master and bundled him unceremoniously around the ring to clinch the greatest victory by a British boxer, anywhere, any time.

He was champion for only 64 days. The rematch at New York Polo Grounds saw Robinson on the brink of defeat because of a gash over his left eye, but then overpowering Turpin in the 10th round.

After that, Randolph never recaptured the fire that made him such a formidable fighting machine.

After losing to Robinson, he held things together well in 1952, stopping Don Cockell in 11 rounds for the British Empire light-heavyweight title, and outscoring George Angelo to take the Empire middleweight crown.

But when he fought Carl "Bobo" Olson for the world title after Robinson had retired in 1953, he seemed like a man treading water for 15 rounds. He was outpointed. The following year he lost the European title he had won before he fought Robinson in one round to Tiberio Mitri of Italy.

He retired in 1958, age 30, and had a couple of near-exhibition comeback fights in his 30s. Beset by personal and business worries, however, he was found dead with gunshot wounds at his home when only 37. The coroner's verdict was suicide.

GLORY DAYS: TURPIN TRAINS AT THE GWRYCH CASTLE NEAR ABERGELE, WALES, IN 1951

SEE ALSO ◆ RAY ROBINSON 278

MIKE TYSON

"I ron" Mike Tyson was a chilling, ferocious storm of a fighter, and at his best in the late 1980s was close to greatness.

"How dare they challenge me with their primitive skills?" he asked during his first championship reign.

But Tyson was a turbulent figure from a chaotic youth, and eventually his inner rage boiled over in alarming circumstances when he was disqualified for biting Evander Holyfield in Las Vegas in June 1997.

Tyson was plucked from reform school by trainer Cus D'Amato and fashioned into the youngest heavyweight champion in history. He was still only 20 when he divided Trevor Berbick from his senses and relieved him of his WBC title in two amazing rounds in November 1986.

He went on to destroy the best heavyweights of the generation, including in a peak performance the undefeated Michael Spinks—in 91 seconds in Atlantic City in June 1988.

But gradually his psychological stability disintegrated. D'Amato and his co-manager Jim Jacobs died, his marriage to actress Robin Givens failed, and he dumped long-time trainer Kevin Rooney. He seemed out of love with life long before his stunning 10th round knockout defeat by James Douglas in Tokyo in February 1990.

Two years later he was jailed for the rape of beauty contestant Desiree Washington, and he was behind bars until 1995. On his release, he returned to boxing, became a world champion by demolishing Frank Bruno, but was stopped in 11 rounds by Evander Holyfield in November 1996. His disgusting display of brutality in the return, when he bit off a chunk of Holyfield's right ear, left his future once more in doubt.

FACT FILE

1966 Born New York City
1986 Beat Trevor Berbick to become the youngest world heavyweight champion
1987 Unified the title by defeating Bonecrusher Smith and Tony Tucker
1988 Knocked out Michael Spinks in one round
1989 Beat Frank Bruno in 5 rounds
1990 Lost world title to Buster Douglas in Tokyo
1992 Jailed for the rape of Desiree Washington
1995 Released from prison, returned to the ring
1996 Stopped Frank Bruno and Bruce Seldon to win WBC and WBA titles, lost to Evander Holyfield

Career record: Fights 47, Won 45, Lost 2

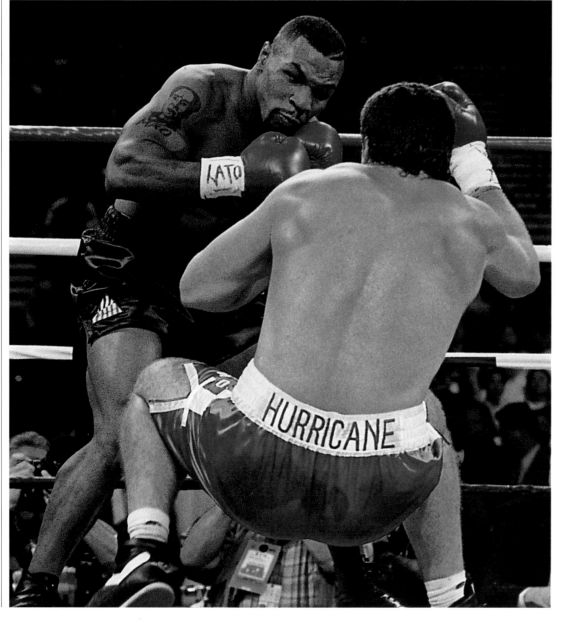

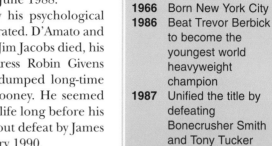

TYSON RETURNS TO THE RING IN 1995 WITH A ONE ROUND WIN OVER PETER MCNEELEY IN LAS VEGAS

SEE ALSO ◆ FRANK BRUNO 44 ◆ BUSTER DOUGLAS 94 ◆ EVANDER HOLYFIELD 159 ◆ MICHAEL SPINKS 302

THE GREAT FIGHTS

MIKE TYSON
V.
MICHAEL SPINKS

CONVENTION CENTER, ATLANTIC CITY.
JUNE 17, 1988.

Hindsight may show us that "Iron" Mike Tyson reached his peak three days short of his 22nd birthday when in front of a 21,000 capacity crowd at the Atlantic City Convention Center he destroyed Michael Spinks in 91 frighteningly one-sided seconds.

Spinks was unbeaten in 31 fights, and had held light-heavyweight and heavyweight titles. As an amateur he had won the Olympic middleweight gold medal in 1976. He knew his trade. Twice he had outpointed Larry Holmes. He had knocked out Gerry Cooney.

Before the fight, some felt Spinks would have the smart, counterpunching style to give Tyson, who had unified the title the previous year, serious problems.

Tyson, a 1-4 favorite, was paid $20 million and Spinks, who said win or lose he would retire, $13 million.

Tyson's personal life was reportedly in turmoil: his co-manager Jim Jacobs had died in March, and his four-month marriage to actress Robin Givens was said to be already in difficulties. As his other manager, Bill Cayton, sat at ringside waiting for the start of the bout, he was handed a letter that revealed Tyson's intention to sue him in order to break their contract.

If all of this had upset or confused the young champion, he put it behind him when he walked to the ring, robeless and sockless, dressed in his menacing black. Tyson won the fight quickly and cleanly, leaving his corner with a kick of his heel, a nervous twist of the neck and ripping into his challenger. Spinks was knocked down twice by savage right hands, the second time for the count.

"I saw the fear in his eyes," explained Tyson.

Spinks said he had not been intimidated, and as he walked away into retirement, he answered the question of Tyson's apparent supremacy.

"There is always somebody on earth who can beat someone else," he said. "No one is invincible."

It would take 19 more, chaotic, roller-coaster months before the prophecy would be borne out.

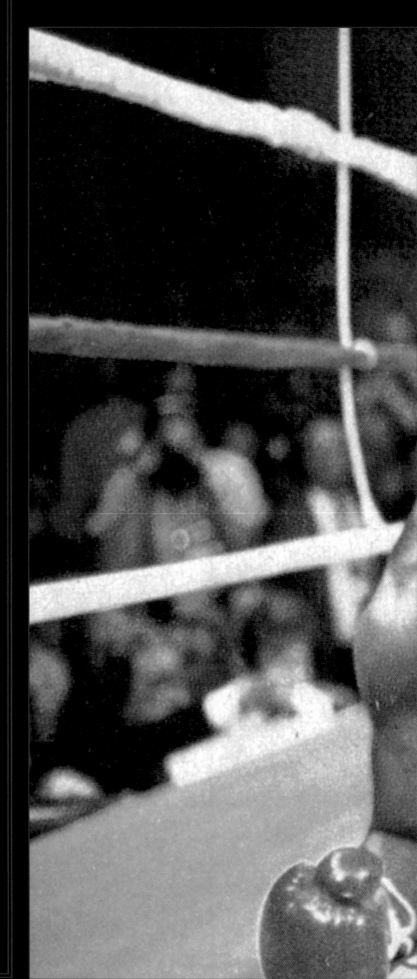

RODRIGO VALDEZ

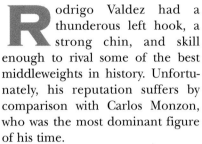

Rodrigo Valdez had a thunderous left hook, a strong chin, and skill enough to rival some of the best middleweights in history. Unfortunately, his reputation suffers by comparison with Carlos Monzon, who was the most dominant figure of his time.

Monzon beat Valdez twice in world title fights, both times on points over 15 rounds in Monte Carlo, in June 1976 and July 1977. In the second fight Valdez dropped the great Argentine, and persuaded him it was time to retire.

Valdez began as a 16-year-old in Cartagena, Colombia, in 1963, and spent the first six years of his career in South America. He began to make an impression in the USA from 1969 onward, and after dropping a 10-round decision to Ralph Palladin in New York in May 1970, did not lose again until Monzon beat him six years later, a run of 27 consecutive victories.

He won the North American middleweight crown with a 12-round decision over Bennie Briscoe in September 1973, and when the WBC controversially stripped Monzon the following year, Valdez won the vacant title by stopping the normally sturdy Briscoe in seven rounds in Monte Carlo.

Although always overshadowed by Monzon, Valdez was a good WBC champion, who disposed of four challengers—Gratien Tonna, Ramon Mendez, Rudy Robles, and Nessim "Max" Cohen.

He performed well enough in defeat to be matched with the aged but still dangerous Bennie Briscoe for the vacant title upon Monzon's retirement. In Campione, Italy, in November 1977, Valdez won the title with a 15-round decision to confirm his superiority over the American.

Having waited so long for recognition, 31-year-old Valdez was surprisingly twice outboxed by dour Argentine Hugo Corro in 1978 and faded away.

VALDEZ (RIGHT) WINS THE WORLD MIDDLEWEIGHT TITLE AGAINST BENNIE BRISCOE IN 1977

SEE ALSO ◆ BENNIE BRISCOE 40 ◆ CARLOS MONZON 222

WILFREDO VAZQUEZ

One of the most enduring fighters of the modern era, Wilfredo Vazquez held three world titles over 10 years.

A competent boxer with a heavy right hand, Vazquez had a steely determination, great courage, and the nerve to fight with consistent success away from home.

Vazquez, a short-armed, stocky fighter, had most trouble with fast, tricky movers, and lost his first world title attempt in 1986 when he was outpointed by Colombian Miguel Lora in a hard-fought 12-rounder in which both men were floored.

A non-title fight which he lost against Antonio Avelar was grandly described by Ring magazine as "one of the greatest fights of all time," but he won the WBA bantamweight belt with a 10th-round stoppage of Chan-yong Park in Seoul in October 1987. Vazquez had another terribly hard fight in Japan in January 1988 when he drew with former champion Takuya Magurama, and lost the title on a bitterly disputed split decision to Khaokor Galaxy in Bangkok in May 1988.

Considered over the hill, he dropped WBA super-bantamweight champion Raul Perez three times for a stunning third-round win before 5,000 partisan fans in Mexico City in March 1992.

He was a fine champion, defending successfully nine times, most impressively a 12-round decision against the highly skilled Orlando Canizales. In May 1995, Vazquez surprisingly lost to the tall, awkward Venezuelan Antonio Cermeno.

Any thoughts that he was finished were dispelled in May 1996, when he overturned a big points deficit to stop defending WBA featherweight champion Eloy Rojas in 11 rounds in Las Vegas.

FACT FILE

1960	Born Rio Piedras, Puerto Rico
1981	Professional debut
1986	Lost first world title bid to Miguel Lora
1987	Beat WBA bantamweight champion Chan-yong Park in 10 rounds in Korea
1988	Lost WBA bantamweight title to Khaokor Galaxy in Bangkok
1992	Knocked out Mexican Raul Perez to win WBA super-bantamweight title
1995	Lost WBA super-bantamweight title to Antonio Cermeno
1996	Won WBA featherweight title by stopping Eloy Rojas in Las Vegas

Career record: Fights 56, Won 46, Lost 7, Drawn 3

VAZQUEZ: ONE OF THE GREAT ROAD WARRIORS OF MODERN BOXING

SEE ALSO ◆ ORLANDO CANIZALES 52

PANCHO VILLA

FACT FILE

1901 Born Francisco Guilledo, Iloilo, Philippines

1919 Boxing professionally in Manila

1922 Beat Johnny Buff for the American flyweight title

1923 Knocked out Jimmy Wilde for world flyweight title

1925 Last fight, lost 10-round decision to Jimmy McLarnin

Died: San Francisco, California, July 14, 1925, age 23

Career record: Fights 105, Won 88, Lost 9, Drawn 5, No Decisions 3

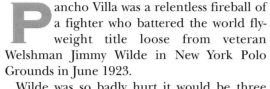

Pancho Villa was a relentless fireball of a fighter who battered the world flyweight title loose from veteran Welshman Jimmy Wilde in New York Polo Grounds in June 1923.

Wilde was so badly hurt it would be three weeks before he could recognize his wife, yet he recovered to live a long life.

Villa, who broke down in tears when he saw the unconscious, apparently lifeless Wilde in the dressing room, was fated to die two years later, while still holding the championship.

The diminutive Filipino was given his ring name—after the Mexican revolutionary—by an enterprising promoter who felt Francisco Guilledo too boring!

In September 1922, shortly after arriving from Manila, Villa knocked out 34-year-old Johnny Buff in 11 rounds for the American flyweight title. Although he lost the championship on a close decision to Frankie Genaro in March 1923, when plans were made for Wilde to defend that summer, Villa was selected as the challenger on financial grounds—he sold tickets; the light-punching Genaro did not.

Villa beat Wilde in seven horribly one-sided rounds, and became one of the stars of the age, cramming 19 fights into the next 12 months, and making four championship defenses by May 1925.

But when he lost to a quick-fisted teenager, Jimmy McLarnin, on July 4, 1925, Villa had only recently had a wisdom tooth out. Three more ulcerated teeth were extracted afterwards, but he ignored orders to rest. He preferred to party. Blood poisoning set in, he collapsed and died in hospital only ten days after his last fight.

VILLA: DIED IN A HOSPITAL BED WHILE STILL WORLD FLYWEIGHT CHAMP

SEE ALSO ◆ FRANKIE GENARO 133 ◆ JIMMY MCLARNIN 246 ◆ JIMMY WILDE 335

KOICHI WAJIMA

Koichi Wajima was 25 and working as a manual laborer when he decided he wanted to box.

He was unorthodox, up to a point self-taught and therefore unpredictable. He was also immensely strong and brave, and his perseverance and fighting spirit made him extremely popular.

Wajima won the Japanese light-middleweight title in his 12th fight, and on October 31, 1971 stunned the boxing world by hustling his way to a 15-round split decision over defending world champ Carmelo Bossi of Italy in the Nihon University Auditorium in Tokyo.

A big puncher with a crouching style, Wajima demolished another Italian, Domenico Tiberia, in 109 seconds in his first defense, and went on to make five more, including a draw with Brazilian Miguel De Oliveira and a majority decision in the rematch.

His first reign ended with a 15th-round defeat by Oscar "Shotgun" Albarado from Texas in Tokyo in June 1974, but he won the rematch seven months later on a unanimous verdict.

Wajima suddenly began to look fragile: Jae-do Yuh of Korea stopped him in the seventh round to take away the championship belt again, by which time the WBC had stopped recognizing him. In a rematch, however, Wajima regained the WBA title with a 15th-round stoppage of Yuh in Tokyo in February 1976.

It was his last win. Spanish substitute Jose Duran knocked him out in 14 rounds to finish his third championship reign in May 1976, and in his farewell fight he was stopped in 11 rounds by Nicaraguan Eddie Gazo in June 1977, again for the WBA belt.

In his retirement Wajima remained a popular, respected man, who became a television boxing commentator.

FACT FILE

1943	Born Nishisanjo, Hokkaido, Japan
1971	Won world light-middleweight title by defeating Carmelo Bossi
1974	Lost world title on 15th-round knockout to Oscar Albarado
1975	Outpointed Albarado to regain title, lost it to Jae-do Yuh
1976	Won WBA belt from Yuh, lost it to Jose Duran
1977	Last fight, lost WBA title challenge to Eddie Gazo, age 34

Career record: Fights 38, Won 31, Lost 6, Drawn 1

WAJIMA REGAINED THE WBA JUNIOR MIDDLEWEIGHT CHAMPION TITLE IN THIS FIGHT AGAINST JAE-DO YUH

THE GREAT FIGHTS

JIMMY WILDE
V.
PANCHO VILLA

POLO GROUNDS, NEW YORK CITY.
JUNE 18, 1923.

Welshman Jimmy Wilde had made up his mind to box no more when American bantamweight Pete Herman stopped him in 17 rounds in London in January 1921. It was only the second defeat in almost 150 recorded contests, and for a long time afterwards, he suffered serious head pains.

But he had held the world flyweight title since 1916 and so when an offer came from New York to defend his championship at the Polo Grounds in June 1923 for £13,000 ($65,000 at the existing exchange rate), he accepted. Although he was 31, he believed he still had the ability, the combination of elusiveness and formidable punching power, to justify his old nickname of "The Ghost With A Hammer In His Hands."

Pancho Villa, a tough, 21-year-old Filipino, was selected as his opponent and 40,000 people paid to watch a living legend take on one of the most exciting newcomers on the scene.

Villa began with a typical whirlwind attack, and both men had been rocked by right hands in round two. After the bell to end that round, the Filipino set himself and floored Wilde with a tremendous right to the head. For some reason, referee Patsy Haley did not even rule a foul, even though fans were roaring for Villa to be disqualified. Wilde was in effect out of the fight from that second. From the fifth there were cries of "Stop it!," but Wilde battled on until the seventh, when he collapsed from a left hook. He was carried from the ring, still unconscious.

Villa visited the dressing room to pay his respects and broke down when he saw the condition the old champion was in. A doctor worked on Wilde for hours until he regained a kind of consciousness. He was taken to a bungalow belonging to bantamweight champion Frankie Burns on a small island near New York, where his wife Elizabeth spoon-fed him milk and ice cream for three weeks, before at last he recognized her. He retired with a total of £70,000 ($350,000) in the bank.

Tragically, Villa died of blood poisoning two years later, while still world champion.

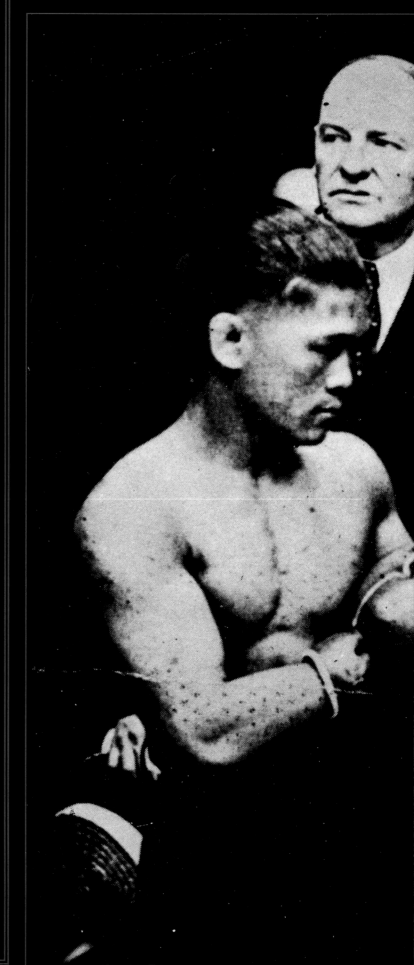

JERSEY JOE WALCOTT

Long before he became world heavyweight champion at the age of 37, Jersey Joe Walcott retired, frustrated by years of toiling as a black boxer in a white man's world.

A clever, beautifully balanced craftsman, Walcott had moves of the highest class, but in the 1930s, before Joe Louis broke the mold, black fighters were "untouchables" because of the anger and hostility which had greeted Jack Johnson's seven-year reign two decades earlier.

As a result men like Walcott learned their craft with little tangible result. A father of six, Jersey Joe quit boxing for jobs in shipyards and on construction sites. At least once, the family were on the New Jersey State welfare list.

His break came in December 1947 when he was pitched in with Joe Louis at Madison Square Garden. Against the expectations of those who had slammed the contest as a rank mismatch, 15-1 outsider Walcott dropped the aging champion twice and was desperately unlucky to lose a split decision. The crowd booed loud and long.

In the rematch before 42,657 fans in Yankee Stadium, he again floored Louis, was ahead on points, but was knocked out in the 11th.

Twice he lost decisions to Ezzard Charles, but produced a textbook left hook—one of the finest shots in heavyweight history—to flatten Charles in the seventh round at Pittsburgh in July 1951. Until George Foreman regained the title in 1994, Walcott was the oldest heavyweight champion.

He lost the title in the 13th round to Rocky Marciano in September 1952 and retired after a dismal first-round defeat in the return. He became a parole officer, refereed the second Ali–Liston fight in 1965, and later became New Jersey State Athletic Commissioner.

WALCOTT OUTPOINTS EZZARD CHARLES IN THE LAST OF THEIR FOUR FIGHTS IN PHILADELPHIA IN 1952

SEE ALSO ◆ EZZARD CHARLES 65 ◆ JOE LOUIS 204 ◆ ROCKY MARCIANO 209

JOE WALCOTT

Joe Walcott was an astonishingly powerful little man who was the best welterweight in the world around the turn of the century, but whose progress was checked repeatedly by the need to cooperate with those who ruled boxing.

As black fighters often were in those days, Walcott was ordered more than once to purposefully lose fights that he reasonably could have won at a stroll. This is almost certainly why Walcott quit abruptly at the end of the 11th round after giving Tommy West a boxing lesson in New York in 1900.

Walcott, who used to employ a skinny, youthful Jack Johnson as a sparring partner, won the world welterweight title in 1901 when he stopped James "Rube" Ferns in five rounds at Fort Erie, Ontario, and stayed champion until 1904 when, in the first all-black world championship, he was beaten on a 20th round foul by Dixie Kid in San Francisco. He was recognized again when Kid moved up in weight, but his claim vanished after two defeats by Honey Mellody in 1906.

Walcott didn't worry about any of the opponents he fought: in 1900 he stopped heavyweight Joe Choynski in seven rounds and also boxed the great Sam Langford to a 15-round draw in September 1904. Three weeks later he drew a 20-rounder with Joe Gans. He also had a rather foul-ridden, six-fight series with Mysterious Billy Smith.

Before he turned professional Walcott was an elevator operator in a Boston hotel, and after his retirement in 1911 he eventually settled down as a handyman at Madison Square Garden. He was killed when hit by a car near Massillon, Ohio.

FACT FILE

1873 Born Barbados, West Indies

1893 Professional debut, age 20

1897 Lost world lightweight title fight to Kid Lavigne

1898 Lost to welterweight champion Mysterious Billy Smith

1901 Won world welterweight title against Rube Ferns

1904 Lost welterweight title on a foul to Dixie Kid, drew with Joe Gans

1906 Lost welterweight title fight with Honey Mellody

1911 Last fight against Henry Hall in Maine

Died: Near Massillon, Ohio, October, 1935, age 52

Career record: Fights 134, Won 74, Lost 30, Drawn 22, No Decisions 5, No Contests 3

THE ORIGINAL WALCOTT: WELTERWEIGHT CHAMP IN THE EARLY YEARS OF THE CENTURY

SEE ALSO ◆ JOE GANS 129 ◆ MYSTERIOUS BILLY SMITH 299

MICKEY WALKER

Mickey Walker loved to fight. He didn't care who was in the opposite corner or what he weighed. The thrill of the rumble was all that really mattered.

He was also a notorious hell-raiser. Legend has it that hours after he lost a bruising 15-rounder with middleweight champ Harry Greb before 65,000 people in the Polo Grounds in 1925, Walker took on Greb outside a speakeasy. And the second fight was even better than the first!

Walker had a weaving, aggressive style that made him hard to hit cleanly, and earned him the name "The Toy Bulldog."

Fighting professionally by the time he was 17, he won the world welterweight title by mauling veteran Jack Britton over 15 rounds in Madison Square Garden in November 1922. He was a good champion, holding it until May 1926 when Pete Latzo, whom he had previously beaten, got a decision over him in Scranton, Pennsylvania.

After Greb's death, Walker won the middleweight title with a terrible decision over Tiger Flowers in December 1926. It has been claimed that Al Capone, who was taking an interest in boxing at the time, was responsible. Whatever the truth of that, Walker remained champion until 1931, when he relinquished the belt.

He was twice outpointed in world light-heavyweight title challenges, in 1929 by Tommy Loughran and in 1933 by Maxie Rosenbloom, and he fought heavyweights. He drew with Jack Sharkey, but was stopped by Max Schmeling.

In retirement he became a widely respected painter, had a spell as a sports editor, sold liquor, and ran a bar. He was married six times. He suffered from Parkinson's Disease in his last years.

THE "TOY BULLDOG" (RIGHT) IN TYPICALLY BARNSTORMING ACTION IN THE 1920S

SEE ALSO ◆ JACK BRITTON 41 ◆ TIGER FLOWERS 115 ◆ HARRY GREB 141 ◆ TOMMY LOUGHRAN 203 ◆ MAX SCHMELING 294 ◆ JACK SHARKEY 296

JIRO WATANABE

A technically brilliant southpaw, Jiro Watanabe exposed the hypocrisy of the world's governing bodies by unifying the super-flyweight division.

Watanabe won an extremely close 12-round decision over Payao Poontarat of Thailand in Osaka on July 5, 1984, adding Poontarat's WBC championship title to the WBA belt he already owned.

The reaction of the WBA was to strip him of their title. All the arguments that the authorities were there for the betterment of boxing disappeared with that single act. Their self-interest was laid bare for all to see.

Watanabe, a clever, precise counterpuncher, continued to be a WBC champion only from that point.

A college graduate, Watanabe was already 24 when he turned professional, but progressed quickly and in April 1981 lost a desperately tight 15-round decision to WBC super-flyweight champion Chul-ho Kim in Seoul. Two judges gave it to Kim by a single point, the other by two points.

The following year, Watanabe's backers tempted WBA champ Rafael Pedroza of Panama to defend in Jiro's home town of Osaka, and this time he succeeded. Again, the fight went the full 15 rounds.

In his first defense Watanabe forced former champion Gustavo Ballas of Argentina to retire after nine rounds in Osaka in July 1992, stopped former flyweight champ Shoji Oguma in the 12th and went on to rattle up 12 consecutive world title wins before he lost the WBC belt in his last fight to Gilberto Roman in Osaka in March 1986, by which time he was 31 years old. A good all-round athlete, before taking up boxing he also excelled in swimming and the martial art, nihon-kenpo.

FACT FILE

1955 Born Osaka, Japan

1981 Lost WBC super-flyweight bid against Chul-ho Kim in South Korea

1982 Won WBA super-flyweight title against Rafael Pedroza in Osaka

1984 Won unification fight with Payao Poontarat in Osaka, stripped of WBA title, continued as WBC champion

1986 Lost WBC title to Gilberto Roman, retired age 31

Career record: Fights 28, Won 26, Lost 2

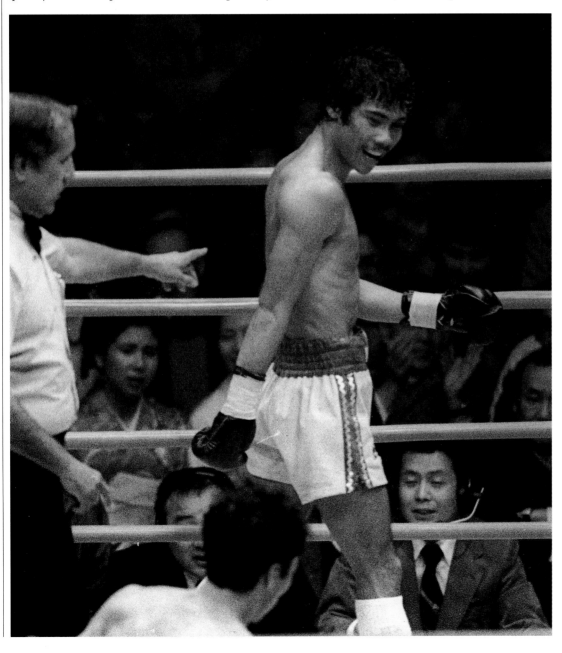

QUALITY ATHLETE: WATANABE WAS A COLLEGE GRADUATE WHO ENJOYED IMMENSE POPULARITY IN FIVE YEARS AS WORLD CHAMP

JIM WATT

A decision to switch his fighting base to London in 1976 changed Jim Watt's destiny.

Frustrated at finding doors closing at every turn, Watt had parted company with his long-time mentor Jim Murray and planned two or three money fights before concentrating full-time on his car business.

But a telephone conversation with manager Terry Lawless persuaded him to change direction—and just three years later he was a world champion.

As a British amateur champion Watt's potential was always there—in the 1968 ABA semi-finals he knocked out John Stracey in 45 seconds. He twice held the British lightweight title, his reigns interrupted by a points defeat against former world champ Ken Buchanan in 1973, and in 1977 he added the European title. Three defenses, one a landslide points win in Spain over former world light-welterweight champ Perico Fernandez, set him up for a shot at the vacant WBC lightweight crown against Alfredo Pitalua of Colombia.

And on an emotional night, Watt delighted his home city fans in the Kelvin Hall with a marvelous display of controlled southpaw boxing, mixing counterpunching with sustained aggression to stop Pitalua in the 12th round.

For the next two years he dominated the division, beating Robert Vasquez of Texas, Irish southpaw Charlie Nash, 1976 Olympic gold medalist Howard Davis, and future WBA champ Sean O'Grady.

Watt's hunger ran out in the fight at Wembley in June 1981 but he was still on his feet at the end of 15 rounds against the great Alexis Arguello. In retirement he remained in the public eye as an expert TV boxing analyst, displaying the same intelligence and incisive thinking that had been an inherent feature of his boxing style.

SOUTHPAW SCIENTIST: WATT HAD TO WAIT FOR HIS BREAK, BUT WHEN IT CAME HE MADE THE MOST OF IT

SEE ALSO ◆ ALEXIS ARGUELLO 20 ◆ KEN BUCHANAN 45

FREDDIE WELSH

A restless, intelligent soul who did things entirely his own way, Freddie Welsh held the world lightweight title for three years during World War I.

The son of a realtor, and born Frederick Hall Thomas, he could not settle in his home town of Pontypridd, and took the boat to America.

He rode the rails, lived on his wits, and eventually, in Philadelphia, found his way into professional fist-fighting. It was the making of him. For several years he switched between Britain and the United States as the job demanded, and not surprisingly, was a mixture of both codes: he had a good, solid jab, was a defensive master, but rolled forward from a low stance like an American, and was, when the mood took him, one of the dirtiest fighters on the scene. His 1910 battle with the great stylist Jim Driscoll descended into an orgy of rule-breaking—Driscoll was eventually disqualified in round 10.

Welsh, who twice held the British lightweight championship, won the world title in July 1914 when he outfought Californian Willie Ritchie at Olympia, London, over 20 rounds. From then on, he lived permanently in America. In 1916 he beat Ad Wolgast on an 11th round foul and also defended his title against Charley White, a ferocious left hooker from Chicago.

But he lost his title in May 1917 when the great Benny Leonard stopped him in nine rounds at the Manhattan Casino, New York. Afterwards he found his manager had gambled on a Welsh victory—using Freddie's entire $5,000 purse!

Welsh, a vegetarian, lost the rest of his money in a health farm venture, and died penniless in New York five years later.

FACT FILE

1886 Born Frederick Thomas, Pontypridd, Wales

1908 Beat world featherweight champion Abe Attell

1909 Won British lightweight title against Johnny Summers

1911 Lost British title to Matt Wells

1912 Regained British title against Matt Wells

1914 Outpointed Willie Ritchie to win world title

1917 Lost world title to Benny Leonard

1922 Last fight in Brooklyn, age 36

Died: New York City, July 29, 1927, age 41

Career record: Fights 163, Won 120, Lost 27, Drawn 16

WELSH: HIS WANDERLUST TOOK HIM TO THE WORLD LIGHTWEIGHT TITLE IN 1914

SEE ALSO ◆ JIM DRISCOLL 95 ◆ BENNY LEONARD 186 ◆ WILLIE RITCHIE 275 ◆ AD WOLGAST 339

PERNELL WHITAKER

A slick, elusive southpaw, Pernell Whitaker was a defensive master whose style was admired by many but adored by few.

Exceptionally fast, he rarely ran, preferring to dart in and out of distance and use an abundance of lateral movement to bewilder and unbalance opponents.

Whitaker was a marvelously talented amateur. He reached the 1982 World Championships finals in Munich as an 18-year-old and won the lightweight gold medal in the Los Angeles Olympics. He won 201 of 215 amateur contests, and then turned professional with the Main Events team, who remained his promoters throughout his career.

Whitaker was robbed in his first world title bid—an outrageous split decision in favor of Mexican WBC champ Jose Luis Ramirez in Paris in 1988. He won the IBF version with an overwhelming points win over Greg Haugen, and then beat Ramirez in Norfolk, Virginia, to straighten out his record. In August 1990, after points wins over both Freddie Pendleton and Azumah Nelson, Whitaker unified the lightweight division by scoring an incredibly rare first-round knockout against the Puerto Rican Juan Nazario.

Weight problems and lack of opposition persuaded him to move up in 1992, when he briefly held the IBF light-welterweight title, and then in 1993 settled into the welterweight division by dethroning WBC champ James "Buddy" McGirt in Madison Square Garden. In September 1993 he fought a hotly disputed draw with Julio Cesar Chavez before a 60,000 crowd at the San Antonio Alamodome. Almost every writer present felt Whitaker won clearly.

He became a four-time world champ when he climbed off the floor to outpoint rugged WBA light-middleweight titleholder Julio Cesar Vasquez in March 1995, then reverted to the welterweight division.

WHITAKER ON HIS WAY TO A FOURTH WORLD TITLE AGAINST WBA LIGHT-MIDDLEWEIGHT CHAMP JULIO CESAR VASQUEZ

SEE ALSO ◆ JULIO CESAR CHAVEZ 67 ◆ AZUMAH NELSON 251

JIMMY WILDE

Jimmy Wilde cut a pale, waif-like figure, and conceded weight even to flyweights, yet was still one of the greatest fighters of all time.

Known as "The Mighty Atom," or "The Ghost With A Hammer In His Hands," Wilde was so light he once weighed in for a British flyweight title fight wearing an overcoat!

He was fast, extremely difficult to hit, and had a repertoire of precise, stinging punches that accounted for 99 of his official 145 opponents inside the distance.

His first title attempt against Tancy Lee of Scotland in January 1915 was ruined by the flu. He lost a terrible struggle in the 17th round, but rebuilt his career and won the world title with a 12th-round stoppage of Joe Symonds in February 1916.

Four months later he stopped Lee in 11 rounds and ended the year by knocking out American claimant Young Zulu Kid in 11. When he beat Joe Conn at Chelsea in 1918, his purse was a bag of diamonds! He won 44 consecutive fights after his defeat by Lee and retired in the summer of 1920.

He agreed to fight American bantamweight Pete Herman in January 1921, but threatened to pull out following a weigh-in dispute. Persuaded to box as a "favor" to the Prince of Wales, who was in the front row at the National Sporting Club, he lost in 17 rounds.

He fought once more. In June 1923 he was butchered in seven rounds by Pancho Villa at the New York Polo Grounds, and was so seriously hurt he did not recognize his wife for three weeks. He recovered and stayed in touch with boxing by writing for a Sunday newspaper. His last years were spent in hospital, his mind wrecked after he was mugged at a train station.

FACT FILE

1892 Born Tylorstown, Wales

1911 Boxing regularly in Pontypridd

1913 Won British 98 lb. title in Glasgow

1916 Won world flyweight title against Joe Symonds

1923 Lost world flyweight title in last fight with Pancho Villa

Died: Cardiff, Wales, March 10, 1969, age 76

Career record: Fights 145, Won 141, Lost 3, Drawn 1

WILDE (LEFT) LOST TO TANCY LEE IN 17 ROUNDS WHEN RIDDLED WITH FLU, BUT WON THE RETURN IN 11

SEE ALSO ◆ PETE HERMAN 156 ◆ PANCHO VILLA 324

IKE WILLIAMS

Even generations after he had slipped out of the ring for the last time, fighters loved Ike Williams.

Williams boxed for the Mob, was brave enough to attempt to start a Boxers' Guild, was ripped off, and blew what money he did make. And he was one of the greatest fighters the world will ever see.

He won the NBA title on a riotous night in Mexico City in April 1945 by knocking out Juan Zurita in two rounds. His manager Connie McCarthy was hit by a brick, and they were mugged for the championship belt. Ike never saw it again.

In August 1947 he knocked out Bob Montgomery in six rounds to win undisputed recognition, and dominated the division until May 1951 when he was stopped and lost his title in 14 to Jimmy Carter.

Williams was ostracized by the Managers' Guild for leaving McCarthy, an habitual drunkard, and attempted to start a similar organization for boxers. Sadly, the big names who could have helped didn't want to know and it failed. Because he couldn't get a fight he signed with notorious mobster Blinky Palermo, who controlled the rest of his career. He beat the best—Johnny Bratton, Kid Gavilan, Beau Jack, Sammy Angott—but what Palermo didn't borrow or subtract from his purses, he lost anyway.

In retirement he worked in various obscure manual jobs, an ordinary man... until he stepped into the ring to take a bow at Madison Square Garden. The place always erupted. But even when he died, an old man alone in a poor area of Los Angeles, somebody broke in and stole his TV set.

WILLIAMS: KING OF THE LIGHTWEIGHTS FOR SIX YEARS

SEE ALSO ◆ KID GAVILAN 132 ◆ BEAU JACK 163 ◆ BOB MONTGOMERY 221

JOHNNY WILSON

A strong, well-organized southpaw, Johnny Wilson knew the men who mattered.

By no means the best fighter New York's Little Italy ever produced, he was nonetheless extremely successful. He understood the way boxing worked and manipulated it for his own benefit.

Many things have been said about Wilson's connections, which included Al Capone, but here was a man who could fight, and who ended up keeping his money. He was one of boxing's winners in all senses of the word.

Wilson began fighting as an 18-year-old. Money was his incentive. He fought under the ridiculous "no-decision" rules mostly and although much of his early record is obscure, he earned well and in May 1920 in Boston he outpointed defending champion Mike O'Dowd over 12 rounds for the world middleweight title. O'Dowd's walk-forward style suited Wilson's left-handed counterpunching, and he won clearly.

He beat O'Dowd again over 15 rounds in New York, and beat Bryan Downey on an extremely dubious foul, after seeming in deep trouble. A betting coup was suspected and the local commission reversed the result, declaring Downey world champion. It didn't stick, however, and Wilson held off Downey a second time with a 12-round draw in Jersey City in September 1921.

After a fallout with promoter Tex Rickard, his title was taken away by the New York Commission and handed to Dave Rosenberg, a former amateur champion. Again, few agreed with that, and Wilson effectively continued to hold the title until Harry Greb outpointed him in August 1923.

He retired in 1926 and went on to own several nightclubs, including the Silver Slipper in New York City.

FACT FILE

1893 Born Giovanni Panica, New York City, March 23, 1893
1911 Professional debut
1920 Outpointed Mike O'Dowd for world middleweight title
1923 Lost world title to Harry Greb
1926 Retired after losing to Maxie Rosenbloom
Died: Boston, Massachusetts, December 8, 1985, age 92
Career record: Fights 123, Won 73, Lost 26, Drawn 8, No Decisions 14, No Contests 2

WILSON (LEFT) IN A RELAXED MOOD BEFORE HIS MIDDLEWEIGHT TITLE FIGHT WITH HARRY GREB IN 1923

SEE ALSO ◆ HARRY GREB 141

HOWARD WINSTONE

FACT FILE

1939 Born Merthyr Tydfil, Wales

1958 ABA and Empire Games bantamweight champion

1961 Won British featherweight title against Terry Spinks

1963 Won European featherweight title against Alberto Serti

1965 Beat Jose Legra, lost world title bid to Vicente Saldivar

1967 Lost twice more to Saldivar in Wales and Mexico

1968 Beat Mitsunori Seki for world title, lost to Legra

Career record: Fights 67, Won 61, Lost 6

A beautiful textbook boxer with a marvelous left hand, Howard Winstone epitomized the British stand-up style. He hit crisply but his power was diluted by an accident at work in a toy factory as a 17-year-old. He trapped his right hand in a machine, which sliced off the tips of three fingers.

Winstone was a joy to watch. He won 80 of 82 amateur contests, his last defeat as a 14-year-old. He was ABA bantamweight champion and Empire Games gold medalist in 1958. Although only 19, he was already married with a family and turned pro to help feed them.

Winstone's skills took him to both British and European featherweight titles, but his name was made by three epic losing battles with swarming Mexican southpaw Vicente Saldivar. Their styles blended perfectly. The first fight at Earls Court was close, but Saldivar took the 15-round decision.

There are those who will always be convinced that Winstone won the second fight, at Ninian Park, Cardiff, in June 1967, but at the end of a pulsating, bruising encounter referee Wally Thom raised Saldivar's arm. "Thanks for British justice," Winstone's manager Eddie Thomas yelled at Thom as the angry Welsh crowd booed and jeered the decision.

Winstone was unable to stay with Saldivar because of the high altitude of Mexico City in October 1967 and was stopped in 12 rounds, but when Vicente retired, he won recognition as world champion in Britain when he beat Mitsunori Seki of Japan on a bad cut in the ninth round at the Albert Hall, London in January 1968.

Six months later, however, he was surprisingly stopped by Jose Legra, whom he had outpointed in his prime, at Porthcawl. He retired in 1969.

MASTER BOXER: WINSTONE'S FLASHING LEFT HAND KEEPS RAFIU KING AT BAY AT WEMBLEY IN 1964

SEE ALSO ♦ JOSE LEGRA 185 ♦ VICENTE SALDIVAR 292

AD WOLGAST

Ad Wolgast was at peace in the ring. He had a concentrated ferocity which flowered there, and he would fight anybody, simply for the pleasure. His enjoyment was to cost him his sanity.

Wolgast hung tough with the best lightweights of his reckless age, and his finest hour was in February 1910 near Port Richmond, California, when he ground the resistance out of defending world titleholder Battling Nelson in a torrid 40-round epic.

Wolgast stopped in turn George Memsic, Anton LaGrave, and Frankie Burns, and knocked out British challenger Owen Moran with a brutally low punch in the 13th round in San Francisco in July 1911. By then he was bringing his own referee along with him, Jack Welch, whose bias reached a scandalous peak in July 1912 when Wolgast fought "Mexican" Joe Rivers. In the 13th round both went down simultaneously in a freak double knockout. Welch pulled the groggy Wolgast to his feet, propped him up, and counted out Rivers with his free hand!

Four months later, Wolgast lost the championship when he deliberately fouled Willie Ritchie in round 16, growling that he wouldn't allow himself be knocked out.

He slid downhill rapidly, although he did fight Freddie Welsh for the title in 1916 and was again disqualified. Horribly exploited for his readiness to fight, he took far too many punches and in 1927, long after he had retired, Wolgast was committed to a hospital for the insane in Camarillo, California. Every day he trained enthusiastically for a fight with the late Joe Gans. He was still in training when he died 28 years later.

FACT FILE

1888 Born Adolph Wolgast, Cadillac, Michigan

1910 Won world lightweight title against Battling Nelson in 40th round

1911 Knocked out Owen Moran in 11 rounds

1912 Controversial win over Joe Rivers, lost title to Willie Ritchie

1916 Retired after 20-round draw with Frankie Russell

1920 One comeback fight, then retired again

Died: Camarillo, California, April 14, 1955, age 67

Career record: Fights 133, Won 80, Lost 33, Drawn 20

THE MICHIGAN BEARCAT: WOLGAST TOOK 40 ROUNDS TO BEAT BATTLING NELSON FOR THE WORLD LIGHTWEIGHT TITLE

SEE ALSO ◆ OWEN MORAN 231 ◆ BATTLING NELSON 251 ◆ WILLIE RITCHIE 275 ◆ FREDDIE WELSH 333

MIDGET WOLGAST

FACT FILE

1910 Born Joseph LoScalzo, Philadelphia

1925 Professional debut, age 15

1930 Won New York recognitioni as world flyweight champion

1935 Lost New York world flyweight title against Small Montana

1940 Last fight in Lancaster, Pennsylvania

Died: Philadelphia, October 19, 1955, age 45

Career record: Fights 199, Won 147, Lost 36, Drawn 16

Astonishingly fast, Midget Wolgast was almost untouchable in his heyday when he was recognized by the powerful New York State Athletic Commission as the best flyweight in the world. Outside the ropes, he was also a remarkable playboy who was once "romantically linked" with Mae West.

He bounced around the ring, inventing things as he went along, switch-hitting as he pleased, delighting fans with his antics and infuriating opponents.

He won New York recognition as champion when he outboxed a Cuban named Black Bill over 15 rounds before a sellout crowd of 18,000 in Madison Square Garden in March 1930. He was still only 19.

He stopped Willie LaMorte in six rounds in his first defense, and drew with Frankie Genaro, who held the NBA belt, in a 15-rounder on Boxing Day, 1930.

He packed 25 fights into the following year, including a 15-round points win over Ruby Bradley in a title defense in Brooklyn, but by the mid-1930s his form became patchy. His marriage failed, his thirst for strong liquor increased, and his attendance at the gym coincided with his desire to take a free shower. Once he was attacked by a wronged lady on the way to the ring—and entered it with blood seeping from a gashed scalp!

His skills eroded enough for him to lose his title to Small Montana at the age of 25 in Oakland, California, in September 1935. He continued until he was a bloated parody of the genius he had once been, enjoyed training youngsters, but perhaps fittingly, died of heart failure while at the Old Locust bar in Philadelphia.

MIGHTY MIDGET: IN HIS PRIME WOLGAST WAS VIRTUALLY UNTOUCHABLE

MYUNG-WOO YUH

Myung-woo Yuh was a clever combination puncher with a tight defense and tremendous fitness. Far East boxing experts were adamant that Yuh would have beaten both of his major rivals, Humberto Gonzalez and Michael Carbajal, but boxing politics kept them apart.

In a poll taken in 1993, he was also voted the best Korean fighter of all time, ahead even of the immensely popular Jung-koo Chang.

A modest, quiet man from Seoul, Yuh won the WBA light-flyweight (108 lb.) title at the age of 21, while still completing his National Service, when he outpointed Joey Olivo of Los Angeles on a split 15-round decision in Taegu in December 1985.

He made 17 successful defenses in the next six years, including wins over other world champions, Jose De Jesus of Puerto Rico (twice), crafty Venezuelan Leo Gamez (twice), and rugged Colombian Rodolfo Blanco.

His tremendous appeal enabled him to defend his championship at home, but when he traveled to Osaka, Japan, in December 1991, he was surprisingly outsped by former strawweight champion and home town hero, Hiroki Ioka.

In a rematch the following November Yuh returned to Japan and showed terrific grit and determination to regain the title with a majority decision.

He said his only remaining ambition was to prove himself against Gonzalez or Carbajal, and when neither fight materialized, Yuh had one farewell defense, a 12-round points win over Yuichi Hosono of Japan in July 1993, after which he retired.

He had lodged his money with his parents after each fight, and had avoided the company of hangers-on. When he left his boxing career behind him, therefore, he was financially secure for life.

FACT FILE

1964	Born Seoul, South Korea
1982	Turned professional, age 18
1985	Outpointed Joey Olivo to win WBA light-flyweight title
1991	Lost WBA light-flyweight title to Hiroki Ioka in 18th defense
1992	Regained WBA title from Ioka
1993	Retired as undefeated champion, age 29

Career record: Fights 39, Won 38, Lost 1

KOREAN HERO: BRUISED BUT VICTORIOUS, YUH SALUTES HIS FANS

TONY ZALE

FACT FILE

1913 Born Anthony Zaleski, Gary, Indiana

1934 Professional debut in Chicago

1940 Won NBA middleweight title against Al Hostak

1941 Beat Georgie Abrams for undisputed world title

1946 Won first classic fight with Rocky Graziano

1947 Lost world title in second fight with Graziano

1948 Regained title from Graziano, lost it to Marcel Cerdan

Died: Indiana, March 20, 1997

Career record: Fights 87, Won 67, Lost 18, Drawn 2

Tony Zale was a proud, upright man who fought his way out of the back-breaking steel mills of Gary, Indiana, and up to the middleweight championship of the world.

Zale was a devout Catholic who left partying to others. As a two-year-old toddler he had been traumatized by the death of his father in a bicycle accident. As an adult, he remained—by the standards of boxers at least!—shy and introverted.

A National Golden Gloves finalist in 1934, Zale was so demoralized in 1936 that he quit the ring and returned to the steel mills. After a 17-month break he tried again, and his persistence was rewarded in July 1940—he won the NBA middleweight title by stopping Al Hostak in 13 rounds in Seattle.

In November 1941 a 15-round decision over Georgie Abrams in a marvelous fight in New York made him undisputed champion. He was a terrific puncher, especially to the body. They labeled him "Man of Steel." It fitted.

During the War, Zale was in the US Navy, but returned in 1946, and his three battles with Rocky Graziano became the stuff of legend. Zale won the first in six amazing rounds before 40,000 fans in Yankee Stadium, New York. In the second, equally breathtaking affair in Chicago in July 1947, Graziano won the title with a sixth-round stoppage. And in the third fight, in Newark, New Jersey, in June 1948, Zale overpowered Graziano easily in round three.

But those wars had taken the fire from his belly. At 35, he was beaten by Marcel Cerdan after 12 rounds in Jersey City in September 1948. He retired, staying in boxing as an amateur trainer, divorced, remarried, and was widowed, then died in a nursing home, age 83.

MAN OF STEEL: ZALE TAKES OUT ROCKY GRAZIANO IN NEWARK, NEW JERSEY, IN 1948

SEE ALSO ◆ MARCEL CERDAN 61 ◆ ROCKY GRAZIANO 140

ALFONSO ZAMORA

If a Mexican government official had not been so budget-conscious, world bantam-weight champion Alfonso Zamora might never even have turned professional.

When he returned from the Munich Olympics with a silver medal, Zamora was praised lavishly, given a private audience with President Luis Echevarria, and promised a car to mark his achievement.

But when it arrived, it was second-hand! Zamora never forgave them the insult and signed a professional contract in disgust.

From a good home, Alfonso gave his parents nightmares because he loved to fight. He was expelled from school, had spells in juvenile institutions, and straightened out only when he was let loose in a boxing gym.

Zamora was a sensational puncher. He won the WBA bantamweight title with his 21st consecutive knockout, in four rounds against Korean soldier Soo-hwan Hong in Los Angeles in March 1975. But already backroom squabbles were demoralizing him. His manager fell out with his father over a public statement that gym rival Carlos Zarate was the better man. There were concerns voiced over certain deals that were done for him.

Alfonso admitted he was interested only in fighting for money—a far cry from those enthusiastic days of youth. He made five successful defenses, but was then exposed by Zarate, who knocked him out in four rounds before a wildly excited, 13,000 crowd in Los Angeles in a non-title fight in April 1977. Seven months later Jorge Lujan of Panama outpointed him to take away his WBA belt. Although he fought on until 1980, his talents had evaporated with his love of the game.

FACT FILE

1954 Born Santa Maria La Redonda, Mexico

1972 Olympic bantamweight silver medal

1975 Won WBA bantamweight title against Soo-hwan Hong of South Korea

1977 Lost non-title fight with Carlos Zarate, lost title to Jorge Lujan

1980 Retired, age 26

Career record: Fights 38, Won 33, Lost 5

ZAMORA STORMS INTO THAILAND'S THANOMJIT SUKOTHAI ON THE WAY TO HIS 23RD CONSECUTIVE WIN

SEE ALSO ◆ CARLOS ZARATE 348

THE GREAT FIGHTS

TONY ZALE
V.
ROCKY GRAZIANO

YANKEE STADIUM, NEW YORK.
SEPTEMBER 27, 1946.

The three-fight series between Tony Zale, the no-nonsense, disciplined "Man of Steel," and wild New York street kid Rocky Graziano was one of the greatest in ring history.

A throng of 40,000 fans gathered at Yankee Stadium in the Bronx, most expecting to see the crowning of 24-year-old Graziano in September 1946. Zale was in good form after a wartime stint in the Navy, but Graziano, who had been thrown out of the Army as unfit to serve his nation, had taken the New York boxing scene by storm and was the betting favorite.

Zale made the odds seem nonsense as he dropped Graziano with a clean, classical left hook for a count of four. Rocky was in deep trouble, but responded in the only manner he knew, piling forward and crashing punches at Zale's head—or any other part of his anatomy that presented itself. Zale reeled around the ring when the bell rang to finish an incredible opening round.

Zale was caught in a crossfire of punches in the second and seemed close to defeat. His lip was split and a barrage of right hands forced him down. The bell rang with the count at three. Zale was literally dragged to his corner by his seconds.

They slogged away, with first one and then the other on the point of defeat, until in round six Zale took everything out of Graziano with a right beneath the heart. He got up, still winded, and had his legs taken away by a left hook to the chin. "The jolt shot from my head to my feet. The feeling went out of my feet and I went whang on the canvas like I didn't have any feet at all," wrote Graziano in his autobiography. Referee Ruby Goldstein counted him out. One of the greatest fights in ring history was over.

They fought twice more. Graziano stopped Zale in six rounds in July 1947, but "The Man of Steel" won the decider in three rounds in Newark, New Jersey, in June 1948.

HILARIO ZAPATA

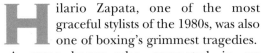

Hilario Zapata, one of the most graceful stylists of the 1980s, was also one of boxing's grimmest tragedies. A great boxer who competed in an incredible 24 world title fights, he made an absolute fortune... and then blew it all on drugs and booze. By 1991 he was living in a hovel without electricity or water, a wretched dope addict with a history of psychiatric illness.

Amazingly, he got himself sorted out and came back, but his plans were crushed by a first-round defeat against Sung-kil Moon in South Korea in Febraury 1993. Afterward, he reportedly returned to his old life in the drug-infested slums of San Miguelito.

In his youth he was a marvelous boxer, and a ring general of the highest order.

A southpaw from Colon, Panama, he was a world champion at 21. He won the WBC light-flyweight title by outpointing defending champion Shigeo Nakajima in March 1980 and retained it eight times, boxing in South Korea, Venezuela, Thailand, and the United States, before losing at home to Mexican puncher Amado Ursua. He was knocked out in two rounds in Panama City in February 1982.

Within five months he was back on top after beating Ursua's successor, Tadashi Tomori. He defeated Jung-koo Chang of South Korea, and Tomori again, before Chang made him look washed-up with a third round stoppage in March 1983.

Zapata became WBA flyweight champion by outpointing Alonso Gonzales in Panama in October 1985, but after five defenses he lost a controversial verdict to Fidel Bassa in Colombia in February 1987. The rematch ended in a draw in Panama City. Zapata said his anguish at the decision in the first fight set him on the road to ruin.

ZAPATA: A WONDERFUL BOXER, BUT A TRAGIC HUMAN BEING

SEE ALSO ◆ JUNG-KOO CHANG 64 ◆ SUNG-KIL MOON 223

DANIEL ZARAGOZA

Daniel Zaragoza, a quiet, businesslike family man, preferred soccer to fighting. "I wanted to be an international soccer star, not a boxer," he said. He was also at law school for a while.

But boxing eventually drew him into its strange world—and was enriched by his southpaw skills and sporting ways.

Zaragoza reached the Moscow Olympic Games in 1980, two years after his first amateur bout. One of a family of 12 children in Mexico City, he earned the respect of his countrymen but his style, in and out of the ring, was not designed to win the kind of adoration afforded big hitting extroverts like Ruben Olivares, Pipino Cuevas, and Julio Cesar Chavez.

Zaragoza was WBC bantamweight champion briefly in 1985, winning the title on a foul against Freddy "Pebble" Jackson, but then losing a decision to the more experienced Colombian Miguel Lora.

In February 1988 he won the WBC super-bantamweight belt when he stopped veteran Carlos Zarate in ten one-sided rounds in Los Angeles. He had a series of bloody battles with Californian Paul Banke, winning the first on a split decision, then losing the second in nine rounds because of cuts. In their third fight in December 1991, Zaragoza established his superiority with another points win.

Zaragoza held the WBC 122 lb. title three times, the last time leaving the boxing world shaking its head in admiration after a points win over Hector Acero-Sanchez of the Dominican Republic in November 1995, when a month short of his 38th birthday. It was his 17th world title fight. In January 1997 he defeated Ireland's Wayne McCullough.

FACT FILE

1957	Born Mexico City
1980	Olympic Games, Moscow
1985	Won WBC bantamweight title on a foul against Freddy Jackson, lost it to Miguel Lora
1988	Beat Carlos Zarate for vacant WBC super-bantamweight title
1990	Lost title to Paul Banke
1991	Outpointed Kiyoshi Hatanaka to regain championship
1992	Outpointed by Thierry Jacob in France
1995	Regained WBC belt with points win over Hector Acero Sanchez

Career record: Fights 64, Won 54, Lost 7, Drawn 3

BORN TO LAST: ZARAGOZA WON HIS FIRST WORLD TITLE IN 1985, AND WAS STILL A CHAMP A DOZEN YEARS LATER AS HE NEARED HIS 40TH BIRTHDAY

SEE ALSO ◆ CARLOS ZARATE 348

CARLOS ZARATE

FACT FILE

1951 Born Tepito, Mexico City

1976 Won WBC bantamweight title by knocking out Rodolfo Martinez

1977 Knocked out Alfonso Zamora in "Battle of Z-Men"

1978 Lost WBC super-bantamweight title fight against Wilfredo Gomez

1979 Lost WBC bantamweight title on disputed decision to Lupe Pintor

1986 Returned from seven-year retirement

1988 Last fight, lost WBC super-bantamweight fight with Daniel Zaragoza

Career record: Fights 65, Won 61, Lost 4

There was a lethal elegance to Carlos Zarate's artistry, a cruel perfection that made him the finest bantamweight of the 1970s.

From one of the poorest barrios of Mexico City, Zarate was an unruly youth who was thrown out of a succession of schools. Like so many others, he straightened out once he found boxing offered a better life.

It was a slow process—he served a short jail sentence even after turning professional—but he won all 33 amateur contests, and went on to become WBC bantamweight title by knocking out fellow Mexican Rodolfo Martinez in nine rounds in Los Angeles in May 1976.

His was a family business. His brother Jorge helped trained him, his sister Marcel was his cook, another brother Ernesto was his financial advisor, and a third brother, Araceli, provided a country retreat.

Although he retained his title nine times, it was his four-rounds non-title win over former gym-mate Alfonso Zamora at the Inglewood Forum, Los Angeles, in April 1977 that sealed his stardom.

And although he lost his unbeaten record when he was stopped by a peak-form Wilfredo Gomez for the WBC super-bantamweight title in Puerto Rico in October 1978, he seemed set to reign for as long as he liked at bantamweight. His subsequent defeat on a split decision to stable companion Lupe Pintor was shocking. The decision was generally accepted as terrible. Even Pintor seemed embarrassed.

Zarate retired in disgust, returning after seven years, by which time his skills had faded. He lost super-bantamweight title bids against Jeff Fenech and Daniel Zaragoza and retired for good in 1988, age 36.

BATTLE OF THE Z-MEN: ZARATE (RIGHT) STOPS ALFONSO ZAMORA IN FOUR ROUNDS IN 1977

SEE ALSO ◆ JEFF FENECH 110 ◆ WILFREDO GOMEZ 136 ◆ LUPE PINTOR 271 ◆ ALFONSO ZAMORA 343 ◆ DANIEL ZARAGOZA 347

FRITZIE ZIVIC

Fouls seemed to come naturally to Fritzie Zivic!

A master at gouging, butting, rubbing the heel of the glove into a wound, low punching on the blind side, somehow he went through 232 fights in 18 years, held the world welterweight title... and was never once disqualified.

Zivic made no apology for his behavior, but never complained if he was on the receiving end. He could box, but by far preferred a white-knuckle, nose-to-nose tearup.

For nine years he was considered no more than a tough club fighter from a tough city. In the winter of 1935–1936, he was outpointed in eight consecutive fights. Hard work, fitness, and sheer desire brought him on.

On the way up he fought Billy Conn, Lou Ambers, and the great middleweight Charlie Burley three times. After beating Sammy Angott in Pittsburgh in August 1940, he was given a world title fight with "Homicide Hank," Henry Armstrong in New York. Zivic, determined to be on his best behavior, fought cleanly for five rounds, even stepping back and saying "Pardon me" when he whacked the champ below the belt. But after they both begun fouling with equal enthusiasm, referee Arthur Donovan left them to it. Zivic enjoyed himself and won the decision.

In a rematch he stopped Armstrong in the 12th round, but lost his title on a 15-round decision to Freddie "Red" Cochrane in July 1941 in Newark, New Jersey. Zivic complained, but was never given another shot. He retired eight years later. He owned a sports stadium for a while, and earned his living as a salesman, a house painter, and eventually a boilermaker.

FACT FILE

1913 Born Pittsburgh
1931 Professional debut in Pittsburgh, age 18
1940 Won world welterweight title against Henry Armstrong
1941 Stopped Armstrong in rematch, lost title to Freddie Cochrane
1949 Last fight in Georgia, age 36
Died: Pittsburgh, May 16, 1984, age 71
Career record: Fights 232, Won 157, Lost 65, Drawn 10

IRON MAN: FRITZIE ZIVIC SHAKES HANDS WITH HENRY ARMSTRONG ON THE SCALES. ZIVIC BEAT HOMICIDE HANK TWICE

SEE ALSO ◆ Lou Ambers 16 ◆ Henry Armstrong 21 ◆ Billy Conn 75

ACKNOWLEDGEMENTS

352

The pictures for this book came from the following suppliers. While every effort has been made to ensure this listing is correct, the Publisher apologizes for any omissions.

Allsport UK
3 Greenlea Park
Prince George's Road
London SW19 2JD
England

Boxing News Ltd
21 Poland Street
London W1
England

The Ring Magazine
P.O. Box 750
Fl. Washington
PA 19034
USA

page 2, **Allsport**; page 12, **Allsport**; page 13, **Bob Mee**; pages 14–15, **Bob Mee**; page 16 (t) **Allsport**, (b) **Boxing News**; page 17, **Allsport**; page 18, **Bob Mee**; page 19 (t), **Bob Mee**, (b) **Boxing News**; page 20, **Boxing News**; page 21, **Bob Mee**; pages 22–23, **Boxing News**; page 24, **Boxing News**; page 25 (t), **Bob Mee** (b), **Boxing News**; page 26 (t), **Allsport** (b), **Bob Mee**; page 27, **Allsport**; page 28, **Bob Mee**; page 29, **Boxing News**; page 30 (t), **Allsport** (b), **Bob Mee**; page 31 (t), **Bob Mee** (b), **Allsport**; page 32, **Bob Mee**; page 33, **Allsport**; page 34, **Boxing News**; page 35, **Allsport**; page 36, **Allsport**; page 37, **Boxing News**; pages 38–39, **Allsport**; page 40, **Boxing News**; page 41 (t), **Allsport** (b), **Boxing News**; 42 (t) **Boxing News** (b), **Bob Mee**; page 43, **Bob Mee**; page 44, **Allsport**; page 45, **Allsport**; pages 46–47, **Boxing News**; page 48, **Ring** magazine; page 49, **Allsport**; page 50 (t), **Allsport** (b), **Bob Mee**; page 51, **Allsport**; page 52, **Allsport**; page 53, **Boxing News**; page 54, **Allsport**; page 55, **Allsport**; pages 56–57, **The Ring** magazine; page 58, **Allsport**; page 59, **Allsport**; page 60, **Bob Mee**; page 61 (t), **Bob Mee** (b), **Allsport**; page 62, **Boxing News**; page 63 (t), **Bob Mee** (b), **Boxing News**; page 64, **Boxing News**; page 65 (t), **Bob Mee** (b), **Allsport**; page 66, **Bob Mee**; page 67 (t), **Allsport**; page 68, **Bob Mee**; pages 68–69, **Allsport**; page 70 (t), **Bob Mee** (b), **Boxing News**; page 71, **Bob Mee**; page 72 (t), **Allsport** (b), **Bob Mee**; page 73, **Boxing News**; page 74, **Allsport**; page 75 (t), **Bob Mee** (b), **Allsport**; pages 76–77, **Ring News**; page 78, **Allsport**; page 79, **Allsport**; page 80 (t), **Allsport** (b), **Bob Mee**; page 81 (t), **Boxing News** (b), **Bob Mee**; page 82, **Allsport**; page 83, **Bob Mee**; page 84, **Bob Mee**; page 85, **Allsport**; page 86, **Boxing News**; page 87 (t), **Boxing News** (b), **Bob Mee**; page 88, **Allsport**; page 89, **Bob Mee**; pages 90–91, **Bob Mee**; page 92, **Bob Mee**; page 93 (t), **Bob Mee** (b), **Boxing News**; page 94, **Allsport**; page 95, **Allsport**; pages 96–97, **Boxing News**; page 98 (t), **Allsport** (b), **Bob Mee**; page 99, **Allsport**; pages 100–101, **The Ring** magazine; page 102 **Boxing News**; page 103, **Boxing News**; page 104, **Ring** magazine; page 105 (t), **Bob Mee** (b), **Ring** magazine; page 106, **Allsport**; page 107, **Allsport**; pages 108–109, **Allsport**; page 110, **Boxing News**; page 111, **Bob Mee**; pages 112-113, **Bob Mee**; page 114, **Bob Mee**; page 115, **Allsport**; pages 116–117, **Allsport**; page 118, **Allsport**; page 119 (t), **Boxing News** (b), **Allsport**; pages 120–121, **Boxing News**; page 122, **Allsport**; page 123 (t), **Ring** magazine (b), **Bob Mee**; pages 125–125, **The Ring** magazine; page 126 (t), **Bob Mee** (b), **Boxing News**; page 127, **Ring** magazine; page 128, **Boxing News**; page 129, **Bob Mee**; pages 130–131, **Bob Mee**; page 132, **Bob Mee**; page 133, **Allsport**; page 134, **Boxing News**; page 135, **Bob Mee**; page 136, **Boxing News**; page 137, **Boxing News**; page 138, **Allsport**; page 139, **Bob Mee**; page 140, **Allsport**; page 141 (b), **Bob Mee** (t), **Allsport**; pages 142–143, **Bob Mee**; page 144, **Allsport**; page 145, **Bob Mee**; page 146, **Boxing News**; page 147, **Allsport**; pages 148–149, **Boxing News**; page 150, **Allsport**; page 151 (t), **Allsport** (b), **Bob Mee**; page 152, **Bob Mee**; page 153, **Allsport**; pages 154–155, **The Ring** magazine; page 156 (t), **Allsport** (b), **Boxing News**; page 157, **Allsport**; page 158, **Allsport**; page 159, **Allsport**; pages 160–161, **Allsport**; page 162, **Allsport**; page 163, **Bob Mee**; pages 164–165, **Allsport**; page 166, **Allsport**; page 167, **Bob Mee**; page 168, **Allsport**; page 169, **Bob Mee**; page 170, **Allsport**; page 171, **Allsport**; pages 172–173, **Bob Mee**, page 174, **Allsport**; page 175 (t), **Allsport** (b), **Boxing News**; page 176 (t), **Bob Mee** (b), **Boxing News**; page 177, **Allsport**; page 178, **Bob Mee**; page 179, **Boxing News**; page 180, **Boxing News**; page 181, **Bob Mee**; page 182 (t), **Bob Mee** (b), **Allsport**; page 183, **Boxing News**; page 184 (t), **Allsport** (b),

Bob Mee; page 185, **Allsport**; page 186 (t), **Allsport** (b), **Boxing News**; page 187, **Allsport**; pages 188–189, **Allsport**; page 190 (t), **Allsport** (b), **Bob Mee**; page 191, **Allsport**; page 192, **Bob Mee**; page 193, **Allsport**; page 194, **Allsport**; page 195 (t), **Allsport** (b), **Boxing News**; page 196, **Allsport**; page 197 (t), **Boxing News** (b), **Bob Mee**; pages 198–199, **Bob Mee**; page 200 (t), **Bob Mee** (b), **Allsport**; page 201, **Boxing News**; page 202, **Bob Mee**; page 203, **Bob Mee**; page 204, **Allsport**; page 205, **Allsport**; pages 206–207, **Bob Mee**; page 208 (t), **Bob Mee** (b), **Boxing News**; pages 209–211, **Allsport**; page 212 (t), **Bob Mee** (b), **Boxing News**; page 213, **Allsport**; page 214 (t), **Boxing News** (b), **Bob Mee**; page 216, **Boxing News**; page 217, **Allsport**; page 218, **Ring** magazine; page 219, **Allsport**; page 220 (t), **Bob Mee** (b), **Allsport**; page 221, **Bob Mee**; page 222 (t), **Boxing News** (b), **Allsport**; page 223, **Bob Mee**; pages 224–225, **The Ring** magazine; page 226 (t), **Bob Mee** (b), **Allsport**; page 227 (t), **Bob Mee** (b), **Allsport**; pages 228–229, **Boxing News**; page 230, **Allsport**; page 231, **Bob Mee**; pages 232–233, **Boxing News**; page 234, **Boxing News**; page 235, **Ring** magazine; page 236, **Bob Mee**; page 237, **Allsport**; page 238, **Allsport**; page 239, **Bob Mee**; page 240, **Bob Mee**; page 241, **Allsport** (b), **Bob Mee**; page 242, **Allsport**; page 243, **Allsport**; pages 244–245, **Allsport**; page 246 (t), **Boxing News** (b), **Bob Mee**; page 247, **Bob Mee**; pages 248–249, **The Ring** magazine; page 250, **Boxing News**; page 251, **Ring** magazine; pages 252–253, **The Ring** magazine; page 254, **Bob Mee**; page 255, **Allsport**; page 256, **Bob Mee**; page 257, **Boxing News**; page 258, **Bob Mee**; page 259, **Allsport**; page 260, **Allsport**; page 261, **Bob Mee**; page 262, **Allsport**; page 263 (t), **Allsport** (b), **Bob Mee**; page 264, **Allsport**; page 265, **Allsport**; page 266, **Bob Mee**; page 267, **Allsport**; page 268 (t), **Allsport** (b), **Bob Mee**; page 269 (t), **Allsport** (b), **Bob Mee**; page 270, **Allsport**; page 271 (t), **Allsport** (b), **Boxing News**; page 272, **Bob Mee**; page 273, **Boxing News**; page 274, **Ring** magazine; page 275, **Boxing News**; pages 276–277, **The Ring** magazine; page 278, **Allsport**; page 279, **Boxing News**; pages 280–281, **Bob Mee**; page 282, **Boxing News**; page 283, **Boxing News**; page 284, **Bob Mee**; page 295, **Boxing News**; page 286, **Allsport**; page 287, **Bob Mee**; page 288, **Allsport**; page 289 (t), **Bob Mee** (b), **Boxing News**; pages 290–291, **Boxing News**; page 292, **Allsport**; page 293, **Ring** magazine; page 294, **Allsport**; page 295, **Boxing News**; page 296, **boxing News**; page 297, **Bob Mee**; page 298, **Allsport**; page 299, **Bob Mee**, pages 300–301, **Bob Mee**; page 302, **Ring** magazine; page 303, **Bob Mee**; page 304, **Allsport**; page 305 (t), **Allsport** (b), **Bob Mee**; page 306, **Bob Mee**; page 307 (t), **Bob Mee** (b), **Boxing News**; pages 308–309, **Boxing News**; page 310, **Allsport**; page 311 (t), **Boxing News** (b), **Bob Mee**; pages 312–313, **Bob Mee**; page 314 (t), **Allsport** (b), **Bob Mee**; page 315, **Allsport**; page 316, **Allsport**; page 317, **The Ring** magazine; page 318, **Allsport**; page 319, **Allsport**; pages 320–321, **Bob Mee**; page 322 (t), **Allsport** (b), **Bob Mee**; page 323, **Ring** magazine; page 324, **Bob Mee**; page 325 (t), **Bob Mee** (b), **Boxing News**; pages 326–327, **Bob Mee**; page 328, **Bob Mee**; page 329, **Boxing News**; page 330 (t), **Allsport** (b), **Bob Mee**; page 331, **Bob Mee**; page 332, **Allsport**; page 333, **Allsport**; page 334, **The Ring** magazine; page 335 (t), **Allsport** (b), **Bob Mee**; page 336 (t), **Allsport** (b), **Bob Mee**; page 337, **Allsport**; page 338, **Allsport**; page 339, **Boxing News**; page 340, **Boxing News**; page 341, **Boxing News**; page 342, **Bob Mee**; page 343, **Boxing News**; page 344, **Boxing News**; page 345, **Bob Mee**; page 346, **Boxing News**; page 347, **Boxing News**; page 348, **Bob Mee**; page 349 (t), **Bob Mee** (b), **Boxing News**.